THE COMPLETE BOOK OF SEWING SHORT CUTS

Claire B. Shaeffer

 Sterling Publishing Co., Inc.   New York

ACKNOWLEDGMENTS

It is with deep appreciation that I wish to thank those who were helpful in many different ways: Elizabeth B. Lawson, Chairperson of the Home Economics Department, College of the Desert; Betty Lou Roche; Pat Wormley; Pat Lee and Dawneen Younghusband.

Library of Congress Cataloging in Publication Data

Shaeffer, Claire B.
   The complete book of sewing shortcuts.
  ISBN 0-8069-7564-4
  Includes index.
  1. Dressmaking   2. Sewing
TT515.S34   1981   646.4   81-8818
                                 AACR2

10 9 8 7 6 5 4 3 2 1

Published by Sterling Publishing Company, Inc.
387 Park Avenue South, New York, N.Y. 10016
© 1981 by Claire B. Shaeffer
Distributed in Canada by Sterling Publishing
℅ Canadian Manda Group, P.O. Box 920, Station U
Toronto, Ontario, Canada M8Z 5P9
Distributed in Great Britain and Europe by Cassell PLC
Villiers House, 41/47 Strand, London WC2N 5JE, England
Distributed in Australia by Capricorn Link Ltd.
P.O. Box 665, Lane Cove, NSW 2066
Manufactured in the United States of America
All rights reserved

Sterling ISBN 0-8069-7564-4

CONTENTS

To my husband, Charlie, for his never-ending patience from the beginning to the end.

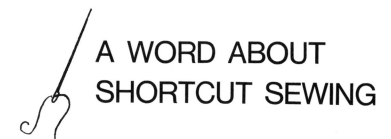

A WORD ABOUT SHORTCUT SEWING

Shortcut sewing is for *everyone*. It's not reserved or limited to jiffy techniques, easy-sew fabrics, and make-it-in-an-hour designs; it's designed for *every* garment you make *every* time you sew. Shortcut sewing will not only save you time, it will also enable you to create fantastic-looking, well-made clothes.

This book is the first book to explain the sewing shortcuts of the fashion industry, the time-saving methods and techniques used in ready-to-wear and designer garments, as well as hundreds of tricks of the trade. The book includes new professional methods to replace old home-sewing methods . . . international sewing secrets . . . tips to make traditional sewing methods easier . . . ready-to-wear techniques and designer details. It also introduces some unusual sewing aids and tells how to solve and avoid problems and how to correct mistakes.

The book contains an extensive collection of alternative methods based on my knowledge of industrial and home-sewing methods, my observations of ready-made garments, and my experiences as a teacher. Since there is no single method that is right for every fabric or design, no one-and-only technique to complete most details and very few always-or-never situations, I have included many techniques so that you can choose the one best suited to your ability, the amount of time you have to sew, and the garment fabric, design, and quality. Each technique is explored in depth and most are totally independent with a minimum of cross-references. Notes on when to use the techniques, shortcuts, variations, and other helpful miscellany are included to ensure professional-looking garments.

THE DIAGRAMS

The hundreds of diagrams throughout the book have been screened to make them easy to read. They have also been simplified and rarely include finishes on the edges of seams, hems or facings. These edges should be finished on the garment.

Right side of fabric

Wrong side of fabric

Reverse side of fabric

Right side of lining and underlining

Wrong side of lining and underlining

Interfacing

Fusible agent

GLOSSARY

Many terms used in the book may be unfamiliar to you. This small glossary will clarify their meanings.

All-in-one facing. A facing that finishes the edges of the neckline and armscye all in one piece. A combination facing.

Apply. Stitch or glue.

Armscye. Armhole.

Backing. Layer of fabric applied to the wrong side of the fashion fabric before the seams are sewn. Underlining or mounting.

Backtack. Backstitch.

Bagging. A method of lining a coat or jacket by machine.

Bias. Any cut which is not on the lengthwise or crosswise grain.

Bight. Width of zigzag stitch.

Bluffed edge. A finished edge which has not been topstitched.

Bobbin stitching. Pulling the thread from the bobbin to thread the needle and machine. Sometimes called continuous-thread stitching.

Butt. Match the edges or folds so that they meet or abut.

Button stand. The distance between the center of the button and the finished edge of the garment. The underlap.

Buttonhole stand. The distance between center front and the finished edge of the garment. The overlap.

Chain stitching. Stitching from one garment section to another without cutting the threads.

Clean finish. A method of finishing hems and seams in which the edge is turned under and stitched.

Clearance above the eye. Flattened area above the eye of the machine. The needle scarf.

Close. Finish stitching a seam by hand or machine.

Coil. A narrow, lightweight, filament coil that secures a zipper. The zipper teeth.

Combination facing. A facing that finishes the edges of the neckline and armscye all in one piece. An all-in-one facing.

Complete. Stitch, press, understitch, trim, clip, and underpress—*anything* that needs to be done to a garment section before it is joined to another section.

Complete pattern. A pattern for the entire garment to be cut out on a single layer of fabric.

Course. "Crossgrain" of knit fabric.

Crimping. A method of easing more fabric into the line of stitching.

Crossgrain. The woof or filling, which runs from selvage to selvage or the course of knitted fabrics.

Crotch. The point on a pair of trousers at which the legs join. The fork.

Crowding. Crimping.

Demarcation line. A ridge or shadow that shows on the right side of the garment.

Ease basting. A method of easing fabric using a tight bobbin tension.

Edgestitch. Stitching $1/16''$ (1.6 mm) from the edge of the garment section.

Enclosed seams. Seams at finished edges which are concealed between the facing and fashion fabric.

Face. (a) The right side of the fabric. (b) To finish the garment edge with a facing.

Fashion fabric. The fabric from which the garment is constructed.

Fell. (a) To join two pieces of fabric with the edges folded together so that they are enclosed. (b) To sew the edges down with an overcasting stitch made by hand.

Findings. Linings, zippers, buttons, thread, snaps, etc.

Finish. (a) Any method for completing the raw edges of seams, hems or facings. (b) To apply the appropriate finish to the raw edges of seams, hems or facings.

Flagging. The clinging of the fabric, as the needle moves up and down, when the fabric isn't held firmly or when the needle is the wrong size.

Flat finish. Any finish that is flat—cut edge, zig-zagged, overlocked, overcast, singed, or taped.

Flat lining. A method of underlining.

Fork. The point on a pair of trousers where the legs join. The crotch.

Glue–baste. Gluing with a washable glue stick to temporarily position a section or sections.

Grainline. The lengthwise grain, parallel to the selvages.

Groove of the seam. The indentation of the seamline on the right side of the garment. The well of the seam.

Hemline. The line on which the hem is finished.

Inside. The part of the garment which is toward the body.

Interlining. Layer of fabric applied to the wrong side of the lining for warmth.

Jigger. A button sewn on the inside of a double-breasted coat. It usually has a long shank.

Key. (a) A guideline on two sections. (b) To match.

Knock-off. An adaptation of a ready-made garment. Manufacturers of less expensive lines make knock-offs of more expensive garments.

Lashing. The hand or machine stitches inside a jacket or coat that hold the facings or linings in position.

Legs of the dart. The stitching lines of the dart.

Lengthwise grain. The warp of the fabric which is parallel to the selvages.

Notch. (a) A small slit cut into the seam allowances of the garment to indicate match points and foldlines and to locate darts, tucks, or pleats. (b) The indentation where the collar joins the lapel.

Open lay. A single layer of fabric; the fabric is opened out to its full width.

Outside. The part of the fabric or garment which will be seen when the garment is worn.

Pick-up line. The foldline of the dart.

Pivot. Insert the needle into the fabric, raise the presser foot, turn the fabric section, and lower the presser.

Placket. Any finished opening in a garment.

Ply. A layer of fabric or strand of thread.

Pretrim. Cut away part of the seam allowances before stitching the seam.

Pseudosuede. Nonwoven fabrics that look like suede, such as Ultrasuede®, Suede 21™, Amara, Feather-suede, and Bellesieme.

Raw edge. Unfinished edge of the garment section.

Rtw. Ready-to-wear.

Sandwich. Place between two layers.

Seam allowance. The width of the fabric between the stitching line and the cutting line.

Seamline. The stitching line.

Secure. Fasten the threads with a knot, backtack, spot tack, or small stitches.

Self. The same fabric as the rest of the garment.

Selvage. Finished edges on woven fabric along the lengthwise grain.

Set. Stitch.

Sew. Sew by hand.

Sightline. Any point on the presser foot, throat plate, or machine bed which can be used as a guide for feeding the material.

Slash. Clip into the fabric.

Spi. Stitches per inch.

Square. Draw a line at right angles to another line.

Staystitch. Stitching with a regular stitch just inside the seamline.

Stitch. Sew by machine.

Stroke. The length of material that can be stitched without stopping.

Swelled edges. An effect created by topstitching an even distance from the finished edge, e.g., ¼″ (6.4 mm), ⅜″ (9.5 mm) or ½″ (12.7 mm).

Tack. Backstitch.

Teeth. Metal or coil hooks that fasten a zipper.

Test. Try on a scrap of the garment fabric.

Topstitch. Stitching from the right side of the garment.

Trim. Cut away excess fabric.

Turn-of-the-cloth. The fabric which is "lost" when a seam is turned right-side-out or when an edge is folded.

Underlining. Layer of fabric applied to the wrong side of the fashion fabric before the seams are sewn. Backing or mounting.

Understitch. Stitching from the wrong side of the garment 1/16″ (1.6 mm) from the seamline at the finished edge, usually through the facing and seam allowances.

Vent. Faced or lined slash for ease such as a sleeve placket.

Wales. The lengthwise "grain" of knitted fabrics.

Well of the seam. Groove of the seam.

YSL. Yves Saint Laurent, the designer.

METRIC MEASUREMENTS

Anticipating the conversion from imperial measurements (inches) to metric measurements, the fashion pattern industry has adopted a Metric Equivalency Chart. The equivalency measurements on the chart have been rounded for your convenience. This will be the industry standard when the change to metric measurements is finalized.

Throughout the book, I have used exact measurements instead of the equivalency chart. I find this is easier for the seamstress who has learned to sew by the metric system and the home sewer who is using a measuring device that indicates both measuring systems.

METRIC EQIVALENCY CHART

CONVERTING INCHES TO CENTIMETRES AND YARDS TO METRES

This chart gives the standard equivalents as approved by the Pattern Fashion Industry.

mm — millimetres   cm — centimetres   m — metres

INCHES INTO MILLIMETRES AND CENTIMETRES
(SLIGHTLY ROUNDED FOR YOUR CONVENIENCE)

inches	mm		cm	inches	cm	inches	cm
⅛	3mm			7	18	29	73.5
¼	6mm			8	20.5	30	76
⅜	10mm	or	1cm	9	23	31	78.5
½	13mm	or	1.3cm	10	25.5	32	81.5
⅝	15mm	or	1.5cm	11	28	33	84
¾	20mm	or	2cm	12	30.5	34	86.5
⅞	22mm	or	2.2cm	13	33	35	89
1	25mm	or	2.5cm	14	35.5	36	91.5
1¼	32mm	or	3.2cm	15	38	37	94
1½	38mm	or	3.8cm	16	40.5	38	96.5
1¾	45mm	or	4.5cm	17	43	39	99
2	50mm	or	5cm	18	46	40	102
2½	65mm	or	6.3cm	19	48.5	41	104
3	75mm	or	7.5cm	20	51	42	107
3½	90mm	or	9cm	21	53.5	43	109
4	100mm	or	10cm	22	56	44	112
4½	115mm	or	11.5cm	23	58.5	45	115
5	125mm	or	12.5cm	24	61	46	117
5½	140mm	or	14cm	25	63.5	47	120
6	150mm	or	15cm	26	66	48	122
				27	68.5	49	125
				28	71	50	127

AVAILABLE FABRIC WIDTHS

25"	64cm	50"	127cm
27"	70cm	54"/56"	140cm
35"/36"	90cm	58"/60"	150cm
39"	100cm	68"/70"	175cm
44"/45"	115cm	72"	180cm
48"	122cm	108"	275cm

AVAILABLE ZIPPER LENGTHS

4"	10cm	10"	25cm	20"	50cm
5"	12cm	11"	28cm	22"	55cm
6"	15cm	12"	30cm	24"	60cm
7"	18cm	14"	35cm	26"	65cm
8"	20cm	16"	40cm	28"	70cm
9"	23cm	18"	45cm	30"	75cm
				36"	90cm

YARDS TO METRES
(SLIGHTLY ROUNDED FOR YOUR CONVENIENCE)

YARDS	METRES	YARDS	METRES	YARDS	METRES	YARDS	METRES	YARDS	METRES
⅛	0.15	2⅛	1.95	4⅛	3.80	6⅛	5.60	8⅛	7.45
¼	0.25	2¼	2.10	4¼	3.90	6¼	5.75	8¼	7.55
⅜	0.35	2⅜	2.20	4⅜	4.00	6⅜	5.85	8⅜	7.70
½	0.50	2½	2.30	4½	4.15	6½	5.95	8½	7.80
⅝	0.60	2⅝	2.40	4⅝	4.25	6⅝	6.10	8⅝	7.90
¾	0.70	2¾	2.55	4¾	4.35	6¾	6.20	8¾	8.00
⅞	0.80	2⅞	2.65	4⅞	4.50	6⅞	6.30	8⅞	8.15
1	0.95	3	2.75	5	4.60	7	6.40	9	8.25
1⅛	1.05	3⅛	2.90	5⅛	4.70	7⅛	6.55	9⅛	8.35
1¼	1.15	3¼	3.00	5¼	4.80	7¼	6.65	9¼	8.50
1⅜	1.30	3⅜	3.10	5⅜	4.95	7⅜	6.75	9⅜	8.60
1½	1.40	3½	3.20	5½	5.05	7½	6.90	9½	8.70
1⅝	1.50	3⅝	3.35	5⅝	5.15	7⅝	7.00	9⅝	8.80
1¾	1.60	3¾	3.45	5¾	5.30	7¾	7.10	9¾	8.95
1⅞	1.75	3⅞	3.55	5⅞	5.40	7⅞	7.20	9⅞	9.05
2	1.85	4	3.70	6	5.50	8	7.35	10	9.15

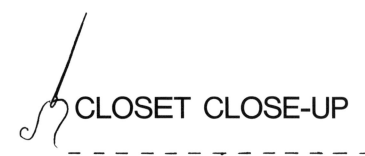

CLOSET CLOSE-UP

Do you have a closet full of clothes and nothing to wear?

Don't make another garment until you inventory and clean out your closet. I know that it is almost impossible to discard those beautiful garments you have made with loving care; but if you are not going to wear them, at least move them.

You will need six boxes to do the job properly. Label them Wash, Dry Clean, Mend, Give Away or Sell, Store to Wear Again, and Store for Reference.

The Store-to-Wear-Again box is for those garments which you do not want to discard but do not intend to wear anytime soon. This includes those outgrown garments you plan to wear when you lose ten pounds. Ideally, you will hang them in a spare closet, but who has a spare closet? Store them in an under-the-bed box.

The Store-for-Reference box is for the garments you have made in a sewing class that reflect your learning experiences.

Look at every garment in the closet honestly. Does it still fit? Is it in style? Does it look worn? Is the color or fabric passé? Do you need it for your lifestyle? Do you plan to wear it this season? Place it in the appropriate box or rehang it.

Once you've cleaned your closet, take an inventory. Do you have a lot of unrelated garments? Plan your new wardrobe to tie them together. Start with the item or items that will update your wardrobe the most.

Decide which garments to make and which to buy. Sew the easy styles and buy the difficult-to-make ones.

When you sew you don't have to be a slave to fashion, but you do want to be informed. Shop around—look at the ready-to-wear in the better stores. Are the new colors and silhouettes flattering to you? If not, can you adapt them so that you will look lovely and be fashionable?

While you are in a cleaning mood, go through the drawer, chest, closet, or room where you store your hoard of beautiful fabrics. Some fabrics never go out of style; others do. Unfortunately, an out-of-date fabric makes an out-of-date outfit.

Have a garage sale or give away those lengths which you'll never use. Be realistic—you know some of them will never be in fashion again, and you cannot make a fashionable garment from a passé fabric; however, good-quality fabrics made of natural fibres will eventually come back into vogue. If your tastes have changed, and you've decided some of those lovely fabrics just aren't for you, sell them.

If you can't bear to part with your fabric collection, try to use it. Go through it carefully at the beginning of each season, select the pieces that can be made into fashionable garments, make those garments before you buy any new fabric, and don't buy anything unless you're going to sew it immediately. Last, but most importantly, repeat to yourself, "I'll never be a fabricholic again!"

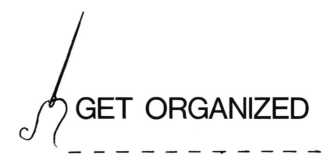

GET ORGANIZED

Organize, organize, organize! This is the key to shortcut sewing and a professional finish.

Organize your sewing area before you start to sew so that you can sew anytime you have a few minutes free. Find a corner or closet where you can keep your sewing machine set up and ready to sew.

Assemble your sewing equipment, notions, and supplies and keep them near the sewing machine. Your small equipment can be kept in a drawer or box. A tackle box is ideal. It's easy to store and opens so that each tray is visible and the contents are easy to see. Everything is together ready to sew or go whenever you are.

Consider having duplicates of some tools to eliminate wasting precious minutes looking for the "one and only."

Learn to use short periods for stitching a seam or two; have your hand-sewing supplies ready to sew so that you can utilize your time whenever you have to wait for others; press while you talk on the telephone. You'll be surprised at how much you can accomplish in your new "found" time.

ASSEMBLE YOUR TOOLS AND SUPPLIES

There are literally hundreds of tools, gadgets, and notions to make sewing easier, but you do not need a lot of fancy or expensive equipment to sew well. You do need good tools, and—this is important—you must know how to make them work for you. Good tools properly used will save you hours of work and frustration. They may not be cheap, but they will last for years.

Cutting Tools
Shears and scissors. Good shears and scissors may be made of stainless or surgical steel, steel alloy, or solid steel which has been plated with nickel or chrome. Shears made of stainless steel or which have serrated edges enable you to cut knits and slippery fabrics quickly and accurately. The only difference between shears and scissors is the shape of the handles—the handles on shears are unequal in size.

You should have a pair of good-quality bent-handled dressmaker shears, seven or eight inches in length, to use for most of your cutting and trimming. They should cut through eight or more fabric thicknesses and all the way to the points. The bent handles permit you to cut without lifting the fabric from the cutting table.

You also need a pair of five-inch embroidery scissors for very close trimming.

If you have a lot of heavy-duty cutting chores, a pair of motor-driven or electric scissors will enable you to finish your work painlessly and quickly.

Cordless shears are easier to use than those with cords. If your electric pair does have a cord, cut the garment sections nearest the outlet first—this eliminates dragging the cord across uncut areas. If your cutting surface is below the dining room chandelier, drape the cord of your electric scissors over the lighting fixture to eliminate dragging the cord around.

Good-quality cutting equipment is not cheap; but, with proper care, it will last a lifetime.

✺ Brush the lint from the blades frequently. Today's easy-care fabrics are more abrasive to your shears than paper.

✺ Keep your shears sharp. Sharpen them regularly to keep them "like new." Dull shears can be damaged easily, and they can damage beautiful fabrics beyond repair.

- Keep the shears dry to avoid corrosion.
- Oil the pivot point regularly.
- Use your sewing shears only for sewing.

Pinking shears. Pinking shears are a luxury, and you can sew very well without them. They are used for finishing and can be used for notching outward (convex) curves, but they should never be used for cutting out garments because a pinked edge is difficult to match and stitch accurately. Furthermore, the blades will quickly become dull, and pinking shears are expensive to have sharpened.

Rotary cutter. The rotary cutter is an innovative cutting tool that looks more like a tracing wheel than a piece of cutting equipment. It will cut through thick or thin fabrics quickly and easily without leaving zigs and zags. It can be used in the right or left hand. It must be used with a cutting board to avoid damaging your table.

The tungsten steel blade is easy to replace to ensure precise cutting.

Seam ripper. A seam ripper should be razor sharp. Replace the seam ripper often. A dull seam ripper must be pushed and urged to cut. That push sometimes becomes a shove, and you cut the fabric.

Cutting table. The cutting table should have a smooth, hard surface and be about 36″ (91.4 cm) high. Most of us do our cutting on a dining table, which is only 30″ (76.2 cm) high, then we wonder why we have a backache.

Cutting board. A cardboard cutting board which can be folded and stored is an optional cutting aid. It can be used on the dining room table to protect it and provide a resilient surface for using a rotary cutter or tracing wheel. Vinyl or felt table pads can be used instead of a cutting board, except when using a rotary cutter.

Measuring Tools
Accurate measuring equipment is essential!

Tape measure. Select a tape measure made of synthetic material that won't stretch and begins its numbering at both ends. Throw away any paper or cloth tape measures you still have—they are often inaccurate.

Flexible plastic ruler. A see-through ruler with a ⅛″ (3.2 mm) grid printed on it is indispensable. Select a 2″ x 12″ (5.1 cm x 30.5 cm) or a 1″ x 12″ (2.5 cm x 30.5 cm) size for easy handling. Check the ruler to be sure the grid is printed evenly and accurately. If your local fabric shops don't stock them, try an art supply or stationery store.

Yardstick. A yardstick is needed to extend grainlines and measure hemlines.

Marking Tools
Dressmaker's chalk. Use only white clay chalk or water-erasable blue chalk. Always test the chalk on a fabric scrap before using it on your garment, to be sure it won't leave a stain.

Soap. A sliver of white soap, without oils or cold cream, is an excellent marking tool. The flat sliver makes a very thin line which vanishes when the garment is pressed. The edge of the soap can be sharpened easily with a nail file. Test to be sure it won't leave a stain.

Water-erasable marking pen. Water-erasable marking pens are relatively new to the seamstress, but quilters have been using them for years. They call them "spit-pens." The ink is water soluble and disappears with a drop of water (spit). Remove the mark from the fabric as soon as possible and do not press over it.

Test the pen on a scrap before using it on your fabric, to be sure the pen won't leave a stain on the fabric, and water won't leave a spot.

Tracing wheel. A needle-point or stiletto tracing wheel can be used to mark most fabrics, even delicate ones. The needle-point tracing wheel is a great tool for patternmaking and can be purchased from a tailoring supply house if your local fabric shop doesn't stock them. If you don't have a needle-point tracing wheel, use a serrated wheel.

Dual tracing wheel. The dual tracing wheel marks the cutting line when you trace the seamline. This adjustable wheel is a great timesaver for patternmaking, adding seam allowances, and matching plaids or stripes.

Tracing carbon. Use only white tracing carbon; colored tracing carbon may leave a permanent mark. The new washable tracing carbon is fine if you don't mind washing your new dress before you wear it.

Miscellaneous Tools and Supplies

Pins. Purchase stainless steel, silk dressmaker pins in large quantities—by the pound or half pound. Throw away all pins that have nicks, burrs, or blunt points. Discard every pin that has been stitched over. When you drop pins on the floor, sweep them out. Don't take a chance on ruining a beautiful garment with a damaged pin worth less than a penny.

Use pins with glass or plastic heads when sewing on knitted or loosely woven fabrics. They are longer, easier to find in the garment and they don't slip out of the fabric easily; but—they aren't as fine, and they are expensive.

Wrist pincushion. You should have at least one wrist pincushion. Keep one for plain pins, one for "fat heads" and a couple of extras in case you misplace one. You'll enjoy the convenience of having pins with you at the cutting table, pressing board, or sewing machine, and they won't all tumble out when you drop them.

Thimble. A thimble is a necessity to hand sew with speed. Its performance depends on the depressions or knurls which should be sharply cut and deep. If the knurls are shallow, the end of the needle will slip when it's pushed.

Select a thimble which fits your middle finger snugly. Learn to use it by pushing with the side of the finger instead of the end.

Needles. Select needles in small sizes (sizes 8 or 9) for most of your hand sewing. Use larger needles for heavyweight fabrics. Short embroidery or crewel needles are best for hemming and finishing and long darners or sharps for basting. Darners have a large eye, unlike the often-used sharps with small eyes. The large eye makes darners easier to thread.

Use a tapestry needle (size 18 or 20) for turning super-thin bias tubing and for cording bound buttonholes; and leather or glover's needles when you sew on leather, vinyl, or pseudosuedes.

Calyx-eyed needles are advised if you have extreme difficulty threading needles. These needles have a slotted opening in the eye, making them easy to thread, but they should not be used when sewing fine fabrics.

Needle threader. A needle threader is not only an aid to use when threading needles but is useful when pulling threads to the wrong side of the garment or repairing fabric snags.

Point turners. Point turners, which help to eliminate the telltale corners so many home sewers produce, are available in two different styles. One style is a plastic or bamboo tool that does an outstanding job on most corners. The other tool is a little gadget that works on the same principle as those used in the fashion industry. It looks like ice tongs. This style will take care of the hard-to-reach corners in belts and can also be used as a tube turner.

If you sew a lot, you'll want both styles. In addition, you should have an orangewood stick like those used for manicures to make turning collars with long points easy.

Mirror. A full-length mirror is an absolute necessity when you sew.

Crumbcloth. Use a clean, old sheet as a crumbcloth to cover the floor in your sewing area. It will protect light-colored fabrics from soil, make cleaning fast and easy at the end of the day, and protect the vacuum and carpet from hard-to-find pins.

Pressing Equipment

Iron. A steam iron is indispensable. If you are purchasing a new iron, select one with a "shot of steam."

Portable steamer. A portable steamer has a nonmetal soleplate which allows you to press fabrics on the right side without scorching or slicking them. This soleplate doesn't become hot when the steamer is steaming and it works when it's held vertically as well as horizontally. My personal choice is the Osrow Steamstress.®

Detachable soleplate. This laminated nonstick plate fits over the soleplate of the iron. It can be used when pressing the right side of fabrics, even naps, without scorching or slicking them; and fusibles won't stick to it.

Adding a detachable plate is an inexpensive way to make an old iron with a "gucky" soleplate like new.

Press cloths. You should have several clean press cloths. See-through cloths are easy to use, but dishtowels or old baby diapers are just as good. Use a woollen press cloth for pressing woollen fabrics and a heavy muslin or drill cloth for tailoring.

Ironing board or pressing stand. The ironing board

should be well-padded and sturdy. If you sew a lot, you will also want a pressing stand which sits on a table. This stand allows you to press the garment with the garment resting on the table, instead of hanging off the ironing board where it might stretch.

Sleeve board. This narrow pressing board allows you to press sleeves and difficult-to-reach sections without creasing them.

Point presser and clapper. The point presser is cut from a ¾″ (19.1 mm) piece of wood and mounted on a heavy stand—the clapper. This narrow pressing board allows you to press seams open without leaving an imprint on the right side of the garment and to press the points of collars and cuffs open without wrinkling adjacent areas. If you do not have a point presser, use a wooden dowel or yardstick.

The clapper is used to pound the steam into resilient fabrics to make a sharp edge or flat seam. If you don't have a clapper, use a fabric-wrapped brick.

Tailor's ham. A tailor's ham is an oblong-shaped cushion used for pressing curved or shaped areas.

Pressing mitt. A small pressing mitt that fits onto the hand or end of the sleeve board is easy to handle when pressing hard-to-reach and small areas.

Pressing pad. A pressing pad made of several layers of polyester fleece will ensure a well-padded surface for pressing matelassé, embroidered fabrics, lace, buttonholes, pockets, appliqués, and other raised surfaces. Cut the layers to the desired size and machine stitch them together at each edge.

Seam roll. This long roll-shaped cushion can be purchased, or you can make your own by wrapping a rolled magazine in a towel. The rounded surface of the seam roll allows you to press the seams open without leaving seam impressions on the right side of the garment.

Notions

Paper. Several kinds of paper are needed when you sew: Pattern paper, drafting, wrapping, butcher, or physician's examining-table paper are all available in convenient-sized rolls to use for patternmaking and other jobs which require large pieces.

Wax paper, a roll of adding machine tape, tissue paper, or typing paper are an aid in eliminating stitching problems.

Nonwoven pattern material. Nonwoven pattern paper is used for tracing multisized patterns, making complete patterns, and preserving your favorite patterns.

Tape. Transparent tape and drafting tape have many uses in the sewing room: Use tape for pattern adjustments and patternmaking. Use it to mark the right side of the fabric when the right and wrong sides look alike. Never press over the tape—it will melt and leave a spot. It shouldn't be used on the right side of napped fabrics because it might pull the nap off. Test to be sure.

Doublestick tape. Basting tapes or regular doublestick tapes can be used to replace hand basting. Never stitch through these tapes or press over them.

Glue. Use a *washable glue stick* obtained from the notions or stationery department for glue basting. The glue will wash out if you get it on the right side of the fabric, and the fabric can be pulled apart without difficulty if you need to reposition the sections of fabric. A glue stick is a great aid when positioning pockets, trims, zippers, interfacings, backings, waistbands, collars, cuffs, and hems. Allow the glue to set for several minutes after gluing before you stitch.

Use a *permanent glue* to apply underlinings, to position trims, and to hem garments. These glues usually dry colorless but they may leave a dark spot on some fabrics. I prefer Sobo.

Rubber cement is best for gluing leather, vinyls, and pseudosuedes; *Velcro adhesive* adheres Velcro® to fabrics.

Test all glues on a fabric scrap before using them on the garment sections.

Fray retardant. A colorless liquid which prevents ravelling is applied to the cut edges and allowed to dry. Be sure to test for discoloration on a fabric scrap before using it on your garment. I prefer one called Fray Check.™

Needle lubricant. A lubricant eliminates skipped stitches. Squeeze it onto the machine needle, thread, and between the tension discs as you work or squeeze several vertical lines onto the spool of thread before filling the bobbin and threading the machine.

Soft-tip pens. Soft-tip pens in a selection of permanent colors can be used to "dye" zippers, organza patches, and interfacing materials which might show on the finished garment.

Thread. For most of your sewing, select long-staple polyester thread in a shade to match your fabric. This thread is spun from fibre lengths 5½″–6½″ (14 cm–16.5 cm) long. These long fibres leave fewer ends for a smoother appearance and less fuzziness than the 1½″ and 2½″ (3.8 cm and 6.4 cm) lengths of short-staple spun cotton on polyester-core threads. Long-staple threads knot and twist less in hand sewing and break less often in machine-stitching. Metrosene, Seralon, Wright's, and Gutermann are just a few of the long-staple threads available.

Nylon threads in clear and dark translucent can be used on many fabrics if you don't have thread to match the fabric. Nylon thread makes an almost invisible stitch and a flat seam. It will melt, however, if pressed with a very hot iron.

Metallic threads, embroidery floss and buttonhole twist in silk or polyester and regular polyester threads in the desired color can be used for topstitching or decorative stitching.

Use special threads for special techniques such as basting, gathering, and tailor tacking. Always use white thread for these techniques—colors sometimes bleed or fade on the fabric.

Embroidery floss is a soft thread without a finish to be used when making tailor's tacks. It won't fall out of the fabric as easily as a thread with a finish.

Silk buttonhole twist is a strong thread which won't break when gathering long strips or turning bias tubings. Its silky quality makes gathering easy.

Silk thread (size A) is a must for basting when it is necessary to press over the basted line, because it won't leave an impression on the fabric.

Fusible bonding agents. There are fusible agents which melt between two layers of fabric when heat and moisture are applied. They are sold by the yard and in narrow widths, and can be used before or instead of stitching.

Fusible Web, Jiffy Fuse,™ Magic Polyweb,® Sav-a-Stitch,® and Stitch Witchery® are the brand names of some of the best-known bonding materials.

Other Timesavers

Sewing log. Keep a record of each garment you make in a small notebook. Include a swatch of the fabric and the interfacing, the pattern number, any changes you made, the pattern size (especially when it is a multisized or child's pattern), the fabric amount, any problems that arose during construction or after the first washing, and anything else that will be helpful when you use the pattern again.

Lamp. A clamp-on desk lamp with an adjustable arm is an invaluable aid. Attach the lamp to your sewing table or sewing-machine cabinet and adjust it to direct the light precisely.

Plastic card. Try using a small, flexible plastic card on top of bulky or fragile fabrics to slide the garment section under the presser foot or buttonhole attachment easily and without damaging the fabric.

If the feed dog on your machine cannot be lowered easily, use another card under the garment section to protect it from the teeth of the feed dog.

Beeswax or a white candle. Eliminate twisting and strengthen the thread by waxing it when you sew by hand. Both of these waxes, however, leave grease stains on some fabrics. Make a test sample and press to check for staining before you use waxed thread on your garments.

White vinegar. Brush white vinegar on the garment with a one-inch paintbrush to save time when setting or removing creases, but test the fabric first for color fastness.

Fingernail polish remover (acetone). Use fingernail polish remover which contains acetone to test acetates. Many acetate fabrics look like polyesters, but they don't have the same washability. Test to be sure. Acetone fingernail polish remover will dissolve acetate fabrics.

Rubbing alcohol or hair spray. Try one of these products to remove ballpoint ink. Test! Test! Test!

Denatured alcohol. Denatured alcohol can be used to remove fusible bonding agent from fashion fabrics. Sponge it onto the fabric sparingly, using a piece of cotton cloth. Denatured alcohol is available at pharmacies.

Laundry soap. Many new fabrics have offensive chemical odors. Wash the fabric with soap, *not detergent,* to remove some or all of the odor.

Aluminum foil. Cover a piece of cardboard with aluminum foil to use when pressing or fusing. The foil will reflect the heat and steam, enabling you to complete the job in less time.

Hot-iron cleaner. Use a hot-iron cleaner to clean the iron while it's hot if you inadvertently fuse interfacing or fusible agent to the soleplate of the iron.

THE SEWING MACHINE

Your most important piece of sewing equipment is a sewing machine. Any machine in good working condition can be used satisfactorily—it doesn't have to be new or elaborate. Even though a machine that makes fancy stitches is fun to use, and it may save you time and effort, most garments can be made easily on an old-fashioned straight-stitch machine.

If you are purchasing a new machine, select a machine that meets your needs and fits your budget. Consider purchasing a reconditioned machine if you can't afford a new one.

Learn to use your machine, study the owner's manual and take the time to master any attachments and extra features. The success of your sewing depends on what *you* can do with your machine—not what the machine costs, nor the number of decorative stitches it will make.

Keep your machine clean, well-oiled, and lubricated for trouble-free sewing.

KNOW YOUR MACHINE

Many exciting features have been added to the sewing machine since it was patented in 1846 by Elias Howe, Jr., but the basic process of forming the stitch is the same: The upper thread, carried by the needle, interlocks with the lower thread, carried by the shuttle hook, to form a locked stitch.

The needle. The sewing machine needle is uniquely designed to penetrate the fabric and to carry the needle thread through the material. The various parts of the needle—the shank, shaft, long groove, eye, scarf, point, and short groove—have each been developed for a specific purpose. (Fig. 1)

The *shank* or upper end of the needle is the part held by the needle clamp. Most needles for home

shaft

point

eye　*long groove*　*shank*

Fig. 1

sewing machines are flat on one side of the shank, making it easy to set the needle correctly.

The *shaft* of the needle extends from the shank to the point. The size of the shaft is determined by the needle size—the smaller the needle size, the thinner the blade.

The *long groove* is on the side of the needle opposite the flat side of the shank. This groove guides and protects the thread between the last thread guide and the needle eye.

The *eye* of the needle is proportioned to the size of the needle or the diameter of the needle blade. It may be larger on special needles for special situations like topstitching.

The *scarf* or *clearance above the eye* permits the needle thread to form a loop so that the stitch can be made.

The *point* of the needle is shaped to penetrate the fabric. The ballpoint is customarily used for woven and knitted fabrics; this type of point causes the fibres to spread without damaging them. A cutting point is usually used for nonfabric materials of low elasticity like leather.

The *short groove* extends a short distance above and below the eye. The short groove and the flat side of the shank are on the same side of the needle.

Bobbin. The bobbin holds the lower thread. It is placed into a bobbin case which is placed in the shuttle. The bobbin case may be a separate case or built into the machine.

Shuttle. The shuttle travels around the bobbin case, and the shuttle hook carries the lower thread through a loop of the upper thread to make a lockstitch.

Race mechanism. The race mechanism holds the bobbin, the bobbin case, and the shuttle.

Tension discs. The tension discs regulate the amount of tension on the needle thread.

Tension regulators. The tension regulator on the top of the machine regulates the tension discs. The tension is easy to adjust if you remember that the tension control is a screw just like any other screw. Turn it clockwise to tighten it and counterclockwise to loosen it.

Some home sewers find it easier to remember that the higher the number on the tension regulator, the tighter the tension on the needle thread.

The tension regulator on the bobbin case is a small screw which adjusts the spring on the case and regulates the bobbin tension. The lower tension is adjusted by tightening or loosening this screw. (Fig. 2)

Fig. 2

Stitch regulators. The numbers on the stitch-length regulator (1, 2, 3, etc.) indicate the number of millimeters in each stitch. A setting of 2½ is approximately 10 stitches to the inch.

On older machines, the stitch length is indicated by the number of stitches to the inch (6, 12, 15, etc.). A setting of 10 indicates 10 stitches to the inch.

The numbers on the stitch-width indicator show the width of the stitch in millimeters.

Presser foot. The presser foot holds the fabric in place. It is also an invaluable gauge for stitching evenly. The outside and inside edges of the straight-stitch foot and zigzag foot can be used advantageously to gauge different widths.

Use the *inside* of the straight-stitch foot to gauge ¹⁄₁₆″ (1.6 mm) from the fold or seamline when edge-stitching, cleanfinishing, understitching, or hemming.

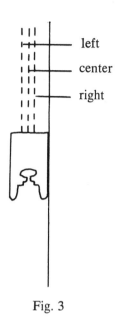

Fig. 3

Varying the needle position also increases the use of the inside edge of the zigzag foot as a guide.

The presser-foot shank is screwed or locked to the presser bar. The shank for most feet is low (Fig. 4a), high (Fig. 4b) or slanted (Fig. 4c). The

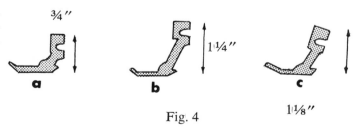

Fig. 4

feet within each group are interchangeable. This allows you to use a foot made by other sewing machine companies on your machine. Bernina has a unique snap-on foot; however, an adapter is available enabling you to use any low shank foot.

Presser-foot lifter. The presser-foot lifter lifts the presser foot and releases the upper tension so that the needle thread can be pulled easily.

The presser foot on some machines can be lifted higher than the regular "up" position by holding the presser-foot lifter up manually. This is advantageous when changing presser feet or inserting fragile or bulky fabrics under the foot.

Throat plate. Most machines have guidelines indicated on the throat plate. Use these guides to stitch accurately. If your machine doesn't have guidelines, place a piece of drafting tape on the throat plate and, using a tape measure, mark guides the desired distance from the needle. (Fig. 5a)

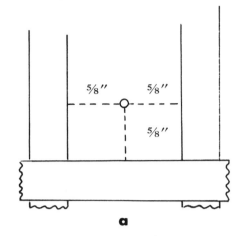

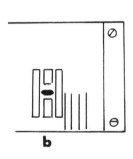

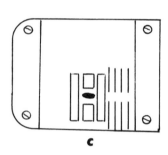

Fig. 5

There are several less conspicuous guides on the throat plate as well—the numbers on the guidelines may be in a line even with the needle (Fig. 5b) or the guidelines may begin in a line directly opposite the needle. (Fig. 5c) Examine the throat plate on your machine. On some machines, the guidelines have crosslines to indicate when to pivot at a corner. (Fig. 5d)

Most zigzag machines have a throat plate with a small hole and one with a large hole. Use the small-hole plate when straight stitching to hold the fabric securely, to prevent the fabric from being pulled down into the hole and to eliminate skipped stitches and puckered seams. Use the zigzag plate or plate with a large hole for zigzag stitching.

Feed dog. The jagged teeth of the feed dog move the fabric backward. While the feed dog is pulling the lower layer backward, the presser foot is pushing the upper layer forward. This is one reason the lower layer creeps and ends up shorter than the upper one.

The amount of creeping is increased if there is too much pressure from the presser foot.

The pulling action of the feed dog can be used to your advantage when you are easing a longer piece to a shorter piece, shaping a seam, stitching a bias piece to a straight piece, or stitching a loosely woven fabric to a firmly woven one.

Lower the feed dog to avoid snagging delicate fabrics when placing them under the presser foot or when stitching a bulky seam or making a buttonhole. Raise the feed dog before you begin stitching.

Pressure regulator. The pressure regulator is used to adjust the amount of pressure on the presser foot. The correct amount of pressure is just enough to hold the fabric firmly, feed it evenly, and make a uniform stitch. Too little pressure makes it difficult to stitch a straight line; too much pressure causes the feed dog to leave an imprint on the fabric, the lower layer to creep excessively, and the seam to pucker.

The pressure is adjusted automatically on many new machines.

Hand wheel. The hand wheel can be turned clockwise or counterclockwise. The hand wheel on most home sewing machines turns counterclockwise when you are stitching.

To avoid making an extra loop which can cause the thread to bubble on the underside of the seam, breaking the thread or jamming the machine, do *not* turn the hand wheel in the reverse direction.

Turn the hand wheel manually for control when stitching difficult seams.

Free arm. The free arm is an optional feature which enables you to stitch hard-to-reach sections easily. Some machines are easier to convert from the flat bed to the free arm and back again than others. This inconvenience tempts many home sewers to do all of their stitching on the free arm, sacrificing speed and precision.

Sewing-machine light. The light on the sewing machine can be used for little pressing jobs, such as the shoulder seams and back-shoulder darts.

Sewing-machine accessories. There are a number of attachments and special feet available for your sewing machine. I have described the ones which I like best. You may not need or want every attachment. Evaluate your needs and purchase only the attachments you'll use.

A *zipper foot* enables you to stitch close to a raised edge. It is an important aid for stitching zippers, cordings, bindings and difficult-to-stitch seamlines. I like a foot that can be adjusted when I want to move it closer to the needle.

An *invisible zipper foot* is required to set invisible zippers. It can also be used as a cording foot.

Hemming feet are available in several sizes to make very narrow hems or seams. The most common size is ⅛″ (3.2 mm).

The *even-feed or walking foot* feeds the top layer of fabric through the machine while the feed dog feeds the bottom layer. Use it for stitching pseudo-suedes, plaids, napped fabrics, thick fabrics such as denim, and for topstitching.

The *roller foot* also feeds the top layer and prevents slippage of some fabrics.

The *blind-hemming foot* moves along the fold of the garment, enabling you to stitch the hem easily.

An *overcast foot* has a tongue which holds the fabric flat and prevents curling as you zigzag the edge.

Snap-on feet are available for some machines. Several feet, packaged with the appropriate ankle, can be purchased for most machines.

A *buttonhole attachment* enables you to make buttonholes on straight-stitch machines and keyhole buttonholes on zigzag machines.

If the manufacturer of your machine doesn't make a buttonhole attachment for it, attachments are available that fit most machines.

Separate gauges, which are screwed to the machine bed, provide a guide for stitching straight or slightly curved seams. They're difficult to use when stitching deeply curved seams.

A *magnet strip* which can be stuck to the top of the machine is handy to hold the extra feet you use most often.

A *foam pad,* like those used under typewriters, will keep a portable machine from sliding on the table. A small foam pad placed under the foot control will hold it in place.

SEWING-MACHINE NEEDLE SELECTION

The success or failure of a garment is sometimes as simple as selecting the proper size and type of needle for the fabric.

Selection of the proper needle size is influenced by the size of the thread and the fabric weight and texture. The thread size determines the minimum needle size. The needle size should be just large enough to penetrate the fabric without bending. Using a needle that is too large may cause fabric distortion, puckered seams, and skipped stitches. Generally, the heavier the fabric weight, the larger the needle required to penetrate it.

The needle type is usually determined by the shape of the needle point, shank, and the clearance cut above the eye. These features of the sewing-machine needle are varied for use on specific fabrics. It is important to understand the variations in order to select the most suitable needle. Examine various needle types with a magnifying glass to see the differences.

Regular, sharp-pointed needles are only used on woven fabrics. (Fig. 6a)

Fig. 6a

Ballpoint needles have slightly rounded points and are recommended for general sewing on knitted and woven fabrics. (Fig. 6b)

Fig. 6b

Universal needles have a longer scarf, or clearance above the eye, than regular ballpoint needles. This flattened area helps to prevent skipped stitches. (Fig. 6c) The flat side of the shank which fits into the needle bar is deeply cut and positions the needle eye close to the point of the shuttle hook to eliminate skipped stitches.

Fig. 6c

Yellow Band Needles (made by Singer), Q Needles (made by Sears) and Schmetz Regular Needles are all universal needles.

Needles for two-way stretch fabrics have a fully-rounded ballpoint for skip-free stitching on coarse knitwear and elastic materials.

Stretch needles have a super-fine ballpoint, an elongated scarf, a deeply-cut shank, and a special eye for stitching synthetics, elastic knitwear, and delicate fabrics such as very fine silk-like jersey.

Leather needles have wedge-shaped cutting points and are designed for stitching leather and vinyl (not for stitching pseudosuedes). (Fig. 6d)

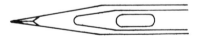

Fig. 6d

Jeans needles have a super-sharp point and are designed to penetrate denim, canvas, and other tightly woven fabrics.

Basting needles have two eyes, one above the other. The upper eye is threaded to produce skip-stitches for basting or topstitching. The lower eye is threaded for regular stitching. (At this time, Bernina is the only manufacturer of this needle.)

Topstitching needles are fine needles with large eyes which will accommodate a heavy or thick thread.

Twin, triple, and wing needles are used for decorative stitching.

Experiment with different brands of needles and different kinds of threads until you find the needle-thread combinations that work well on your machine.

Keep a variety of needles in several sizes on hand. Change the needle often; synthetic fabrics dull the needle quickly.

Most stitching problems are caused by needles that are the wrong size, damaged or inserted incorrectly.

BABY-LOCK MACHINES

Baby-Lock and Juki machines have recently been introduced to the home sewer. These machines trim the fabric edge and make an overcast stitch on the edge like a commercial overlock machine. There are two different-style machines available. One machine requires three spools of thread, the other requires four. Admittedly, they are an extravagance, but if you can afford one, and you sew a lot, you'll want one of these machines to save time and to make a truly professional finish.

The three-thread machine has a single needle, which carries one thread, and two loopers, which carry the other two threads. As you sew, the three threads intertwine to overcast the edge. The four-thread machine has two needles, each carrying a thread, and two loopers, carrying the other two threads. Two threads intertwine to overcast the edge and two threads make a chain-stitched seam.

Since I use this machine just to finish the edges, I prefer the three-thread machine because it makes a more attractive finish.

BASIC SEWING SKILLS

The basics of sewing—machine stitching, hand sewing, pressing and assembling—are especially important when you're using shortcuts. Your ability to handle these elements determines the success of the garment you make and how much time you'll save.

MACHINE TECHNIQUES

Good machine stitching is the biggest difference between the finish of a professional and the look of an amateur. It determines the appearance and durability of every garment, and it cannot be overemphasized. The most valuable timesaver you'll ever learn is how to use your sewing machine to the best advantage. Learn to stitch it right the first time—it's time-consuming and boring to rip it out and stitch it again!

Adjust the Machine for the Fabric

Insert the correct size and type of needle. This procedure is made easy for the home sewer since the shank of the machine is flat on one side with the long groove on the other side. The needle is always placed in the machine so that the thread is inserted into the long groove. This groove always faces the last thread guide on the machine. (Fig. 7)

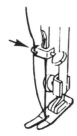

Fig. 7

Thread the machine. Place the spool of thread on the spool spindle so that the slash is at the bottom of the spool to prevent the thread from catching in the slash. If there isn't a small felt circle under the spool, place one under it so that the thread will feed off the spool properly through the guides, tension discs, and take-up lever. To thread the needle, cut the thread at an angle. The thread should be relaxed when you cut it. If it is taut, the end will unravel and require further trimming. Slide the end of the thread down the groove of the needle until the thread slides into the needle hole. All you have to do then is catch the end on the other side and pull the thread through. If you have difficulty seeing the needle eye, hold a white card behind the needle.

Fill the bobbin and place it in the **bobbin case.** The slash on the bobbin case indicates the proper way to insert the bobbin. The thread comes off the bobbin in the direction of the slash (Fig. 8)

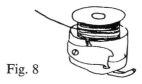

Fig. 8

Pull the bobbin thread up through the needle hole by holding the needle thread firmly in your left hand and turning the hand wheel with your right hand. The needle will enter the needle hole and bring the bobbin thread up. Pull both threads—bobbin and needle—back and under the presser foot about 6″ (15.2 cm).

If the bobbin on your machine *isn't* filled through the needle, you can use this industrial timesaver—

set up a bobbin spool for filling and let it fill while you are stitching so that you will be ready for the next garment.

Use the straight-stitch foot and small-hole throat plate instead of the zigzag foot and plate when straight stitching for greater control, speed, and accuracy.

Check the stitching. Before beginning each new garment, make a line of stitching across the bias through two layers of fabric to check the tension, thread color and size, needle size and sharpness, stitch length, and stitch formation.

Adjust the tension. Stitch seams with a balanced tension so that the stitches look the same on both sides of the work. Loosen the upper tension for ease-basting and some topstitching.

Regulate the pressure. The fabric should feed evenly and smoothly.

Set the stitch length. The stitch length is important in all stitching. Most seams are stitched with 10–12 stitches per inch or a 2–2½ mm stitch. This length is sometimes referred to as regular, regulation, or permanent stitch.

A longer stitch, 6–10 stitches per inch (2½– 4 mm), is needed on vinyl, leather, suede, and pseudosuede fabrics to avoid cutting the material. Heavy or bulky fabrics also require a longer stitch because the fabric thickness causes the stitch to shorten.

A short stitch, 20 stitches per inch (1.25 mm), is used for reinforcing.

A very short stitch, 30 stitches per inch (.75 mm), is used for security.

A basting stitch, 6 stitches per inch (4 mm), is used to hold two or more layers together temporarily and to mark garment sections.

The stitch length can be changed anytime to meet your needs. If you near the end of a stitching line and see that another stitch will carry the line too far, adjust the stitch length to a shorter length. Apply this technique whenever you must stop precisely, as when you are stitching buttonholes or setting pockets.

Set the stitch width. Adjust the stitch width for the desired stitch pattern. The stitch width on most zigzag machines can be adjusted from 0–4 mm. One mm is a narrow width, 2 mm is medium, and 3–4 mm is wide. Replace the straight-stitch foot and small-hole throat plate with the zigzag **foot and** plate, and set the stitch pattern.

The Sewing Procedure
Approximately 75 percent of your time is spent getting ready to sew and cleaning up after you sew, leaving only 25 percent for stitching. If you rip a lot, you may stitch as little as 10 percent of the time.

Save a little clean-up time with advance preparation. Spread the floor with a crumbcloth and place a wastebasket near the machine.

Don't waste time. Have everything you need on hand, ready to sew, when you begin working. Organize your work into units so you won't waste time looking for pieces. Place the sections you plan to stitch first in your lap; place the other sections on a nearby table.

Work with a positive attitude. Strangely enough, it is easier to get a professional finish in less time when you expect it.

Arranging Your Work
Position the fabric under the presser foot with the bulk to the left. When you set waistbands and stitch shell hems, position the bulk to the *right* of the presser foot.

Match the cut edges of the fabric layers unless directed otherwise. Match the notches, clips, or other indicators as you work.

Complete all small sections such as pockets, flaps, and collars first.

Stitch directionally. Arrange the garment sections so that you will be stitching with the grain. This will preserve the grainline and prevent stretching. Generally, stitch from the wide part of the garment section to the narrow part when stitching directionally. (Fig. 9)

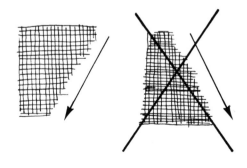

Fig. 9

Shoulder seams especially should always be stitched directionally from the neckline to the armhole. This not only preserves the grain in the shoulder area, it also ensures matching the seam exactly at the neckline. If the seam is off ⅛″ (3.2 mm) at the armhole, it is less critical than if it is off ⅛″ (3.2 mm) at the neckline.

Directional stitching is especially important to prevent rippling when seams are self-finished. Self-finished seams include French, standing-fell, and flat-fell seams.

Arrange as you go. Arrange only the first inch or less for stitching before placing the work under the presser foot; anchor it by lowering the needle into the fabric and the presser foot down; then arrange the next section, which may be 6″–10″ (15.2 cm–25.4 cm) on straight sections or 1″–2″ (2.5 cm–5.1 cm) in intricate areas. Try to arrange from one notch to the next without pinning. If you need a lot of pins to hold the fabric in place, hand baste instead. Pin basting takes more time than you realize because you must remove the pins as you stitch. Do *not* stitch over pins.

Arrange your work so that you always stitch *away* from difficult-to-match points instead of toward them.

Sew flat. Complete as much as possible on each section *before* joining it to another. Set the pockets, zipper, collar, finish the unnotched facing edges, and apply any trims while the sections are flat.

When you are stitching a loop seam such as an armscye, sleeve, or pant leg, stitch inside the loop or circle. Overlap the stitching line at the beginning and end for ½″ (12.7 mm) instead of using a backtack.

Stitching

Hold the needle and bobbin threads securely behind the needle to eliminate a thread bubble or an unthreaded needle when you begin stitching.

Fasten the stitching securely at the beginning and at the end of the stitching line. There are several ways to fasten the thread. Use the method which is easiest for you and most suitable for the garment.

⚙ Make a backtack or backstitch by stitching forward ½″ (12.7 mm), then backward, then forward again. Stitch backward by reversing the machine or by pulling the work *forward* to prevent the fabric from feeding normally. Several stitches will be made over the first stitches.

⚙ Spot tack by stitching with the stitch length set at 0, by lowering the feed dog or by holding the fabric in front of the presser foot so that the fabric doesn't move. Spot tacking doesn't always make a satisfactory knot.

⚙ Stitch ½″–1″ (12.7 mm– 25.4 mm) with very short (30 spi, .75 mm) stitches.

⚙ Knot the threads. Twist the two threads together and make a tailor's knot at the end of the stitching line. This method is used most often at the ends of darts.

⚙ Thread the ends of the thread into a needle or needle threader and hide them between the fabric layers.

If you begin stitching in the middle of a seam which won't be pressed open, it isn't necessary to backtack. Begin the new stitching line at the cut edge and overlap the previous stitching ½″ (12.7 mm). (Fig. 10)

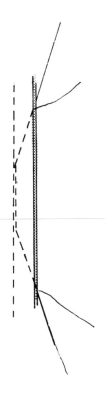

Fig. 10

Seams which will be trimmed should be secured where the seamlines will cross, instead of at the edge of the section, to avoid trimming away the backtack. (Fig. 11)

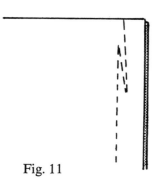

Fig. 11

When a section of the stitching line has been ripped, restitch so that the ends of the stitching are in the seam allowance. (Fig. 12)

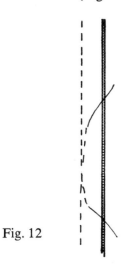

Fig. 12

Match and control the fabric as you work, interrupting the stitching procedure as needed. Anchor your work when you stop to adjust it by lowering the needle into the needle hole to avoid an irregularity in the stitching.

Work with dexterity, using your hands to control the fabric. Hold fabrics that creep or slip firmly in front and back of the presser foot so that the material is taut to eliminate excessive feeding of the underlayer and puckered seams. This technique often eliminates skipped stitches, too.

I also use my fingers as an aid in controlling the fabric. To do this, I place my index and middle fingers flat on either side of the presser foot, holding the upper layer flat when stitching. To avoid the possibility of running the needle through my fingers, I stop the machine each time I reposition them. (Fig. 13a)

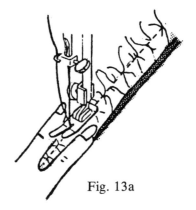

Fig. 13a

Use your index finger for crimping. This is sometimes called crowding, staystitching plus, or ease plus. Hold your index finger firmly behind the presser foot as you stitch. (Fig. 13b) This causes the

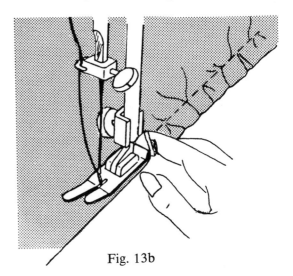

Fig. 13b

fabric to pile up and make small pleats, forcing more fabric into each stitch than usual. Use this technique to clean-finish curved areas and to ease shoulder seams, sleeves, waistlines, or darts. Woollens and permanent press fabrics do not actually crimp; however, the crimping action usually forces more fabric into each stitch. If there is too much crimping, break some of the threads to remove the extra ease.

Use your scissors to position difficult-to-stitch sections. Holding the blades of the scissors together in the palm of your hand, use the points to adjust fullness and hold the upper layer of fabric flat in front of the presser foot or push it up to the foot.

Stitch at an even speed. Use the speed dictated by the garment design and fabric. Stitch long seams at full speed, stitch difficult-to-handle sections, such as corners and curves, slowly. Turn the hand wheel manually to walk the machine around intricate seams.

Use a gauge to keep the stitching line an even distance from the cut edge. The presser foot is the easiest gauge to use, and you can utilize the inside and outside edges of the foot as a guide. Lines marked on the throat plate permanently or with tape are also convenient. Metal seam guides are helpful for straight seams, but they have limited use when the seams are curved.

Use gauge stitching to mark difficult-to-match and difficult-to-stitch sections.

Key and *quarter* the garment sections so that they are easy to match and stitch accurately.

Chain stitch. Stitch continuously from one section to the next section, connecting them with a thread chain. Stitch to the edge of one section or seam; secure the threads with a backtack; then stitch onto the next section without cutting the threads or raising the presser foot. A thread chain bridges the two sections. Stitch as many pieces as possible before cutting the threads. Chain stitching is the most effective way to release the work from under the presser foot, and it eliminates thread bubbles which might form at the beginning of the stitched line. It also eliminates unthreaded needles. As you finish one seam, feed another under the presser foot and keep stitching. (Fig. 14a)

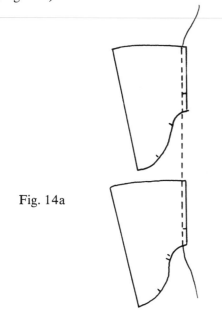

Fig. 14a

When you don't have another section ready to be stitched onto, stitch onto a small scrap of fabric to continue the chain. (Fig. 14b)

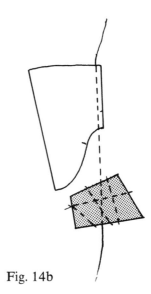

Fig. 14b

Chain stitching requires stitching a short distance without fabric between the presser foot and the feed dog. This will not damage your machine.

If chain stitching is impractical when the stitching line is ended, raise the presser foot and the take-up lever to the highest point, then pull the stitched section to the back of the machine to avoid breaking the needle or the upper thread.

If you are not chain stitching when you begin a stitching line, hold the needle and bobbin threads behind the presser foot securely.

Stitching Techniques
These techniques, used regularly, will not only improve the quality of your work, they will also make sewing quicker, easier, and more fun.

Staystitching. Staystitching is a line of stitching through a single layer of fabric to preserve the grain of the garment section, to provide a guide for clipping and joining, and to prevent stretching.

Staystitch with the grain just inside the seamline $\frac{9}{16}''$ (14.3 mm) from the cut edge.

If you rip a lot, staystitching will help preserve the garment shape. If you are an experienced seamstress and rip rarely, you can safely eliminate most staystitching except at the neckline.

25

Edgestitching. Edgestitching is often used on garments. Stitch along the folded or finished edge of the garment section so that the folded or finished edge moves along the inside of the presser foot, making the stitching line 1/16″ (1.6 mm) from the edge. (Fig. 15)

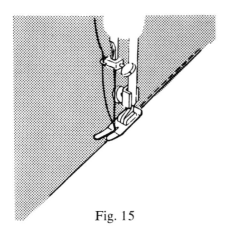

Fig. 15

Understitching. Understitch faced edges to prevent the seamline from rolling to the outside and to hold the seam allowances in the desired position.

With the facing face-up, stitch through the facing and seam allowances 1/16″ (1.6 mm) from the seamline, using the inside of the presser foot as a guide. (Fig. 16)

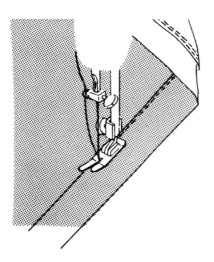

Fig. 16

Most garments are understitched *before* the seam is trimmed, clipped, and pressed.

Understitching usually eliminates the need to press seams open; however, the seams of extra-special garments should be pressed open, then understitched, trimmed, and clipped.

Understitch delicate fabrics by hand with a tiny backstitch.

Stitch-in-the-ditch. This technique is sometimes called crack stitching or ditch stitching. Stitch-in-the-ditch to secure waistbands, facings, linings, bindings and elastic. From the right side of the garment, stitch in the groove or well of the seam. (Fig. 17)

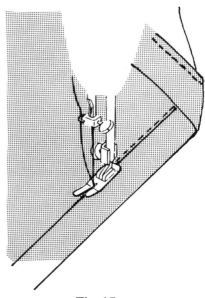

Fig. 17

If the fabric is bulky and a ridge is formed when the seam allowances are pressed to one side, use a zipper foot.

Ease basting. The success of this method is the uneven tension which causes the bobbin thread to float on the underside of the fabric and the short stitch which prevents pleating. If you accidentally pull the needle thread or stitch from the wrong side of the fabric, you must rip the stitching out and begin again.

Ease basting can be used to control ease on any fabric.

1. Loosen the upper tension.
2. Set the stitch length to 10–12 spi (2.5 mm). On lightweight fabrics, use a shorter stitch. Do not use

a long basting stitch except on heavyweight fabrics. The fabric will pleat in a long stitch.

3. From the *right side* of the garment section, place a line of stitching just inside the seamline.

4. Pull the *bobbin* thread to ease the fabric.

Gauge stitching. It is more difficult to gauge a width of ⅝″ (16 mm) than a width of ¼″ (6.4 mm) or ⅛″ (3.2 mm). Gauge stitching is used to mark difficult-to-match and difficut-to-stitch sections.

Place a line of gauge stitching in the seam allowance ⅜″ (9.5 mm) or ½″ (12.7 mm) from the cut edge to help you locate the seamline when matching plaids, setting zippers, or stitching lapped seams.

Paper stitching. To eliminate puckered seams, skipped stitches, creeping underlayers, and curling fabric, insert paper between the fabric and the feed dog before stitching.

I prefer papers like wax paper, adding-machine paper, or typing paper because they're easier to tear away than tissue paper. However, these papers cannot be used successfully on some machines because the feed dog won't feed properly with heavier papers. Many times you can insert the paper between the fabric and *presser foot* instead to stitch a perfect seam.

If you must use tissue paper, remember that paper has a grain just like fabric. It will tear away more easily when you stitch with the lengthwise grain than when you stitch with the crosswise grain. Make a sample to determine which is which.

Bartack. Using a very short, narrow zigzag stitch (W 1-L,.5), stitch ¼″–½″ (6.4 mm–12.7 mm) at stress points to make a bartack.

Bobbin stitching. Bobbin stitching eliminates a knot at the point of a dart.

1. Thread the machine and pull up the bobbin thread 15″–20″ (38.1 cm–50.8 cm).

2. Tie the bobbin and needle thread together. (Fig. 18)

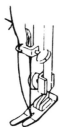

Fig. 18

3. Wind the needle thread onto the spool, pulling the bobbin thread through the needle, up to the machine and to the spool.

4. Stitch the dart from the point to the garment edge.

5. Rethread the machine to stitch the next dart.

Keying

Keying is a method of marking the seamlines which will be matched on corresponding sections. Collars, zipper tapes, and plackets are marked on the seamlines to ensure both sides are finished the same length.

Keying zippers. Close the zipper. Stitch across the ends of the tape ⅜″ (9.5 mm) above the zipper teeth, chain stitching from one side of the zipper to the other. (Fig. 19a)

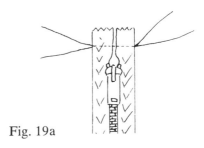

Fig. 19a

Cut the thread chain and set the zipper, matching the keyed lines to the stitching line on the garment neckline, armscye, or waistline.

Keying collars. Fold the collar in half at the center back and match the ends of the collar. Measure an even distance from the collar points to the neck edge and mark the stitching line at the neck. Unfold the collar and chain stitch from one side of the collar to the other at the marked points. (Fig. 19b)

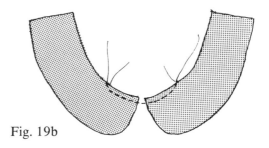

Fig. 19b

Cut the chain and set the collar to the garment neckline, matching the keyed lines to the stitching lines at the neck edge.

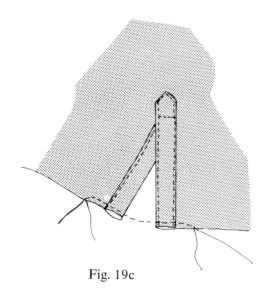

Fig. 19c

Keying plackets. Match the sides of plackets. Mark the seamline on each side of the placket. Chain stitch from one side of the placket to the other. (Fig. 19c)

Cut the chain and set the cuffs, collar, or waistband.

Quartering

Divide collars, cuffs, waistbands, and the edges they match into quarters if there are no notches. Match and pin the marked points, then stitch them together. *Note:* The quarter points on a collar won't match the shoulder seams and the quarter points on a waistband may not match the side seams.

TOPSTITCHING

Topstitching is a decorative detail which emphasizes the structural lines of a garment. It also serves an important and practical function by holding seams and facings in place and by keeping edges flat.

Thread

Regular thread is suitable for most topstitching. For greater emphasis, however, use thread from two spools. Thread the two as if they are one. Some machines don't have two spool spindles—fill two bobbins and stack them on the spindle with a small circle of felt between them. The felt circle keeps the top bobbin from spinning and feeding the thread too quickly.

You can also use two strands of thread on the bobbin. Fill the bobbin carefully, feeding both threads through the guide evenly.

Use polyester buttonhole twist and topstitching threads to greatly emphasize stitching lines or silk

buttonhole twist for a high luster. Metallic threads provide an interesting effect on dressy garments and sportswear.

The color of the thread can be matching or contrasting. A shade lighter than the fabric often gives a subtle emphasis.

Needles

Select a needle one size larger than usual for topstitching with regular thread. Universal needles perform consistently well.

Use a size 100 (16) or 110 (18) needle when you are topstitching with buttonhole twist. If the large needles leave holes in your fabric, try a topstitching needle, a smaller needle with a large eye. If a topstitching needle is unavailable, fill the bobbin with decorative thread and stitch from the wrong side of the fabric.

Use twin, triple, or wing needles for special effects. Loosen the tension if you don't want a raised fold between the stitched lines. The upper and lower tension should be tighter than normal when stitching pin tucks or the creases in slacks. The tighter the tension, the greater the ridge between the two lines.

Twin needles can be used with decorative stitches, but the stitch width is limited by the width of the hole in the throat plate. Check the width setting by turning the hand wheel manually to be sure the needles won't strike the throat plate.

Do not pivot with twin needles in the fabric. Raise the needles so that they rest on the fabric surface. Lift the presser foot halfway, take one stitch, turn the fabric again, lower the presser foot, and finish topstitching.

Pressure, Tension, and Stitch Length

Loosen the pressure on the presser foot when topstitching to avoid pushing the upper layer of fabric. If a drag line still forms, use an even-feed foot or roller foot.

Balance the tension to form a perfect stitch. If you want the stitches to make a noticeable indentation in the fabric, loosen the upper tension slightly so that the tension will no longer be balanced. Experiment with the loosened upper tension; if the bobbin thread is too tight, the seam will pucker.

Use long stitches for sportswear and very short stitches on dressier garments. The French stitch you find on those little $400 silk blouses is a stitch one millimeter long, that is, twenty-five stitches in every inch.

A very narrow, close zigzag stitch on tweeds and

heavy fabrics will create a solid line and an elastic straight stitch will create a heavy line.

Gauges

The edge of the straight-stitch or the zigzag foot is the easiest, most convenient gauge. It can be used to gauge distances from $1/16''-3/8''$ (1.6 mm–9.5 mm).

The three important variables are the needle position (L-C-R), the inside of the foot, and the outside of the foot. Decide on the desired width and experiment with the two feet until you find a satisfactory gauge.

If you are using an even feed foot or roller foot to eliminate a drag line, use it as a gauge.

Tape on the machine bed and scoring on the throat plate are convenient gauges for topstitching along the edge of the garments.

Seam guides that attach to the machine bed with a screw or magnet are helpful for beginners to stitch along straight edges. The guides can be set to use on curved edges, but they are cumbersome.

Other aids for gauging include quilting gauges and quilting feet. The simplest quilting guide is secured to the presser bar with the screw that holds the presser foot. The snap-on foot assortment includes a quilting guide which can be inserted into the ankle and used with any of the snap-on feet. Some quilting feet are not available with a hinged ankle, making stitching over seams even more difficult than usual. Some machines are designed so that the quilting gauge can be inserted into the presser bar.

Use chalk, soap, basting thread, drafting tape, transparent tape, and special topstitching tapes to mark intricate stitching lines. Stitch *next* to the marked line, not on it.

A cardboard template secured with doublestick tape can be used to outline stitching lines. Stick it to the garment and stitch around it.

Irregularities are less likely to show and occur when the stitch length is short than when it's long.

Stitching

Always test stitch to check the needle, thread, tension, pressure, and stitch length. Stitch through as many layers of fabric and interfacing as you will have on the garment. This may be as many as eight layers of fabric and four layers of interfacing.

Whenever possible, topstitch one garment unit before joining it to another. Stitch with the grain. Stitch each side of a seam in the same direction. If the fabric has a nap, stitch *with* the nap.

Topstitch with the right side of the garment up. An exception is a jacket with a lapel. Begin stitching at the lower edge of the jacket on the facing, stitch up the front, around the collar, and down the other front. The stitches on the collar and lapel are stitched from the right side. These are most noticeable since they frame the face.

Leave long lengths of thread at the beginning and end of the stitching line. Pull the threads to the wrong side of the garment, knot them, and thread them into a needle. Insert the needle where the thread comes out of the fabric. Take a $1/2''$ (12.7 mm) stitch. Give the thread a quick tug to make the knot disappear between the facing and garment. Hold the threads taut and clip them close to the garment to make them disappear to the inside of the garment.

If you find that you have almost finished your line of topstitching and there is no more thread on the spool, tie the end of the thread to the thread on another spool and continue stitching. This technique enables you to finish most jobs. Use this secret on mending day when you are changing thread colors often.

If you have to stop topstitching in the middle of a line, resume stitching by inserting the machine needle precisely into the last hole stitched. Later, secure all threads.

With practice, you'll develop not only the skill but also the confidence to topstitch with precision.

Stitching Problems

The three most common reasons for stitching problems are improper threading, a dirty machine, and a damaged needle.

When you clean the machine, be sure to remove the throat plate and brush out all lint which has accumulated on top of the feed dog.

Clean and oil the machine after every eight hours of stitching.

Insert a new needle after making a garment in a synthetic fabric, after stitching over pins, and before topstitching.

Improper tension. The proper tension for one fabric may not be right for another fabric. The softness and weight of the fabric, the number of fabric layers, and the stitch type and its length may cause the tension to be too tight, too loose, or unbalanced.

A perfect stitch is formed when the threads interlock in the center of the fabric layers. (Fig. 20a) If the upper tension is too tight, the upper thread lies

Fig. 20

flat on top of the fabric. (Fig. 20b) If the lower thread is too tight or the upper thread too loose, the lower thread lies flat along the surface. (Fig. 20c)

Using the type of thread, needle, and stitch length you've selected for the garment, stitch for several inches across the bias of two layers of the fashion fabric.

Look at the stitched line. If the thread floats on top of the fabric layers or the threads interlock toward the top layer, the upper tension is too tight. Loosen the upper tension by turning the tension regulator to a lower number.

If the thread floats on the underside or the threads interlock toward the bottom layer, the upper tension is too loose. Tighten the upper tension by turning the tension regulator to a higher number.

Sometimes you can't tell if the tension is balanced just by looking at the stitched line. Hold the stitched line between your thumb and index finger, spacing your hands 2″–3″ apart. Pull sharply. If the thread breaks evenly, the tension is balanced. If the thread on the upper layer breaks, the upper tension is too tight. If the thread on the lower layer breaks, the upper tension is too loose.

If the stitching line puckers even though the stitch is interlocked in the center of the fabric layers, both tensions, upper and bobbin, are too tight. This happens frequently when the fabric is a lightweight synthetic.

Loosen the bobbin tension by turning the screw in the bobbin case ¼ or ½ turn. (Fig. 21) Be careful;

Fig. 21

if the screw falls out, it may be lost forever. If the bobbin case is built into your machine, use the sewing-machine manual to help you locate the screw.

If the stitches are loose and don't hold the fabric together securely, tighten both tensions.

Needle thread breaks. It isn't difficult to prevent the needle thread breaking once you know what causes the problem. Here are the most common reasons:

- The tension is too tight.
- The machine is improperly threaded.
- The needle is bent or damaged.
- The needle is improperly set.
- The thread is too coarse or too fine for the needle or fabric.
- The thread has slubs or knots.
- The thread is old and brittle.
- There are damaged surfaces (guides, tension disc, take-up lever, etc.) over which the thread passes.
- The thread is tangled on the thread spindle, a guide, or the spool slash.

Bobbin thread breaks. Eliminate bobbin-thread breaking by finding the probable reason for it in this list.

- The tension is too tight.
- The bobbin is wound unevenly or too tightly.
- The bobbin is placed in the case or sewing machine incorrectly.
- The machine is threaded improperly.
- The throat plate is damaged.
- Lint or dust is in the machine or bobbin case.
- The bobbin-case screw has worked out and is catching the thread as the bobbin turns.

Puckered seams. Lightweight, permanent press, and tightly woven fabrics cause the most problems, and all fabrics pucker most when stitched in the direction of least stretch—lengthwise.

Use one or more of these suggestions to eliminate puckered seams.

- Use a small ballpoint or universal needle.
- Use a polyester or polyester-core thread.
- Use a finer thread. The thread may be too thick for the fabric.

☼ Use the same size and kind of thread on the needle and bobbin.

☼ Correct the tension. It may be uneven or too tight. Loosen the tension on both the bobbin and needle threads if necessary.

☼ Lighten the pressure on the presser foot slightly.

☼ Use the straight-stitch foot and small-hole throat plate.

☼ Set the needle position in the right-hand position if the machine doesn't have a straight-stitch foot.

☼ Hold the fabric firmly in front and back of the needle so that the machine can't feed too much fabric too quickly.

☼ Stitch at a moderate speed.

☼ Stitch with a piece of paper between the fabric and the feed dog. (Typing paper or wax paper is easier to tear away than tissue paper.)

Skipped stitches. Understanding the cause of skipped stitches is the key to solving this problem. The fabric clings to the needle when the needle penetrates the needle hole in the throat plate. This causes the thread to stay so close to the needle that it doesn't make a loop large enough to allow the shuttle hook to catch it and make a stitch.

☼ Thread the machine properly.

☼ Use a new needle. The old needle may be bent, blunt, or coated with sizing or lint. It may be the wrong size or type. Use the smallest needle size possible for the fabric.

☼ Use a universal needle, a topstitching needle, or a needle with a medium or large ballpoint.

☼ Use a larger needle. A small needle may not make a large enough hole in a resilient fabric. Sometimes the reverse is the case—a large needle may cause fabric distortion which causes skipped stitches. Then try a smaller ballpoint needle. Different fabrics react in different ways.

☼ Set the needle properly. It may not be inserted all the way into the needle clamp, or it may need to be lowered a fraction so that a bigger loop is formed.

☼ Increase the pressure. The increased pressure holds the fabric more firmly so as to make it less likely to cling to the needle.

☼ Use the straight-stitch foot and small-hole throat plate.

☼ If the machine doesn't have a straight-stitch foot, set the needle position in the right-hand position.

☼ Cover the large hole on the throat plate with tape if the machine doesn't have a small-hole plate.

☼ Loosen the upper tension.

☼ Stitch evenly.

☼ Use a lubricant on the needle, thread, bobbin, and fabric. Test first for spotting.

☼ Level the presser foot. The machine will skip stitches when the presser foot isn't level. Hold the toes of the presser foot down as you stitch. If this doesn't solve the problem, make a leveler of lightweight cardboard. Place the leveler under the presser foot as needed to balance it.

Creeping underlayer and drag lines. The sewing machine moves the fabric to the back of the machine each time a stitch is made. The fabric is held in place by the presser foot which pushes the upper layer forward while the feed dog pulls the lower layer backward. It is this basic design of the machine which causes the underlayer to creep and become shorter than the upper layer at the end of a seam. When you are topstitching, this action causes drag lines.

Use one or more of these suggestions to prevent creeping.

☼ Stitch with the grain.

☼ Lighten the pressure on the presser foot.

☼ Pull the bottom layer forward with the right hand while pushing the upper layer back with the left hand.

☼ Hold the fabric taut when stitching.

☼ Use the points of the scissors to push the upper layer toward the needle or to hold the upper layer firmly against the lower layer.

☼ If the two sections are uneven in length, position them so that the longer one is on the bottom.

☼ Place a piece of wax paper between the lower layer of fabric and the feed dog.

☼ Use an even-feed foot or a roller foot.

☼ When topstitching, pin, glue, or baste the seam allowances or facing to the garment. Use the points of your scissors to gently push the top layer toward the needle.

RIPPING

To rip or unpick, clip a stitch every inch with the seam ripper. If possible, clip the thread that was on the needle when the seam was stitched, so that the bobbin thread will pull out easily.

If the stitches are difficult to see, rub them with soap to highlight them.

Use a small brush or transparent tape to remove the clipped threads from the fabric.

Do *not* slide the seam ripper along the seam between the fabric layers. The ripper is difficult to control, and it may cut the fabric.

Press the garment sections before restitching the seam.

HAND-SEWING TECHNIQUES

Most garments require some hand work, even in shortcut sewing. There are some tricks of the trade which will speed you along, and show you how hand sewing, properly used, can be a shortcut.

Position your work. Work at a table when you are sewing by hand. Allow the bulk of the garment to rest on the table or in your lap. Hold the section on which you are working in your hands, resting your arms on the table so that you will not tire. If you are right-handed, hold the edge of the garment in your left hand as you sew with your right. (Fig. 22)

single strand of thread, knot the end and begin the stitching line with a backstitch to prevent pulling the knot through the fabric, leaving a hole. (Fig. 23a)

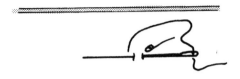

Fig. 23a

If you don't want a knot under a button or snap, secure the thread with several small stitches on top of each other. This is easier to do if you begin with a knot ½" (12.7 mm) away from the button loca-

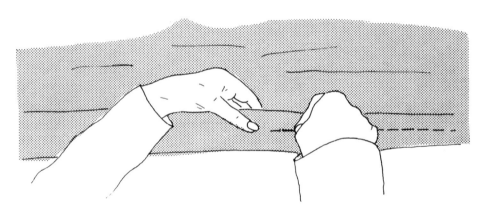

Fig. 22

Threading the needle. To eliminate knotting and twisting the thread when you sew by hand, wax the thread with beeswax, or a white candle, or coat it with lubricant; then thread the needle.

When cutting the thread, cut at an angle and make sure the thread is relaxed. If it is taut, the thread will unravel. Cut a 30" (76.2 cm) length of thread (approximately an arm's length from the spool) when you are basting to give you a working length of 18"–20" (45.7 cm–50.8 cm). Cut a shorter length when you are making finishing stitches such as hemming, buttonhole, blanket, or slipstitches.

Most hand sewing is done with a single strand of thread. Use long needles such as darners for basting and short needles such as crewel or embroidery needles for finishing (hemming).

Secure the thread. Begin and end securely. Using a

tion, make several small stitches to secure the thread under the button, then cut off the knot. (Fig. 23b)

Secure the thread at the end of the stitching line with a tailor's knot. Twist the thread ends together,

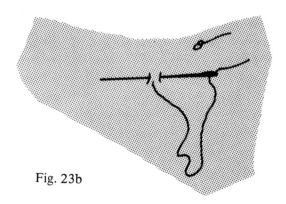

Fig. 23b

loop them around your index finger, then roll the ends through the loop with the thumb. If you have difficulty forming the knot exactly at the end of the stitching line, insert a pin in the loop. (Fig. 23c)

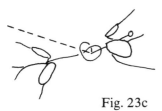

Fig. 23c

Insert the needle into the fabric as close to the knot as possible, take a ½″ (12.7 mm) stitch, and give the thread a sharp pull. This will make the knot disappear between the fabric layers. (Fig. 23d)

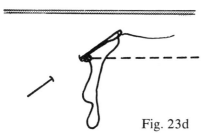

Fig. 23d

Begin and end basting stitches with a single backstitch, without a knot. (Fig. 23e)

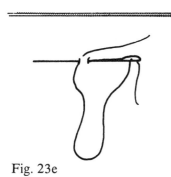

Fig. 23e

Hand Stitches

Backstitch. The halfstitch, prickstitch, and pickstitch are all variations of the backstitch. These stitches are the strongest of hand stitches and used to repair seams in hard-to-reach places, to understitch delicate garments, and to set zippers by hand.

Working from right to left, secure the thread, then take a small stitch by inserting the needle to the right of the thread. (Fig. 24)

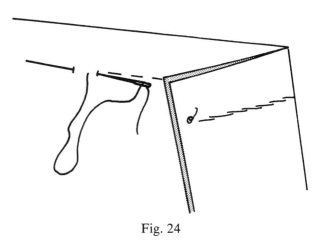

Fig. 24

Basting stitches. Few enjoy hand basting, but the right stitch at the right time can be a timesaver. It guarantees a perfect seam the first time you stitch it, ensures a professional finish, and eliminates redoing seams, stretched garments, and frayed nerves.

When basting a garment edge that requires pressing, position your stitches ¼″ (6.4 mm) from the finished edges, thereby avoiding an edge that ripples. When basting a faced edge, work from the *wrong* side of the garment and roll the seamline to the underside as you baste.

Remove basting stitches whenever possible before you press. This is especially important when seams are pressed open. If you cannot remove the basting, use silk thread to avoid leaving pressing impressions.

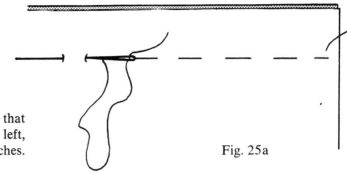

Fig. 25a

Even basting is used to hold seams together that require close control. Working from right to left, take short, ¼″ (6.4 mm), evenly spaced stitches. (Fig. 25a)

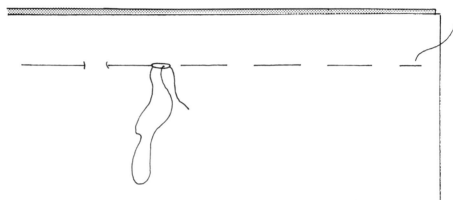

Fig. 25b

Uneven basting is used during construction and fitting for straight or slightly curved seams. It combines a long stitch of ½″–1″ (12.7 mm–25.4 mm) and a short stitch of ¼″ (6.4 mm). (Fig. 25b)

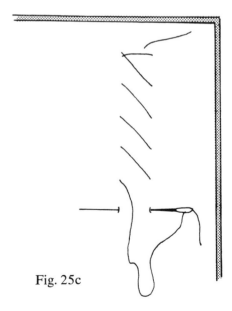

Fig. 25c

Diagonal basting is used to hold two layers or edges together during construction or pressing. Working from left to right or top to bottom, make the parallel stitches large or short. (Fig. 25c).

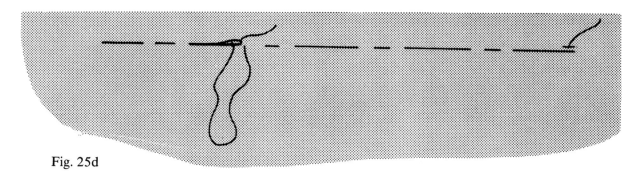

Fig. 25d

Dressmaker's basting is used to baste long seams with little or no stress and to mark placement or guidelines. Take one long stitch (1″ or 2.5 cm) and two short stitches (¼″ or 6.4 mm). (Fig. 25d)

Slip basting is used to match stripes, plaids, or prints and to make fitting adjustments from the right side of the garment.

Working with the garment *right*-side-up, turn under the seam allowance of one section and pin the folded edge so that it meets the stitching line of the adjoining section, matching the fabric design. (Fig. 25e)

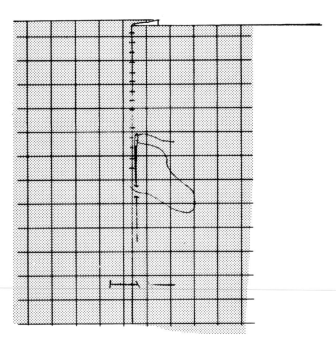

Fig. 25e

If you can't estimate the width of the seam allowance accurately, gauge stitch ½″ (12.7 mm) from the cut edge or mark the stitching line on the right side of the fabric with a soap sliver or chalk.

Working from right to left, take a ¼″ (6.4 mm) stitch in the folded edge of the upper layer, then a stitch in the lower layer. Make several stitches forming a ladder, then pull the thread taut. (Fig. 25f)

The ladder is the secret that prevents the layers from shifting and ensures a matched seam. Each stitch must begin *exactly* opposite the end of the last stitch, thereby making the stitches between the two layers straight, not slanted.

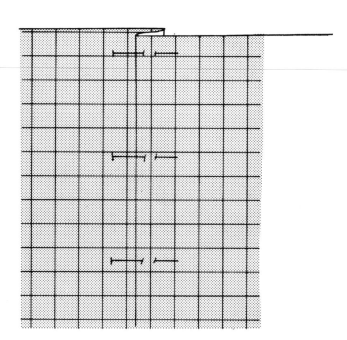

Fig. 25f

Blanket stitches. Blanket stitches are used to finish an edge decoratively or to make French tacks, belt carriers, and thread eyes.

Working from left to right, insert the needle into the right side of the fabric the desired distance from the edge. Loop the thread under the needle point. Pull the needle through to form a stitch at the fabric edge. (Fig. 26)

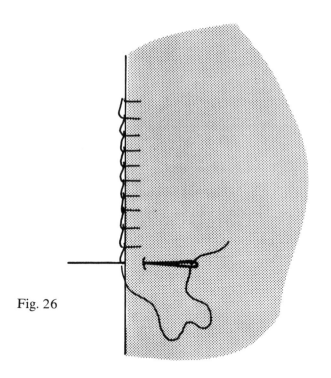

Fig. 26

Buttonhole stitches. Working from right to left, insert the needle into the wrong side of the fabric ¹⁄₁₆″–⅛″ (1.6 mm–3.2 mm) from the edge. Loop the thread behind the needle eye and under the point. Pull the needle through to form a purl stitch at the fabric edge. (Fig. 27)

Cross stitches. Make cross stitches to secure lining pleats. Work from left to right or top to bottom. Secure the thread, take a small stitch ¼″ (6.4 mm) to the right and ¼″ (6.4 mm) below the knot. Take the next stitch ¼″ (6.4 mm) to the right and ¼″ (6.4 mm) above the last stitch. Continue the stitches the desired distance. (Fig. 28)

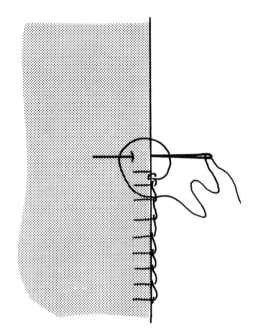

Fig. 27

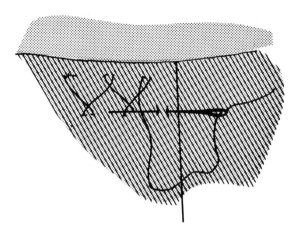

Fig. 28

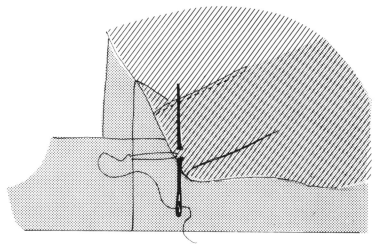

Fig. 29a

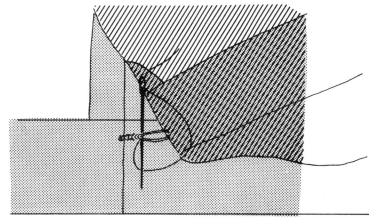

Fig. 29b

French tacks. French tacks are used to secure the lining to the garment at the hem. Secure the thread in the hem of the garment. Take a stitch in the hem of the lining opposite the first stitch. The thread between the two layers should be 1″–1½″ (2.5 cm–3.8 cm) long. Take another stitch in the garment hem, leaving the thread the same length. (Fig. 29a)

Cover the stitches with blanket stitches and fasten the thread. (Fig. 29b)

Hemming stitches. Most better garments are hemmed with a *blindstitch*.

Working from right to left, secure the thread in the hem or seam allowance. Pick up *one thread* in the garment, take a small stitch in the hem ½″ (12.7 mm) to the left. Alternate stitches between the garment and the hem. Do *not* pull the stitches too tightly. The stitches will look like small "v's" and the hem will be inconspicuous on the right side of the garment. (Fig. 30a)

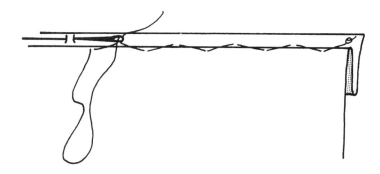

Fig. 30a

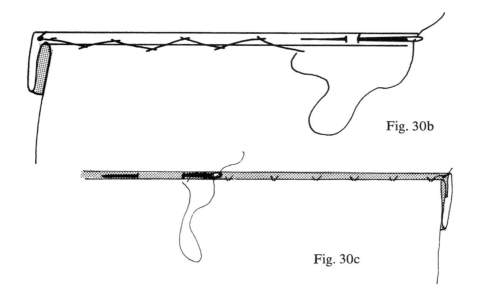

Fig. 30b

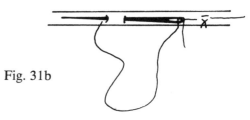

Fig. 30c

The *catch stitch* is used in tailoring and in hemming heavy fabrics.

Working from *left to right,* secure the thread in the hem or seam allowance. Pick up one thread in the garment ½″ (12.7 mm) to the right, then make a small stitch ½″ to the right on the hem. Alternate stitches between the garment and the hem. Do *not* pull the stitches too tightly. The stitches will look like "x's." (Fig. 30b)

The uneven *slipstitch* is used to hem garments that are finished with a clean finish or folded edge.

Working from right to left, secure the thread in the hem or seam allowance. Pick up *one thread* in the garment, take a ½″ (12.7 mm) stitch in the fold of the hem. Alternate stitches between the garment and hem. Do *not* pull the stitches too tightly. The stitches will look like small "v's." (Fig. 30c)

The *figure-eight stitch* is used to hem knits, crepes, and all other fabrics that are difficult to hem invisibly. Each stitch takes more time, but the stitches can be spaced farther apart.

1. Working from right to left, secure the thread in the hem or seam allowance. Take a ⅛″ (3.2 mm) stitch in the hem. (Fig. 31a)

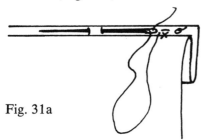

Fig. 31a

2. Take another stitch on top of the first one. (Fig. 31b)

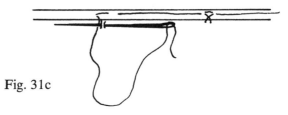

Fig. 31b

3. Pick up *one thread* in the garment directly opposite the two stitches in the hem. Do *not* pull the stitch too tightly. It should be slack, about ⅛″ (3.2 mm) long. (Fig. 31c)

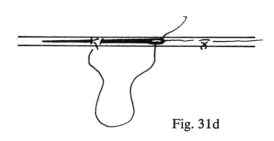

Fig. 31c

4. Take a third stitch on top of the first two stitches in the hem. The completed stitch will look like a figure eight. (Fig. 31d)

Fig. 31d

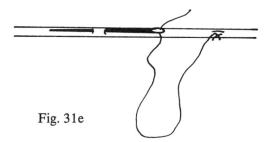

Fig. 31e

Even slipstitches. When it is necessary to finish seams from the right side of the fabric, use even slipstitches.

Turn one seam allowance under and pin it to the other seam allowance, matching the stitching lines. Working from right to left, take a small stitch in the folded edge, then a stitch in the underlayer. Make several stitches, then pull the thread taut. (Fig. 34)

5. Make the next stitch ¾″–1″ (19.1 mm–25.4 mm) to the left, beginning again in the hem. Allow the thread between the stitches to be slack. (Fig. 31e)

Overcasting. Working from left to right, space the stitches ⅛″–¼″ (3.2 mm–6.4 mm) apart. Use the thumb on your left hand to hold each stitch on the diagonal. (Fig. 32)

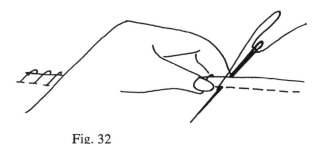

Fig. 32

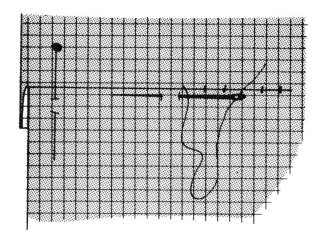

Fig. 34

It is easier to make the stitches the same depth if you gauge stitch ⅛″ (3.2 mm) from the cut edge.

Running stitches. Frequently you can use this short, even stitch (Fig. 33) instead of a slipstitch. A running stitch is made from the wrong side of the garment and a slipstitch is made from the right side. Reposition the garment so that you can sew from the wrong side to make a running stitch. You will find it is much quicker and easier to make running stitches than slipstitches.

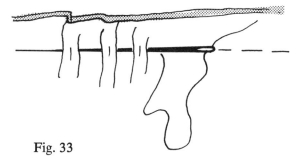

Fig. 33

Stabstitching. Stabstitching is a loose stitch between two layers that is used to hold two seamlines together or shoulder pads in place. The stitches are made vertically in the groove of a seam from the right side of the garment. (Fig. 35)

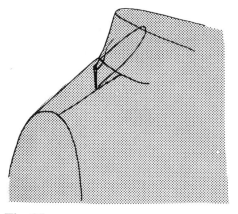

Fig. 35

Thread loops. There are two varieties of thread loops, chain or blanket-stitched loops. They are used for belt carriers, lingerie straps, button loops, thread eyes, and instead of French tacks.

Chain Loops:

1. Secure the thread, then take a small stitch to make a loop. Reach into the loop with your left thumb and forefinger. Hold the thread end taut with the thumb and forefinger of the right hand. (Fig. 36a)

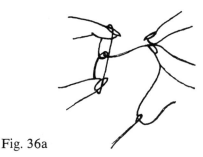

Fig. 36a

2. Use the middle finger of your left hand to make a new loop. Pull it through the first loop (Fig. 36b)

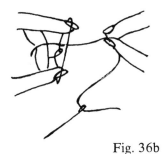

Fig. 36b

3. Allow the first loop to slip off the fingers. Open the new loop as you pull the first loop taut on the chain. (Fig. 36c)

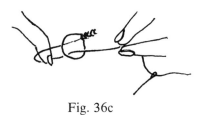

Fig. 36c

4. Repeat until the chain is the desired length.

5. Finish the chain by taking a small stitch on the garment *before* you slip the needle through the last loop of the chain, then secure the thread to the garment.

Quick thread chains can be made with a small crochet hook but they will be looser and less firm than the handmade chains.

Blanket-Stitched Loops:

1. Using a single strand of thread, make a 3–4 strand bar. (Fig. 36d)

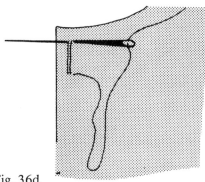

Fig. 36d

2. Cover the bar with blanket stitches, securing the thread at the end. (Fig. 36e)

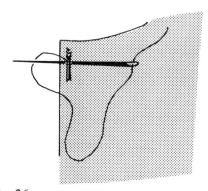

Fig. 36e

ASSEMBLING TECHNIQUES

In order to get a professional finish, home sewers often have to baste before machine stitching. In addition to hand and machine basting, you can use glue, tape, pins, or fusible bonding agent to hold the sections together temporarily. With practice, you'll learn to save time by machine stitching without basting.

Baste with a washable glue stick to secure interfacings and underlinings, position trims and pockets, align stripes and plaids, eliminate drag lines when stitching-in-the-ditch, lap seams, and trial fit. Do not glue baste seams which will be pressed open.

Baste with doublestick tape to fit, match plaids, set zippers, and position trims or pockets. Position the tape so that it is out of the line of stitching; always remove the tape after stitching. Do *not* use tape on velvets and velveteens without testing—tape may pull off the nap.

Baste with regular tape to hold collars and cuffs in place while you machine stitch them permanently. When using the tape on fabrics like Ultrasuede®, avoid leaving a napless spot by pulling the tape down with the nap to remove it.

Baste with pins. Place the pins so that they are out of the line of stitching whenever possible. Do *not* stitch over the pins if you can avoid it. *Remember:* Every time you insert a pin you'll have to stop the machine and pull it out before continuing the stitching line. If you cannot pin baste sparingly, use another basting method.

Baste with fusible bonding agents to hold pockets, appliqués, and trims in place. Position narrow strips of the fusible between the garment and the applied section. (Fig. 37) Cover the area with a press cloth;

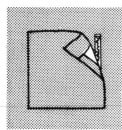

Fig. 37

then steam it 2–3 seconds to baste the two layers together. Apply the fusing agent to only one layer before fusing it to another layer by holding the steam iron or portable steamer an inch above the fusible until the fusible is sticky. Position the section as desired on the garment and finger press or steam it until it is basted.

Baste by machine using a long stitch to trial fit garments. Hold the fabric taut as you stitch, to eliminate puckered seams. Baste using a regular stitch to secure interfacings and to hold the seam allowances of pockets, collars and cuffs in position for the final stitching.

Don't overlook hand basting. It is an easy way to position the fabric layers exactly where you want them, enabling you to stitch accurately by machine.

Place the basting stitches next to the permanent stitching line to avoid stitching over them.

If you've been using hand stitches to permanently finish collars, cuffs, bindings, and plackets because you're afraid your machine stitching won't be perfect, use a basting step to eliminate them. Remember that ready-made garments have few or no hand stitches and when you finish your garments by hand, you're putting a tag on it that says homemade.

You will be surprised to find the basting-machine-stitching combination requires less time than the old-fashioned method of using permanent hand stitches to finish the garment. In addition to the time saved, your garments will look professional and wash and wear better.

PRESSING TECHNIQUES

Pressing is as important as stitching. Pressing as you sew is an imperative for the home sewer who wants a professional-looking garment. This doesn't mean you should stitch a seam and jump up to press it before stitching another seam. Stitch as much as possible, press everything you've stitched, then stitch some more.

Pressing is an up-and-down motion; ironing is a back-and-forth, sliding motion. *Press, don't iron,* when you sew. Don't overpress. Overpressing is worse than not pressing enough.

Pressing can be used to stretch, shrink, shape, mark, and fuse. It's an aid that will save time and make your sewing easier.

Using Your Equipment
The iron and portable steamer. Set the iron at the desired temperature. Too much heat will scorch or melt some fabrics; too little heat won't set creases and flatten seams. Check the fibre content and care label when in doubt.

Test the effects of pressure, moisture, and temperature on a scrap of fabric before pressing the garment sections. Use a large scrap so you can compare pressed and unpressed areas. If you don't have a scrap, press the garment in an inconspicuous area such as a seam allowance.

Allow the steam iron or steamer to heat completely before using it, to avoid spitting.

Use moisture when pressing linen and cotton fabrics to remove wrinkles, and on woollens to avoid damaging the fibres, causing them to become dry and brittle.

Use extra pressure when pressing thick or bulky

fabrics. Set the iron at a lower temperature when pressing lightweight fabrics.

Press cloths and soleplates. Different fabrics require different pressing cloths. Commercial press cloths, see-through cloths, old diapers, or tea towels are good for most pressing jobs. Wet the cloth and wring out all the excess water so that the cloth is barely damp.

Use a heavy muslin or drill cloth for tailoring when you will be using lots of pressure and moisture. Wash the cloth five or six times to remove *all* the sizing before using it. Lay the dry cloth on top of the area to be pressed. Using a very wet, almost dripping sponge, sponge the area, then press.

Use a woollen press cloth when pressing woollen garments. Lay the dry woollen cloth on top of the area to be pressed, cover it with a damp all-purpose cloth, then press.

Use a pile, such as a velvet or velveteen, cloth for pressing pile or such deeply textured fabrics as lace, matelassé, embroidered, or beaded materials. Place the cloth face-up on the pressing pad and the garment face-down on the cloth. Cover the section to be pressed with another pile cloth, then press, using a little pressure and a lot of steam.

Always use a press cloth when pressing with a dry iron.

Keep your press cloths clean and store them with your pressing equipment.

A detchable soleplate will allow you to do much of your pressing without a press cloth. It has the added advantage of not sticking to fusibles, eliminating "gucky" soleplates, and it's an inexpensive way to renovate an old iron.

Pressing pads, mitts, and point pressers. Use a tailor's ham to press and mold curved or shaped areas. Position the garment or garment section over the ham so that the garment curve fits smoothly over the curve of the ham. Use a pressing mitt to press hard-to-reach or small areas which are difficult to press on the ham. Place the mitt on the end of the sleeve board or on your hand.

Use a seam roll to press straight seams open. Position the garment sections wrong-side-up with the stitching line on the seam roll. Using the point of the iron, press only along the stitching line. Because the cut edges aren't pressed against the garment, they won't leave an imprint that shows on the right side of the garment. If you don't have a seam roll, make one using a magazine wrapped with a towel or insert

paper strips between the seam allowances and the garment to avoid making an imprint. Strips of adding-machine paper are a convenient width to use when pressing.

Use a point presser, wooden dowel, or yardstick to press open seams in hard-to-reach areas like collars, flaps, pockets, and belts. If you don't have any of these, use this technique: Place the section on the pressing board with the facing up. Open the seam allowances and press the facing seam allowance toward the facing. (Fig. 38) Turn the section over and repeat the process. Turn the section right-side-out, using a point presser. Underpress.

Fig. 38

Clapper or beater. The clapper or beater is used most often in tailoring. Occasionally, you'll need one for setting pleats and flattening seams and garment edges. Press the garment, using lots of steam or a damp press cloth. Pound the section once or twice with the clapper; then hold the clapper on the section with pressure until the fabric is cool and dry. If you don't have a clapper, use a brick that is wrapped in fabric.

Tips

If the garment sections are wrinkle-free when you begin construction, if you handle them carefully, if you hang them when you're not working on them, and if you press as you sew, you'll find that you have very little pressing to do when the garment is finished.

⚙ Use a well-padded surface or pressing pad to prevent press marks on pockets, buttonholes, and hems.

⚙ Press as much as possible from the wrong side of the garment. When you press from the face side of the garment, always use a press cloth.

⚙ Underpress from the wrong or facing side, rolling the seamlines at the edges to the underside of the garment.

⚙ Press with the grain except when pressing naps; then, press with the nap.

⚙ Quick-press short seams with your thumbnail, scissors, or the sewing-machine light. Open the seam allowances and press the seamline with your nail or the handles of the scissors, or hold the opened seam against the sewing-machine light to press it.

☀ Remove pins and bastings before you press. If you will be pressing over basting threads, baste with silk thread. Don't press over pins, hooks, eyes, or snaps—they may leave a permanent imprint on the right side of the garment. Don't press over zippers—nylon coils may melt and metal zippers may cut or mar the fabric.

☀ Do not press sharp creases until you check the garment fit.

☀ Eliminate a wavy foldline when pressing a narrow strip in half lengthwise by pressing a fold on a large scrap; then trim the strip to the desired width.

☀ Place a piece of aluminum foil on the pressing board under the fabric to reflect the steam and heat when you're fusing.

☀ Do not press soft pleats, shirring, smocking, or gathers flat.

☀ Do not press over soil, perspiration spots, or stains.

☀ Do not overpress—the fabric should retain its original texture and finish when you are pressing the finished garment.

Darts and Seams

☀ Do not press darts and seams until you've checked the garment fit.

☀ Press darts and seams flat to marry the stitches to the fabric and to smooth the stitching line before pressing the seam open or to one side.

☀ Press darts and seams before crossing them with another seam.

☀ Open seams with your fingers as you press. Move them along the seam just ahead of the steam iron or steamer. Be careful not to burn your fingers.

☀ Press enclosed seams open for a sharper seamline. This can usually be eliminated if the section is understitched.

☀ For a sharper line, press welt and topstitched seams open before pressing them to one side.

☀ Press straight seams on flat surfaces and shaped seams over curved surfaces to shape the garment. Clip or notch shaped seams as needed to make them lie flat. (Fig. 39)

Fig. 39

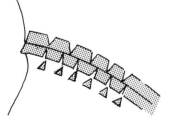

☀ Slash the darts in bulky fabrics and press them open for a custom finish.

REMEDIES FOR PRESSING PROBLEMS

Hem imprints on the right side of the fabric can often be removed. With the garment wrong-side-up, press under the edge of the hem, using the point of the iron. (Fig. 40)

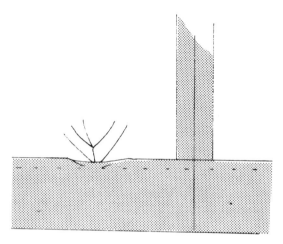

Fig. 40

An unwanted shine on the right side of the fabric can often be removed. Brush the fabric with a solution of 1–2 tablespoons of white vinegar to 1 quart of water. Cover the garment with a press cloth and press lightly. Before using vinegar on the garment, test the fabric for color fastness.

Needle holes are sometimes difficult to remove in napped fabrics. Press the fabric, using lots of steam, then brush over the needle holes with a toothbrush. Repeat the process until the needle holes no longer show.

Stubborn creases, hemlines, and seamlines must be removed before a garment is altered. Use a very damp press cloth to press out the crease. If it still shows, use a sponge or paintbrush to brush on vinegar or a vinegar-and-water solution. Test a fabric scrap or a seam allowance for color fastness first.

To clean the soleplate of the iron when you inadvertently press over fusible agent or on the fusible side of interfacing, use hot-iron cleaner or this quick method: Sprinkle salt between two layers of wax paper. Iron the wax paper sandwich until the soleplate is clean.

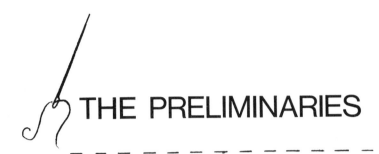

THE PRELIMINARIES

FABRIC AND PATTERN SELECTION

Shortcut sewing is not just quick-sew patterns and easy-sew fabrics, but you will save time and temper and ensure success if you combine easy-to-make styles with difficult fabrics and easy-to-sew fabrics with intricate or complicated designs.

Every time you combine a fabric and a pattern you are a designer. Many of your designs will be first-class, some will be mediocre, and a few may even be failures.

Analyze ready-made garments to help you recognize successful fabric-design combinations and analyze your wardrobe to ascertain which fabric-design combinations are your favorites.

Use the fabrics recommended by the pattern companies as a guide to select an appropriate fabric for each design. It's impossible for the pattern companies to list every suitable fabric, but you can easily compare the characteristics of the suggested fabrics with the characteristics of the fabric you like.

If you do have an occasional failure, don't despair—the professionals have them, too. For every design you see in the stores, many others were eliminated. Sometimes you see these discards at sample sales.

Consider these factors when selecting patterns and fabrics for speed sewing or if your sewing skills are limited.

⚙ Garments with a minimum of design details and seams are quick and easy to sew.

⚙ Collarless garments take less time than those with collars.

⚙ Round necklines are easier to finish than square ones.

⚙ Shawl collars can be assembled more quickly than notched ones.

⚙ Kimono, raglan, and shirt sleeves are easier to sew and fit than traditional set-in sleeves.

⚙ Loose-fitting styles are easier to fit and sew than fitted garments.

⚙ Dresses without waistline seams can be sewn faster than those with seams.

⚙ Skirts and slacks with elastic casings are easier to stitch and fit than those with waistbands.

⚙ Barrel cuffs take less time than cuffs with plackets.

⚙ Patch pockets are more time-consuming than in-the-seam pockets.

⚙ Dresses that slip over the head are easier to make than those with zippers or buttonholes.

⚙ Patterns with few pieces are easy to sew but may be difficult to fit.

⚙ Unlined jackets and coats are usually quicker to make than lined ones, but they can be more time-consuming if the seams require finishing. In addition, if you decide to line a garment which doesn't include a lining pattern, it will take time to make a pattern.

⚙ Blouses usually take longer to make than skirts.

⚙ Evening gowns are quicker to make than suits.

⚙ Skirts and slacks usually take less time to make than jackets.

⚙ Mistakes are less noticeable on small all-over print fabrics.

⚙ Firmly woven or knitted fabrics are easier to sew than fabrics which are slippery, soft, or loosely woven.

⚙ One-way designs, napped fabrics, and fabrics which require matching take longer to lay out and sew.

⚙ Fabrics which ravel are harder to sew and require special finishes.

THE PATTERN
Pattern Preparation
Press the pattern. Remove all of the pattern pieces from the pattern envelope. Select the ones you'll need and cut them apart as needed.

Open out the largest pattern sections and lay them flat, one on top of the other. Stack the smaller pieces on top of the larger ones.

Smooth the stack of pattern pieces with your hand or press them with a dry iron from the center to the edges.

Trim the pattern. To trim or not to trim the margins on the pattern before cutting out a garment is a decision you must make each time you use a new pattern. It is time-consuming to trim away the excess paper, but it often saves time later. You'll find you get fewer zigs and zags when you cut out the fabric if you have trimmed away the excess tissue. When cutting thick or heavy fabrics, trimming the pattern before you cut allows you to cut without distorting the cutting line. If you plan to cut the garment out using the tailor's cutting method, you *must* trim away the excess tissue. When you trim away the excess paper, cut off the notches printed in the margin. If you reuse the same pattern for several garments, you can avoid this boring chore.

Fitting the Pattern
Adjust and alter every pattern before you cut out the garment. This not only saves time, it prevents disaster.

Fitting a basic pattern. If you have difficulty fitting garments and adjusting patterns, make and fit a basic garment with a dart-fitted bodice, straight skirt, and long set-in sleeves. Each of the major companies offers a pattern in this basic style with instructions on how to fit the garment. Make the garment in a good-quality gingham. Fit it carefully, but avoid over-fitting—some figure irregularities should be camouflaged, not fitted, to create an illusion of perfect fit.

After the basic garment has been altered to fit you perfectly, carefully rip it apart. Transfer the alterations to the original paper pattern—this perfected pattern can be used to adjust *every* pattern you make.

I cut a copy of my basic pattern in lightweight cardboard and use it to alter every new design I make. I punched some large holes in it so that it could be conveniently stored on a coat hanger. You might prefer to cut yours in nonwoven pattern fabric or interfacing material, or you could fuse interfacing to the altered paper pattern to preserve it.

The scope of this book doesn't include pattern adjustments or how to alter a garment. There are several complete guides to help you solve each and every fitting problem. In addition to these books, many stores offer classes in fitting patterns.

Fitting a basic pattern to perfection can be very time-consuming, but its importance cannot be over-emphasized. It will eliminate multiple fittings every time you make a garment; it will also eliminate excessive handling of the garment during the garment construction; it will ensure a better fitting garment, and it will save you time every time you sew.

Fitting the commercial pattern. If you don't have a basic pattern, you can fit many paper patterns satisfactorily. This allows you to check the pattern size and make minor adjustments before you cut out the fabric, but it won't eliminate fitting as you sew.

Fit the pattern with the printed side out.

1. Trim away the excess paper around the pattern front, back, and sleeve sections. Clip curved seam allowances as needed.
2. Press the pattern with a warm, dry iron.
3. Pin the darts or tucks outward on the stitching lines.
4. Pin yokes and other details within a section in place before pinning the section to another major section.
5. Pin shoulder seams outward on the stitching lines. Repeat at the side seams. Pin other vertical seams together so that the pattern sections overlap and the stitching lines match. Pin the waistline seam outward.
6. Pin the center of a 36″ (91.4 cm) strip of twill tape to the center back of the paper pattern at the waistline.
7. Carefully, try on the pattern.
8. Tie the tape at the front.
9. Pin the pattern to the tape at the center front.
10. Check the pattern fit, silhouette, and design lines. Check the ease, spacing of darts, garment length, and hang. Decide on adjustments and mark where the changes are to be made.
11. Remove the pattern and adjust it by slashing and spreading or slashing and overlapping.
12. Pin the darts and underarm seam of the sleeve outward. Then pin the sleeve into the armscye at the shoulder seam, circles, and notches, matching the seamlines and overlapping the pattern sections.
13. Carefully try the pattern on again.

14. Check the sleeve length, fit, ease, and location of the darts and indicate adjustments to be made.

15. Remove the pattern and adjust the sleeve.

16. Try on the pattern for a final fit check.

Measure the paper pattern. Some patterns can be adjusted successfully by comparing your body measurements to the pattern measurements. This method has limitations if you want a perfect fit but it will eliminate cutting garments too small, too short-waisted, or too short.

Take your body measurements, then measure the pattern, allowing some ease for movement. Adjust as needed. Don't over-adjust—most patterns have design ease in addition to ease for movement.

Fit a complete or expanded pattern. Most commercial patterns include a pattern for the right half of the garment. (Fig. 41a) This pattern is then laid onto two layers of fabric. A complete or expanded pattern is for the entire garment, and it is cut from a single layer of fabric. (Fig. 41b)

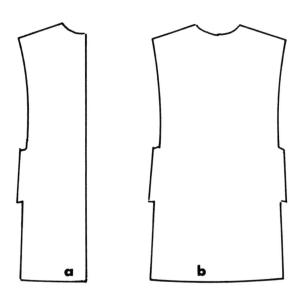

Fig. 41

Fitting a complete pattern is an easy way to check the pattern fit for a jacket, coat, or any garment to be made from an expensive fabric. Cut the complete pattern in a material similar in weight and drapability to the fashion fabric. Nonwoven interfacing or pattern materials are easy to work with, but you can use a woven fabric if you treat the edges with a fray retardant. Cut out a complete pattern for the

major garment sections. Mark the pattern carefully to designate the right and left sides. Sew or pin the pattern sections together for fitting.

True the pattern. After the paper pattern or complete pattern has been adjusted and new stitching lines have been established, check the pattern carefully, and draw the new cutting lines, using a see-through ruler, so that they are parallel to the stitching lines.

1. Place the ruler on the stitching line so that the long edge of the ruler is ⅝″ (16 mm) from the line. Mark the cutting line along the edge of the ruler. (Fig. 42a)

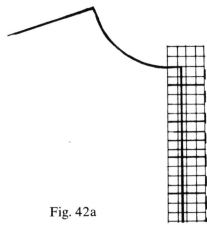

Fig. 42a

2. To mark a cutting line parallel to the neckline, armhole, or any curved seamline, place the ruler on the stitching line so that the end of the ruler is ⅝″ (16 mm) from that line. The line on the ruler will overlap the stitching line for a very short section (⅛″ or 3.2 mm). Mark a point at the edge of the ruler directly across from the overlapped lines. Reposition the ruler and repeat around the curved line. Connect the marked points. (Fig. 42b)

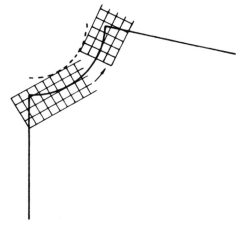

Fig. 42b

3. Measure stitching lines which will be joined together to be sure they are the same length.

4. True the darts. Fold each dart into the position it will have in the finished garment. Trim the dart even with the cutting line of the seam to shape the dart at the edge of the pattern.

Design Using Commercial Patterns

Use the same pattern several times to eliminate altering patterns and fitting garments. Learn to design with commercial patterns to maximize pattern use, save time, and create your own originals.

To copy a pattern, place the pattern paper on a resilient surface such as a cutting board, piece of cardboard, magazine, or table pad. Lay the pattern on top of it. Using a tracing wheel, trace the desired stitching and/or cutting lines, the notches, the grainlines, the center lines, and all other construction marks. Use a ruler to keep the straight lines straight.

Lengthen or shorten patterns. Increase the use of patterns by lengthening or shortening them. Because all horizontal lines below the waist, such as the hemline, that are parallel to the floor are parallel to each other, you can use a blouse pattern to make a dress, long or street length (Fig. 43a), or use a dress pattern to make a blouse, tunic, or tennis dress. (Fig. 43b)

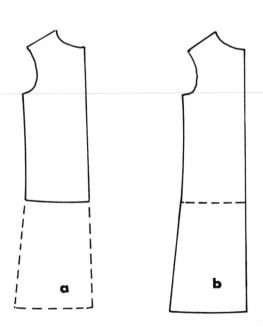

Fig. 43

1. Draw a new cutting line parallel to the pattern hem edge by measuring the desired distance with a tape measure or ruler from several points along the pattern edge. Connect the points and draw a new cutting line.

2. Extend the vertical seamlines and foldlines to the new cutting line. Be sure stitching lines which will be sewn together are equal in length.

3. If you are lengthening a pattern, check the width of the pattern at the hipline and adjust it if needed.

Bias designs. Cut some garment sections on the bias for a new design. Place the see-through ruler so that the diagonal of a one-inch (2.5-cm) square on the ruler is on the pattern grainline. Draw a new grainline along the edge of the ruler. (Fig. 44)

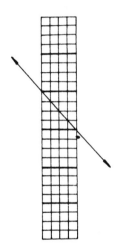

Fig. 44

Pattern Preservation

Preserve often-used patterns by bonding them to inexpensive interfacing or a pattern preserver. Roll them up and store them in cardboard tubes.

Patterns are folded and inserted into the pattern envelope by hand at the factory—a fact that is hard to believe when you are trying to stuff one of those super-bargain patterns with a hundred pieces back into the envelope. Cut your pattern envelope open and tape it onto a large manila envelope, new or used. The pattern will fit into the larger envelope easily.

Pattern Guide Sheets

Pattern guides are just that: guides.

Use the guide sheet to help you but do not be its slave. Remember, a guide is written for millions to use—novice or expert. Home sewers use many different kinds of fabric to make the same pattern. There is no way the pattern companies can write specific instructions for every type of fabric; you must use your experience and knowledge to supplement the guide sheet.

Read the entire guide sheet before you begin the garment; sometimes, even the experts make mistakes. The guide sheet for one current designer pattern instructs you to set the patch pockets *after* you complete the blouse body!

THE FABRIC

Get ready. Have everything—interfacing, lining, notions, and so forth on hand, prepared and ready to sew. Make a shopping list of anything you are missing, pin a fabric swatch to the list, and put it in your billfold.

Prepare the fabric. Prepare the fabric as soon as you purchase it. If you plan to wash and dry the garment, wash and dry the fabric before you cut out the garment to shrink it and to remove any resin-like finish which might gum the needle. If you plan to dry clean the garment, the fabric is probably needle-ready. If it isn't needle-ready, ask your dry cleaner to steam and shrink it.

Many garments will retain their beauty longer if they are dry cleaned, even though the fabrics are washable.

Preshrink the interfacing. Preshrink the interfacing materials before cutting them. Purchase four-yard lengths of interfacing in different weights to have on hand ready to sew. Most interfacings do shrink, even nonwovens and fusibles. Do not dry fusible interfacings in the dryer before bonding them to the fabric—hang them over the shower rod instead.

Examine the fabric. Examine the fabric carefully for flaws and irregularities before you lay it out. Hold the fabric up against a bright light or window to examine it. Flaws and holes will show plainly. Mark them carefully. Expensive fabrics, produced in limited quantities, often have more flaws than moderate-priced fabrics which are mass-produced. If the fabric has a number of flaws, return it to the retailer.

Block or straighten the fabric. If the ends of the fabric haven't been torn, straighten them by pulling a crosswise thread and cutting along the line formed by the pulled thread.

Check the crosswise grain—it should be at right angles to the lengthwise grain or selvage. Fold the fabric in half lengthwise. If the ends of the top layer are on top of the ends of the bottom layer, the fabric is grain perfect and doesn't require blocking. (Fig. 45a) If the ends are not on top of each other, the

Fig. 45a

fabric is off-grain and must be blocked. (Fig. 45b)

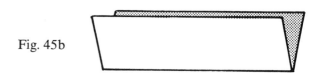

Fig. 45b

Unfortunately, off-grain fabrics cannot be blocked if they have a permanent-press finish.

To block the fabric, pull the short ends of the fabric diagonally. This often requires two people to do it properly. (Fig. 45c)

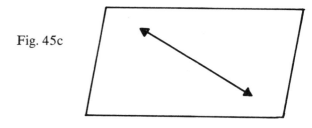

Fig. 45c

Check fabric content. If the content of the fabric is unknown and you are unsure of its washability, you can identify the fibre by burning a small scrap.

For safety, work over a lavatory or sink. Hold a small piece of fabric horizontally with tweezers when you ignite it.

The combined reaction to the flame and resulting ash will identify the fibre.

Identify the right side of the fabric. The right side of the fabric is often difficult to distinguish from the wrong side, but the position of some fabrics on the bolt makes it easier. Generally, cottons and linens are folded with the wrong side together and woollens are folded with the right sides together or rolled with the wrong side out.

If the fabric is not on a bolt, examine the selvage —the smooth or finished side is usually the right side; however, if pins have been inserted in the sel-

FABRIC BURN TEST

Fibre	Reaction to the Flame	Ash
Cellulose Cotton Linen Rayon	Burns rapidly with a yellow flame, leaving an afterglow when the flame is removed.	Soft, grey ash
Protein Wool Silk	Burns slowly, curling away from the flame. Sometimes extinguishes itself when flame is removed. Smells like hair.	Crushable, black ash
Acetate Acrylic	Burns and melts, continues to burn and melt when the flame is removed.	Hard brittle black bead
Nylon	Shrinks from the flame, burns slowly and melts. Self-extinguishing.	Hard brittle black bead
Polyester	Shrinks from the flame, burns slowly with black smoke, melts. Usually self-extinguishing.	Hard brittle black bead

vage during the manufacturing process, they are usually inserted from the wrong side.

If these clues don't identify the face side, select the side you prefer and mark it with a small piece of tape on each garment section. Marking the right side of the fabric eliminates finding a piece of tape on the inside of a finished cuff or collar.

If you use tape on napped fabrics, remove the tape by pulling it down with the nap. It is better, however, to mark napped fabrics on the reverse side; the tape may pull the nap off when you remove it. Test to be sure. Use chalked arrows on the wrong side to indicate the direction of the nap. (Fig. 46)

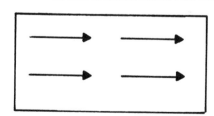

Fig. 46

LAYOUTS

Lay out and cut several garments in one session. Even the lucky sewers with a sewing room usually cut out their garments in the dining room. It takes the same amount of time to set up and clean up for several garments as it does for one. Cut interfacings, linings, backings, and so forth when you cut the fashion fabric.

Lay the fabric on the table so that it doesn't hang off the table. Many woven and knitted fabrics will stretch out of shape when hanging free, then they will "shrink" after the garment is completed.

If the fabric has a center crease that cannot be removed, lay the fabric so that you can cut around the crease so the crease will be inconspicuous in the finished garment.

Determine the Lengthwise Grain

If the selvage has been cut away, you can easily determine the lengthwise grain; remember, the lengthwise grain always has less stretch than the crosswise grain.

Hold the fabric securely along one grainline, spacing your hands only an inch apart. Pull. (Fig. 47)

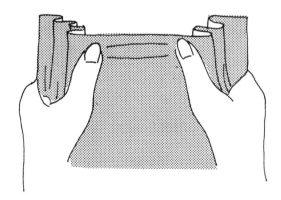

Fig. 47

Repeat in the other direction. The grain that stretches least is the lengthwise grain.

Spread the Fabric

The fabric is usually folded with the *right* sides together when you cut out the garment. Position the wrong sides out for easy marking with tracing wheel and paper, tailor's tacks, or pins. In addition, center-front and back seams will be properly aligned for machine stitching.

Fold the fabric with the *wrong* sides together when you plan to mark with chalk, soap, or water-erasable pen, or if it is a fabric with a nap.

Spread the fabric face-up in a single layer to cut out fabrics that require matching or are very expensive. This layout requires a complete pattern. It eliminates folding the fabric several different ways to save fabric, and it eliminates cutting blindly. Be sure to place each pattern section right-side-up on the fabric to avoid cutting two right fronts or two left sleeves.

Lay Out the Pattern

The success of the finished garment begins with laying out the pattern. Follow the layout on the pattern guide sheet or devise your own layout. Carefully measure the distance from the selvage or fold to the grainline to ensure accuracy on each piece.

When the design, width, or weave of the fabric makes the use of the pattern guide impractical or impossible, these suggestions will help you develop a new layout.

☼ If possible, lay the pattern pieces on the fabric so that the top of each piece is in the same direction even though the fabric does not have an apparent nap, directional print, or weave. The difference in some fabrics is so subtle that the difference in direction is not noticeable until the garment is completed.
☼ Lay the large pieces in place first so that the cutting lines meet but don't overlap; then, place the smaller pieces on the fabric. Dovetail the pieces wherever possible.
☼ Position pattern pieces with seams on the lengthwise grain along the selvage of the fabric. Clip the selvage if it does not lie flat.

Pin the Pattern to the Fabric

Position all the pattern pieces before you pin them in place. If you have to rearrange them, you won't have to unpin them first.

Pin the pattern to the fabric by placing pins first at each end of the grainline or foldline. Place the remainder of the pins within the seam allowances *parallel* to the grainline. Use as few pins as possible so that the pattern and fabric won't pucker. Five or six pins are usually enough for each garment section.

Pins may leave holes in very delicate fabrics like satin. Instead of pins, use very fine needles (sizes 9 or 10). Place the needles *only* in the seam allowances.

Weights. If you trimmed the excess paper from around the pattern, you may prefer to use drapery weights or dinner knives instead of pins to hold the pattern in place.

Too Little Fabric

Position all the pattern pieces before you begin cutting to be sure you have enough fabric. If you are short of fabric, don't despair—one of these suggestions will often solve the problem.

☼ Shorten the pattern length instead of the garment.
☼ Shorten the sleeve length.
☼ Allow a 2″ (5.1 cm) hem instead of the 3″ (7.6 cm) hem indicated on most patterns, use a machine hem which requires even less than 2″ (5.1 cm) or face the garment with scrap fabric or packaged bias.
☼ Change patch pockets to flaps, welts, or bound pockets.
☼ Change the grainline from the lengthwise grain to the crossgrain or from the bias to the straight grain.
☼ Cut facings, pockets, and casings from another fabric. Contrasting fabrics can be used to provide design interest as well as to solve the too-little-fabric problem on collars, cuffs, plackets, and yokes.
☼ Eliminate waistbands and face the garment with another fabric or grosgrain.
☼ Eliminate nonfitting seamlines by pinning the pattern pieces together on the stitching lines. In addition to saving fabric, you'll save time with this technique. (Fig. 48a)

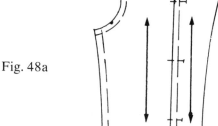

Fig. 48a

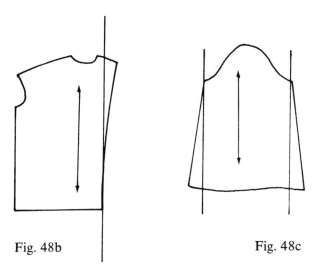

Fig. 48b   Fig. 48c

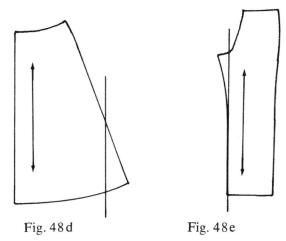

Fig. 48 d   Fig. 48 e

✿ Reshape the facing. (Fig. 48b)

✿ Pretrim the seam allowances of enclosed seams to 3/8″ (9.5 mm).

✿ Piece the garment inconspicuously. (Fig. 48c, d, e)

✿ Replace buttons and buttonholes with a zipper.

CUTTING

Mistakes in cutting are very difficult to correct, and if you don't cut the garment out accurately, you cannot sew it together accurately. *Never* use pinking shears to cut out a garment.

Cut precisely along the outer edge of the cutting line, trimming away the notches printed in the margin.

When you cut, do not close the points of the shears. Cut almost to the ends of the points, then slide the shears forward to take another bite. For a smooth cut, keep the point of the shears *on* the table all the time.

Cut Directionally

Cut directionally with the grain whenever possible but avoid twisting and turning the fabric in order to do so. Walk around the table, use a combination of dressmaker's and tailor's methods for cutting, or block-cut around the garment sections first.

Cut Everything

To save time, cut out everything—the interfacing, lining, backing, and stays—when you cut out the fashion fabric.

If you are unsure of the fit, do not cut the lining fabric until you have fitted the garment. Alter the lining pattern as needed, then cut the lining fabric.

Pretrim the Seam Allowances

Necklines and armscyes. Pretrim enclosed seams, those seams which form a finished edge at the neckline and armscye. In the past, you've stitched these seams, then trimmed them.

Narrow seams are easier to stitch with greater accuracy. In addition, if you should have to rip out a seam after it's stitched, the seam can be restitched with greater accuracy because the seam allowances are cut evenly and the notches haven't been trimmed away.

Trim the seam allowances of the garment and facing at the neckline or armscye to 3/8″ (9.5 mm).

Collars and flaps. Pretrim the seam allowances at the finished edges of the under collar or flap facings 1/8″ (3.2 mm), making the facing seam allowance 1/2″ (12.7 mm). Trimming the facing causes the finished seamline to roll to the underside. To stitch the seams together, match the cut edges and stitch a 1/2″ (12.7 mm) seam—the additional 1/8″ (3.2 mm) on the upper layer will be absorbed in the turn of the cloth. Trim the stitched seam to 1/4″ (6.4 mm).

Since most home sewers can stitch the facing edges of collars, flaps, and tabs more accurately and faster if they pretrim the facing seam allowance 1/8″ (3.2 mm) and match the cut edges, this method is used throughout the book; however, the off-set method is popular with many home sewers.

The off-set method is when the facing edges extend 1/8″ (3.2 mm) beyond the edges of the garment section. Hold or pin the seam allowances as you stitch a 5/8″ (16 mm) seam, measuring from the cut edge of the *facing.* (Fig. 49) Trim the stitched seam to 1/4″ (6.4 mm).

If the off-set method works for you, pretrim *all* enclosed seams to 3/8″ (9.5 mm). Off-set the facing edges ⅛″ (3.2 mm) and stitch a ⅜″ (9.5 mm) seam.

Dressmaker's cutting method. The dressmaker places her left hand on the pattern and cuts with her right hand, keeping the cutting line on the pattern in sight at all times. (Fig. 50a)

Tailor's cutting method. The tailor holds the fabric to be cut away in his left hand; the blades of the shears obscure the cutting line. To avoid a jagged cutting line and ensure accuracy, trim the excess margins from the paper pattern before laying out the pattern. (Fig. 50b)

Fig. 49

Fig. 50

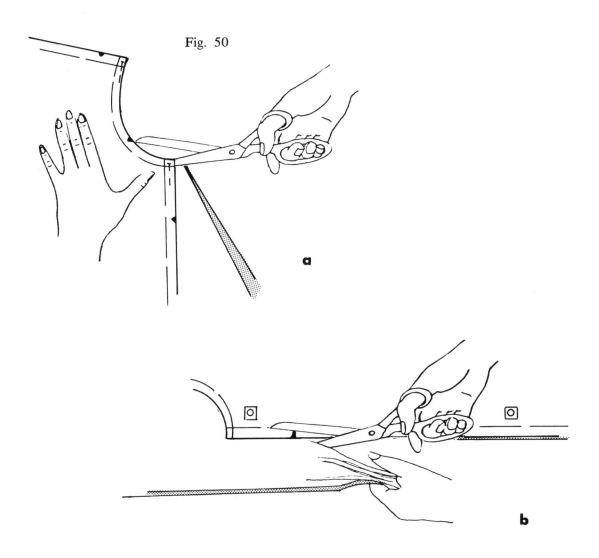

a

b

MARKING TECHNIQUES

Mark, mark, mark! Five minutes spent marking often saves lots of sewing time and it ensures accuracy.

Mark everything as soon as you finish cutting so that you won't waste time later dragging out the pattern to look for the piece which you need in order to mark the garment.

Different fabrics and different patterns require different marking techniques. The cut edges of most garment sections can be marked with clips. Pins, chalk, soap, water-erasable pen, tracing wheel and paper, tailor's tacks, thread tracing, or pressing can be used to indicate intricate stitching lines, construction symbols, darts, foldlines, and placement lines on the body of the garment.

Generally, I use a combination of clips and pins to mark garments quickly and easily; however, special fabrics and garments sometimes require more time-consuming methods to ensure a professional finish.

Clips

Many garments can be marked entirely with small clips. Clip into the seam allowance ⅛″ (3.2 mm) to mark the notches. Clips will not weaken the seam allowance. Notches cut away from the stitching line are often inaccurate, and the cutting line may be distorted when you twist and turn the fabric to cut the notches.

Clip everything. The notches, garment centers, foldlines (top and bottom or both sides), dart legs, pleats, tucks, any seamline that is not a standard ⅝″ (16 mm), the circles indicated on the seamlines of the sleeves and garment, the hemline, waistline location, inseam pockets, belt-carrier locations, the zipper length, shoulder points on the collar, and other special details indicated on the pattern should be clipped. (Fig. 51)

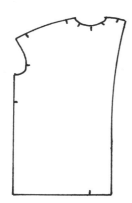

Fig. 51

Clip properly. Only scissors that cut to the ends of the blades can be used. Hold the blades between your thumb and forefinger. Position the scissors so that the points are exactly where you want the clip to be. *Clip*. If you position your scissors correctly, you will *never* clip too far.

Pins

Use pins to indicate dart points, placement symbols, and points to be matched on the body of the garment when you plan to make the garment immediately. Don't leave pins in the garment for a long time; they may leave permanent marks.

Lay the fabric out with the *right* sides together.

1. Insert pins vertically into the pattern and both layers of fabric at each symbol to be marked.
2. Turn the garment section over to mark the other layer with a pin at each marked point. (Fig. 52)

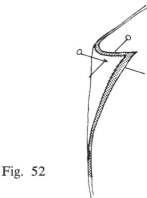

Fig. 52

3. Before you remove the pattern push the head of each pin through the paper pattern.
4. Set the pins so that they won't fall out.

Chalk, Soap, or Water-erasable Pen

Darts and other details on the body of the garment can be marked with chalk, soap, or water-erasable pen. White clay chalk or a sliver of soap, which has no oil or cold cream, can be used on most fabrics. Colored chalks may leave a permanent stain. Water-erasable pens cannot be used on fabrics that water-spot. Always check before using the pen to be sure it won't stain the fabric permanently. Never press over water-erasable-pen markings.

Lay the fabric out with the *wrong* sides together.

1. Insert pins vertically into the pattern and both layers of fabric at each symbol to be marked.

2. Separate the fabric layers carefully so that the pins won't fall out.
3. Mark the location of each pin with chalk, soap, or pen. (Fig. 53)

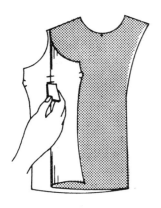

Fig. 53

Tracing Wheel and Tracing Paper

Use a tracing wheel and white tracing paper to mark intricate stitching lines, placement lines, darts, and underlinings. Colored tracing paper may permanently stain the fabric or show on the finished garment. For best results, always use white tracing paper, especially on white fabrics. Test to be sure the tracing wheel won't damage the fabric.

Staple the tracing paper to a piece of cardboard 20″ (51 cm) by 26″ (66 cm) with the wax side of the paper up. Use several sheets if the paper is not that large.

Lay the fabric out with the *right* sides together.

1. Place the cut-out garment sections on the tracing paper with the pattern pinned to the fabric.
2. Trace the pattern on all lines to be marked. Use a ruler for accuracy and mark each construction symbol through the center to form an "x." (Fig. 54)

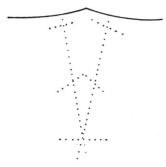

Fig. 54

3. Remove the paper pattern, leaving the fabric sections together.
4. Carefully turn the garment sections over on the tracing paper so that the marked layer is face-up.
5. Using the marked lines as a guide, trace all markings to transfer them to the underlayer.

This method gives you a clearer, more accurate marking than when you mark both layers at the same time; furthermore, the tracing paper will last much longer.

Some fabrics can be marked using the tracing wheel without tracing paper.

Tailor's Tacks

Use tailor's tacks to mark delicate, loosely woven and some napped fabrics.

Lay the fabric out with the *right* sides together.

1. Using white embroidery floss, sew through the pattern and two fabric layers with a long, loopy basting stitch. (Fig. 55a) Do not use colored thread

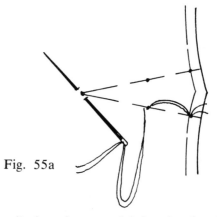

Fig. 55a

to make tailor's tacks; some fabrics absorb color and some colored threads crack.
2. Clip the loops between each stitch. (Fig. 55b)

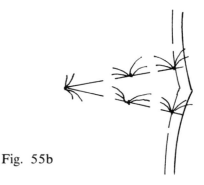

Fig. 55b

3. Remove the pattern. Separate the fabric layers carefully and cut the threads between them. (Fig. 55c)

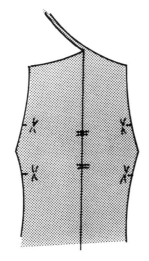

Fig. 55c

Thread Tracing or Basting
Mark grainlines, center lines or placement symbols on the right side of the fabric with thread tracing or basting. Marked grainlines and garment centers will help you fit garments quickly and accurately.

☼ Mark placement lines on the wrong side of the garment sections with a tracing wheel and tracing carbon. Using an uneven or dressmaker's basting stitch, baste along the traced line to mark the right side of the fabric. (Fig. 56a) Use a machine-basting

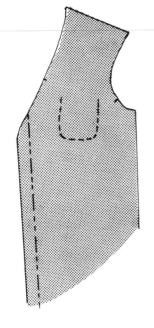

Fig. 56a

stitch to mark fabrics which won't be marred by needle holes.

☼ Fold the garment section on the foldline and baste along the fold. (Fig. 56b)

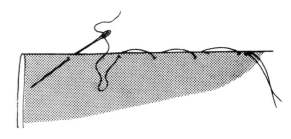

Fig. 56b

Press Marking
Mark straight lines for placket and casing locations, folds, and hems by pressing lightly with the iron. (Fig. 57)

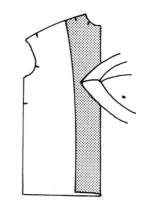

Fig. 57

Mark each end of the line to be marked with a small snip. Fold the garment section so that a snip is at each end and press carefully along the folded edge.

INTERFACINGS
A garment without interfacing is like a cake without leavening—it sags. Interfacing is the invisible ingredient that makes the garment a success.

The interfacing is positioned between the garment section and the facing to give shape, body, and support. It is used to preserve the garment shape in areas of stress, to prevent stretching, to add body and stiffness to certain garment sections and limp fabrics, to build an unusual silhouette, to cause the garment-facing seamline to roll to the underside, and to prevent a seam shadow.

Select interfacings to complement and reinforce, not overwhelm. They should have the same care requirements as the fashion fabric, be lighter in weight, shrink, and wrinkle-resistant.

Commercial interfacing fabrics are available in woven, knitted, and nonwoven fabrics, fusibles, and sew-ins. They range from soft and sheer to crisp and heavy.

If you keep a variety of interfacings on hand, you can experiment with several before you make the final choice on each garment. Carefully mark each interfacing for washability and keep any instructions for fusing with the appropriate interfacing.

Nonwoven Interfacings

Nonwoven interfacings were introduced in the early fifties by the Pellon® Corporation. Today, many people call all nonwoven interfacings "pellon"; actually, Pellon® is the trademark of one manufacturer.

The nonwoven interfacings of today bear little resemblance to their predecessors of the fifties. They've lost their "paper" quality and no longer crumble after they're washed. Today, they are soft and flexible, finishing edges almost as well as their woven cousins. They don't ravel, making them easy to apply and lovely to look at after repeated launderings. Contrary to popular opinion, they do shrink and should be prewashed.

There are three kinds of nonwoven interfacings: stable, stretch, and all bias.

Stable nonwoven interfacings have little or no give in any direction. The interfacing section can be cut out on any grain with success.

Stretch nonwoven interfacings are stable in the lengthwise direction and stretch in the crosswise direction. Cut these fabrics in either direction to utilize the stretch most effectively on your garment. Eliminate buttonholes that stretch out of shape by interfacing the buttonhole area so that the lengthwise direction of the interfacing is *parallel* to the buttonholes.

All bias interfacings have some give in all directions. They are not suitable for interfacing buttonholes.

Nonwovens are a good choice to use with knits and nonwoven fabrics; however, woven interfacings are preferred for better garments.

Woven Interfacings

Many washable woven interfacings are available to meet your everyday needs. Preshrink them before cutting. Hair canvas, lamb's wool, collar linen, and wiggan can be purchased for tailoring and haute-couture details.

Other fabrics that can be used to interface the garment include muslin, colored organdy, lining fabrics, self-fabric, flannel, and nylon net.

Cotton and linen interfacings with potato starch stiffening have been replaced with synthetic fibers and permanent-press finishes, enabling woven interfacings to retain their shape and appearance for the life of the garment. Cut the unnotched edges with pinking shears to retard fraying.

Knit Interfacings

Knit interfacings are soft and silky. They can be used to stabilize the entire garment or a section without adding bulk, weight, or crispness.

Fusibles and Sew-in Interfacings

Fusible interfacings are easy to apply, easy to sew, and retain their shape after extended use and abuse. However, the adhesive changes the fashion fabric's characteristics, adding extra body and some rigidity. Fusible interfacings sometimes overwhelm the fashion fabric. If they are not properly applied, the section will blister when the garment is washed or dry cleaned. A slight ridge may show through on the right side of the garment at the edge of the interfacing if the entire section hasn't been interfaced. This ridge is more visible on light-colored or lightweight fabrics.

Fusibles shrink, too, so soak them in very hot water and line-dry.

Sew-in interfacings preserve the shape of the garment and the qualities of the fabric. They never stiffen or blister.

Which is better—a fusible or sew-in interfacing?

It depends on what you're making, the results you desire, and what works best for you. Always use a sew-in, not a fusible, interfacing on designer garments when you want structure with haute-couture subtlety. Use fusibles for a more structured look. Do not use fusibles on corduroy, velvet, velveteen, crepe, gauze, sheers, or silks.

It is easy but tedious and time-consuming to fuse the interfacings in place; however, the interfaced sections can be stitched together quickly and easily. Avoid using fusibles where a demarcation line (ridge) shows unless you interface the entire garment section.

Nonfusible interfacings can be applied quickly with a washable glue stick. Assembling the garment takes only a little longer than when fusible interfacings are used.

How to Cut Interfacings

Cut nonfusible interfacings by the facing pattern or in 1″ (2.5 cm) bias strips for easy application and fabric economy.

Cut fusible interfacings by the facing or the garment pattern. Fuse a piece of interfacing to a fabric scrap to check for a demarcation line. This line is less noticeable on some fabrics if you pink the unnotched edge. If the line still shows, interface the entire garment section or the facing section, or substitute a sew-in interfacing.

Generally, do not trim away any seam allowances from the interfacing, except in tailoring.

How to Apply Interfacings

Sew-in interfacings. Set sew-in interfacings on the wrong side of the garment section, using a washable glue stick.

1. With the interfacing section wrong-side-up, apply the washable glue sparingly. If the fabric is lightweight, the glue may show until the first washing. Avoid this by applying the glue only in the seam allowances.
2. Position the interfacing on the wrong side of the garment and smooth it in place.

If you should inadvertently get glue on the right side of the fabric or apply too much, it will wash out.

Fusibles. Fused interfacings must be applied by the manufacturer's directions to avoid blistering after the garment is washed. *Always* make a sample to check the amount of stiffness and to look for a demarcation line. Wash the sample if possible before making a decision.

All fusing directions clearly indicate: *Do not slide the iron.* Sliding the iron rearranges the fusing agent, leaving some sections bare. These bare sections will bubble when the garment is washed.

Overlap the iron on fused sections carefully to avoid missing an area.

Place a piece of aluminum foil on the press board to reflect the steam and heat, ensuring a good bond. If you have two irons, use both to save time.

These directions can be used if there are no manufacturer's directions:

1. Set the iron at "Wool" and allow it to preheat.
2. Place the garment section on the press board wrong-side-up.
3. Place the interfacing on top of the garment section with the resin side next to the fabric.

4. Cover the interfacing with a *wet* press cloth.
5. Press each area a full 10 seconds, overlapping areas until the interfacing and fabric are bonded together on the entire section. *Do not slide the iron.*
6. Turn the section over, cover with a damp press cloth, and repeat the fusing process.
7. Allow the fabric to cool and test the bond by trying to lift one corner. If necessary, press 5–10 seconds longer on each side.

Fusible agent. Fuse a sew-in interfacing to the fashion fabric with a fusible agent. Always make a sample to check the amount of stiffness and to look for a demarcation line.

1. Cut a piece of interfacing and a piece of the fusible agent from the facing pattern.
2. Sandwich the fusible between the wrong side of the fabric and the interfacing.
3. Fuse them together according to the manufacturer's directions. The fusible agent will stiffen the section slightly, but it rarely blisters.

If there are no directions with the fusible agent, handle it as a fusible interfacing.

Bias strips. Stitch 1″ (2.5 cm) bias strips of interfacing into the garment-facing seamline as you stitch the seam by sandwiching the garment between the bias strip and facing. Clip the bias so that it will lie flat against the garment.

This ready-to-wear technique has been overlooked by most home sewers. It is the perfect answer for subtle shaping at necklines and armholes. Designers often use cotton flannel strips to shape a soft edge on silk and woollen garments.

Where to Apply Interfacings

Interfacings are usually applied to the garment rather than to the facing, except in tailoring and with some fusibles.

Collars. The interfacing for a collar is usually cut from the upper-collar pattern and applied to the upper collar.

If the collar and undercollar are cut in one piece, fold the pattern in half lengthwise to use as a pattern to cut the interfacing. (Fig. 58a) Apply the interfacing to the upper collar. (Fig. 58b)

Fig. 58a

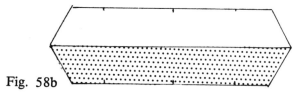

Fig. 58b

If the collar is cut with a separate band, the interfacing is applied to the upper collar and band section next to the neck. The other band section may also be interfaced.

Garment fronts. When the facing is cut as an extension on the garment, the interfacing is cut to fit the extended facing (Fig. 59a) or it may be cut as a straight strip. (Fig. 59b)

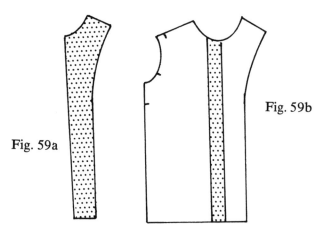

Fig. 59a

Fig. 59b

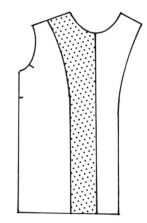

Fig. 59c

interfacing edges can be finished neatly by facing the facing (see FACINGS) or by using a flat-edge finish.

If the garment is *collarless,* apply the interfacing to the garment. Glue baste to hold the facing until the buttons and buttonholes are set, thus eliminating the need to secure it by hand along the garment-facing foldline. (Fig. 59c)

If the garment does not have buttons and buttonholes, stitching the interfacing into the neckline seam and hem is adequate for most garments. Permanent glue can be used sparingly on some fabrics. Test to be sure it won't show on the finished garment.

If the garment has a *turned-back lapel,* apply the interfacing to the facing. (Fig. 59d) The facing and

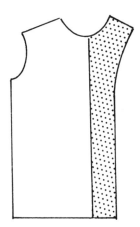

Fig. 59d

Welts, flaps, and pockets. Apply the interfacing to the section that will be uppermost on the finished garment.

Waistbands and cuffs. Interface these sections as you would collars.

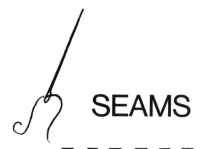

SEAMS

Seams are the basic element of construction. The simple process of joining two or more pieces of fabric together must be executed perfectly if you want a professional-looking garment. Try to stitch every seam flawlessly the first time to avoid ripping and overhandling. Before stitching the seams of the garment, make a test seam on a fabric scrap to check the tension, pressure, stitch length, and stitch formation. If a seam is not perfect, don't hesitate to rip it out immediately. It won't improve with age.

PLAIN SEAMS

Plain seams are stitched with the right sides together so that they are on the wrong side of the finished garment. The cut edges are matched and the seam is stitched the desired distance from the edges. This distance or seam-allowance width is ⅝″ (16 mm) on all American-made patterns unless otherwise indicated.

Seam Finishes

The primary function of a seam finish is to prevent fraying, but it can also improve the appearance and comfort of the garment. The finish is determined by the characteristics of the fabric (washability, weave, and thickness), the use and type of garment (custom, utility, theatrical, or lined), the position of the seam on the garment and the amount of time you want to spend sewing.

Cut Edge or *Raw Edge* is appropriate for lined garments, knits, tightly woven fabrics, and such nonwoven fabrics as felt, vinyl, leather, suede, or pseudosuede. (Fig. 60a)

Singed Edge is an easy finish to use on synthetic fabrics. Hold the edge of the seam just *above* a lighted candle. The fabric edge will melt slightly, sealing the edge. Be very careful to avoid burning the garment. This finish is often used on ski wear.

The singed edge forms a hard bead on some fabrics which may be irritating if it's next to the skin.

Pinked or *Stitched and Pinked* is a quick and easy finish that can be used on fabrics that ravel slightly. (Fig. 60b)

Stitch the seam allowance ¼″ (6.4 mm) from the edge, then pink the edge. Omit the stitching line if the fabric doesn't fray.

Zigzagged can be used on loosely woven fabrics. Zigzag finishes are suitable for washable garments.

Use a zigzag stitch (W,2-L,2) to stitch near but not over the edge. (Fig. 60c) Lightweight fabrics may roll when you zigzag the single layer. Use an overcast guide foot or stitch over paper to prevent rolling.

The seam allowances can be zigzagged together and pressed to one side if the fabric is light or medium weight.

Overedged or *Overlocked* is very similar to a zigzag finish. (Fig. 60d)

Use a zigzag stitch (W,2-L,2) and stitch so that the needle swings over the edge to complete the stitch off the fabric. The seam edge will roll slightly.

Clean-finished, either *edgestitched* or *turned and stitched,* is a good finish for lightweight fabrics that ravel. This finish washes well and provides a neat finish. It is often used on unlined jackets and very expensive garments. The guide sheets of most patterns recommend clean-finishing the seams, but this finish is *not* appropriate for sheer, medium, or heavyweight fabrics. (Fig. 60e)

Allow a ¾″–1″ (19.1 mm–25.4 mm) seam allowance so that the finished seam allowances won't be skimpy. Turn under ¼″ (6.4 mm) and edgestitch from the right side of the fabric.

When you are clean-finishing outward (convex) curves, the amount to be turned under along the cut edge is greater than the seam or upper layer under

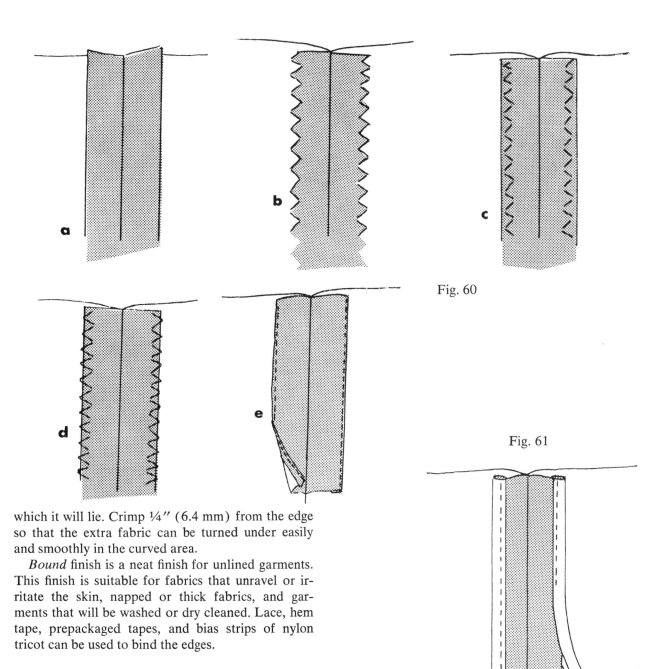

Fig. 60

Fig. 61

which it will lie. Crimp ¼″ (6.4 mm) from the edge so that the extra fabric can be turned under easily and smoothly in the curved area.

Bound finish is a neat finish for unlined garments. This finish is suitable for fabrics that unravel or irritate the skin, napped or thick fabrics, and garments that will be washed or dry cleaned. Lace, hem tape, prepackaged tapes, and bias strips of nylon tricot can be used to bind the edges.

1. Fold the binding lengthwise with the wrong sides together so that one edge is a little narrower than the other. Prepackaged tapes are already pressed with an off-center fold.
2. Enclose the cut edge of the seam allowance with the tape.
3. Set the machine for a straight or zigzag stitch (W,2-L,2). Stitch the tape to the seam allowance, using the inside of the presser foot as a gauge to stitch closely to the edge of the tape. (Fig. 61)

Hong Kong finish is neat and elegant but time-consuming. This finish is suitable to use on any fabric that unravels, napped fabrics, garments that will be washed or dry cleaned, and unlined jackets. (Fig. 62a)

1. Cut bias strips of lightweight lining fabric 1″ (2.5 cm) wide.

2. Stitch the strip to the right side of the seam allowance ¼″ (6.4 mm) from the edge. (Fig. 62b)

3. Trim to ⅛″ (3.2 mm). (Fig. 62c)

4. Press the strip up and over the cut edge. (Fig. 62d)

5. Stitch-in-the-ditch. (Fig. 62e) Glue the strip to the wrong side of the fabric before you stitch-in-the-ditch to avoid a drag line.

Overcast the edges by hand if you want a flat finish without stiffness. This easy finish takes lots of time and is only used on the finest garments. (Fig. 62f)

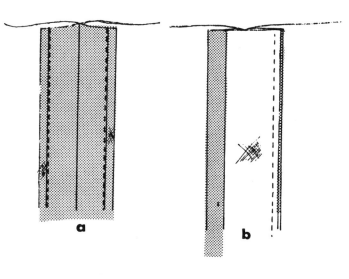

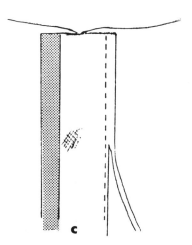

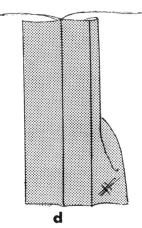

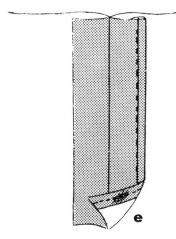

Fig. 62

Machine stitch ⅛″ (3.2 mm) from the edge. Working from left to right, space the stitches ⅛″–¼″ (3.2 mm–6.4 mm) apart. Use your left thumb to hold each stitch on the diagonal.

If you like this finish, practice will build speed.

STITCHING SPECIAL SEAMS
Enclosed Seams
Enclosed seams are those seams which join an upper layer and an underlayer to form a finished edge, such as the seams at the neckline, armscye, and around the edges of collars. The seam is stitched, clipped, and trimmed, then pressed in the same direction and enclosed by the garment and facing.

The seamline which joins these sections should never show from the right side of the garment; instead, it should roll to the underside. Cut and stitch the upper layer slightly larger than the underlayer.

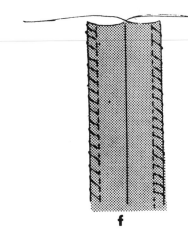

Collars
1. Pretrim the seam allowances on the collar facing ⅛″ (3.2 mm). If the fabric is bulky, pretrim the

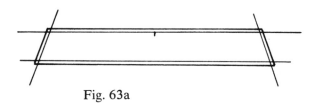

Fig. 63a

seam allowances on the facing ¼″ (6.4 mm). (Fig. 63a)

2. Cut the interfacing by the collar pattern unless otherwise instructed.

3. Fuse or glue the interfacing to the upper collar.

4. Match the cut edges of the two sections by easing the upper collar and stretching the collar facing. Use a pin at each corner to control the fullness easily. (Fig. 63b)

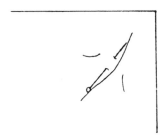

Fig. 63b

5. With the facing on top, stitch a *½″ (12.7 mm) seam* even though the seam allowance on the upper collar is ⅝″ (16 mm). The additional ⅛″ (3.2 mm) will be lost in the turn-of-the-cloth.

6. Understitch, trim, and clip as needed.

7. Turn the collar right-side-out, using a point turner.

8. Underpress, rolling the seamline to the underside of the collar.

Curved seams. Stitch curved seams with a short stitch for reinforcement and easier handling.

Use a soft-tip pen to mark the seam allowance width on the throat plate with a dot *directly opposite* the needle. This is the *only* point that will be an accurate gauge. (Fig. 64)

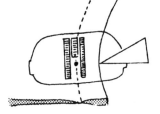

Fig. 64

Stitch slowly or walk the machine in order to gauge the width accurately. A separate gauge on the machine base is not recommended. It is almost impossible to position the gauge accurately, and it is awkward to stitch around it.

Corner seams. To achieve a well-formed point at a corner, shorten the stitch 1″ (2.5 cm) on each side of the point. Take a diagonal stitch or two, or more, across the corner; the bulkier the fabric or the sharper the point, the greater the number of stitches required across the point. (Fig. 65) If the sections to be joined have been pretrimmed so the facing is smaller than the upper layer, match the cut edges and use a pin at each corner to control fullness.

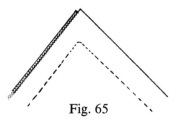

Fig. 65

Eased seams. An eased seam is formed when two seam allowances of unequal length are stitched together without puckers or gathers. An eased seam replaces small darts at the shoulder, bust line, elbow, and armscye.

Seams at the shoulder, sleeve underarm, and waistline can be eased by stitching the two sections together with the longer piece next to the feed dog. The action of the feed dog eases the longer seam allowance to the shorter one.

The armscye seam of shirt sleeves can be stitched in the same manner, but most regular set-in sleeves require crimping or ease basting to control the ease smoothly.

When ease basting is used to control the fullness, the section to be eased should be placed on top of the shorter section. This positioning allows you to adjust the easing with the points of the scissors as you stitch to prevent pleating or puckering. Use the index and middle fingers of your left hand to hold the fullness flat on each side of the presser foot. Be sure to position your fingers carefully and do not move them while stitching to avoid making your fingers part of the seam.

Reinforced Seams and Stays

Seams which will stretch out of shape need to be reinforced with a stay to preserve the shape of shoulder and waistline seams and necklines. Seam tape, twill tape, linen tape, selvage cut from lining or underlining fabrics, or bias tape with the stretch pressed out can be used as a stay.

Shoulder stay. Using the paper pattern as a guide, cut the shoulder stay the length of the front shoulder seam. (Fig. 66) Stitch the stay to the wrong side of the garment section on the seamline.

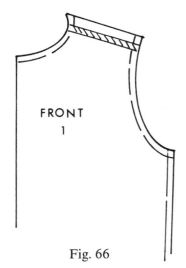

FRONT
1

Fig. 66

If it is an eased seam, the back or longer section can be eased to the stay, then stitched to the shorter section; otherwise, the stay is stitched to the front section.

Waistline stay. Usually this stay is cut the length of the waistline and stitched into the seam with the waistband or bodice to prevent stretching. However, it can be used to control the fit of the garment by easing the waistline seam to the stay and fastening the stay with a hook and eye at the garment opening.

1. Cut the stay 3″ (7.6 cm) longer than the waistline measurement to allow 1″ (2.5 cm) ease and 2″ (5.1 cm) to finish the ends.

2. Position and stitch the stay on top of the waistline seam on the wrong side of the garment skirt, leaving 2″ (5.1 cm) free on each side of the zipper. If the garment has buttons and buttonholes, stitch the stay to the waistline seam, stopping at the edges of the facing.

3. Hem the ends of the stay and add a hook and eye.

Neckline stay. Use a stay to work a miracle on necklines that gap. (Fig. 67a)

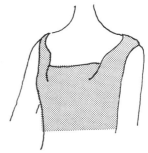

Fig. 67a

1. With the garment on, pin small tucks at the neck edge to control the excess fullness. (Fig 67b)

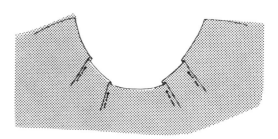

Fig. 67b

2. Measure the distance between the first and last tuck.

3. Cut the stay the measured length plus 2″ (5.1 cm).

4. Pin the stay to the neckline seam on the wrong side of the garment beginning 1″ (2.5 cm) before the first tuck. Place pins at right angles to the seamline between each tuck. (Fig. 67c)

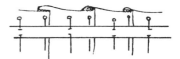

Fig. 67c

5. Unpin the tucks.

6. Ease the garment to the stay as you stitch on the seamline. Baste if necessary.

7. Use the garment-front pattern to make a new facing pattern. Pin small tucks at the neckline of the pattern equal to those pinned on the garment. Trace the pattern, indicating the stitching and cutting lines. Cut a new facing.

8. Stitch the facing to the garment with the tape uppermost.

Some fabrics will not ease as smoothly as others. Only you can decide which you like better, gathers or gaps!

Shaped Seams
Shape as you stitch when you are making shoulder shapes or inserting featherboning. Hold the garment sections in a curved position so that the bottom layer has greater length than the top layer. The action of the feed dog will cause more length to be stitched into the bottom layer. (Fig. 68)

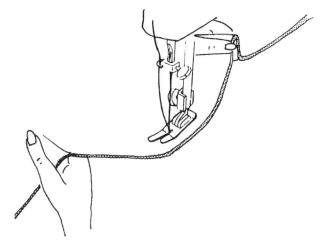

Fig. 68

If you are making a custom garment, apply this technique when you are setting the undercollar to a collar, cuff facing to the upper cuff, facings to the garment, or linings to pockets.

Loop Seams and Tunnelling
Garments are circular in shape. Always work inside the loop or circle for easier stitching and better results. (Fig. 69a)

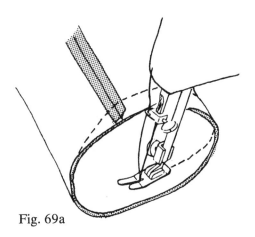

Fig. 69a

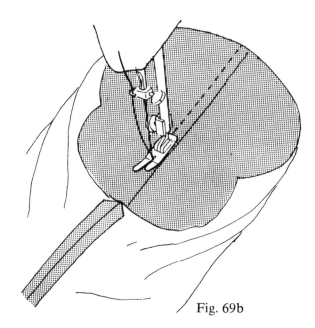

Fig. 69b

The sleeves, pant legs, skirt, and garment form a tunnel when the vertical seams are stitched. (Fig. 69b) Turn the garment or garment section *wrong-side-out* so that you can work inside the tunnel (circle) when you topstitch hems or seams, zippers, and cuffs from the *right side* of the garment.

Tunnelling eliminates stitching unwanted layers, pleats, or tucks into the stitching line.

Stitching a Curved Line to a Straight Line
Neckline seams which join a straight collar to a curved neck edge or waistline seams which join a circular skirt to a straight bodice edge are easier to stitch if you staystitch and clip the curved edge.

The stitching lines of the two sections are equal in length, but the cut edges are unequal. The cut edge of the curved section is shorter than the seamline.

1. Staystitch the curved line just inside the seamline. Clip the seam allowance to the staystitching so that the curved line can be held straight. (Fig. 70a)

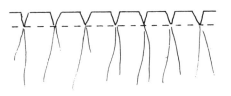

Fig. 70a

Fig. 70b

2. With the right sides together and the curved section on top, pin and stitch the sections together, using the staystitching line as a guide. (Fig. 70b)

Stitching an Inward (Concave) Curve to an Outward (Convex) Curve

The most common seam that joins an inward curve to an outward curve is the princess seam, but it is not the only one. Seams that join curved yokes to the bodice (Fig. 71a), skirt, or slacks (Fig. 71b), and standing or tailored collars to necklines, also fall into this group. (Fig. 71c)

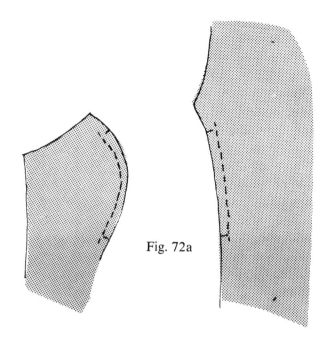

Fig. 72a

1. Staystitch the curved lines just inside the seamline. (Fig. 72a)

2. Clip the seam allowance of the inward curve to the staystitching in several places.

3. With the right sides together and the inward curve on top, pin and stitch the sections together. (Fig. 72b)

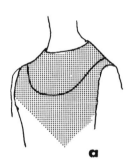

a

Fig. 71

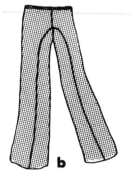

b

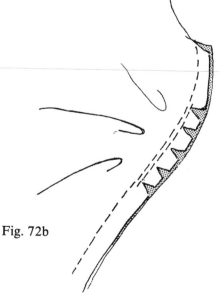

c

Fig. 72b

The stitching lines of the two sections are usually equal in length, but the cut edge of the inward curve is shorter than the stitching line and the cut edge of the outward curve is longer than the stitching line.

4. If the outward curve has gathers or easing, place it on top when you stitch the seamline.

Stitching a Bias Edge to a Straight Edge
Stitch the two sections together with the bias edge next to the feed dog and the straight edge on top.

Stitching a Seam with an Inward Corner
Godets (Fig. 73a), gussets, shawl collars, and seams that join square or pointed yokes to the bodice (Fig. 73b), skirt, or slacks have inward corners.

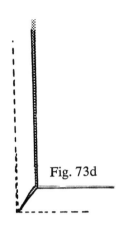

Fig. 73

Fig. 73d

Shortcut:
1. Use short stitches to staystitch the corner to be clipped. (Fig. 73c)

4. Pivot the sections so that the cut edge of the section with the inward corner matches the cut edge of the other section. (Fig. 73e)

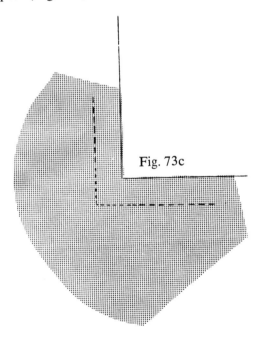

Fig. 73c

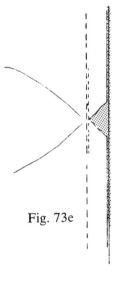

Fig. 73e

2. Clip the corner to the staystitching.
3. With the right sides together and the section with the inward corner on top, pin and stitch the seamline to the corner. Stop with the needle down. The clipped corner is only a thread away. (Fig. 73d)

5. Pin, then finish stitching the seam.

Custom method. The custom method for stitching a seam with an inward corner takes more time and effort. Better garments warrant this special attention.

1. Face the inward corner, using a piece of lightweight lining fabric or underlining fabric for the facing. Silk organza and sheer nylon tricot are ideal because they are transparent and easy to shape. Cut the facing 3″ (7.6 cm) square.

2. Mark the stitching line on the wrong side of the fabric with soap, chalk, thread tracing, or tracing paper.

3. Place and pin the facing over the corner on the *right* side of the garment.

4. With the garment uppermost, stitch the facing to the corner *one thread* inside the seamline. Stop with the needle down at the corner, pivot and continue stitching. (Fig. 74a)

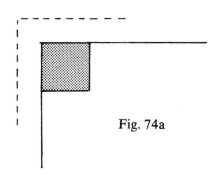

Fig. 74a

5. Clip the corner to the stitching line. Understitch the facing to the seam allowances. Trim the facing so that it is ⅝″ (16 mm) wide. The facing seam allowance will fill the clipped corner. (Fig. 74b)

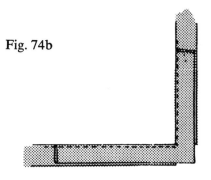

Fig. 74b

6. With the right sides together and the faced section uppermost, *begin stitching at the corner* next to the "little seam." (Fig. 74c) Stitching from the corner,

the most intricate point, will ensure a perfect corner. In order to stitch one side of the corner, the bulk of the fabric will be to the right of the needle.

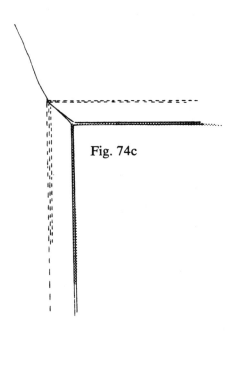

Fig. 74c

7. Tie the two needle threads on top of the seam together with a tailor's knot; then tie the bobbin threads together. (Fig. 74d)

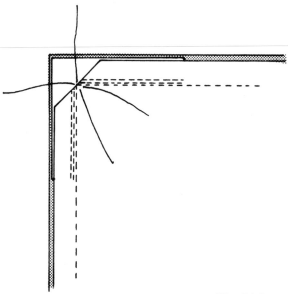

Fig. 74d

Reversing the Seams

Reverse the seams for a custom finish when setting turned-back cuffs or when setting the facing to the outside of the garment. This finish eliminates any seam allowances which might "peek out" at the garment edge. (Fig. 75a)

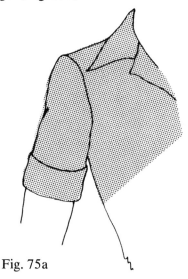

Fig. 75a

The seam is stitched in the usual position, right sides together, to a point that will be under the facing or cuff; then it is stitched with the wrong sides together. (Fig. 75b)

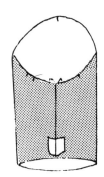

Fig. 75b

The procedure for sleeves also applies to slacks and faced garments.

1. Measure the width of the finished cuff or facing at the underarm seam. On the underarm seamline, mark this distance less ½" (12.7 mm) from the cut edge of the sleeve. For a 2" (5.1 cm) cuff, mark the sleeve 1½" (3.8 cm) from the cut edge. (Fig. 75c)

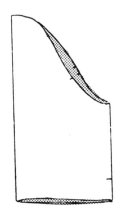

Fig. 75c

2. With the right sides together, stitch the seam from the underarm to the marked point. Backtack. (Fig. 75d) Clip the seam allowances to the end of the stitching line. (Fig. 75e)

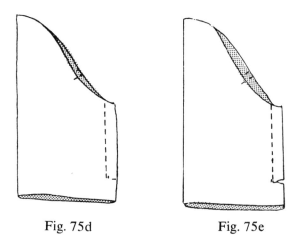

Fig. 75d   Fig. 75e

3. Reverse the unstitched section of the seam so that the *wrong* sides are together. Backtack and stitch to the garment edge. (Fig. 75f) Press and

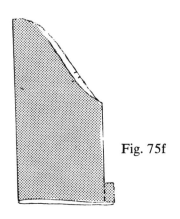

Fig. 75f

trim the reversed seam allowances to ¼″ (6.4 mm).

4. Set the cuff or facing with the right side of the cuff or facing to the *wrong* side of the garment. Press, trim, and understitch *the garment* and seam allowances.

5. Fold the cuff or facing to the right side of the garment. Topstitch or stitch-in-the-ditch to hold it in place.

MITRED CORNERS

This is a never-fail technique for any shape corner to be mitred.

1. Press the seam allowances to the wrong side of the section.

2. Where the seam allowances meet, clip the inner edges ⅛″ (3.2 mm) toward the point. (Fig. 76a)

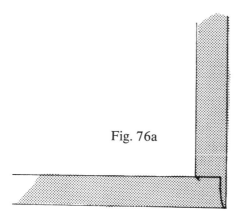

Fig. 76a

3. Mark the corner with a pin.

4. Refold the corner so that the right sides are together.

5. Stitch from the clips to the corner. (Fig. 76b)

6. If the fabric is bulky, trim the seam. (Fig. 76c)

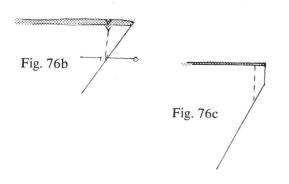

Fig. 76b

Fig. 76c

7. Turn the corner right-side-out and underpress.

TRIMMING AND GRADING
Enclosed Seams

If the seam allowances of enclosed seams are pre-trimmed to ⅜″ (9.5 mm) when you cut the garment out, they will rarely require additional grading. In addition, the narrow seam allowance allows you to stitch more quickly and with greater accuracy.

If the seam allowances were not pretrimmed, trim the stitched seams to ¼″ or ⅜″ (6.4 mm, 9.5 mm). Grade as needed.

Grading Seams. To prevent a ridge on the outside of the garment, enclosed seam allowances sometimes need to be graded or trimmed to different widths.

The seam allowance closest to the outside of the garment should be the longest. If you have set the interfacing to the garment section, the widest seam allowance will be the interfacing. (Fig. 77)

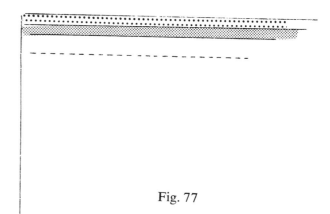

Fig. 77

The seam allowance in garments made of lightweight and some mediumweight fabrics may not require grading. The heavier and bulkier the fabrics, the greater the need to grade.

The seam allowances of some garments can be graded with a single cut. Position the garment so the facing or layer which will be shortest is on top. Hold the scissors so they are almost parallel to the upper layer; then trim through all the seam allowances.

Corners. If the fabric is bulky, trim the seam allowances diagonally across the corner. (Fig. 78a)

Some lightweight and mediumweight fabrics should not be trimmed at the corners. The seam allowances actually support the corner for a sharper point. This is especially true when one side of the

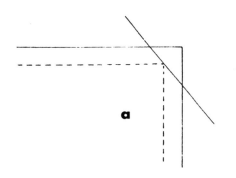

a

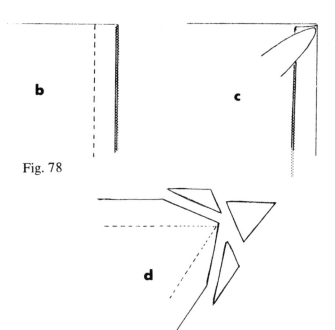

b

c

Fig. 78

d

corner is a fold, such as the corners on a one-piece cuff or collar. (Fig. 78b) Open the seam allowances and position the point turner between the seam allowances at the corner, or fold the seam allowances toward the facing and position the point turner on top of them to turn the corner right-side-out. (Fig. 78c)

Sharp points need to be trimmed with an additional diagonal cut on each side of the corner. (Fig. 78d) Use an orangewood stick to turn a collar with a sharp point.

Curves. Inward curves like necklines and armholes must be clipped in order to lie flat when the garment is turned right-side-out. (Fig. 79a)

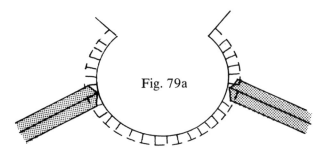

Fig. 79a

Space the clips closer together on sharper curves to ensure a smooth edge. (Fig. 79b) Position the

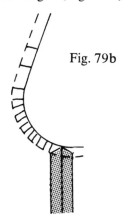

Fig. 79b

scissors points carefully so that the stitching line is not clipped.

Notch outward curves like collar edges to remove the extra bulk and eliminate ripples that show through. Pinking shears can be used to notch curved edges quickly and easily. (Fig. 79c)

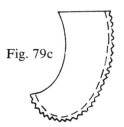

Fig. 79c

Trimming seam allowances. Most seamlines will be crossed by another seam or a hem. Trim the seam allowances to reduce bulk before stitching over them. (Fig. 80)

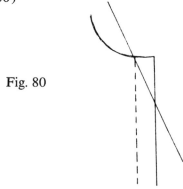

Fig. 80

Clipping and notching. Clip or notch the seam allowances of shaped seams so they can be pressed flat. (Fig. 81)

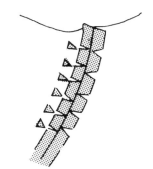

Fig. 81

DECORATIVE SEAMS

Decorative seams accentuate the lines of a plain garment for a finished, professional look.

Topstitched Seams

The topstitched seam is the easiest decorative seam to make and the seam with the greatest variety. Accent the seamlines of the garment with one line or several lines of topstitching. The seams can be pressed open or to one side.

If the seams are pressed to one side, these guidelines will help you decide in which direction to press them. Press horizontal seams up, press shoulder and side seams to the back, press other vertical seams to the center, press center-front seams to the right, and center-back seams to the left. Occasionally, the design of your garment may be improved by disregarding these standards. If so, be brave and stitch them the way you want.

Welt Seams

Welt seams are topstitched seams with some of the bulk removed. Use the guidelines for pressing topstitched seams to determine the position of welt seams.

1. With the right sides together, stitch a plain seam.
2. Press the seam allowances to one side.
3. Trim the seam allowance next to the garment to ⅛″ (3.2 mm).
4. Topstitch the garment and untrimmed seam allowance ¼″ (6.4 mm) from the seamline so that the trimmed seam allowance is encased. (Fig. 82)

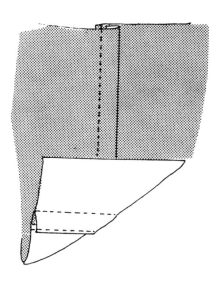

Fig. 82

Lapped Seams

The lapped seam is not only an attractive design but an easy way to match plaids and set yokes. Halston introduced a variation of the lapped seam on Ultrasuede® garments. His variation features raw edges, utilizing the no-fray quality of Ultrasuede®. Generally, seams lap top-over-bottom, front-over-back, center-over-side, right-over-left at center front, and left-over-right at center back. Cuffs lap over sleeves, and collars lap over garments.

Plain lapped seams. The plain lapped seam is suitable for woven and knitted fabrics.

1. Mark the seamlines on the right side of the fabric with soap or chalk or gauge stitch ⅛″ (3.2 mm) from the seamline.
2. Press the seam allowance of the overlap under. If the seam is curved, ease baste, crimp or clip ½″ (12.7 mm) from the edge.
3. Working from the right side of the garment, glue, baste, tape, or pin the overlap to the adjoining section, matching the stitching lines. The cut edges of the sections will match on the underside. Edgestitch the overlap in place. (Fig. 83)

Flat lapped seam. The flat lapped seam is an innovative seam that utilizes the unique feature of nonwoven fabrics. The seam can be constructed with one of the following methods:

Trim-and-Stitch Method:

The trim-and-stitch method is used on commercial patterns for nonwoven fabrics. This method is also

71

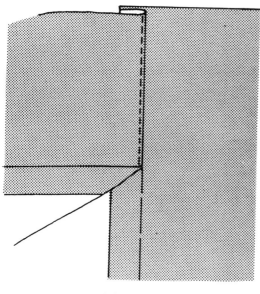

Fig. 83

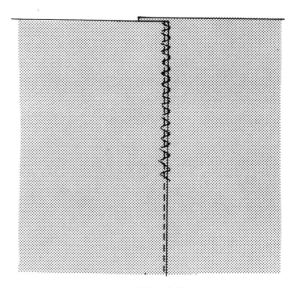

Fig. 84b

recommended for darts and seams on interfacing materials.

1. Cut away the ⅝″ (16 mm) seam allowance on the overlap.
2. Mark the seamline on the right side of the underlap with soap or chalk.
3. Working from the right side of the garment, glue, tape, pin, or baste the overlap so that the cut edge of the overlap meets the seamline of the underlap. (Fig. 84a) Edgestitch the overlap in place.

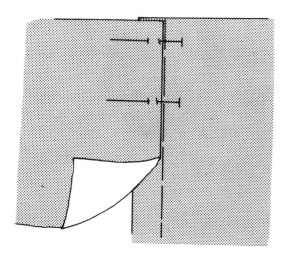

Fig. 84a

Variation: Zigzag (W,2-L,2) the edge of the overlap, allowing the needle to swing over the edge.

(Fig. 84b) Strange as it may seem, this variation will make an attractive finish on knitted and firmly woven fabrics.

Stitch-and-Trim Method:
This seam eliminates bulk and is only suitable for such nonwovens as suede, leather, vinyl, felt, and pseudosuedes.

Many home sewers have difficulty cutting out nonwoven fabrics so that the edges don't have zigs and zags. They also find it hard to stitch straight and close to the edges of these spongy fabrics. This method requires a very small seam allowance which will be trimmed away after the seam is stitched.

1. Cut away ½″ (12.7 mm) of the seam allowance on the overlap.
2. Mark the underlap with soap ¾″ (19.1 mm) from the cut edge.
3. Position the overlap so that it meets the marked line. This positioning covers the seamline ⅛″ (3.2 mm). Glue, tape, pin, or baste the sections together. If you want to check the fit, carefully try on the garment.
4. Topstitch the sections together ⅛″ (3.2 mm) from the edge of the overlap. (Fig. 85a) Topstitch again ⅜″ (9.5 mm) from the edge if you want to simulate a flat-fell seam. (Fig. 85b)
5. Use embroidery scissors to trim the overlap close to the stitching line. (Fig. 85c)
Lace seams. Many designs can be sewn attractively with this variation of a lapped seam because the

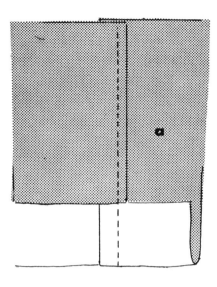

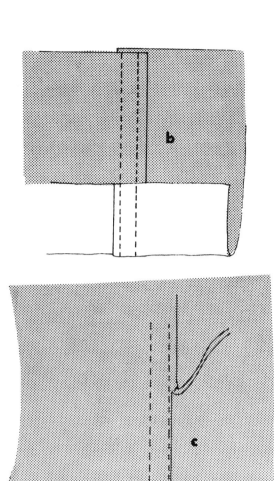

Fig. 85

construction details of the garment are hidden by the design of the lace.

1. Use a complete pattern *without* seam allowances. Pin the pattern pieces on the lace so that the motifs are positioned attractively with several inches between each section. The motifs on corresponding sections do not have to match exactly.

2. Cut around the large motifs in the lace when you cut the sections out. The cutting lines will be *very* crooked, and the seam allowances will be uneven. (Fig. 86a)

3. Mark the stitching lines on each section with a basting thread. (Fig. 86b)

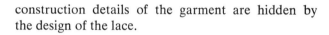

4. Lap one section over the other. Match the traced lines and pin them together. Using thread to match

the lace, baste a line around the lace motifs on the right side of the garment. This line will be very irregular. If it enhances the design, the front can lap over the back for part of a seam and the back can lap over the front for the remainder of the seam. It isn't necessary to lap the entire seam in one direction.

5. Whipstitch or zigzag (W,2-L,2) over the basted line to seam the two layers.

6. Trim each layer close to the whipped seam. The seamline will look like an irregularity in the lace.

Piped Seams

Piped seams really add pizazz to a plain garment. They are used to outline edges and accentuate seamlines. These decorative seams aren't difficult to make, but corners and curves require a little know-how.

The piping can be corded or not. If cording is used, shrink it before making the piped strips.

Fig. 86

1. Cut bias strips the required length. Determine the width of the strip by the diameter of the cord to be inserted or by the desired finished width of the piping plus two seam allowances. (An easy, accurate method is to cut a wide bias strip, stitch the piping, then trim the seam allowances to the desired width.)

2. Stitch the piping with the wrong sides together the desired distance from the folded edge or make cording by wrapping the bias strip around the cord with the right side of the bias out. Stitch close to the cord, using a zipper foot. Trim the piping to the desired seam allowance, ⅝″ (16 mm) for regular seams and ⅜″ (9.5 mm) for enclosed seams (Fig. 87a)

3. Match the cut edges of the piping to those of the garment and stitch the piping to the right side of one garment section with the zipper foot.

4. With the right sides of the garment together and the piping sandwiched between, stitch through all layers. This line of stitching should be slightly closer to the cording than the previous stitching line to eliminate stitches showing on the right side of the garment.

5. Clip the seam allowance of the piping to the stitched line before you apply it to curved edges like collars, flaps, and pockets. (Fig. 87b) Ease the seam

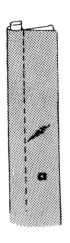
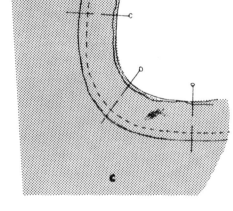

Fig. 87

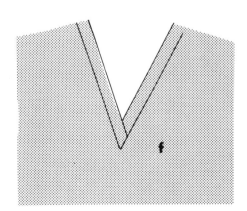
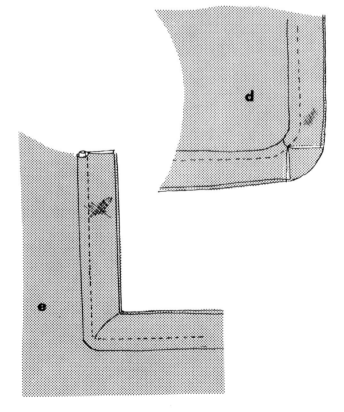

allowance of the piping to inward curves such as necklines and armscyes. (Fig. 87c) Remember that the stitched line on the piping is the key; it should be exactly the same length as the garment seamline.

6. Piping around the corners of pockets and collars must be clipped to the stitching line at the corner. Round each corner slightly by taking several stitches around it. (Fig. 87d)

7. Fold a pleat in the seam allowance of the piping when stitching it to a squared neckline. (Fig. 87e) Clip the seam allowance of the garment and facing to the corner. The stitching line on the piping must be the same length as the garment seamline.

8. The point of a V-neckline is one of the few times the piping begins and ends at a corner. Position the piping so that the right end overlaps the left end. (Fig. 87f)

9. When using corded piping to trim a neckline which has a zipper placket, pull the cord out at each end and trim away ⅝″ (16 mm) to avoid stitching the cord into the placket area.

SELF-FINISHED SEAMS
French Seams

French seams were formerly used on all expensive garments made of lightweight fabrics. This seam takes time to construct, and care must be taken to avoid having "fuzz" sticking out of the seam on the right side of the garment.

Most designers are now using other seams such as standing fell, quick flat-fell, and overlocked seams, all of which are quicker and cheaper to make.

1. With the *wrong* sides together, stitch a ¼″ (6.4 mm) seam. (Fig. 88a)

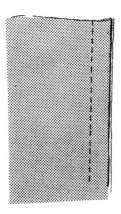

Fig. 88a

2. Press the seam to one side.
3. Trim the seam to ⅛″ (3.2 mm).
4. Turn the seam so that the right sides of the garment are together and stitch another ¼″ (6.4 mm) seam, enclosing the first one. (Fig. 88b)

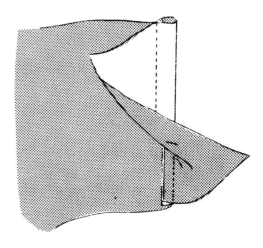

Fig. 88b

You have stitched only ½″ (12.7 mm) of the ⅝″ (16 mm) seam allowance; however, the difference will be absorbed in the turn-of-the-cloth.

Drapery French Seams

The drapery French seam is softer than a regular French seam and it is constructed so that there is no possibility of fuzz in the seamline.

This seam was formerly used on custom-made draperies. Most drapery manufacturers have replaced it with the quick-to-make overlocked seam. You can use it on garments instead of French seams.

1. With the *wrong* sides together, stitch a ¼″ (6.4 mm) seam.
2. Fold the seam to one side. (Fig. 89a)

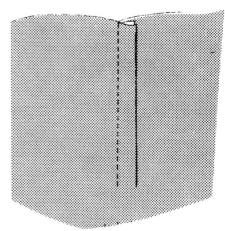

Fig. 89a

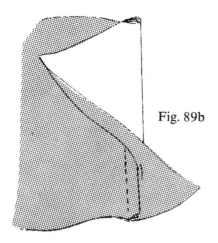

Fig. 89b

positioning the garment sections so that the seams will be stitched directionally.

2. Fold the lower layer to the left, over the top layer. (Fig. 90b)

3. Fold both layers to the left ¼″ (6.4 mm). Pin. (Fig. 90c) Stitch through all layers, using the inside of the presser foot as a guide. Arrange as you go without pinning the entire seam. (Fig. 90d)

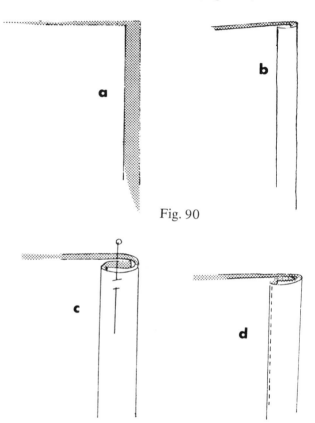

Fig. 90

3. Fold the fabric over the cut edges of the seam so that the right sides of the fabric are together. The first stitching line is ¼″ (6.4 mm) from the folded edge. (Fig. 89b)

4. Stitch from the wrong side of the garment in the well of the seam. (Fig. 89c)

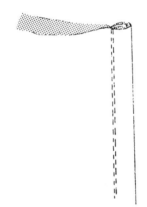

Fig. 89c

Standing-fell or Self-bound Seams

The standing-fell seam is a super-fast, ·hassle-free seam to make on any garment made of a lightweight fabric that ravels. Substitute it for French seams and make two garments in the time it would take you to make one. This seam is used on some designer blouses.

Do not make clips in the seam allowances to indicate the notches, but it won't be a disaster if you've already made the clips before deciding to use standing-fell seams.

1. With the right sides together, place the edge of the upper layer so that the lower layer extends ¼″ (6.4 mm). (Fig. 90a) Avoid a twist in the seam by

Modified Standing-fell Seams

The modified standing-fell seam was developed for the less-experienced seamstress and for seamlines that are more difficult to handle than straight or slightly curved seams.

1. Stitch the seam with a ⅝″ (16 mm) seam allowance.

2. Trim *one* seam allowance to ⅛″ (3.2 mm). (Fig. 91a)

3. Fold the other seam allowance to the left so that the cut edges meet (Fig. 91b), then fold it again enclosing the cut edges. Stitch along the folded edge, using the inside of the presser foot as a guide. (Fig. 91c)

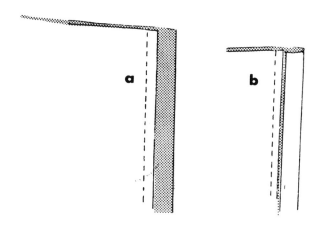

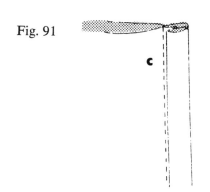

Fig. 91

Modified Standing-fell Seams for Ruffles

Seams with ruffles can be finished with a modified standing-fell seam or by this method which forces the seam allowances to stand up and improves the way the ruffle hangs. This finish has less bulk than a standing-fell seam, but it isn't a true self-finished seam.

1. Stitch the seam with a ⅝″ (16 mm) seam allowance.

2. Trim the seam allowance of the ruffle to ⅛″ (3.2 mm). (Fig. 92a)

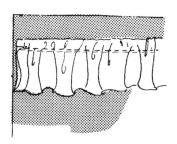

Fig. 92a

3. Fold the untrimmed seam allowance over the trimmed edge (ruffle). (Fig. 92b)

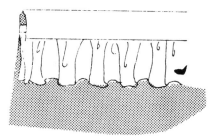

Fig. 92b

4. Stitch from the reverse side on top of the first stitching line. (Fig. 92c)

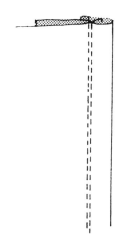

Fig. 92c

The edge of the untrimmed seam allowance remains unfinished.

Quick Flat-fell Seams

Flat-fell seams are used on tailored, reversible, and unlined garments as well as on work clothes.

Traditional flat-fell seams on ready-made garments are stitched on double-needle machines and have two rows of stitching on the right *and* wrong sides of the fabric. This cannot be duplicated exactly on the home sewing machine.

The old-fashioned, home-sewing method is difficult to make because you're turning one seam allowance under and stitching it in place in one step. Take a tip from designers Chanel and Yves Saint Laurent and use a quick flat-fell seam instead. Do not make clips in the seam allowances.

If you want two rows of stitching on the right side of the garment, start with the wrong sides to-

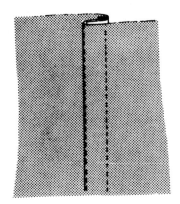

Fig. 93a

gether. (Fig. 93a) If you want one row of stitching on the right side, start with the right sides together. (Fig. 93b)

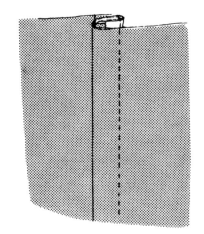

Fig. 93b

1. Place the edge of the upper layer so that the lower layer extends ½″ (12.7 mm). (Fig. 93c)

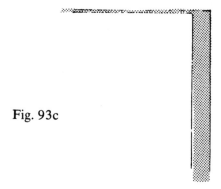

Fig. 93c

Avoid a twist in the seam by positioning the garment sections so that the seams will be stitched directionally.

2. Fold the lower layer over the edge of the upper layer. Stitch ⅜″ (9.5 mm) from the folded edge. It is more important to keep the stitching an even distance from the fold than it is to catch every little bit of the exposed cut edge. (Fig. 93d)

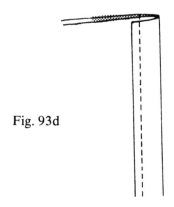

Fig. 93d

3. Open the garment flat. Fold the seam to the left, enclosing the cut edge. Edgestitch the folded edge to the garment using the inside of the presser foot as a guide. (Fig. 93e)

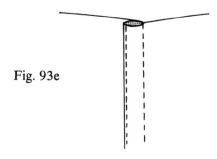

Fig. 93e

Heavy fabrics require ¾″ (19.1 mm) seam allowances to accommodate the turn-of-the-cloth. Extend the lower layer ⅝″ (16 mm), fold it over and stitch ½″ (12.7 mm) from the folded edge.

Lightweight fabrics look better with a narrow seam. Allow ½″ (12.7 mm) seam allowances. Extend the lower layer ⅜″ (9.5 mm), fold it over and stitch ¼″ (6.4 mm) from the folded edge.

Modified Quick Flat-fell Seams
The modified quick flat-fell seam is constructed with only one line of stitching on the right side of the garment. It looks like a welt seam on the right side, but it is self-finished and the welt seam is not.

1. With the right sides together, stitch the seam with a ⅝″ (16 mm) seam allowance.
2. Trim one seam allowance to ¼″ (6.4 mm). (Fig. 94a)

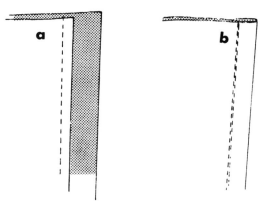

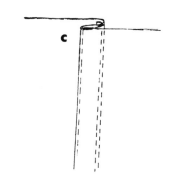

Fig. 94

3. Fold the other seam allowance over the trimmed edge and stitch from the reverse side on top of the original seamline. (Fig. 94b) Open the garment flat and edgestitch the folded edge to the garment. (Fig. 94c)

Flat-fell Seams for Nonwoven Fabrics

This easy seam for pseudosuedes is the answer if you can't decide which way the seam should lap or if you want to try on the garment before you trim the seam allowance.

1. Allow a 5/8″ (16 mm) seam allowance.
2. With the *wrong* sides together, stitch a 5/8″ (16 mm) seam. Try the garment on to check the fit, if desired.
3. Trim the underlap to 1/8″ (3.2 mm). (Fig. 95a)
4. Fold the overlap over the trimmed layer and glue baste.
5. Topstitch the overlap 1/4″–3/8″ (6.4 mm–9.5 mm) from the seamline. (Fig. 95b)
6. Trim the overlap close to the stitched line with embroidery scissors.

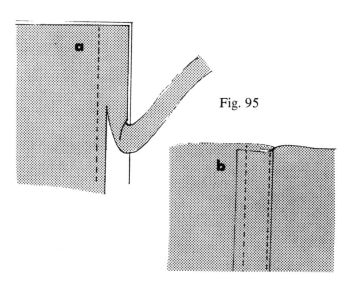

Fig. 95

OTHER SEAMS
Double-stitched Seams

Double-stitched seams are especially suited to transparent fabrics or such intricate enclosed seams as collars or scallops.

1. With the right sides together, stitch on the seamline with a short, straight stitch.
2. Stitch the seam allowances again 1/16″ (1.6 mm) from the first stitching line, using the inside of the presser foot as a guide.
3. Trim the seam allowances to 1/8″ (3.2 mm) *total*. (Fig. 96)

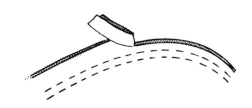

Fig. 96

Do not use this technique on fabrics that unravel unless the seam is enclosed and protected between the garment and the facing.

Hairline Seams

Despite its fragile appearance, the hairline seam is a very sturdy one, and it's especially lovely on sheers, lace, and lingerie. Ungaro, the designer, uses this tiny seam on silk evening gowns. It can be used also on any enclosed seam, eliminating bulk on intricate style lines.

1. Stitch on the seamline with a short, straight stitch.
2. Trim the seam allowance to 1/8″ (3.2 mm).
3. Zigzag (W,2-L,1) over the trimmed edge. The

needle stitches off the fabric each time it swings to the right. (Fig. 97)

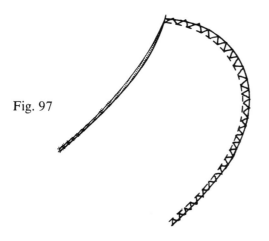

Fig. 97

Don't forget to use this technique to stitch darts, too.

Overlocked or Zigzagged Seams

This seam simulates the seam made on commercial overlock machines. Surprisingly, it is easy to duplicate and is found on many expensive garments.

1. Stitch on the seamline.
2. Trim the seam allowances to ¼" (6.4 mm).
3. Zigzag (W,3-L,2) over the trimmed edge. Stitch with the grain when you zigzag to reduce the fraying at the edge. If the fabric rolls, stitch with paper or use an overcast foot. (Fig. 98)

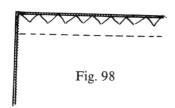

Fig. 98

Narrow or Rolled Seams

The narrow or rolled seam is made, using a hemmer foot. The ⅛" (3.2 mm) hemmer foot makes a beautiful, narrow straight seam on sheer fabrics. Use it on straight or almost-straight seams; it is very difficult to stitch on shaped seams.

1. Allow a ⅝" (16 mm) seam allowance.
2. With the right sides together, stitch a plain seam ½" (12.7 mm) from the cut edges, leaving long threads at the beginning and end of the stitching.

3. Trim the seam allowances to ⅛" (3.2 mm) from the stitching line. This should be done just before you make the rolled seam, to eliminate fraying. If the edges fray while you're making the seam, trim the unraveled threads before they go through the hemmer foot.
4. Use the threads at the beginning of the stitching line to pull the seam into the spiral of the hemmer foot so that you will be stitching directionally. (Fig. 99a)

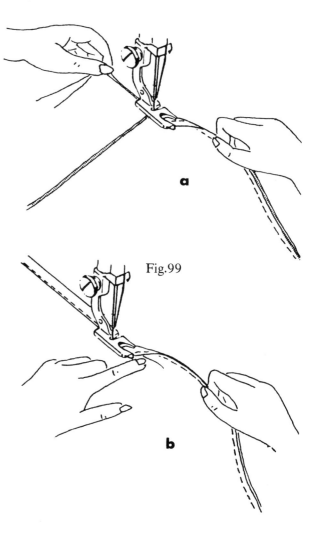

a

Fig. 99

b

5. As you begin stitching the seam, gently pull the threads in back of the hemmer foot. Hold the fabric taut in front of the foot.

The fabric edge in front of the foot is held perpendicular to the machine bed with the right hand. The index finger of the left hand is inserted between the seam and garment immediately in front of the foot to position the seam as it enters the foot. The way the fabric is held is an important key to the success of the finished seam. (Fig. 99b)

Strap Seams

A strap seam is an easy way to add a designer look to any garment. It is especially attractive on reversible garments and on garments made of see-through fabrics as net, lace, mesh, open-weave knits, and wovens. A strip of bias tape, contrasting fabric, or pseudosuede covers the seamline and seam allowances on the right side of the garment.

1. Cut the strap the desired length and width—½″ (12.7 mm) or wider plus two seam allowances, if necessary.
2. Allow ⅝″ (16 mm) seam allowances on the garment.
3. With the *wrong* sides of the garment together, stitch the seam.
4. Trim the seam to ¼″ (6.4 mm).
5. Press the seam open or press it to one side, depending on the width of the strap.
6. Glue, pin, or baste the strap in place, covering the seam allowances of the garment. If the strap is a woven or knitted material, turn under the seam allowances on each side. Edgestitch the strap to the garment. (Fig. 100)

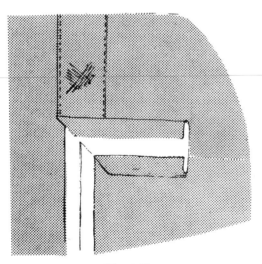

Fig. 100

Stretch Seams

The seams in garments made of stretchy knits should have some elasticity so they won't break when the garment is worn.

Straight stitch. Seams made with a straight stitch are difficult to stitch because the edges roll, and they are more likely to break when the garment is worn. If you don't have a zigzag machine, this is the best method.

1. Loosen the tension and set the machine for a short stitch, 15–20 spi or 1.5 mm. Shortening the stitch and loosening the tension allows more thread to be stitched into each stitch, and it increases the elasticity of the seam.
2. Hold the fabric in front and back of the presser foot. Stretch the fabric slightly as you stitch. Most knits will roll which makes the seam difficult to stitch evenly.
3. Stitch the seam again ¹⁄₁₆″ (1.6 mm) from the first line of stitching, stretching as you stitch.

Narrow zigzag stitch

1. Stitch the seam the desired distance from the edge using a narrow zigzag stitch (W,1-L,1.5). Hold the fabric taut as you stitch. (Fig. 101)
2. Press the seam flat, then press it open.

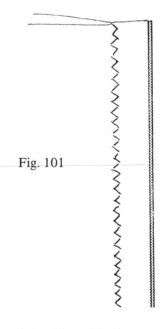

Fig. 101

Wide zigzag stitch. The wide zigzag stitch makes a very elastic seam which can be used on lingerie, but the stitches will show on the right side of the garment.

1. Trim the seam allowances to ¼″ (6.4 mm). Most lingerie patterns already have ¼″ (6.4 mm) seam allowances.

2. Zigzag (W,4-L,1) over the cut edge. The needle should stitch off the fabric each time it swings to the right. (Fig. 102)

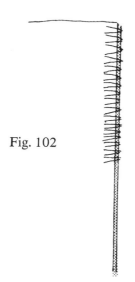

Fig. 102

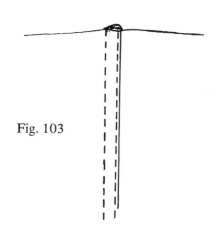

Fig. 103

Stretch stitch. If your machine has a stretch stitch, set it the desired length and width to stitch this seam.

Seams for Single-ply Reversible Fabrics

Many fabrics can be used for reversible garments because both sides of the fabric look the same or because the wrong side of the fabric is attractive. A few fabrics are printed with one pattern on one side of the fabric and another pattern on the other side. All of these fabrics are a single thickness or single-ply fabrics.

Flat-fell seams, strap seams, and lapped seams for nonwoven fabrics are often used on reversible garments. Other seams—French, drapery French, and plain seams—can be adapted for reversible garments.

French seams for reversible garments. This seam will look like a flat-fell seam on one side of the garment and a topstitched seam on the other.

1. Construct the French seams in the usual manner.
2. Press the finished seams toward the back of the garment.
3. Edgestitch the seam to the garment, using the inside of the presser foot as a guide. (Fig. 103)

Plain seams for reversible garments. This seam is especially attractive when one side of the fabric is a solid and the other is a print or a solid in a different shade or color.

Nonwoven or Firmly Woven Fabrics:
1. Stitch a ⅝″ (16 mm) seam.
2. Press the seam open.
3. Pin, glue, or baste the seam allowance to the garment. Stitch directionally when you stitch the seam allowances to the garment. (Fig. 104a)

If the material is a woven fabric, zigzag (W,2-L,2) over the edges of the seam allowances. (Fig. 104b)

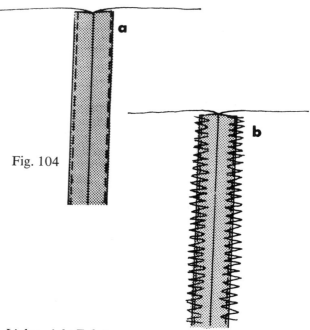

Fig. 104

Lightweight Fabrics:
1. Allow ¾″ (19.1 mm) seam allowances.
2. Stitch a ¾″ (19.1 mm) seam.
3. Press the seam open.
4. Turn the edge of each seam allowance under ¼″ (6.4 mm). Pin, glue, or baste it to the garment, then edgestitch it in place. (Fig. 105)

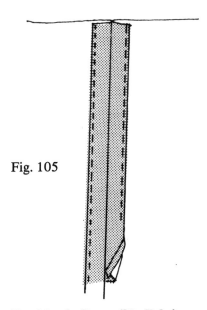

Fig. 105

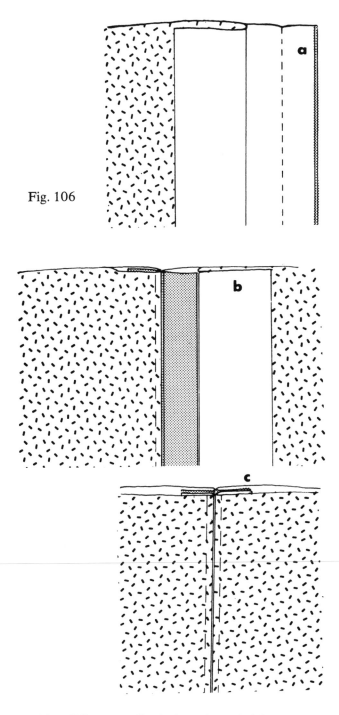

Fig. 106

Seams for Double-ply Reversible Fabrics

Many reversible fabrics have two layers or plies which are sewn, bonded, or woven together. If they are woven together, they must be handled as single-ply reversibles. If they are bonded or sewn together, they can be stitched as single-ply fabrics, or each layer can be stitched separately.

Stitched-slipstitched reversible seams. The seams on each layer of stitched-slipstitched reversible seams are completed separately; one layer is stitched by machine, then the other layer is finished by hand.

1. Separate the layers for 1¼" (3.2 cm) or twice the seam width at each edge to be seamed. If the layers are sewn together, clip the threads between them. If you separate them a little more or an uneven distance, it won't show; but you must separate the layers for at least twice the seam width.
2. Pull the layers apart to separate the layers if they are bonded together. They must be separated an even distance from the edge to avoid an uneven and unsightly demarcation line. Use an even basting stitch through both layers to mark a guideline 1¼" (3.2 cm) from the cut edge. Separate the layers to the basted line.
3. With the right sides of the outer layer together, machine stitch a ⅝" (16 mm) seam. (Fig. 106a)
4. Press the seam open.
5. Turn in one of the underlayer seam allowances so that the folded edge meets the stitched line. Baste the seam allowance in place so that the basted line is ¼" (6.4 mm) from the folded edge. If you place the basted line closer to the folded edge, the seam

will be difficult to slipstitch and the finished seamline may be crooked. (Fig. 106b) Turn in the other seam allowance and baste it in place. (Fig. 106c) Slipstitch the seams together.
6. Topstitch both sides of the seamline if desired.

If the fabric is bonded, topstitching on the demarcation line, ⅝" (16 mm) from the seamline, makes the separation line less noticeable.

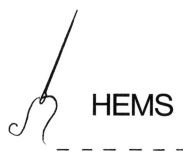

HEMS

The primary purpose of a hem is to finish the edge of the garment. It is usually turned to the wrong side of the garment, but it can be turned to the right side or left unturned. The hem also adds weight to the edge to improve the appearance of the garment. Well-made hems are inconspicuous unless they are decorative.

HEMMING THE GARMENT

The hem is usually measured at the last fitting after all changes have been made and the garment has been pressed. Circular, flared, and bias-cut garments should hang at least 24 hours before the hem is measured.

The hemming sequence for all garments is the same:

1. Mark the hemline of the garment.
2. Fold the hem to the wrong side of the garment, matching the seamlines and centers.
3. Pin or baste ¼″ (6.4 mm) above the hemline to hold the hem allowance in place.
4. Insert brown paper or adding-machine paper strips between the hem allowance and the garment to avoid making impressions on the right side of the garment and to prevent shrinking the garment.
5. Press the hem lightly with the lengthwise grain, being careful not to press over the pins, and shrinking out as much fullness in the hem as possible. Removing the fullness in the hem allowances may cause the hem depth to widen. (Fig. 107a)
6. Measure the hem depth with a cardboard gauge or tape measure. Use chalk or a soap sliver to mark the desired depth. (Fig. 107b)
7. If the skirt is flared, control the excess fullness with crimping, ease basting, or buttonhole twist.

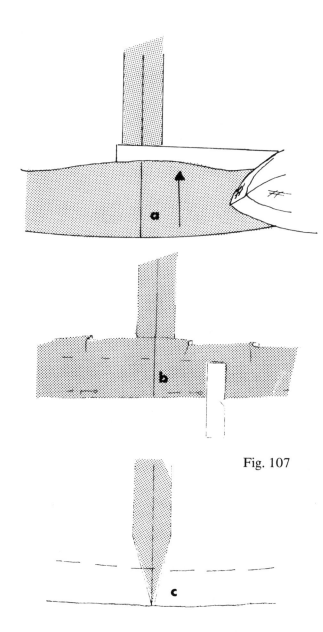

Fig. 107

8. If the fabric is bulky, trim the seam allowances in the hem area. (Fig. 107c)
9. Finish the cut edge of the hem appropriately for the fabric and garment.
10. Hem the garment by hand, machine, gluing, or fusing.
11. Press.

MARKING THE HEMLINE

Use a yardstick or meter stick to mark the hemlines. The small end of the stick is easier to fit between the feet than a skirt marker, and it is long enough to mark the hems of jackets and blouses.

Stand on a table and have someone mark the garment for you. While you stand still, the person marking should move around you. The hem should be marked quickly so that the person standing does not tire and shift position during the marking process.

Pins should be placed every four or five inches at the hemline parallel to the floor. After the hemline is marked, pin the hem up before removing the garment. The hem should *look* level; adjust it until it appears level, even though it may not be.

Remove the garment and lay it on a table right-side-up. Correct slight irregularities in the placement of the pins for a smooth hemline. (Fig. 108a)

Mark the hemline on the face side of the fabric with pins, soap, chalk, or basting thread. (Fig. 108b)

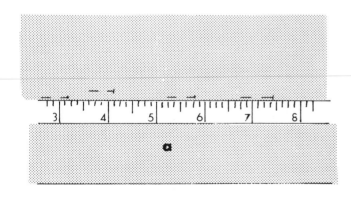

Fig. 108

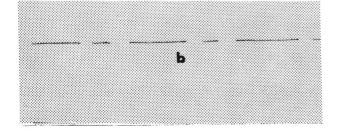

Marking a Floor-length Garment
A floor-length garment is often difficult to mark evenly. Use this method on any garment that will not be marred by pin or needle holes.

1. Place pins around the skirt 10″ (25.4 cm) from the floor. (Fig. 109a) Use very fine needles to mark delicate fabrics.

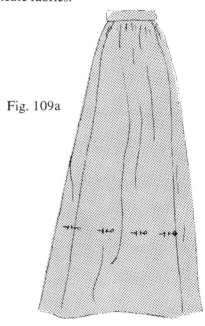

Fig. 109a

2. Remove the garment and measure the hemline 9½″ (24.1 cm) below each pin for the desired length. The garment will float ½″ (12.7 mm) above the floor. (Fig. 109b)

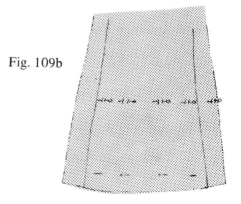

Fig. 109b

3. If you want the skirt to be ankle length, adjust the distance below the pins accordingly.

CONTROLLING HEM EASE

When the hem allowance on a flared or circular skirt is turned under, the cut edge of the hem has more fullness than the garment. The excess fullness in the hem must be controlled so that the hem will lie flat against the skirt.

There are several ways to control the ease, depending on the fabric and garment quality. One or more technique can be used to get the desired result.

Reduce the Hem Allowance

The amount of fullness increases with the hem depth. If the hem is narrow, there is less fullness to shrink out.

1. Fold the hem to the wrong side of the garment.
2. Mark the hem depth ⅝″–1¼″ (16 mm–3.2 cm).
3. Finish the edge of the hem and hem the garment.

Reshape the Seamlines

These quick-and-easy methods are suitable for everyday garments and quick projects. In order to reduce the ease in the hem area by reshaping the seamline, the excess fullness must be localized at the vertical seamlines such as on an A-shaped skirt or bell-bottom pants. The vertical seamlines will be reshaped to remove the excess fabric. The seamlines must be ripped and restitched if the garment is to be lengthened.

Method one. If the hemline can be marked from the pattern, reshape the side seams before stitching them.

1. Notch the hemline fold at each seamline.
2. Fold and press the hem to the wrong side of the garment section at the hemline notch. (Fig. 110a)
3. Trim away the excess hem allowance.

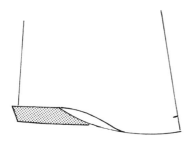

Fig. 110a

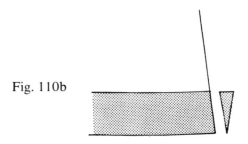

Fig. 110b

4. Stitch the side seam.

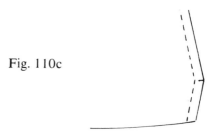

Fig. 110c

5. Press the seam open.
6. Turn the hem to the wrong side of the garment.
7. Finish the edge of the hem and hem the garment.

Method two. If you need to assemble the garment and try it on to mark the hemline, reshape the side seams after stitching them.

1. Mark the hemline.
2. Fold the hem to the right side of the garment at the hemline. (Fig. 111a)

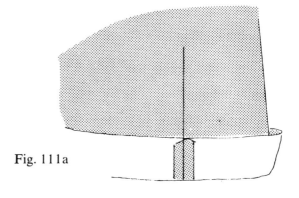

Fig. 111a

3. Pin the seam together at the cut edge of the hem to remove the fullness. (Fig. 111b) Notch the cut edge of the hem at the pinned seam.

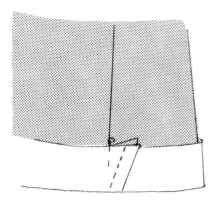

Fig. 111b

4. Stitch the side seam from the hem edge to the hemline fold, continue stitching 1"–2" (2.5 cm–5 cm) to secure the stitching line. (Fig. 111c)

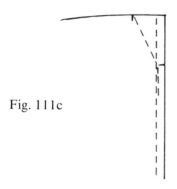

Fig. 111c

5. Trim the seam allowances in the hem area if you do not plan to lengthen the garment.
6. Rip out any of the original side seam that remains in the hem area so that you can press the seam open.
7. Press the seam open.
8. Press the hem to the wrong side of the garment.
9. Finish the edge of the hem and hem the garment.

Press and/or Shrink Out the Fullness
The ease in the hem is easily controlled if the garment has little or no flare or if the fabric shrinks easily. Press and steam to reduce the bulk in the hem.

1. Fold the hem to the wrong side of the garment.
2. Pin or baste ¼" (6.4 mm) above the folded edge.
3. Insert heavy paper or lightweight cardboard between the hem and garment to prevent shrinking the garment and to avoid a pressing imprint on the garment.
4. Using steam, press the hem allowance with the grain from the hemline to the cut edge of the hem. Do *not* press over pins.
5. Mark the hem the desired depth.
6. Finish the edge of the hem and hem the garment.

Crimp
Crimp the cut edge of the hem if you need to remove a moderate amount of fullness. This method is especially suitable for circular skirts. Even though these skirts have a lot of fullness, the fullness is evenly distributed.

1. Fold the hem to the wrong side of the garment.
2. Pin or baste ¼" (6.4 mm) above the folded edge.
3. Press out as much fullness as possible. Do *not* press over pins.
4. Mark the hem the desired depth.
5. Crimp the flared sections of the hem or the entire hem on the marked line to control the fullness.
6. Finish the hem edge with hem tape, lace, or a Hong-Kong finish to cover the ease and hold it in place.
7. Hem the garment.

Ease Baste
Ease basting can be used to control the ease on any fabric or garment, but it is time-consuming.

1. Fold the hem to the wrong side of the garment.
2. Pin or baste ¼" (6.4 mm) above the folded edge.
3. Press out as much fullness as possible. Do *not* press over pins.
4. Mark the hem the desired depth.
5. Ease baste the flared sections or the entire hem by tightening the upper tension so that you can stitch from the right side of the hem on the marked line. Stop and start the ease basting at each seamline.
6. Pull the thread on the right side of the fabric to adjust the fullness so that the hem will lie flat against the skirt. (Fig. 112)

Fig. 112

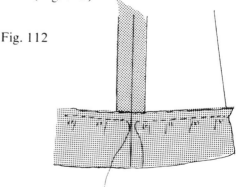

7. Finish the hem edge with hem tape, lace, or a Hong-Kong finish to cover the ease and hold it in place.

8. Hem the garment.

Buttonhole Twist

Zigzag over cord to adjust hems with a lot of fullness quickly and easily.

1. Fold the hem to the wrong side of the garment.
2. Pin or baste ¼″ (6.4 mm) above the folded edge.
3. Press out as much fullness as possible. Do *not* press over pins.
4. Mark the hem the desired depth.
5. Zigzag (W,3-L,2) over the buttonhole twist on the marked line. Stop and start again at each seamline. (Fig. 113a)

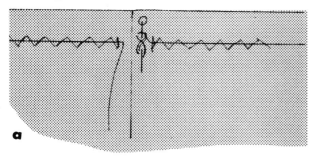

Fig. 113

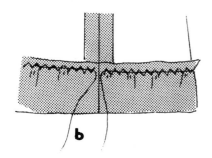

6. Pull the buttonhole twist to gather in the fullness. (Fig. 113b)
7. Finish the hem edge with hem tape, lace, or a Hong-Kong finish to cover the cord and hold the ease in place.
8. Hem the garment.

HEM FINISHES

The hem finish is determined by the style of the garment and the characteristics of the fabric: knit, woven or nonwoven, fray quality, washability, weight, and opaqueness. Finish the edge as flatly as possible and still prevent fraying.

This simple detail—finishing the edge of the hem —can make a garment a success or failure.

Cut or Raw Edge

The cut edge is an appropriate finish for most lined garments and unlined garments of knitted, firmly woven, and nonwoven fabrics: felt, vinyl, leather, suede, or pseudosuede. (Fig. 114)

Fig. 114

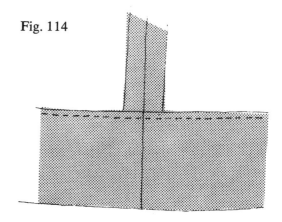

1. Fold the hem to the wrong side of the garment and press out as much fullness as possible.
2. Mark the hem allowance the desired depth.
3. Trim on the marked line.
4. Stitch ⅛″–¼″ (3.2 mm–6.4 mm) from the edge if desired. If the hem is to be fused, a ½″–1″ (12.7 mm–25.4 mm) wide strip of a fusible agent can be stitched to the wrong side of the hem at this time. The fusible agent used should not be wider than the hem.
5. Hem the garment by gluing, fusing, or stitching (hand or machine).

Pinked or Stitched and Pinked

Use a pinked edge on fabrics that ravel slightly. Stitch the edge, then pink it to finish hems on fabrics that fray moderately. (Fig. 115)

Fig. 115

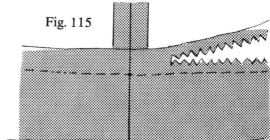

1. Fold the hem to the wrong side of the garment and press out as much fullness as possible.
2. Mark the hem allowance the desired depth and at least ¼″ (6.4 mm) from the cut edge.
3. If desired, stitch on the marked line.
4. Pink just above the marked or stitched line.
5. Hem the garment.

Zigzagged or Stitched and Zigzagged
The zigzagged finish is suitable for garments made of loosely woven fabrics and washable fabrics that fray. (Fig. 116) Lightweight fabrics will roll when zigzagged.

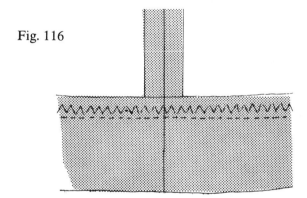

Fig. 116

1. Fold the hem to the wrong side of the garment and press out as much fullness as possible.
2. Mark the hem allowance the desired depth and at least ¼″ (6.4 mm) below the cut edge.
3. Stitch on the marked line with a zigzag stitch (W,2-L,2); or stitch on the marked line with a straight stitch, then stitch again just above it with a zigzag stitch. (If the fabric rolls, use an overcast foot or stitch with paper. The fabric will roll less if the zigzag stitch isn't right on the edge of the hem.)
4. Trim above the zigzagged line.
5. Hem the garment.

Tape or Lace
Tape or lace is an attractive finish that washes well, controls fullness neatly, and prevents fraying.

1. Fold the hem to the wrong side of the garment and press out as much fullness as possible.
2. Mark the hem allowance the desired depth and at least ¼″ (6.4 mm) from the cut edge.
3. If the hem has fullness to be eased, crimp or ease baste on the marked line.
4. Position the edge of the tape along the marked or eased line and stitch it to the hem allowance. (Fig. 117a)

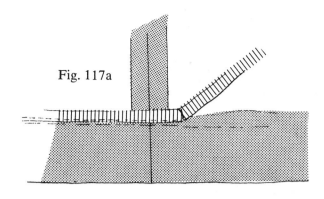

Fig. 117a

5. Trim away any excess fabric under the tape. (Fig. 117b)
6. Hem the garment.

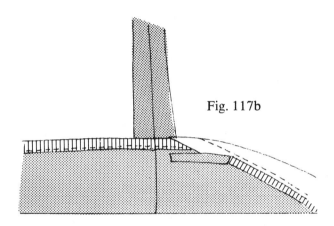

Fig. 117b

Iron-on Hem Tape
Iron-on hem tape can be used to finish the edge and hem lightweight, everyday garments. It washes well, prevents fraying, and is quick to apply. It should not be used on flared hems and it may show on the right side of the garment. Test before applying it.

1. Fold the hem to the wrong side of the garment and press it.
2. Mark and trim the hem allowance the desired depth.
3. Pin the hem in place, placing the pins away from the cut edge.
4. Position the iron-on hem tape so that it covers the cut edge of the hem allowance ¼″ (6.4 mm).
5. Using a dry iron, set at *cotton* for cotton or linen fabrics or at *wool* for other fabrics, and press the hem tape lightly.
6. Use the edge of the iron to bond the tape permanently to the hem allowance and garment. Apply pressure until the bond lines appear.

7. Allow the hem to cool and do not wash or dry-clean the garment for twelve hours.

Clean-finished Edge or Turned Under and Stitched

The guide sheets of most patterns recommend the clean-finished edge. However, it is *only* appropriate for lightweight washable fabrics that ravel. It is *not* suitable for knitted, heavy or mediumweight fabrics, or sheers. This finish washes well and looks neat on the right fabrics.

1. Fold the hem to the wrong side of the garment and press out as much fullness as possible.
2. Mark the hem allowance the desired depth plus ¼″ (6.4 mm).
3. Trim on the marked line.
4. Turn the hem edge under ¼″ (6.4 mm) and edgestitch from the right side of the fabric. (Fig. 118)
5. Hem the garment, using a slipstitch.

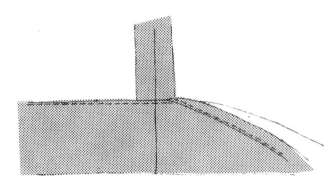

Fig. 118

Folded Edge or Turned Under

The folded edge is also appropriate for lightweight fabrics that fray. It should not be used on flared hems.

1. Fold the hem to the wrong side of the garment and press.
2. Mark the hem allowance depth plus ½″ (12.7 mm).
3. Trim on the marked line.
4. Fold the hem edge under ½″ (12.7 mm). (Fig. 119a)
5. Hem the garment, using a slipstitch.

Double the hem on sheer garments with straight lines for shadow-proof hems. Double-fold hems can be as deep as one-third the skirt length.

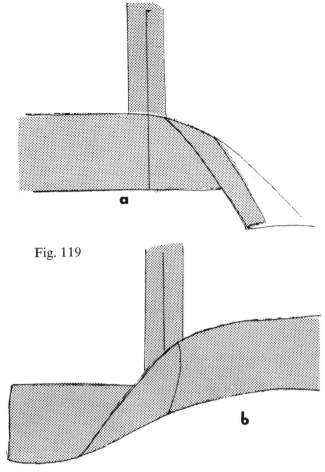

Fig. 119

1. Fold the hem to the wrong side of the garment and press on the folded edge.
2. Mark the hem allowance twice the finished width of the hem.
3. Trim on the marked line.
4. Fold the hem allowance in half and press the folded edge. (Fig. 119b)
5. Hem the garment, using a slipstitch.

Hong-Kong Finish

A Hong-Kong finish, sometimes called a welt-finished edge, is suitable for any fabric that ravels, garments to be washed or dry-cleaned, and unlined jackets. It is very time-consuming to make.

1. Cut bias strips of lightweight lining fabric 1″ (2.5 cm) wide.
2. Fold the hem to the wrong side of the garment and press out as much fullness as possible.
3. If there is little fullness, mark and trim the hem allowance the desired depth. If the hem has a lot of fullness, mark the hem depth at least ¼″ (6.4 mm)

below the cut edge. Crimp, ease baste, or zigzag over buttonhole twist on the marked line. Trim the hem allowance evenly ¼″ (6.4 mm) above the marked line and ease the fullness to fit the garment.

4. Stitch the strip to the right side of the hem ¼″ (6.4 mm) from the edge. Do not stretch the strip unless you want to ease some of the hem fullness to it. (Fig. 120a)

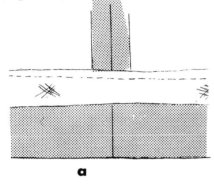

a

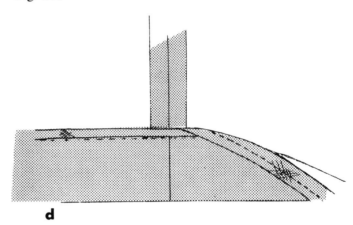

b

Fig. 120

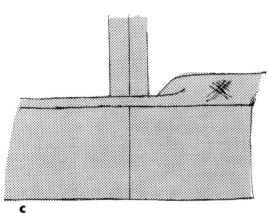

c

d

5. Trim the bias-hem seam ⅛″ (3.2 mm). (Fig. 120b)

6. Press the strip up and over the cut edge of the hem. (Fig. 120c) Glue or pin the strip to the wrong side of the fabric to avoid a drag line. Stitch-in-the-ditch. (Fig. 120d)

8. Hem the garment using a blindstitch or catch-stitch.

Bound Finish

A bound edge is a neat finish for unlined garments, garments made from fabrics that ravel, and garments to be washed or dry-cleaned. This finish is less elegant than a Hong-Kong finish, but it takes less time and is easier to stitch. (Fig. 121a)

1. Fold the hem to the wrong side of the garment and press out as much fullness as possible.

2. Mark and trim the hem allowance to the desired width.

3. Use prepackaged bias tape or hem or lace tape. Press the tape so that one side is slightly narrower than the other. Some prepackaged tapes are already pressed with an off-center fold. (Fig. 121b)

Fig. 121a

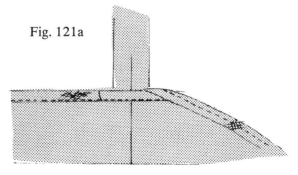

Fig. 121b

4. Enclose the cut edge of the hem with the tape so that the narrow side of the tape is on top.
5. Stitch the tape to the hem allowance with a straight or zigzag stitch (W,2-L,2). Overlap the tape ½" (12.7 mm) at the end. (Fig. 121c)

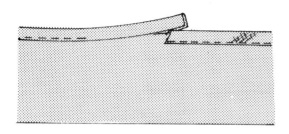

Fig. 121c

6. Hem the garment using a blindstitch or catch-stitch.

Overcasting by Hand

Overcast the edges by hand for a flat finish without stiffness. This elegant finish requires more time and effort than any other finish. It is a favorite in the salons of the French couture, but you won't find it in the boutiques or in the ready-to-wear collections of any designer. (Fig. 122) You'll learn to over-cast quickly with a little practice.

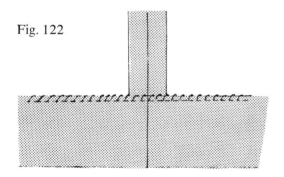

Fig. 122

1. Fold the hem to the wrong side of the garment and press out as much fullness as possible.
2. Mark the hem allowance the desired depth at least ⅛" (3.2 mm) from the cut edge of the hem.
3. Stitch on the marked line.
4. Trim ⅛" (3.2 mm) above the stitched line.
5. Working from left to right, overcast the edge of the hem. Space the stitches ⅛"–¼" (3.2 mm–

6.4 mm) apart. Use the thumb of your left hand to hold each stitch on the diagonal.
6. Hem the garment.

HEMMING TECHNIQUES
Fusing

Fusing is one of the quickest ways to hem a garment. This method of hemming is used most often on non-woven fabrics which can be finished with a cut edge. It can also be used with a pinked or zigzagged finish. Fusing usually stiffens the hem.

Test the fusible agent between two layers of fabric to see if a demarcation line will appear on the right side of the garment. As a general rule, light colors are more likely to have a line than dark colors.

Super Shortcut:
1. Cut the fusible agent into strips ¼"–½" (6.4 mm–12.7 mm) wide. Roll a piece of fusible agent like a newspaper, then cut strips the desired width. (Fig. 123)

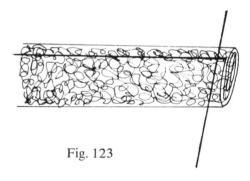

Fig. 123

2. Mark and trim the hem allowance the desired depth.
3. Stitch the strips to the wrong side of the hem, matching the cut edges of the hem and the fusible agent.
4. Fuse the hem in place according to the manu-facturer's directions.

Shortcut:
This method of fusing will stiffen the hem and can sometimes be used instead of interfacing.

1. Mark and trim the hem allowance the desired depth.
2. Cut the fusible agent into strips ¼"–½" (6.4 mm–12.7 mm) *narrower* than the hem depth.

3. Insert the fusible between the hem and garment so that the edge of the fusible is at the folded edge of the garment.
4. Fuse the hem in place according to the manufacturer's directions.

Gluing

Gluing is another quick and easy method for hemming a garment. It is used most often on leather, suede, nonwoven, and pseudosuede fabrics. It can be used on thick or mediumweight fabrics. Test to be sure it won't show on the right side of the finished garment.

1. Mark and trim the hem allowance the desired depth.
2. Fold the hem to the wrong side of the garment.
3. Use a permanent white glue for woven or knitted fabrics and rubber cement for nonwovens to glue the hem in place. Follow the glue manufacturer's directions.

Hemming by Machine

Narrow topstitched hems. Narrow topstitched hems are easy to make and a great idea if you are short of fabric or when the skirt is flared.

1. Allow a ⅝″ (16 mm) hem allowance.
2. Fold the hem to the wrong side of the garment. If you have difficulty gauging a ⅝″ (16 mm) hem allowance, mark the hemline with soap, chalk, or gauge stitch ½″ (12.7 mm) from the cut edge of the hem.
3. Finish the hem edge if desired.
4. Topstitch ¹⁄₁₆″ (1.6 mm) and ½″ (12.7 mm) from the folded edge. (Fig. 124a)
5. Press the hem.

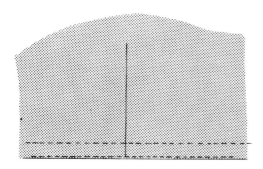

Fig. 124a

Wide topstitched hems. Wide hems can be topstitched with a straight or decorative stitch to add interest at the hemline. Use this attractive variation design by Jean Muir or create your own variation.

1. Allow a 2¼″ (57.2 mm) hem allowance.
2. Mark the hemline with chalk, soap, or gauge stitching.
3. Fold the hem allowance to the wrong side of the garment and press the folded edge.
4. Topstitch ¹⁄₁₆″ (1.6 mm), ⅜″ (9.5 mm), 1⅝″ (4.1 cm), and 2″ (5.1 cm) from the edge of the garment. (Fig. 124b)

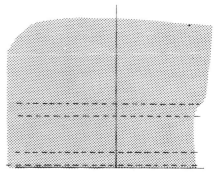

Fig. 124b

Machine-rolled hem. This goof-proof hem can be used instead of a hand-rolled hem. Julio, the designer, uses it at the neckline as well as at the hemline. It's a super-quick method for hemming ruffles and scarves.

1. Allow ⅝″ (16 mm) hem allowance.
2. Fold the hem under ½″ (12.7 mm) and edgestitch from the right side of the garment.
3. Trim the hem allowance as closely as possible to the stitching line with embroidery scissors—the narrowness of the finished hem depends on how closely you trim. (Fig. 125a)
4. Fold the hem to the wrong side again and edgestitch on top of the first line of stitching. For best results, stitch from the wrong side of the garment. (Fig. 125b)

Fig. 125

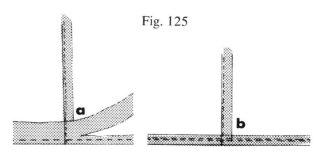

The hemline does not have to be straight, enabling you to use this hem on points or curves. If the edge is shaped, clip the hem allowance as much as necessary before edgestitching in order to turn it under smoothly.

Narrow or rolled hem, using a hemmer foot. Hemmer feet are available in several sizes from $\frac{3}{32}''$–$\frac{1}{4}''$ (2.4 mm–6.4 mm). The most common width is $\frac{1}{8}''$ (3.2 mm). Use the hemmer foot to make an attractive narrow hem on sheers and lightweight fabrics.

1. Allow a $\frac{5}{8}''$ (16 mm) hem allowance.
2. Trim the seams in the hemmed area to $\frac{1}{8}''$ (3.2 mm). Do *not* press the seams open.
3. Place a line of straight stitching $\frac{1}{2}''$ (12.7 mm) from the cut edge of the hem. Stitch from the *wrong* side of the garment and fold the seams toward you as you stitch over them. (Fig. 126a) Leave long threads at the beginning of the stitching line.

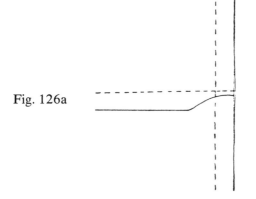

Fig. 126a

This stitching line prevents stretching when hemming on the bias or crossgrain, provides a guideline for the hem placement, serves as an aid for stitching the hem evenly, and, if desired, can furnish stiffness if you use a nylon filament thread on the bobbin.
4. Trim the hem allowance $\frac{3}{8}''$ (9.5 mm), making the stitching line $\frac{1}{8}''$ (3.2 mm) from the trimmed edge.
5. Use the long threads at the beginning of the stitching line to thread the hem into the spiral of the hemmer foot. (Fig. 126b)
6. As you begin stitching the hem, gently pull the threads in back of the hemmer foot. Hold the fabric taut in front of the foot.
  The way you hold the fabric in front of the hemmer foot is one of the keys to success. The edge of the fabric is held perpendicular to the machine bed with the right hand several inches in front of the

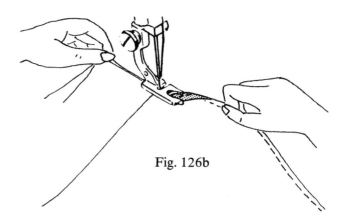

Fig. 126b

foot. The index finger of the left hand is inserted between the hem and garment immediately in front of the foot to position the hem as it enters the spiral. (Fig. 126c)

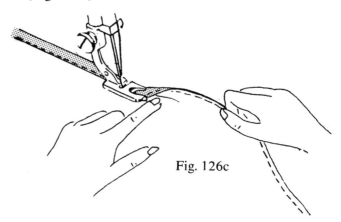

Fig. 126c

7. If you are hemming a scarf or ruffles with corners, trim a small triangle from the corner before you stitch the guideline. Stitch the guideline to the corner; do *not* pivot at the corner. Stop, cut the threads and begin a new stitching line, leaving long threads at the beginning of it. (Fig. 126d)
8. Follow the same procedure for each corner.

Fig. 126d

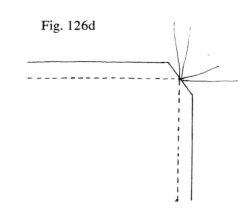

Some hemmer feet are designed so that you can zigzag the hem if desired. To do this, set the zigzag stitch at W,4-L,3. Tighten the tension if you want to make a scalloped hem.

Narrow shirttail hem. This narrow ¼″ (6.4 mm) hem is often used on blouses or shirts made of light-weight fabrics. (Fig. 127)

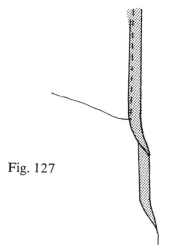

Fig. 127

1. Allow a ⅝″ (16 mm) hem allowance.
2. Crimp curved edges ¼″ (6.4 mm) from the cut edge.
3. Working from the wrong side of the garment, fold ¼″ (6.4 mm) over twice to make the hem. One-eighth inch (3.2 mm) will be absorbed in the turn-of-the-cloth.
4. Edgestitch the hem in place.

Satin-stitch hem. The satin-stitch hem can be used on woven or knitted fabrics and on any garment edge. Try it on all of the edges of a sheer blouse, in-cluding the pockets, for a designer look.

1. Allow a ⅝″ (16 mm) hem allowance.
2. Fold the hem allowance to the wrong side of the garment and edgestitch to prevent rippling in bias areas and to provide a pretty finish.
3. Zigzag (W,3-L, almost 0) over the folded edge.
4. Trim away the excess hem allowance close to the stitches with embroidery scissors.

Lettuce or ripple edge. Lettucing, an innovation of New York designer Stephen Burrows, produces a rippled edge on knit fabrics. Four inches of fabric must stretch from 2″ (5.1 cm) to 6″ (15.2 cm) more for good results. The amount of stretch deter-mines the amount of rippling. (Fig. 128)

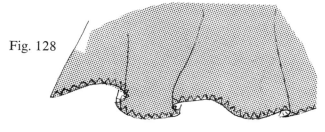

Fig. 128

Single knits will run when stretched. Eliminate runs in the hem by constructing the garment so that the fabric runs down from the neck to the hem.

1. Allow a ⅝″ (16 mm) hem allowance.
2. Fold the hem allowance to the wrong side of the garment.
3. Hold the fabric firmly in back and front of the needle, stretching the hem edge as much as possible. Zigzag (W,3-L,.5) *over* the folded edge.
4. Trim away the excess hem allowance close to the zigzagged stitches.

Scalloped finish. Zigzag the edge to produce a scal-loped edge on knitted or firmly woven fabrics. The scalloped edge is a nice detail for collars or ruffles and can be used on fabrics which do *not* stretch. (Fig. 129)

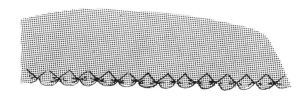

Fig. 129

1. Allow a ⅝″ (16 mm) hem allowance.
2. Fold the hem allowance to the wrong side of the garment.
3. Tighten the upper tension.
4. Zigzag (W,3-L,2) over the folded edge.
5. Trim away the excess hem allowance close to the stitches.

Shell hem. The shell hem is created by using a hem-ming stitch. (Fig. 130)

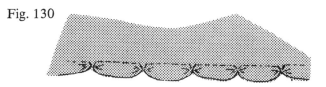

Fig. 130

1. Allow ⅝″ (16 mm) hem allowance.
2. Fold the hem allowance to the wrong side of the garment.
3. Tighten the upper tension.
4. Set the machine to make a blind hemming stitch. The length and width will determine the size of the scallop. Make several samples with different combinations.
5. With the bulk of the garment to the *right* of the needle, stitch so that the zigzagged stitch is off the edge of the garment, forming scallops.

Machine blindstitch. Blind hemming is easy to do on the sewing machine when you position the fabric correctly.

1. Allow a 1″–3″ (2.5 cm–7.6 cm) hem allowance.
2. Fold the hem allowance to the wrong side of the garment and press out as much fullness as possible.
3. Mark the hem allowance the desired depth.
4. Finish the edge of the hem with a finish appropriate to the fabric and garment.
5. Pin the hem in place. Place the pins at least 1″ (2.5 cm) from the top edge of the hem. (Fig. 131a)

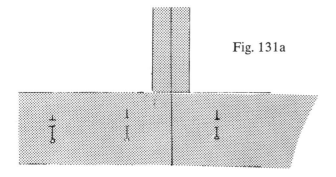

Fig. 131a

6. Fold the garment with the right sides together just below the finished edge of the hem. (Fig. 131b)

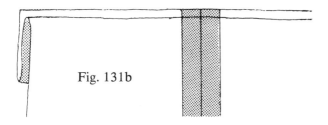

Fig. 131b

7. Set the machine for a hemming stitch (W,2-L,2) and use a blind-hemming foot or zigzag foot. Place the garment under the foot so that the bulk of the garment is to the left of the foot. The machine will make several straight stitches on the hem allowance and one zigzag stitch on the fold of the garment. The hem will be almost invisible from the right side of the garment if the zigzag stitch barely catches the fold of the garment. (Fig. 131c) Make several stitches before you thread the needle to check the garment placement.

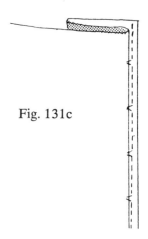

Fig. 131c

If you do not have a zigzag machine, blindstitch manually with a straight-stitch machine by swinging the fabric.

Blind-hemming knit fabrics. This technique is widely used on ready-made shirts made of single-knit fabrics.

Single knits roll to the right side of the fabric at any cut edge such as a hem. To reduce the rolling and finish the hem smoothly, use a regular zigzag stitch instead of a blind-hemming stitch. (Fig. 132)

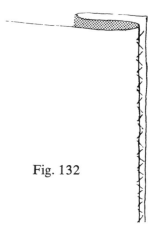

Fig. 132

Use this hem on casual knits, children's slacks, and skirts which won't be lengthened—it's difficult to put a foot into it and rip it out. Do not use it on flared hems.

1. Allow a 1"–1½" (2.5 cm–3.8 cm) hem allowance.
2. Finish the edge of the hem with a cut edge.
3. Fold the hem to the wrong side of the garment and press.
4. Pin the hem in place close to the folded edge of the garment.
5. Fold the garment for blind hemming.
6. Set the machine to zigzag (W,4-L,4), using a blind-hemming foot or zigzag foot. Place the garment under the foot so that the bulk of the garment is to the left of the foot. Each zigzag stitch should barely catch the fold of the garment. Make several stitches *before* threading the needle to check the garment placement.

Hemming by Hand

The regular hems of better garments are hemmed inconspicuously by hand. Make the stitches as long and loose as possible, yet hold the hem in place.

1. Fold the hem to the wrong side of the garment and press out as much fullness as possible.
2. Mark the hem allowance the desired depth, control the fullness as needed, and finish the edge.
3. Hold the garment upside down with the wrong side toward you. Fold the garment with the right sides together so that the fold is ¼" (6.4 mm) below the finished edge of the hem. (Fig. 133a) If the

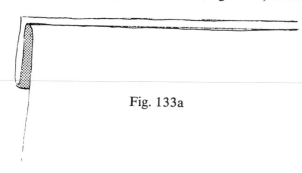

Fig. 133a

fabric creases easily, avoid a foldline on the garment by folding the hem back ¼" (6.4 mm) instead. (Fig. 133b)

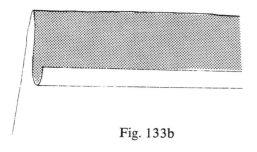

Fig. 133b

4. Hem the garment loosely. Do not pull the stitches too tightly. The hem finish and/or garment fabric will determine the appropriate hemming stitch. Slip-stitch garments with a clean-finished or folded edge. (Fig. 133c) Blindstitch most quality garments.

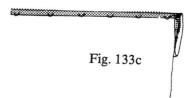

Fig. 133c

.(Fig. 133d) Catchstitch hems on tailored garments

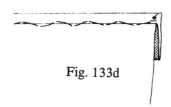

Fig. 133d

or heavy fabrics. (Fig. 133e) Use a figure-eight

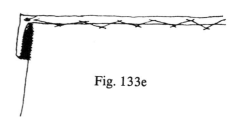

Fig. 133e

stitch on knits, crepes, and other fabrics which are difficult to hem invisibly. (Fig. 133f)

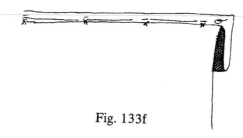

Fig. 133f

Hand-rolled hems. Occasionally, you will make an exquisite garment that deserves the very best—a hand-rolled hem. Apply one of these methods to hem your next luxurious garment.

Rolled Edge:
This is the ultimate, most beautiful rolled hem.

1. Allow a ⅝" (16 mm) hem allowance.
2. Trim the vertical seam allowances in the hem area

to ⅛″ (3.2 mm). Do not press the seam allowances open.

3. With the wrong side of the garment up, stitch ½″ (12.7 mm) from the cut edge.

4. Trim away ⅜″ (9.5 mm) on the hem allowance for 4″–6″ (10.2 cm–15.2 cm). To avoid excessive ravelling, do *not* trim all the hem allowance at once.

5. Roll the trimmed section between your thumb and index finger, enclosing the stitching line. The hem will roll easily if you moisten your forefinger slightly with the tip of your tongue.

6. Hold the rolled edge over the forefinger, stabilizing it with your thumb and middle finger.

7. Using silk or a lightweight polyester thread, take a small stitch in the roll, then pick up a single thread in the garment. (Fig. 134) If you want the thread to

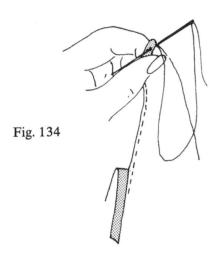

Fig. 134

match exactly, pull a lengthwise thread from a fabric scrap to use for hemming.

8. Hem the trimmed section, then trim and hem the next section until the hem is finished. This technique of trimming just in the area you're hemming reduces fraying as you work and eliminates the need to re-trim.

9. Press the garment up to the hem. Do not press the hem flat when you press the garment.

Easy-Rolled Hem:
This hem is easier to make than a rolled edge but the finished hem is a little flatter than the rolled edge.

1. Allow a ⅝″ (16 mm) hem allowance.

2. Trim the vertical seam allowances in the hem area to ⅛″ (3.2 mm).

3. With the wrong side of the garment up, stitch ½″ (12.7 mm) from the cut edge.

4. Press the hem to the wrong side of the garment on the stitched line.

5. Trim the hem allowance ⅜″ (9.5 mm).

6. Secure the thread in the hem. Take a small ⅛″ (3.2 mm) stitch along the fold, then pick up a single thread on the garment next to the cut edge of the hem.

7. Repeat for several stitches, then pull the thread taut to create a roll. (Fig. 135)

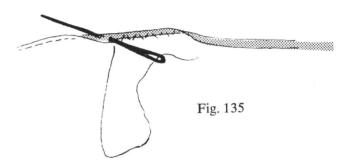

Fig. 135

Faced Hems
Faced hems can be used to reduce the bulk in hems on heavy fabrics. They can also be used when there isn't enough fabric for a folded hem, or when the hem is shaped and a folded hem is undesirable.

1. Allow a ⅜″ (9.5 mm) seam allowance below the hemline.

2. Use prepackaged bias hem tape, bias strips made from lightweight fabric, a shaped facing, or net strips to face the hem. Cut the facing 1″–2½″ (2.5 cm–6.4 cm) wide. Seam the facing as needed to make a strip the desired length.

3. With the right sides together, stitch the facing to the garment with a ¼″ (6.4 mm) seam. Overlap the ends ½″ (12.7 mm) or seam the ends to fit the edge.

4. Fold the hem to the wrong side of the garment, understitch and underpress.

5. Finish the edge of the facing if needed and hem the garment.

No-hem Finishes
Cut edges, pinked edges, and zigzagged edges are the most popular no-hem finishes.

Cut edges and pinked edges. Cut edges and pinked edges are often used today on nonfray fabrics such as pseudosuede, suede, vinyl, and felt.

A little-known fact is that these finishes have been used on woven fabrics for hundreds of years. The fraying quality was sometimes used as a design feature and other times minimized by the use of bias cuts, twill weaves, and firmly woven fabrics. When you use a cut or pinked no-hem on a woven fabric instead of a hem, dry clean the garment to prevent excessive fraying.

Zigzagged edge. The zigzagged edge is an innovative, no-hem finish used by designer Sonia Rykiel on knitted and woven fabrics.

1. Cut the garment with no hem allowance.
2. Zigzag (W,4-L,2) over the edge of the fabric. Use the overcast foot to minimize the fabric rolling when you zigzag the edge. If you don't have an overcast foot, use paper when you stitch. Minimize fraying by stitching with the grain. The fraying which does occur creates an interesting effect.

French Hemming
Heavy fabrics and deep hems make heavy hems that require French or double-stitched hemming.

1. Press the hem in place, mark the depth, control the fullness, and finish the edge.
2. Baste or glue through the center of the hem. (Fig. 136a)
3. Fold the hem down at the basting line so that the finished edge of the hem and the hemline of the garment are even. (Fig. 136b)
4. Blindstitch (Fig. 136c) or catchstitch (Fig. 136d) the hem by hand. Do not pull the stitches too tightly. Some garments can be blindstitched by machine. (Fig. 136e)
5. Hem the garment at the finished edge of the hem by hand or machine. (Fig. 136f)

Fig. 136

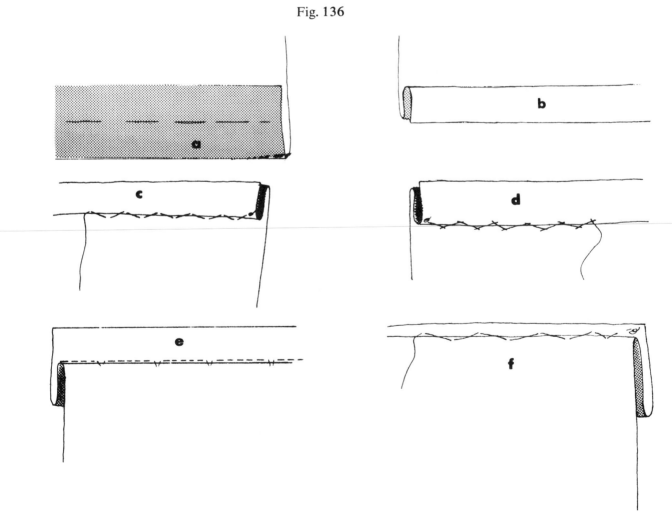

Interfaced Hems

Interface the hem to preserve the shape of better garments. Use an interfacing material, muslin, or silk organza for crisp hems and cotton flannel or polyester fleece for soft ones.

Fusing. Fusing the interfacing is a quick-and-easy method used in better ready-to-wear. It is especially appropriate for washable, unlined garments.

1. Cut a piece of bias-woven or knitted fusible interfacing the width of the hem and the desired length. If the hem is shaped, cut the interfacing by the garment pattern so that it is the exact shape of the hem allowance.
2. Fuse the interfacing to the *hem allowance* (Fig. 137)

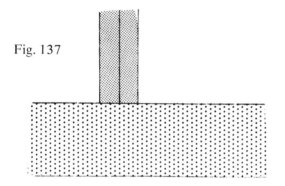

Fig. 137

3. Press the hem in place and hem the garment. Most lined garments can be hemmed by securing the hem only at the seams with fusible agent or permanent glue or stitching-in-the-ditch.

Stitching the seams. In ready-made garments, the interfacing is often applied to the flat garment sections before the sections are joined together. This simple method allows you to set the interfacing to the flat garment sections.

1. Cut one bias piece of interfacing for each garment section so that the bias width is equal to the hem depth, and its length is equal to the section width. The interfacing is sewn into the seams using several short pieces of interfacing instead of one long length.
2. Position the interfacing on the wrong side of the garment sections so that the interfacing extends into the hem allowance ½″ (12.7mm). (Fig. 138a) If the hemline is shaped, press and shape a bias strip or cut a shaped interfacing.

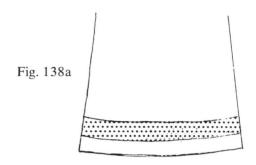

Fig. 138a

Glue the strips to the garment sections. If the sections are wide, hand baste the interfacing to the section on the hemline using a very long stitch. Pick up only one thread on the garment so that the stitches won't show. (Fig. 138b)

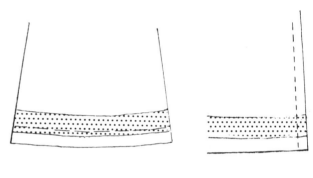

Fig. 138b   Fig. 138c

3. Assemble the garment. (Fig. 138c)
4. Press the hem into place, finish the hem edge, and hem the garment.

Designer method. Use this designer method to interface the hem on extra-special garments. These garments are usually lined.

1. Cut a piece of bias interfacing the desired length and the width of the hem plus 1″ (2.5cm).
2. Mark the hemline with thread.
3. Position the interfacing on the wrong side of the garment so that the interfacing extends into the hem allowance ½″ (12.7mm). Press and shape the interfacing to fit the hemline, if needed. Use an uneven basting stitch to baste the interfacing to the garment at the hemline. Pick up only one thread on the garment so that the stitches won't show from the right side of the garment.
4. Sew the upper edge of the interfacing to the garment with a catchstitch. (Fig. 139)
5. Pin or baste the hem in place, then hem it to the interfacing.

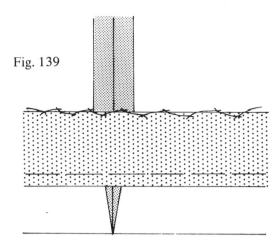

Fig. 139

Hemming Lined Garments

In order to secure the lining to the garment hem by machine, the garment must be hemmed so that the edge of the hem is free to stitch a seam. This is easy to do in several ways:

☼ Hem the garment at the center of the hem allowance instead of close to the hem edge. The center of the hem is one-half the hem depth. If the garment has a 2″ (5.1cm) hem, place the hemming stitch 1″ above the hemline.

Fold the hem of the garment so that the cut edge of the hem is even with the edge of the garment. Hem by hand or machine before lining the garment. (Fig. 140a, b, c)

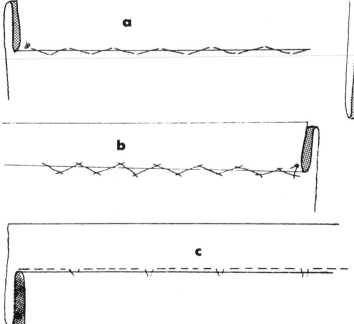

☼ Cut a piece of fusible agent one-half the width of the hem. Place the fusible agent in the hem so that it fills only the lower half of the hem. Fuse the hem. Fusing stiffens the hem slightly and, in some garments, can replace hem interfacing. (Fig. 140d)

☼ Place a small piece of fusible agent between the seam allowances of the hem and garment. Fuse them together. (Fig. 140e)

☼ Machine stitch the seam allowances of the garment and hem together—reach between the garment and hem, grasp the seam allowances and pull them out so that you can stitch them together. (Fig. 140f)

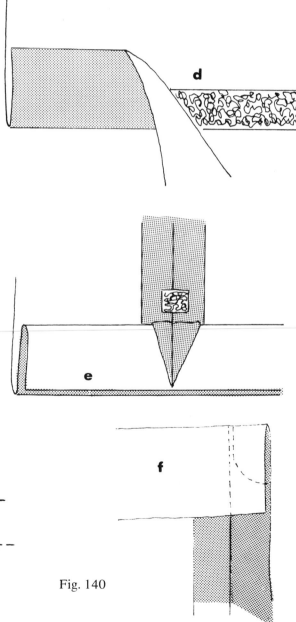

Fig. 140

PRESSING TIPS

Use a press cloth when you press the hem.

Avoid making an imprint of the hem allowance on the right side of the garment by inserting brown paper between the hem allowance and the garment.

If there is an imprint of the hem edge on the right side of the gament, press the garment from the underside, allowing the tip of the iron to press under the hem edge. (Fig. 141)

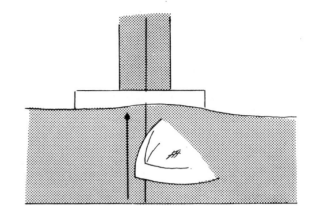

Fig. 141

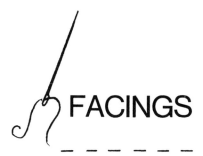

FACINGS

Facings are used to finish the edges of necklines, armholes, garment openings, and waistlines. They sometimes replace hems on skirts, slacks, or sleeves. They are usually cut from the fashion fabric but can be cut from a lightweight fabric to reduce bulk, a firm fabric to give body, a contrasting fabric to create design interest, or a less expensive fabric to economize.

The facing may be fitted or bias. Fitted facings are cut by a pattern to the size and shape of the garment edge to be faced. Bias facings are cut in strips.

In general, fitted facings are easier to apply and add to the quality of the garment. On sheer garments and sportswear, a bias facing is preferable to a fitted one.

FACING-EDGE FINISHES

All conventional methods for finishing seam allowances—clean-finished zigzagged, pinked, bound, Hong-Kong, and overcast by hand—are suitable for use on the unnotched edges of the facing. In addition, the unnotched edges of the facing can be faced for a custom finish.

Face the Facing

Faced facings are ideal for fabrics which fray easily. Use self-fabric, lining fabric, or regular interfacing material to face the facing.

1. Complete any seams in the facing and interfacing.
2. With the right sides together, stitch the facing and interfacing together along the edge(s) to be finished with a ¼″ (6.4 mm) seam. (Fig. 142)
3. Understitch, trim, and clip.
4. Turn the facing right-side-out.
5. Pin and stitch the facing to the garment with the right side of the facing to the right side of the garment.

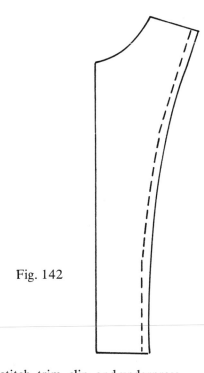

Fig. 142

6. Understitch, trim, clip, and underpress.

FITTED FACINGS
Patterns

A fitted facing duplicates the garment section which it faces. Pattern alterations, changes in the garment design, or changes in construction techniques require making a new facing pattern for the area to be faced.

Fitted Facing Patterns

1. Draw the facing on the garment pattern. Mark the unnotched edge of the facing so that the facing is 3″ (7.6 cm) wide at the narrowest point. This width includes the seam allowances.
2. Mark the grainlines on the facing pattern parallel to the garment grainline. (Fig. 143a)

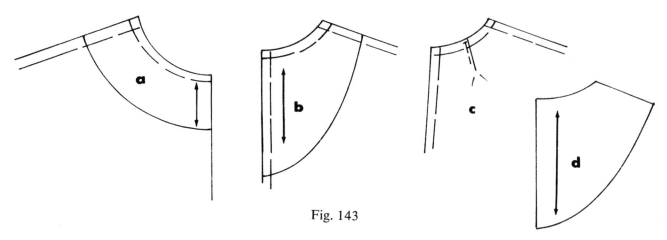

Fig. 143

3. Mark the back-neck facing so that it is 5″–7″ (12.7 cm–17.8 cm) deep at the center back. This deeper facing protects the garment from body oils and makes the garment hang better. (Fig. 143b)

4. Fold out any darts on the garment pattern in the area to be faced. The garment pattern will bubble slightly. (Fig. 143c)

5. Place and pin the pattern on top of a piece of pattern paper or wax paper.

6. Using a tracing wheel, trace the cutting, stitching, and fold lines for the facing pattern. Trace the grainline and any notches carefully. (Fig. 143d)

All-in-One or Combination Facing Patterns

An all-in-one facing or combination facing finishes the neckline and armhole in one piece. For a smooth finish use this facing to replace the separate neckline and armhole facings supplied with many patterns.

1. Draw the facing on the garment pattern. Mark the unnotched edge with a smooth curve for easy finishing so that the facing is 3″ (7.6 cm) wide at the narrowest point and so that it doesn't extend into the bust or shoulder blade area. (Fig. 144a)

2. Fold out any darts on the garment pattern in the area to be faced. The garment pattern will bubble slightly.

3. Place and pin the pattern on top of a piece of pattern paper or wax paper.

4. Using a tracing wheel, trace the cutting lines and foldlines for the facing pattern. Trace the grainline and any notches carefully. Trace the stitching lines if needed.

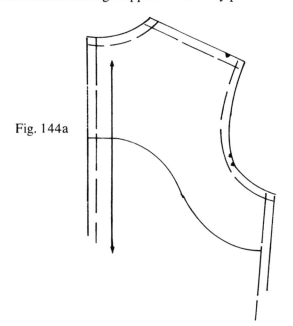

Fig. 144a

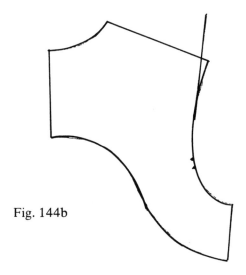

Fig. 144b

5. Trim the armscye of the facing ¼″ (6.4 mm) at the shoulder on the front and back armhole. (Fig. 144b)

FITTED FACING APPLICATIONS

The general procedure is the same for setting all facings that finish a garment.

1. Interface the garment or facing appropriately for the fabric, style, and type of interfacing.
2. Pretrim the enclosed seam allowances, the garment and facing seam allowances which will be joined together, to ⅜″ (9.5 mm). Pretrimming will enable you to stitch the curved seams accurately and easily.
3. Complete any seams on the facing as indicated. The facing fits inside the garment better if it is slightly smaller than the edge which it faces. Think of the garment as a circle. If you draw another circle inside the garment circle, the second circle has to be a little smaller. Stitch a larger seam allowance— ¾″ (19.1 mm) instead of ⅝″ (16 mm)—at each facing seam.
4. Finish the unnotched edge of the facing.
5. With the right sides together and the facing uppermost, pin and stitch the facing to the garment, using a short stitch. (Fig. 145)

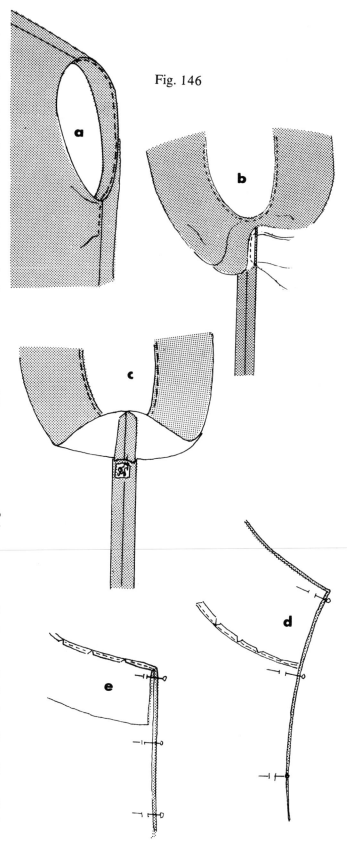

Fig. 146

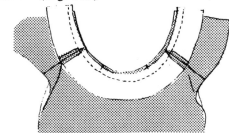

Fig. 145

6. Understitch, trim, clip, and underpress. If you do not trim closely and clip often, the facing will "flip" out.
7. Secure the facing to the garment.

Securing the Facings

There are several ways to secure the facings so that they won't peek out when you wear the garment. Select the one most appropriate for your garment.

✿ *Edgestitch or topstitch* the faced edge. Match the color of the thread and garment carefully if you want the stitching to be inconspicuous. If you prefer, select a contrasting color to trim the garment.

✿ *Stitch-in-the-ditch* from the right side of the garment through all layers. (Fig. 146a)

✿ *Stitch the seam allowances* of the garment and facing together by machine. (Fig. 146b)

✿ Use a piece of *fusible agent* between the seam allowances of the garment and facing. Fuse according to the manufacturer's directions. (Fig. 146c)

✿ *Stitch the facing with the seam.* On sleeveless garments, secure the armhole facing when you stitch the side seam. This finish can be very bulky since four seam allowances are on top of each other, but it's a good technique to use on children's wear and lightweight fabrics.

1. Set the facing *before* stitching the underarm seams of the garment and facing.
2. Pin the underarm seams together from the unnotched edge of the facing to the hem of the garment, matching the armscye seamline. (Fig. 146d)
3. Fold the facing down onto the body of the garment just below the armscye seamline. (Fig. 146e) Stitch the underarm seam.

Lapel Facings

A lapel facing is larger than the edge which it faces since the facing is the outside circle. (Fig. 147a)

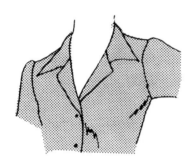

Fig. 147a

1. Extend the neckline of the facing at the shoulder seam ⅝″ (16 mm) to insure a smooth roll on the lapel. (Fig. 147b)

Fig. 147b

2. Interface the lapel instead of the garment front.
3. Pin the neckline of the lapel to the collar and garment, easing the fullness of the lapel to the other sections. (Fig. 147c)

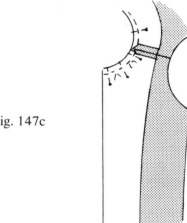

Fig. 147c

Facing Zipper Plackets

When a garment is finished with a facing at the top of the zipper, the facing should be finished *before* the zipper is stitched in place.

Facing for a slot zipper. These directions for a dress or blouse with a jewel neckline can be applied to a skirt with a faced waistline.

1. Notch the neck edge of the facing ⅞″ (22.2 mm) from the ends. Notch the neck edge of the garment sections at the seamline ⅝″ (16 mm) from the edge.
2. Fold the ends of the facing to the wrong side at the notches.
3. With the right sides together, pin the facing on top of the dress so that the garment sections extend ⅞″ (22.2 mm) beyond the facing sections. (Fig. 148a)
4. Fold the dress to the right side at the notches, covering the facing. Stitch the neckline seam to the notches on the neck edge. (Fig. 148b)

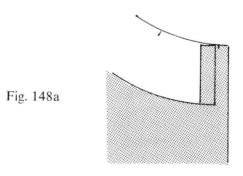

Fig. 148a

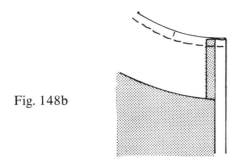

Fig. 148b

5. Turn the garment right-side-out.
6. Set the zipper.
7. Complete the shoulder seams of the garment and facing.
8. Complete the neck edge of the garment and facing.

Facing for a lapped zipper. These directions for a dress with a jewel neckline can be applied to a skirt with a faced waistline.

1. Notch the neck edge of the garment facing underlap ½″ (12.7 mm) from the end. If the zipper laps right over left, the underlap is the left back; if it laps left over right, the underlap is the right back. Notch the facing for the overlap ⅞″ (22.2 mm) from the end.
2. Fold the ends of the facing to the wrong side at the notches.
3. With the right sides together, pin the facing for the underlap on top of the garment back. The dress will extend beyond the facing ½″ (12.7 mm)
4. Fold the dress to the right side at the notches, covering the facing ½″ (12.7 mm). Stitch the neckline seam to the notches on the neck edge.
5. With the right sides together, pin the facing for the overlap on top of the garment back. The dress will extend beyond the facing ⅞″ (22.2 mm).
6. Fold the dress to the right side at the notch ⅝″ (16 mm) from the edge, covering the facing. Stitch the neckline seam to the notches on the neck edge.
7. Turn the garment sections right-side-out.
8. Set the zipper.
9. Complete the garment and facing.

All-in-one or Combination Facings
The neckline and armscye of a garment can be faced with separate facings. However, they are bulky, difficult to set smoothly, require more time to apply, and often make the garment look homemade.

An all-in-one or combination facing finishes the neckline and armscyes in one piece. There are many methods for applying all-in-one facings, but those employing hand stitches are little better than the separate facings which they replace. A knowledge of several applications will enable you to handle any situation with professional results.

Flip facing. This super-easy method requires a center-back or front opening and shoulder seams wide enough, 4″ (10.2 cm) or wider, to turn the garment through. The fabric should not be bulky nor the garment full.

1. Pretrim the seam allowances of the neckline and the armscyes on the garment and facing to ⅜″ (9.5 mm).
2. Complete the shoulder seams of the garment and facing. Do *not* stitch the vertical seams.
3. Finish the unnotched edges of the facing sections.
4. With the right sides together, pin and stitch the facing to the garment around the neckline and armholes, making a ⅜″ (9.5 mm) seam. (Fig. 149)

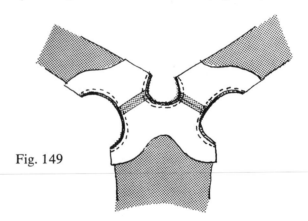

Fig. 149

5. Clip the seam allowances as needed.
6. Turn the garment right-side-out by pushing it through the shoulder seams.
7. Understitch and underpress.
8. Complete the side seams.

Narrow-shoulder method. This method for an all-in-one facing can be used on any garment with very narrow shoulder seams. It can also be used on a halter neckline; however, the garment cannot have a collar or piping around the neckline.

1. Pretrim the seam allowances of the neckline and armscyes on the garment and facing to ⅜″ (9.5 mm).

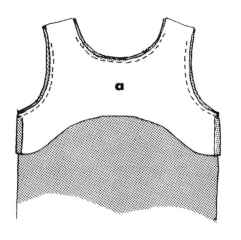

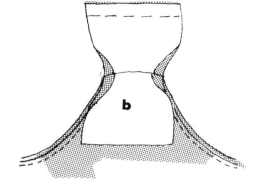

Fig. 150

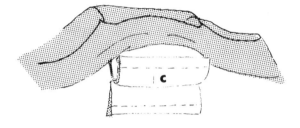

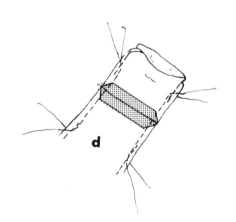

2. Complete all vertical seams in the garment and facing. Do *not* stitch the shoulder seams.

3. Finish the unnotched edge of the facing.

4. With the right sides together, pin and stitch the facings to the garment at the neckline with a ⅜″ (9.5 mm) seam, beginning and ending 2″ (5.1 cm) from the shoulder. Repeat at the armholes. (Fig. 150a)

5. Clip as needed.

6. Turn the garment right-side-out.

7. Stitch the shoulder seams of the garment together with a ⅝″ (16 mm) seam. (Fig. 150b).

8. Reach between the back of the garment and facing, grasp the shoulder seam, and pull it out until the facing is exposed.

9. Stitch the facing shoulder seams with the right sides together, making a ⅝″ (16 mm) seam. (Fig. 150c)

10. Adjust the shoulder so that you can complete the unstitched portions of the neckline and armholes. Overlap the previous stitching line and eliminate backtacking. (Fig. 150d)

11. Turn the garment right-side-out.

12. Understitch the neckline and armholes wherever possible. Clip and underpress.

Facing with a collar. This method for an all-in-one facing can be used on a garment with a collar or piping at the neckline. It does not require a center opening, but the shoulders must be 2″ (5.1 cm) wide or wider.

1. Pretrim the seam allowances of the neckline and armscyes on the garment and facing to ⅜″ (9.5 mm).

2. Finish the shoulder and side seams of the garment and facing.

3. Finish the unnotched edge of the facing.

4. Set the collar to the garment with the right sides of both face-up.

5. With the right sides of the garment and facing together, pin and stitch the neckline seam.

6. Understitch, trim, and clip.

7. Turn the garment right-side-out.

8. If the facing is wider than the garment at the armscye, trim away the excess.

9. Fold the cut edges at the armholes to the wrong side of the garment at the shoulder seam. Turn in a *generous* amount and pin. (Fig. 151)

10. Reach between the garment back and its facing and grasp the seam allowances of the armscye at the shoulder. Pull the seam allowances out so that you can stitch a ⅜″ (9.5 mm) seam around the arm-

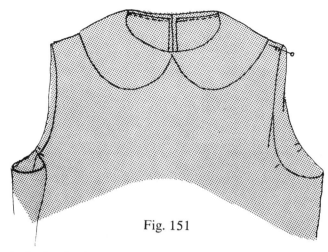

Fig. 151

hole, beginning and ending at the shoulder seam. (This looks very confusing! Match the notches and seams and everything will turn out right. If you must, use a few pins.)

11. Understitch, clip, and underpress.

In less expensive garments and children's wear, the side seams are left open until the facing is finished.

Stitch the shoulders together. This easy method is often used on inexpensive ready-to-wear and children's garments; however, the facing is difficult to finish without a slight "step" at the shoulder seams.

1. Pretrim the seam allowances of the neckline and armscyes on the garment and facing to 3⁄8″ (9.5 mm).
2. Stitch the vertical seams in the garment and facing. Do *not* stitch the shoulder seams.
3. Finish the unnotched edge of the facing.
4. Place the facing on top of the garment with the right sides together. Stitch around the armholes and neckline. (Fig. 152a)

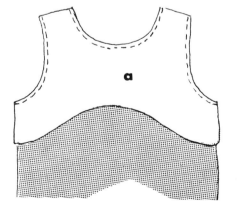

Fig. 152

5. Turn the sections right-side-out. Understitch, clip, and underpress.
6. Reach between the shoulder of the garment front and its facing. Grasp the back shoulder and pull it through, turning the front wrong-side-out.
7. Position the shoulder seam so that all the cut edges match. The back and its facing are sandwiched between the front and its facing. Stitch the shoulder seams through all layers. (Fig. 152b)
8. Turn the garment right-side-out.
9. Underpress.

Variation for vests with unfaced fronts. Lace, leather, suede, and pseudosuede fabrics do not require a facing. These materials and fabrics are often used only on the front of a vest for economy, comfort, and design.

1. Cut an all-in-one facing for the garment back.
2. Pretrim the seam allowances of the neckline and armscyes on the garment back and back facing to 3⁄8″ (9.5 mm).
3. Finish the unnotched edge of the facing.
4. With the right sides together, stitch the facing to the garment back around the back neckline and armholes. (Fig. 153a)

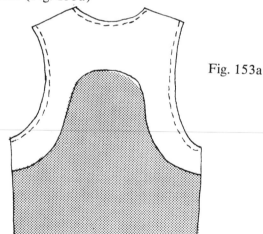

Fig. 153a

5. Insert the front between the back and its facing, so that the right side of the front faces the right side of the back. Match and pin the cut edges of the shoulder seam.
6. Stitch the shoulder seam through the three layers. (Fig. 153b)

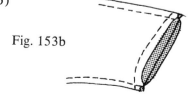

Fig. 153b

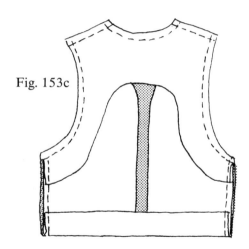

Fig. 153c

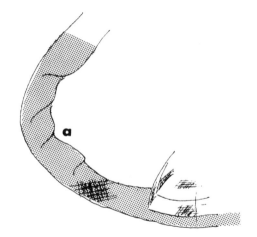

Fig. 154

7. With the right sides together, match the side seams of the front and back. Fold the armscye facing and the hem so that the right sides of the facing and hem are next to the wrong side of the front. Stitch the side seams. (Fig. 153c)

8. Turn the garment right-side-out.

9. Press the side seams to the back.

BIAS FACINGS

Fitted facings are easy to apply, but they are often a telltale sign of a homemade garment. In addition, they are very unattractive when used on sheer garments. Eliminate fitted facings and face the edges with a bias strip for a slick, ready-to-wear look.

Without proper preparation, bias facings are easy to set incorrectly. The bias strip must be moulded and shaped to fit the curved edge so that it will lie flat against the garment.

The edge of an armhole is an inward (concave) curve—the stitching line is shorter than the garment section which it faces.

The edge around a collar is an outward (convex) curve—the stitching line is longer than the garment section it faces.

These suggestions will help you to set bias facings properly and smoothly.

☼ Pretrim the seam allowances of the garment to ⅜″ (9.5 mm).

☼ Use a narrow bias strip to minimize the difference between the length of the stitching line and the faced section.

☼ Ease the bias into the stitching line of an inward curve and stretch the bias when you stitch it around an outward curve.

☼ Preshape the bias with a steam iron before applying it for a custom finish. (Fig. 154a)

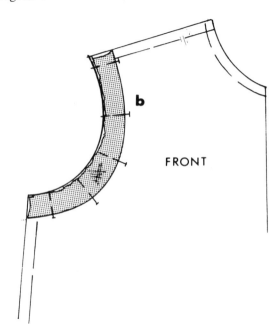

FRONT

☼ Shape deep curves by pinning the bias to the paper pattern, then press and steam it into the desired shape. (Fig. 154b)

Single-bias Facings

These suggestions for setting bias facings at the armscye can be used to face any edge of the garment.

Armscye facings. Fitted facings at the armhole are rarely used on ready-made garments because they flap in and out of the garment.

1. Pretrim the seam allowances of the armhole to ⅜″ (9.5 mm).

2. Complete the shoulder seams on the garment. Do *not* stitch the underarm seams.

110

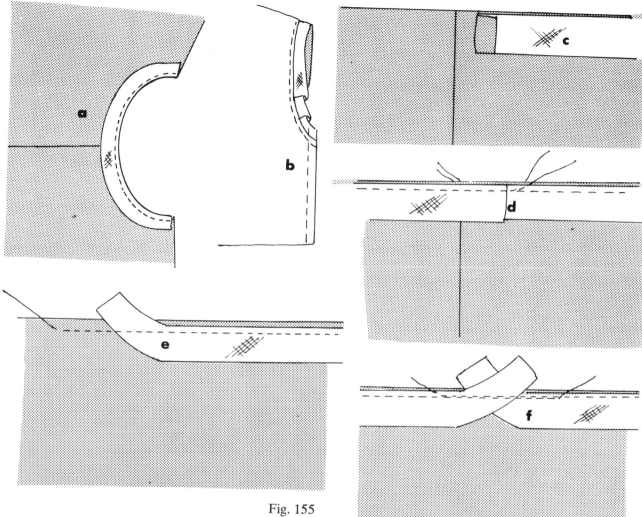

Fig. 155

3. Cut a bias strip the desired length and 1″ (2.5 cm) wide. (If you are facing a neckline the bias can be wider.)

4. Press the bias to shape.

5. Beginning at the armhole, place the bias on the garment with the right sides together. Match and pin the cut edges and stitch a ⅜″ (9.5 mm) seam. (Fig. 155a)

6. Understitch and clip as needed.

7. Complete the side seams. (Fig. 155b)

8. Fold the bias to the wrong side of the garment.

9. Edgestitch and/or topstitch ¼″ (6.4 mm) from the edge.

Variations: Use one of these methods to finish and secure the facing.

⚙ Omit the topstitching. Secure the facing at the shoulder and side seams by stitching in the well of the seam or by fusing the bias to the garment.

⚙ Complete the side seams before applying the bias. At the underarm, fold the end of the bias up ⅜″ (9.5 mm) before you begin stitching. (Fig. 155c) Stitch the strip around the armhole and lap it over the folded end ⅝″ (16 mm). (Fig. 155d) Fold the bias to the wrong side of the garment and secure it.

⚙ Position the bias so that the end is well into the seam allowance at the underarm. Stitch around the armhole on the seamline. (Fig. 155e) Curve the other end into the seam allowance so that the bias ends overlap. (Fig. 155f) Fold the bias to the wrong side of the garment and secure it.

Double-bias Facings

Double-bias facings can be made of medium- and lightweight fabrics. The raw edge is eliminated on the inside of the garment, which makes it an attractive finish for jackets, vests, and sheer garments.

1. Pretrim the seam allowances of the armhole to ⅜" (9.5 mm).
2. Complete the shoulder seams on the garment. Do *not* stitch the underarm seams.
3. Cut a bias strip 1¾" (4.5 cm) wide from a lightweight fabric.
4. Fold the bias in half lengthwise with the wrong sides together. Press the bias to shape it.
5. Place the bias on the right side of the garment. Begin at the underarm and stitch a ⅜" (9.5 mm) seam, matching the cut edges of the bias and the garment.
6. Understitch and clip.
7. Complete the side seams.
8. Fold the bias to the wrong side of the garment.
9. Edgestitch and/or topstitch ¼" (6.4 mm) from the edge or use one of the variations for a single bias facing.

Piping
Face the edges with piping to make a simple garment look fantastic.

1. Allow a ⅜" (9.5 mm) seam allowance on the garment edge to be finished.
2. Cut a bias strip twice the finished width of the piping plus two ⅜" (9.5 mm) seam allowances, and the desired length plus 1¼" (3.2 cm).
3. Make the piping strips.
4. Set the piping to the garment as you would a bias facing.
5. Clip as needed.
6. Fold the seam allowances to the wrong side and secure them with topstitching.

Variation: Use one of these ideas to vary the garment design.

✿ Use cord inserted into the bias strip. Cut the bias 3"–4" (7.6 cm–10.2 cm) wide, fold it around the cord and stitch close to the cord with a zipper foot. Trim the seam allowances to ⅜" (9.5 mm). (Fig. 156a) Eliminate bulk by removing the cord anywhere it overlaps or joins.
✿ Use two or more cords in the piping. Cut the bias strip 3"–4" (7.6 cm–10.2 cm) wide. Cord the strip as before, add another cord, and stitch close to it with the zipper foot. Trim the seam allowances to ⅜" (9.5 mm). (Fig. 156b)
✿ Use two or more corded strips of different colors. Complete each strip separately. Position the strips so that the strip which will touch the garment edge is

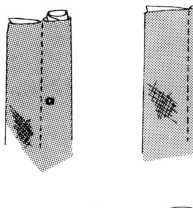

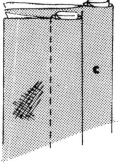

Fig. 156

on top of the other one. Stitch the strips together and trim the seam allowances to ⅜" (9.5 mm). (Fig. 156c) Place the strips face-down on the right side of the garment. Pin and stitch them to the garment on the seamline.

Braid or Lace
European designers often use braid or lace to face garments. It's remarkably easy to trim and finish a garment with this technique.

1. Select a narrow trim ⅜"–⅝" (9.5 mm–16 mm) wide.
2. Trim the seam allowance on the garment edge to be faced so that it is ⅛"–¼" (3.2 mm–6.4 mm) less than the width of the trim. If you want the braid to show ⅛" (3.2 mm), cut the seam allowance for a ½" (12.7 mm) braid ⅜" (9.5 mm) wide. If you want the braid to show ¼" (6.4 mm), cut the seam allowance ¼" (6.4 mm) wide.
3. With the right sides together, match the edge of the trim to the cut edge of the garment. Stitch them together on the seamline.
4. Fold the trim to the wrong side of the garment. (Fig. 157)
5. Topstitch around the edge ¹⁄₁₆" (1.6 mm) from the seamline.

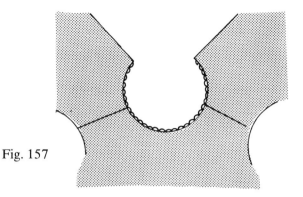

Fig. 157

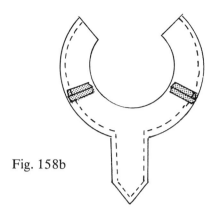

Fig. 158b

FACINGS TO TRIM

Facings are usually applied so that they are on the inside of the finished garment, but they can be applied to the right side of the garment for design as well as to finish the edge.

The old-fashioned method for applying a facing to trim required turning the unnotched edge of the facing under and sewing it to the garment by hand or machine. Face the facing to finish the unnotched edge quickly and neatly. The curved edges and points, which were difficult to handle the old-fashioned way, can now be secured easily. (Fig. 158a)

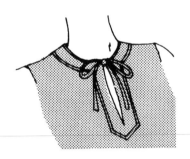

Fig. 158a

1. Cut the facing from the desired fabric. Cut the facing lining from a lightweight lining or interfacing fabric.
2. Complete the seams in the facing and its lining.
3. With the right sides together, stitch the facing and its lining together with a ⅜″ (9.5 mm) seam at the unnotched edge. (Fig. 158b)
4. Understitch, trim, and clip.
5. Turn the facing right-side-out.
6. Complete the seams of the garment.

For a custom finish, reverse the seams, which will be under the facing, to avoid having the seam allowances "peek out" at the neckline.

Better ready-made garments usually have clean-finished seams or quick flat-fell seams. Narrow seams

with the edges overcast together are used on less expensive garments; trim the seam to ¼″ (6.4 mm) and zigzag the edges together to duplicate this inexpensive finish.

7. Pin and stitch the facing to the garment with the *right* side of the facing to the *wrong* side of the garment. The faced side of the facing is up. (Fig. 158c)

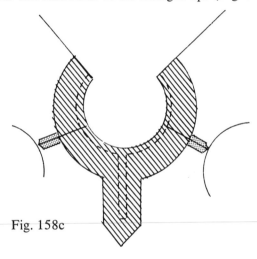

Fig. 158c

8. Understitch the *garment* and seam allowances, clip and press.
9. Turn the facing to the right side of the garment. Baste the facing in place with glue or by hand and topstitch it to the garment. (Fig. 158d)

Fig. 158d

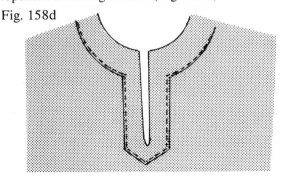

Variations: Use one of these ideas to create a new design.

✿ Insert piping between the seam allowances of the facing and facing lining and/or between the garment and facing at the neckline. Use a zipper foot to topstitch the facing in place.

✿ Use a very expensive or unusual fabric such as jewelled or embroidered fabrics or fake furs for the facing. Baste the facing to the garment by hand or pin it in place ¼″ (6.4 mm) from the free edge. Working from the inside of the garment, secure the edge of the facing permanently with a running stitch. (Fig. 158e)

✿ Set an all-in-one facing to the right side of the garment.

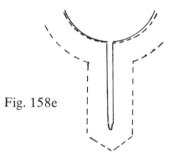

Fig. 158e

Reminder: The all-in-one pattern was trimmed ¼″ (6.4 mm) at the top of the armscye so that the seamline will roll to the underside of the garment. Do *not* trim this ¼″ (6.4 mm) from the facing since it will be the outside section; instead, trim ¼″ (6.4 mm) from the top of the armscye on the garment front and back.

Front Facings
Jewelled, fur, embroidered, and other fancy facings may be used to trim *only* the garment front. A regular facing will be used to finish the garment back. (Fig. 159a)

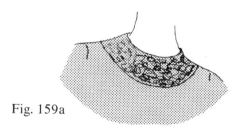

Fig. 159a

1. Pretrim the neckline seam allowances to ⅜″ (9.5 mm).
2. Face the front facing.

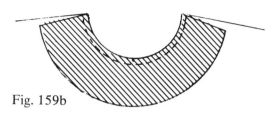

Fig. 159b

3. Stitch the neckline of the facing and the garment front together with the right side of the facing to the wrong side of the garment. (Fig. 159b)
4. Understitch the garment front and seam allowances. Clip and press.
5. Fold the facing to the right side of the garment and sew the free edge in place.
6. Finish the unnotched edge of the back facing.
7. With the right sides together, stitch the facing and garment together at the back neckline. (Fig. 159c)

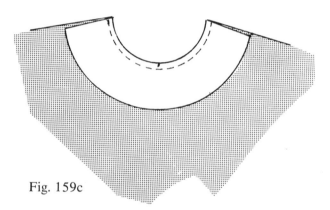

Fig. 159c

8. Understitch, clip, and press.
9. With the right sides together, stitch the shoulder seams of the front and back garment sections together. The back facing will extend beyond the garment front. (Fig. 159d)
10. Fold the back-neck facing so that the right side of the facing is next to the wrong side of the garment

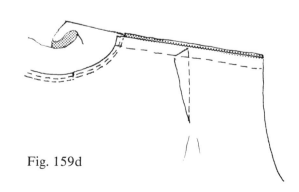

Fig. 159d

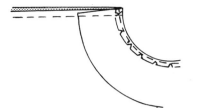

Fig. 159e

front. Pin it securely to avoid a "step" at the neckline. Stitch on the shoulder seam to secure the facing. (Fig. 159e)

11. Turn the garment right-side-out.

This technique can be used to finish garments made from such fabrics as lace, pseudosuede, or leather and do not have a front facing. It also can be used when the back neckline is finished with a yoke facing.

CUT-EDGE FACINGS

Cut-edge or raw-edge facings are often used on garments made of nonwoven fabrics. This facing is an attractive, flat finish for no-fray fabrics.

1. Cut the garment and facing sections with a ¼" (6.4 mm) seam allowance around the outside edges. Commercial patterns designed for synthetic suedes and leather have no seam allowances on the edges to be matched. No matter how carefully you cut, it is almost impossible to match these cut edges exactly.
2. With the wrong sides together, stitch the sections together ¼" (6.4 mm) from the cut edge.
3. Use embroidery scissors to trim away the seam allowances close to the stitched line. (Fig. 160)

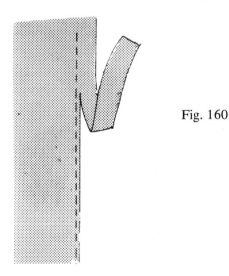

Fig. 160

BINDINGS

Bindings are a substitute for facings. They add interest to the garment and they are quick and easy to apply. Woven bindings are usually cut on the true bias (45°); knit bindings can be cut on the crossgrain, true bias, or 5° bias.

Single Bindings

1. Cut away the seam allowances of the garment edges to be bound.
2. Leave one seam open so that the bias can be applied flat.
3. Cut the binding on the bias—the bias cut ravels little or not at all and shapes easily. (Some knit fabrics are easier to shape on the crossgrain or 5° bias.) Cut the strips the desired length and five times the finished width of the binding. Cut a strip 1¼" (3.2 cm) wide for a ¼" (6.4 mm) finish.
4. Preshape the binding by pressing it with the iron before applying it to the garment.
5. With the right sides together, place the binding on top of the garment so that the end of the binding extends 1" (2.5 cm) beyond the edge of the garment. Matching the cut edges, stitch the bias to the garment with a seam the width of the finished binding— ¼" (6.4 mm) for a ¼" finish. (Fig. 161a)

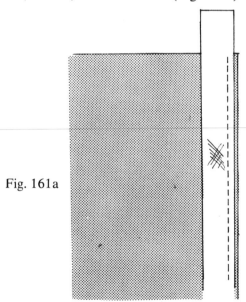

Fig. 161a

Even though the bias was preshaped with the iron, you may need to stretch the bias at the stitching line as you apply the binding to inward curves or ease it as you apply it to outward curves.

6. Press the binding toward the garment edge, then fold and press the binding over the cut edge of the garment. Glue or pin it in place. (Fig. 161b) Using

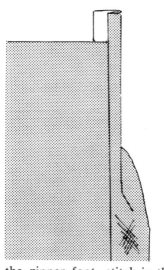

Fig. 161b

the zipper foot, stitch-in-the-ditch or topstitch the binding. If you topstitch, position the zipper foot on *top* of the binding. (Fig. 161c)

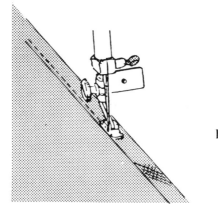

Fig. 161c

7. Stitch the open seam. Use the 1″ (2.5 cm) extension on the binding as a handle to align the seam exactly. (Fig. 161d)

8. Trim away the extension.

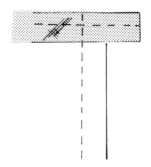

Fig. 161d

French Bindings or Double Bindings

French bindings finish the garment edge on both sides of the garment. They are an attractive finish to use on jacket edges, sheer fabrics, and lace garments.

1. Cut away the seam allowances of the garment edges to be bound.

2. Leave one seam open so that the bias can be applied flat.

3. Cut the bias the desired length and nine times the finished width. Cut the strip 2¼″ (5.7 cm) wide for a ¼″ (6.4 mm) finish.

4. Fold the bias in half lengthwise with the wrong sides together. Preshape the bias with the iron.

5. Place the bias on the right side of the garment and match the cut edges, leaving 1″ (2.5 cm) extension at each end. Stitch the seam the width of the finished binding—¼″ (6.4 mm) for a ¼″ finish. (Fig. 162a)

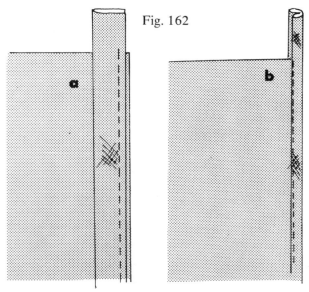

Fig. 162

6. Press the binding toward the garment edge, then press and fold the binding over the cut edge of the garment. Glue or pin it in place. Using the zipper foot, secure the binding by stitching-in-the-ditch or topstitching. (Fig. 162b)

7. Complete the open seam, using the handle to align it exactly.

8. Trim away the extensions.

Narrow French Binding

A ⅛″ (3.2 mm) French binding is an elegant finish for a beautiful garment. Lightweight fabrics of silk and cotton are the best selections for this binding.

1. Trim the seam allowances on the garment edges to be bound to ⅛″ (3.2 mm)

2. Cut the bias strips 1″ (2.5 cm) wide and the desired length.

3. Fold the bias in half lengthwise with the wrong sides together. Preshape the bias.

4. Place the binding on the right side of the garment. Match the cut edges of the binding and garment, leaving a 1″ (2.5 cm) extension at each end. Stitch a ¼″ (6.4 mm) seam.
5. Trim the seam *evenly* to ⅛″ (3.2 mm).
6. Press the binding up and over the garment edge. Pin or baste it in place.
7. Sew the folded edge of the binding in place by hand. Insert the needle into the threads of the stitching line of the seam instead of into the garment.
8. Complete the open seam. Trim away the bias extensions.

DOUBLE-FOLD BINDINGS—
MACHINE APPLICATION

This one-step machine application utilizes a pre-packaged or custom-made double-fold binding. The fold of double-fold bindings must be slightly off-center for the method to be successful.
1. Cut away the seam allowances of the garment edges to be bound.
2. Leave one seam open so that the bias can be applied flat.
3. Preshape the binding by pressing it with the iron before applying it to the garment.
4. With the garment face-up, enclose the garment edge so that the wider fold of the binding is on the underside and the binding extends 1″ (2.5 cm) at each end. Ease the binding around outward curves and stretch it on inward curves. Do not stretch the binding on straight edges. Baste, pin, or glue as needed. Position the zipper foot on top of the binding to edgestitch the binding to the garment. Adjust the foot to stitch ¹⁄₁₆″ (1.6 mm) from the edge of the binding.
5. Complete the open seam and trim away the extension.

Binding Corners
Outward corners

1. Apply the binding as directed for single or double bindings.
2. Stitch to the pivot point at the corner and backtack. The pivot point is determined by the width of the binding. The distance between the pivot point and the cut edge equals the finished width of the binding. (Fig. 163a)
3. Fold the binding so the underfold is diagonal and the upper fold is even with the cut edge. Pin. Begin stitching at the binding fold, continue to the end of the strip. (Fig. 163b)
4. Press the binding over the edge.
5. Mitre the corner on the underside in the opposite

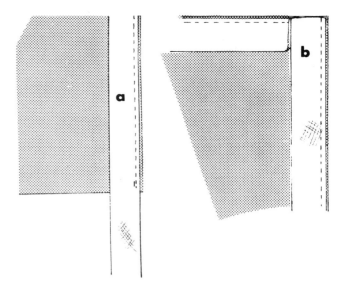

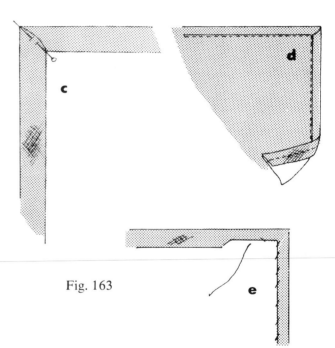

Fig. 163

direction by using the point of a needle to push it into place; pin the corner in place. Glue or baste the binding as needed. (Fig. 163c)
6. Secure the binding by topstitching or stitching-in-the-ditch. (Fig. 163d) For a custom finish, turn under the cut edge of single bindings and sew them by hand to the stitching line. (Fig. 163e)

Inward corners

1. Apply the binding as directed for single or double bindings, stitching with the garment on top and the binding to the base of the machine. Cut single bind-

117

ings five times the desired width. Cut doubled bindings seven times the desired width.

2. Pin and stitch to the pivot point, stopping with the needle down. (Fig. 164a)

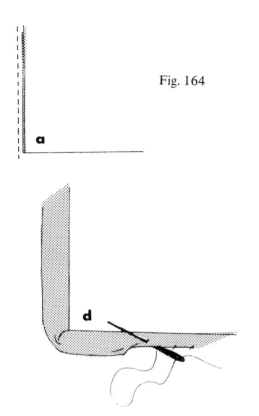

Fig. 164

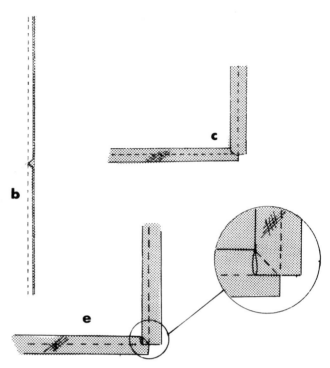

3. Raise the presser foot; clip the garment at the corner to the needle. Align the cut edges of the binding to the unstitched garment edge when you pivot the garment and binding. (Fig. 164b) Finish setting the binding.

4. Press the binding up and over the garment edge. Pin, glue or baste the binding as needed.

5. Secure the binding by one of these methods:

Topstitch or stitch-in-the-ditch single bindings. Clip the binding to the stitching line at the corner so that it will lie flat. (Fig. 164c)

Turn under the cut edge of single bindings and hand sew the binding to the stitching line. (Fig. 164d)

Sew the folded edge of the double binding to the stitching line by hand.

6. Miter the binding at the corner on the wrong side of the garment and stitch a small dart. (Fig. 164e)

Finishing the Ends of Binding

The ends of the binding can be finished several ways.

Open seam. Leaving a seam open so that the binding can be applied flat is the simplest way to finish the binding ends. Leave a shoulder seam open when binding the neckline, an underarm seam open when binding the armscye or edges of a jacket or vest, and a side seam open when binding the hem.

Easy Method:

1. Set the binding to the right side of the garment, leaving a 1″ (2.5 cm) "tail" at each end.

2. Fold binding to the wrong side of the garment. Secure it by hand, topstitching, or stitching-in-the-ditch.

3. Complete the open seam using the binding tail to align the seam exactly. Trim away the tail.

Designer Method:

1. Leave one seam open so that the binding can be applied flat.

2. Set the binding to the right side of the garment.

3. Close the open seam.

4. Fold the binding to the wrong side of the garment and secure it by hand, topstitching, or stitching-in-the-ditch.

Seam the Binding:

1. Leave the ends of the binding free to make a seam. Stitch the binding to the garment, leaving 1″ (2.5 cm) free at the beginning. Stop 1″ (2.5 cm) before the starting point.

2. Extend the bias ends to be joined.
3. Fold the garment so that the strips are at right angles to it. (Fig. 165)

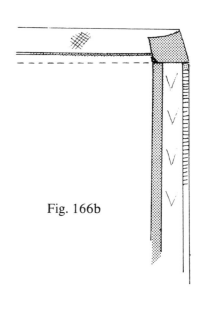

Fig. 166b

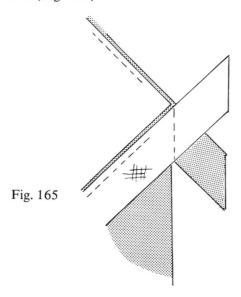

Fig. 165

4. Stitch the strips on the lengthwise grain so they fit the garment. Trim as needed. Press.
5. Complete the binding application.

Openings:
1. Set the zipper or complete the placket before applying the binding.
2. With the binding extending ½" (12.7 mm), match the cut edges of the garment and stitch the binding to the garment. (Fig. 166a)

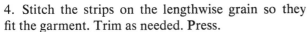

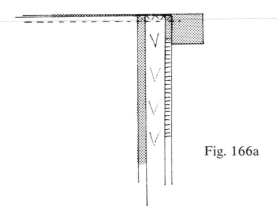

Fig. 166a

3. Fold the end of the binding around the placket to the wrong side of the garment. (Fig. 166b)
4. Fold the binding to the wrong side of the garment and complete the binding application.

BRAID
Folded braid is another substitute for a facing. It's a quick finish for the edges of jackets, vests, and wrap-around skirts. If you don't know how to apply it, the garment will certainly look homemade.

Commercial folded braids are folded so that one edge is a little wider than the other edge. If you are making a custom braid with ribbon, flat braids, or nonwoven materials like leather, vinyl, suede, or pseudosuede, fold the braid lengthwise with the wrong sides together so that one edge is ⅛" (3.2 mm) wider than the other.

1. Cut away the seam allowances of the edges on the garment and facing to be bound.
2. Leave one seam open so that the braid can be applied flat. With the wrong sides together, stitch the garment and facing together ¼" (6.4 mm) from the edge.
3. Preshape the braid by pressing it with the iron before applying it to the garment.
4. With the garment face-up, enclose the garment edge so that the wider fold of the braid is on the underside and the braid extends 1" (2.5 cm) at each end. Ease the braid around outward curves and stretch it on inward curves. Do not stretch the braid on straight edges. Baste, pin, or glue as needed. Using the zipper foot, edgestitch the bias to the garment. Position the foot so that it rests on the braid. Adjust the foot so that the edge of the foot can be used as a guide to stitch the braid ¹⁄₁₆" (1.6 mm) from the edge.

CONTROLLING FULLNESS

Darts, tucks, elastic, casings, and gathers are used to shape flat pieces of fabric into figure-fitting garments. These shaping devices can be decorative as well as functional.

DARTS

Short straight darts can be stitched quickly and easily without pinning or basting when you use these industrial shortcuts.

Shortcut One
1. Mark the machine base with a piece of tape from the needle straight forward. (Fig. 167a)

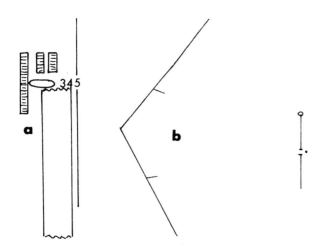

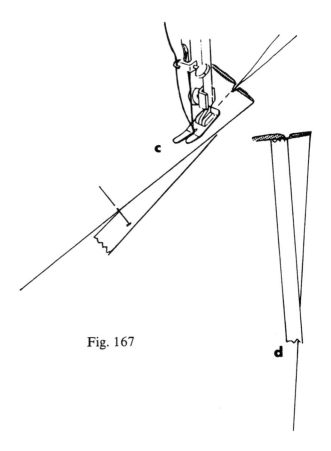

Fig. 167

2. Mark the stitching lines of the dart with two snips at the cut edge and with a pin 1/8″ (3.2 mm) from the point. (Fig. 167b)
3. Lower the sewing-machine needle into the needle hole. Fold the dart in half with the right sides together, matching the snips. Slide the snips up to the needle. Place the pin at the dart point on the taped line. Lower the presser foot, hold the threads behind the foot, and stitch from the snips toward the point, keeping the pin on the edge of the tape all the way to the needle. (Fig. 167c) Remove the pin and take one stitch along the foldline to the point.

4. Chain-off at the dart point for several inches before stitching onto another section. The long chain will be easy to tie into a tailor's knot at the dart point. Do not backtack—backtacks accent the dart point, add stiffness and bulk, and are difficult to rip out when refitting is necessary.

Until you master this technique, mark the stitching line of the dart with a piece of tape. Stitch next to, not on, the tape. (Fig. 167d)

Shortcut Two
Use the threads from the machine as a guide to stitch the dart straight.

1. Mark the stitching lines of the dart with two snips at the cut edge and with a pin ⅛″ (3.2 mm) from the point.
2. Pull up 10″–12″ (25.4 cm–30.5 cm) of thread from the needle and bobbin.
3. Fold the dart with the right sides together and begin stitching at the snips on the cut edge. Lay the threads on top of the garment from the cut edge to the pin to indicate the stitching line. Wrap the threads around the pin at the dart point to form a figure eight. (Fig. 168) Stitch along the thread guideline. Remove the pin and take one stitch along the foldline at the point.
4. Chain-off at the dart point for several inches before stitching onto another section. Tie a tailor's knot at the dart point.

This same technique can be used if you stitch from the dart point to the cut edge.

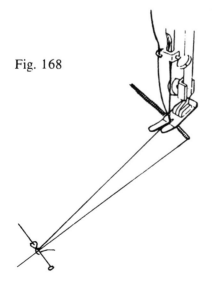

Fig. 168

Long or Intricately Shaped Darts

1. Using a tracing wheel and white tracing paper or tailor's tacks, mark the stitching lines of the dart, Mark each of the matchpoints (circles) and the end of the dart with a cross mark. Mark the stitching lines of the dart at the cut edge with two snips.
2. With the right sides together, match and pin the stitching lines of the dart together. Insert the pins so that they can be removed as you stitch without stopping the machine.
3. Baste the dart together by hand or machine if the garment requires fitting.
4. Using a regular stitch, stitch the dart from the cut edge to the point. Stitch the point carefully with a stitch or two along the fold to avoid a pucker.
5. Chain-off at the dart point for several inches before stitching onto another section. Tie a tailor's knot at the dart point.

TUCKS

Tucks can be stitched on the right or wrong side of the garment.

1. Mark the stitching lines with snips at the cut edge. Mark the foldline with a small V-shaped notch at the cut edge. Mark the ends of the stitching lines with a pin, soap, chalk, water-erasable pen, or tailor's tacks.
2. Mark the foldline on the right side of the fabric if the tucks will be stitched on the right side; mark it on the wrong side if they will be stitched on the wrong side.
  Use soap or water-erasable pen to draw the fold-line which connects the V-shaped notch at the cut edge and the mark at the end of the tuck. Be sure to test the water-erasable pen on a fabric scrap before using it on the garment.
  (It is not necessary to mark the foldline if the fabric has a design or stripe that can be used as a guideline. Many designer blouses are made from signature fabrics. The signature or design is woven so that it makes inconspicuous vertical and horizontal stripes. Tucks are extremely easy to mark and sew when the fabric has a stripe in the pattern or weave.)
3. Fold the tuck on the foldline, matching the snips. Press the foldline. Do not press beyond the end of the tuck. Lower the sewing-machine needle into the needle hole. Slide the snips up to the needle and lower the presser foot. Hold the threads behind the foot and stitch from the snips to the pin at the end of the tuck. (Fig. 169)

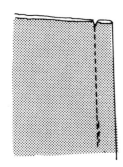

Fig. 169

4. Pull the threads to the wrong side and tie them at the end of the tuck.

5. If the fabric is sheer, bobbin-stitch the tuck. Begin at the end of the tuck and stitch to the snips. Position the garment under the presser foot so that the end of the tuck is *directly below* the needle before pulling the bobbin thread up and threading the machine.

Pin Tucks

Pin tucks are stitched $\frac{1}{16}''$ (1.6 mm) from the fold on the right side of the garment. (Fig. 170)

Fig. 170

1. Mark the beginning of the foldline at the cut edge with a snip. Mark the end of the tuck with a pin, chalk, soap, or water-erasable pen. If necessary, mark the foldline with soap or water-erasable pen.

2. Fold the tuck with the wrong sides together.

3. Stitch from the cut edge to the point, using the inside of the straight-stitch presser foot as a guide.

4. Pull the threads to the wrong side and tie them at the end of the tuck.

5. Bobbin-stitch pin tucks on sheer fabrics.

GATHERS

Gathers can be soft and draped or puffed and bouffant. Either way gathering is one method to control garment fullness.

Loosen the Tension

Use this shortcut method for gathering light- and mediumweight fabrics.

1. Loosen the upper tension, making the bobbin thread tight.

2. Set the stitch length at 10 spi or 2.5 mm—a long basting stitch will make pleats instead of gathers.

3. To avoid breaking, use a heavy or strong thread in the bobbin: polyester, silk, or nylon. A cord with a silky or smooth finish pulls more easily than a coarse cord. The color does not have to match.

4. Stitching from the *right* side of the fabric, stitch just inside the seam allowance. Stop and start again at each seamline when gathering long lengths. (Fig. 171a) Stitch difficult-to-handle fabrics again $\frac{3}{8}''$ (9.5 mm) from the cut edge for greater control.

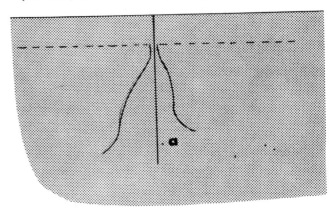

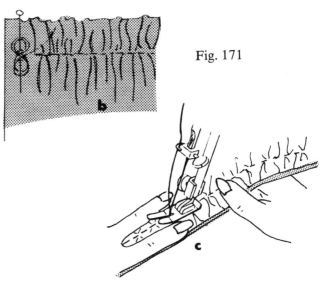

Fig. 171

5. Pull the bobbin thread from each end, sliding the gathers toward the center.

6. With the right sides together, pin the gathered edge to the corresponding edge, matching the

notches. (If the sections have no notches, make some in each section by dividing it into quarters or eighths *before* pulling the bobbin thread.)

Secure the bobbin thread at the beginning of the first gathered section by winding it around a pin in a figure eight. (Fig. 171b)

7. Adjust the gathers only between the first two pins.

8. With the gathered section on top, begin stitching the seam. Stitch to the first pin. Hold the gathers flat while stitching with your index and third finger placed on either side of the presser foot. (Fig. 171c) Do not move your fingers when the machine is in motion. Hold the fabric behind the presser foot firmly with your other hand.

9. Stop, with the needle down, and adjust the gathers between the next two pins, using the points of the scissors. Adjusting as you go is quicker than adjusting all the gathers before you begin stitching. This is one of the few times you will stitch over pins. *Walk* the machine over each pin to prevent damage to the needle, machine, fabric, or yourself.

10. Adjust and stitch the remaining sections. When you reach the last notch, adjust the gathers and secure the thread at the end of the section by winding it around the pin. Finish the seamline.

Zigzag over Cord

Gathering heavy fabrics, pseudosuedes, dust ruffles, and curtains is quick and easy with this method.

1. Set the machine for a medium zigzag stitch (W,2-L,2); use a longer and wider stitch on heavy fabrics. A medium-width stitch will seldom show on the finished garment.

2. Use a silk, nylon, or other strong cord. A cord with a silky or smooth finish pulls more easily than a coarse cord.

3. With the garment wrong-side-up, position the cord just above the seamline. Secure the cord at the beginning with a pin or knot. Zigzag over the cord. Do *not* stitch on it. If you cannot avoid stitching on the cord, increase the stitch width. (Fig. 172)

4. Pull the cord to adjust the gathers.

5. Pin and stitch the gathered section to the corresponding section, keying the seams and notches.

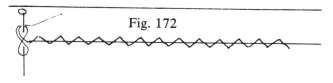

Fig. 172

Machine Gathering

Occasionally, you need to gather very long lengths of fabric, which do not need to be absolutely precise, such as ruffles on dance costumes, curtains, and bedspreads.

This industrial technique will allow you to gather 2″ (5.1 cm) of fabric into 1″ (2.5 cm) of stitching. The fabric *cannot* be adjusted along the stitching line.

1. Finish the hem on the section to be gathered before gathering it.

2. Tighten the upper tension slightly and use a short stitch.

3. With both index fingers in front of the presser foot and the foot centered between the fingers, push the fabric toward the needle as you stitch, forcing extra fabric into each stitch. *Be very careful* not to push your fingers under the needle. Continue until the gathered piece is the desired length. (Fig. 173)

4. Pin and stitch the gathered piece to the corresponding section.

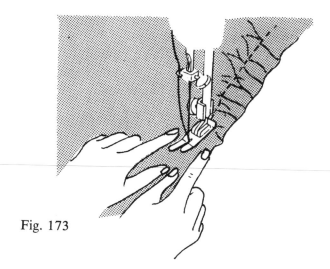

Fig. 173

ELASTIC

The appearance of many straight garments is improved when the fullness is distributed evenly. Stitch elastic or elastic thread at the waistline or wrist to regulate the fullness.

Stitch elastic to the wrong side of garments to eliminate casings, save time, reduce bulk, and space the gathers evenly. A zigzag stitch will create an attractive "smocked" look on the right side of the garment.

Elastic at the Waistline with the Side Seams Open

1. Select a soft, narrow elastic ¼"–½" (6.4 mm–12.7 mm) width which won't become narrower when stretched. Elastic webbing and woven elastics retain their width when stretched; braided elastics don't.

2. Measure your waistline length. Cut the elastic the measured length. Divide the elastic into two sections, making the elastic for the front one inch longer than the elastic for the back. Cut the elastic into two pieces and mark the center of each piece with a marking pen or a straight pin.

3. Use the paper pattern to mark the location line for the elastic at the side seams with ⅛" (3.2 mm) snips. Use pins to mark the waistline centers on the wrong side of each garment section.

4. Pin the longer piece of elastic to the location line on the wrong side of the garment front. Match the ends to the cut edges of the garment, then match the centers. Pin the other piece of elastic to the garment back. Each piece of elastic has only three pins. Use more, if needed. Learn to stitch using fewer pins whenever possible. Stopping to remove pins takes more time than you realize.

5. Using a zigzag stitch (W,2-L,2) or straight stitch, apply the elastic to the garment, stretching it as you stitch. Do *not* stretch the first or last ⅝" (16 mm) which will be stitched into the side seam. Chain stitch from one garment section to the other.

6. Complete the side seams, the elastic will be secured in the seamline stitching.

7. Many times the garment can't be marked from the paper pattern. Use this fitting idea so that you can apply the elastic to flat garment sections and avoid working in a loop or circle.

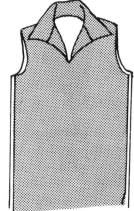

Fig. 174

Finish the shoulder seams and the neckline of the garment. (Fig. 174) Try on the garment. Pin the underarm seams together as needed. Tie a string or narrow tape around your waist and adjust the fullness as desired. Mark the waistline with pins at the center and side seams. Remove the garment. Compare the side seams for accuracy. They should be the same distance from the armscye unless you are lopsided.

The length of the elastic on the finished garment is 2½" (6.5 cm) less than your waistline measurement. This is comfortable for most people because elastic which is stitched in a stretched position never completely returns to its original length. Some elastics lose less stretch when stitched and/or have less springiness to begin with than others. These are important considerations if you hate too tight a waistline.

Elastic at the Waistline in a Finished Garment

1. Select a soft, narrow elastic that won't become narrower when stretched. Cut the elastic so that it measures 2" (5.1 cm) less than your waistline. Mark the center of the elastic and fold it again with the free ends extending ¼" (6.4 mm) beyond the center fold. Mark the foldlines. (Fig. 175)

Fig. 175

2. Mark the waistline on the wrong side of the garment with pins or soap. Divide the waistline into quarters.

3. Pin the elastic to the wrong side of the garment, matching the quarter marks and overlapping the ends of the elastic ½" (12.7 mm).

4. Using a zigzag (W,2-L,2) or straight stitch, stitch the elastic to the wrong side of the garment, stretching the elastic as you stitch.

Elastic at a Sleeve Edge

If the elastic can be stretched to the sleeve width, use elastic on the edges of the sleeves instead of making a casing. Apply the elastic before stitching the underarm seam.

1. Measure the sleeve width at the edge to be finished. Measure the elasticity of the elastic to determine if the elastic can be stretched that amount. If the elastic can't be stretched enough, pin as many small pleats as needed at the edge of the sleeve to remove the excess fullness. Space the tucks evenly, and they won't show on the finished garment.

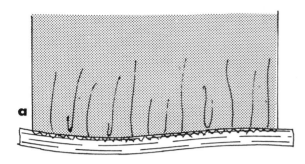

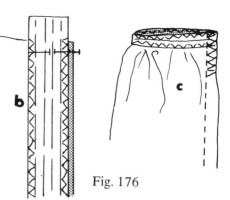

Fig. 176

2. Allow a ¼″ (6.4 mm) hem on the sleeve edge. Mark the hemline on the right side of the sleeve.

3. Select a ⅜″–½″ (9.5 mm–12.7 mm) wide elastic which won't become narrower when stretched. Mark the length of the wrist or arm measurement on the elastic. Do *not* cut the elastic; it is easier to apply when it has a "tail."

4. Divide and mark the elastic into quarters. Divide and mark the sleeves into quarters.

5. Place the elastic on the right side of the sleeve, matching the edge of the elastic to the marked hemline. Pin the elastic to the sleeve at the marked points. Use a zigzag (W,2-L,2) or straight stitch to apply the elastic, stretching the elastic as you stitch. (Fig. 176a)

6. Fold the hem and elastic to the wrong side of the sleeve and pin it in place. Using a zigzag (W,2-L,2) or straight stitch, stitch the elastic to the wrong side of the sleeve. (Fig. 176b)

7. Stitch the underarm seams. Cut off the elastic tail.

8. Trim the seam allowances of the underarm seam to ⅛″ (3.2 mm) for 1″ (2.5 cm) at the sleeve edge. Using a zigzag stitch (W,3-L,1), overlock the seam edge. (Fig. 176c)

Sleeve with a Ruffled Edge

This easy finish makes a pretty ruffle on long or short sleeves. (Fig. 177) Apply the elastic before stitching the underarm seams.

Fig. 177

1. Measure the sleeve width at the edge to be finished. Measure the elasticity of the elastic to determine if it will stretch the required amount. If the elastic can't be stretched enough, pin as many small pleats as needed at the edge of the sleeve to remove the excess fullness. Space the tucks evenly so they won't show on the finished garment.

2. If the pattern doesn't have a ruffle, add the width of the desired ruffle to the edge of the pattern.

3. Hem the sleeve with a narrow hem.

4. Using a ⅛″–⅜″ wide elastic (3.2 mm–9.5 mm), mark but do not cut it the desired length. Divide and mark the elastic into quarters.

5. Mark the stitching line on the wrong side of the sleeve. Divide and mark the sleeve into quarters.

6. Pin the elastic to the sleeve, matching the marked points. Using a zigzag (W,2-L,2) or straight stitch, stitch the elastic to the wrong side of the sleeve, stretching the elastic as you stitch.

7. Complete the underarm seams with a standing-fell, quick flat-fell, or zigzagged seam. Cut off the elastic tail.

ELASTIC THREAD

Elastic thread can be used to make a soft, gathered waistline on straight garments, but the elastic thread often loses some of its elasticity with wear, age, and washing.

1. Fill the bobbin by hand with elastic thread. Stretch the thread slightly as you wind it onto the bobbin.

2. Mark the location line for the gathers at the side seams with ⅛″ (3.2 mm) snips. If the line is straight, press mark between the two snips. If the line is curved, mark the *right* side of the garment with soap or pins, using the paper pattern.

3. From the right side of the garment section, stitch on the marked line. Pull out enough elastic at the end of the stitched line so that it won't spring back into the needle hole when you cut the threads.

4. Complete the side seams, the elastic thread will be secured in the seamline stitching. If the side seams were stitched before the elastic waistline, tie the ends of the elastic thread together to secure them.

Shirring

Shirring consists of several decorative rows of gathering. Elasticized shirring is attractive and comfortable to wear.

1. Wind the bobbin by hand with elastic thread so that there is a slight tension on the elastic.

2. Experiment with a piece of fabric to determine the stitch length—a longer stitch shirrs the fabric more than a shorter stitch. Six stitches per inch reduces the fabric width by half; twelve stitches per inch reduces it by one quarter.

3. Mark the lines to be shirred on the right side of the fabric with soap or chalk. They can be spaced evenly (Fig. 178a) or in groups or they can form diamonds by crossing each other. (Fig. 178b)

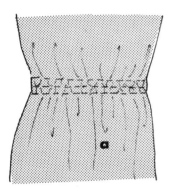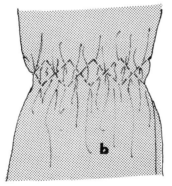

Fig. 178

4. Place a piece of paper under the garment section.

5. Stitching from the right side of the fabric, stitch the desired number of shirring rows with the fabric held taut. Begin and end in the seam allowances.

6. Do not change the stitch length during the stitching process and be sure to pull out enough elastic at the end of each stitched row so that it won't spring back into the needle hole. Knot the elastic and thread at each end of the stitching lines.

7. Rip away the paper.

8. Complete all seamlines which cross the shirred rows.

CASINGS

Garment fullness can be adjusted and controlled with elastic or a drawstring in a casing.

Baste the seam allowances in the casing area to the wrong side of the garment with glue or machine stitching to avoid catching the drawstring or elastic in them during insertion.

Casing Openings

Complete casing openings like eye slits, buttonholes, or eyelets before making the casing.

Reinforce the openings with a small piece of nonwoven interfacing. Glue the interfacing to the wrong side of the garment to hold it while you make the openings.

Fold-over Casings

Fold-over casings or self-casings are often used at the neckline, waistline, and sleeve edges when the edge is straight or slightly shaped. The garment edge is extended the amount required to fold it over and encase the drawstring or elastic.

Clean-finished edge. A clean-finished or folded edge can be used to finish the edge of casings if the garment is made from a lightweight fabric. This finish is especially attractive on a neckline edge which will be worn open, exposing the inside of the garment and the casing.

The casing allowance must be at least as wide as the elastic or drawstring to be inserted, plus a ¼" (6.4 mm) seam allowance and an additional ⅛"–¼" (3.2 mm–6.4 mm) ease. The casing allowance shouldn't be less than ⅝" (16 mm) wide.

1. The casing allowance for a 1" (2.5 cm) elastic at the waistline of slacks or skirts will be 1½" (3.8 cm).

The casing allowance for a tie at the neckline, wrist, or waist will be ⅝"–1¼" (16 mm–3 cm), depending on the width of the drawstring.

2. Mark the casing foldline with a clip in the seam allowance at each side of the garment section.

3. Complete any casing openings like eye slits, buttonholes, or eyelets. Complete the vertical seams.

4. Glue the seam allowances in the casing area to the garment.

5. Press the casing allowance to the wrong side of the garment.

6. Turn under the ¼" (6.4 mm) seam allowance at the edge of the casing, pin, and stitch the casing to the garment. If there are no casing openings leave

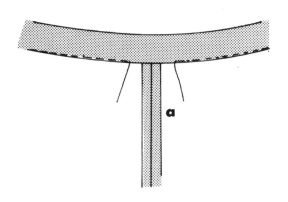

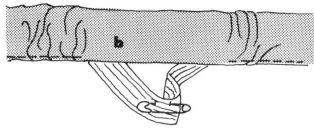

Fig. 179

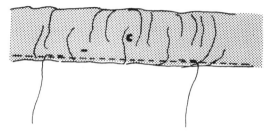

the casing unstitched for 1″–1½″ (2.5 cm–3.8 cm). (Fig. 179a)

7. Insert a drawstring or elastic the desired width and length, using a safety pin or tapestry needle. For the waistlines of slacks and skirts, select a non-roll elastic.

8. Overlap the ends of the elastic. Use a safety pin to fasten the elastic ends together and wear the garment once or twice before stitching it permanently. (Fig. 179b) Adjust the elastic if needed. If your waist measurement fluctuates, use the safety pin to adjust the garment waistline.

9. If desired, complete the stitching on the casing or use a permanent glue to secure it. (Fig. 179c)

Zigzagged or cut edge. If the fabric is too heavy or bulky to turn the casing edge under, if the casing won't be seen, if you want a very flat finish, or if you're in a hurry, leave the cut edge raw on fabrics that won't unravel. Zigzag the edge on fabrics that will ravel.

1. The casing allowance is the width of the elastic or drawstring plus ½″ (12.7 mm).
2. Mark the casing foldline with a clip in the seam allowances.
3. Make any casing openings.
4. Zigzag the edge of the casing, if required or if desired.
5. Glue the seam allowances in the casing area to the garment.

6. Press the casing allowance to the wrong side of the garment.
7. Pin and stitch the casing to the garment ¼″ (6.4 mm) from the cut or zigzagged edge. If there are no casing openings, leave the casing unstitched 1½″ (3.8 cm).
8. Insert the elastic or drawstring and finish the casing.

Applied Casings
Lace, prepackaged bias tapes, ribbon, lining fabrics, nonwoven materials, and lightweight knits can be used to make casings. The casing can be applied to the inside or face side of the garment.

Inside applied casings
1. The casing width is the width of the elastic or drawstring plus ½″–1″ (12.7 mm–2.5 cm).
2. On the wrong side of the garment, mark the casing location at the garment centers and seamlines.
3. If the garment has a drawstring, finish any openings before applying the casing.
4. Complete the side seams of the garment and glue the seam allowances in the casing area to the garment.
5. With soap or chalk, connect the marked points on the garment to indicate the casing location.
6. Center the casing over the marked line using several pins to hold it in place. If you are using a woven fabric for the casing, finish the edges with a clean finish or a zigzag stitch before applying it.
7. If the garment has elastic and has no openings, fold one end under for the first ½″ (12.7 mm) of the casing strip. Pin and stitch one long edge of the casing to the garment. Finish the end of the casing by folding it under so that the two folded ends meet. (Fig. 180) Stitch the other side of the casing to the garment.
8. Insert the elastic or drawstring.
9. Secure the ends of the elastic.

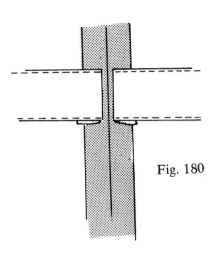

Fig. 180

1. Use a ⅛″–¼″ (3.2 mm–6.4 mm) wide elastic.
2. Slash the paper pattern at the casing location and insert a strip of paper that is three times the width of the elastic.
3. Mark the top and bottom of the tuck at the cut edges of the garment sections with snips.
4. Complete all vertical seams except one.
5. With the right sides of the garment together, pin and stitch the tuck, matching the snips. (Fig. 181)

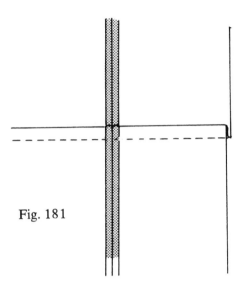

Fig. 181

Outside applied casings

1. If the casing is made of a woven or knitted fabric, the casing width is the width of the elastic or drawstring plus 1½″ (3.8 cm). If the casing is ribbon, lace, vinyl, suede, or pseudosuede, the casing width is the width of the elastic or drawstring plus ¾″ (19.1 mm).
2. On the right side of the garment, mark the casing location at the garment centers and seamlines with pins. With soap or chalk, connect the marked points on the garment to indicate the casing location.
3. Center the casing over the marked line and pin or baste it in place.
4. Fold the end of the casing strip under for the first ½″ (12.7 mm). Stitch one long edge of the casing to the garment. Finish the end of the casing by folding it under ½″ (12.7 mm). Stitch the other side of the casing to the garment.
5. Insert the drawstring.

Casing Tucks

A tuck on the inside of the garment is a quick, easy-to-make casing on garments made of lightweight fabrics.

6. Insert elastic the desired length into the casing. Pin it in place at each end.
7. Complete the open vertical seam, securing the elastic.

Casing Seams

French, quick flat-fell seams, and welt seams can be used for casings when elastic or a drawstring is used at a seamline.

If the insertion is narrow, no changes are required in the width of the seam allowances. If the insertion is wide, make the seam allowances wide enough to accommodate it.

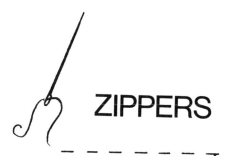

ZIPPERS

Can you imagine how long it took to make button-holes and sew on buttons or hooks and eyes before the invention of the zipper? The forerunner of this convenient fastener was invented in 1891 by Whitcomb L. Judson to replace the buttons on shoes, but it wasn't widely used on garments until Schiaparelli popularized it in the thirties.

Today's zippers bear little resemblance to those early heavy metal zippers. There is a zipper suitable for every weight fabric and any style garment. Metal, plastic, and filament coil zippers in a variety of sizes and colors can be set as conspicuously or as inconspicuously as you choose.

These professional techniques apply to all zipper applications:

☸ Use a filament coil zipper for inconspicuous plackets in medium and lightweight fabrics. The lightweight coil is narrow in width and flexible, and it resists snagging. Select a heavier zipper for heavyweight fabrics.

Be sure your zipper has a shrink-proof tape, 100% polyester, to avoid a "roller-coaster look." Zippers *cannot* be preshrunk; only the tapes shrink. When the zipper tape shrinks, the zipper ripples and looks terrible. It makes little difference whether the zipper was preshrunk or shrank after the first washing—if the tape shrinks, the zipper will buckle.

☸ Press the zipper tape before setting the zipper. Using a cool iron and a press cloth, press the tape to the teeth; do not press over the teeth.

☸ Key the zipper ⅜" (9.5 mm) above the top stop to ensure that both sides are the same length. Key the garment on the seamline. (Fig. 182a)

☸ Shorten the zipper if you don't have a zipper the desired length. Measure and mark the correct length on a longer zipper. Make a new bottom stop by sewing across the teeth by hand several times. Cut away the excess zipper about ½" (12.7 mm) below the new stop.

Shorten fly zippers and separating zippers from the top. To avoid being left with a zipper in one hand and a zipper tab in the other, do *not* rezip the zipper until it is completely set in the garment.

☸ Eliminate bulk in any seams which are crossed by the zipper placket. (Fig. 182b)

☸ If, as in a neckline, a facing finishes a garment edge, set the zipper into an open placket *after* the facing has been applied so that the top of the teeth are ⅜" (9.5 mm) below the finished neckline.

☸ If a band finishes the garment edge as with some waistlines, set the zipper into an open placket *before* the band is set so that the top of the teeth will be ⅛"–¼" (3.2 mm– 6.4 mm) below the band.

☸ Press the seam allowances of the placket to the wrong side of the garment before setting the zipper.

If you can't gauge the seam allowance width precisely, mark the stitching line on the right side of the fabric with soap or gauge stitch ⅜"–½" (9.5 mm– 12.7 mm) from the cut edges of the placket. Gauge stitching will stay the placket and prevent stretching at the opening.

☸ Baste the zipper to the seam allowances using pins, a glue stick, doublestick tape (Fig. 182c), regular tape (Fig. 182d), hand or machine basting, or if it is a self-basting zipper by pressing. (Self-basting zippers have a thin line of adhesive that sticks to the fabric when the zipper is pressed to the garment.)

☸ Open the zipper and set it into an open placket. This allows you to use the guidelines on the machine throat plate as a stitching gauge. When you are stitching the zipper into the garment, allow the folded edge of the placket to move along the guideline to ensure success.

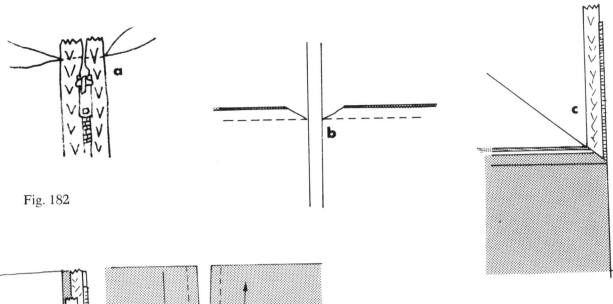

Fig. 182

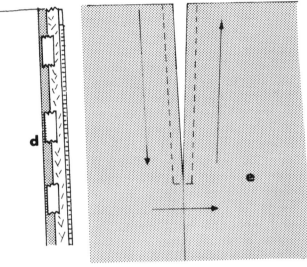

Begin stitching at the top of one side, stitch to the bottom, across the bottom, and up the other side. (Fig. 182e) If the fabric is loosely woven, napped, stretchy, or requires matching, stitch each side of the zipper from the top to the bottom.

☼ When you stitch the zipper in place, do *not* stitch around the zipper tab. Stop the machine with the needle down, raise the presser foot, and move the tab up or down as needed.

☼ Do not stretch the fabric when you set a zipper; instead, ease the garment to the zipper tape. Depending on the placket length and garment fabric, you may ease as little as ⅛″ (3.2 mm) or as much as 2″ (5.1 cm).

☼ If you are replacing a broken zipper, measure the placket length before you rip the zipper out.

☼ Ideally, the zipper is stitched into the placket from the right side of the garment with the garment and zipper face-up; however, this is sometimes easier said than done, especially when you are sewing on stretchy fabrics. Reverse the positions putting the zipper on top and the garment toward the machine base to take advantage of the pulling action of the feed dog. Tighten the upper tension slightly to make an attractive stitch on the right side of the garment.

☼ To match plaids and stripes, stitch one side of the zipper in place, close the zipper and baste the unstitched zipper tape with glue or tape to the other seam allowance, matching the fabric pattern. Stitch both sides from top to bottom.

☼ Whenever possible, set the zipper when the garment sections are flat. Complete the seam below the placket and immediately set the zipper into the opening. If this isn't feasible, set the zipper as soon as possible. Try to avoid stitching a zipper into an almost completed garment.

SLOT ZIPPERS OR CENTERED APPLICATIONS

The slot zipper is centered in the opening and looks the same on each side of the zipper. The zipper is very easy to set by this method and it is usually used at the center back of garments although many French designers use this application at the side seam.

Skirt with a Waistband

The finished skirt placket should be 7″ (17.8 cm) long—a longer placket is a telltale sign of "loving hands at home." If a 7″ (17.8 cm) placket is too short, use another kind of closure, unless you're tall, then you can cheat and use an 8″ (20.3 cm) placket.

The slot zipper is frequently used on skirts which have waistbands. These directions can also be used on blouses or dresses which have collars.

1. Key the zipper ⅜" (9.5 mm) above the zipper stop. Key the skirt at the skirtband seamline.
2. Stitch the seam below the placket, backtacking at each end of the seam.
3. Press the seam allowances of the placket to the wrong side of the garment when you press the seam open.
4. Open the zipper. Place it face-down on the garment seam allowances, matching the edges of the zipper teeth to the pressed lines and the keyed lines on the zipper to the keyed lines on the garment. The edges of the zipper teeth must match the pressed lines exactly. (Fig. 183) Pin, glue, press, or baste the zipper to the seam allowances.

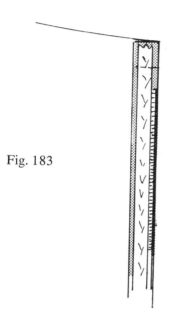

Fig. 183

5. If the fabric has a pattern to be matched, close the zipper to check the alignment. Reopen the zipper after checking the seam.
6. Glue the seam allowances to the wrong side of the garment.
7. Using the zipper or straight-stitch foot, stitch the zipper into the placket ¼" (6.4 mm) from the folded edge.

The completed zipper will have a slight ridge at the center where the two folded edges meet. This ridge will disappear when the garment is on the body. If there is no ridge, the teeth or coil will show when the garment is worn.

Dress with a Facing
The slot zipper is used on dresses which have collarless or jewel necklines and are finished with facings.

The application can also be used for a slot zipper on a skirt with a facing or lining.

Easy method
1. Finish the neckline of the dress with a facing (see FACINGS). (Fig. 184a)
2. Key the zipper ⅜" (9.5 mm) above the zipper stop.
3. Stitch the seam below the placket, backtacking at each end of the seam.
4. Press the seam open and press the seam allowances of the placket to the wrong side of the garment.
5. Open the zipper and place it face-down on the garment seam allowances, matching the edges of the zipper teeth to the pressed lines with the keyed lines of the zipper ⅛" (3.2 mm) below the garment edge. Fold the zipper tape under at the keyed line. (Fig. 184b) Pin, glue, press, or baste the zipper to the seam allowances.
6. If the fabric has a pattern to be matched, close the zipper to check the alignment. Open the zipper after checking the seam.
7. Glue the seam allowances to the wrong side of the garment. Fold the facing to the wrong side of the garment. (Fig. 184c)

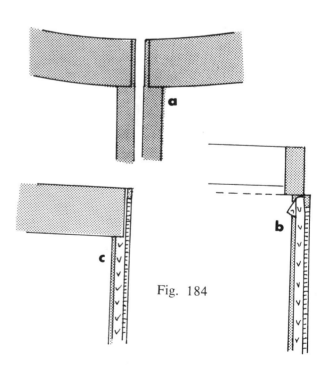

Fig. 184

8. Using the zipper or straight-stitch foot, stitch the zipper into the placket ¼″ (6.4 mm) from the folded edge. The stitching line should catch the folded edge of the facing.

9. Finish the placket with a hook and eye above the zipper.

Zippers in inexpensive garments are often set so that the top of the zipper teeth is even with the edge of the garment, eliminating the need for a hook and eye.

Designer method

1. Key the zipper ⅜″ (9.5 mm) above the zipper teeth. Key the facing at the neckline seamline.

2. Stitch the seam of the garment below the placket, backtacking at each end of the seam.

3. Press the seam open and press the seam allowances of the placket to the wrong side of the garment.

4. Open the zipper. Place it face-down on the garment seam allowances, matching the edges of the zipper teeth to the pressed lines and the keyed lines on the zipper tape to the keyed lines on the garment. The edges of the zipper teeth must match the pressed lines exactly. Glue, tape, press, or baste the zipper to the seam allowances.

5. If the fabric has a pattern to be matched, close the zipper to check the alignment. Open the zipper after checking the seam.

6. Notch the neck edge of the facings ⅞″ (22.2 mm) from the ends. Fold the ends of the facing to the wrong side at the notches.

Position the folded edge of the facing on the back of the zipper tape, matching the keyed lines on the zipper tape to the keyed lines at the facing. The zipper teeth and tape will be exposed ¼″ (6.4 mm) between the facing and garment. Stitch the facing to the back of the zipper (185a)

8. Fold the facing and the seam allowances of the garment placket to the right side of the garment, enclosing the zipper and facing seam allowances. Match and pin the notches at the neck edge. Stitch the neckline seam. (Fig. 185b)

9. Trim and clip as needed.

10. Turn the garment right side out and glue the seam allowances of the placket to the wrong side of the garment.

11. Using the zipper or straight-stitch foot, stitch the zipper into the placket ¼″ (6.4 mm) from the folded edge.

12. Finish the placket with a hook and eye above the zipper.

LAPPED ZIPPER OR WELT APPLICATIONS

The lapped zipper is applied so that one side of the garment is stitched close to the zipper, and the other side is lapped over the zipper and the underlap stitching line. (Fig. 186)

This application is usually used at the side seams of dresses and skirts on American designs; French designers, however, rarely use it. If you have difficulty setting lapped zippers, don't—pretend you're a French designer and forget them.

The zipper laps right-over-left on the garment front, front-over-back at the side seam and any way you want on the garment back. Ready-to-wear garments usually lap left-over-right, but designer dresses may lap right-over-left.

Skirt with a Waistband

This application is usually used at the side seams of skirts, but it can be used at the center back. It can also be used to set zippers on slacks, blouses, or dresses with collars.

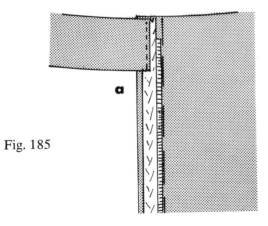

Fig. 185

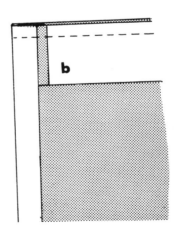

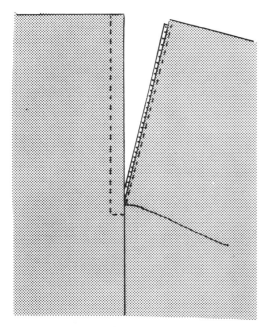

Fig. 186

1. Key the zipper ⅜″ (9.5 mm) above the zipper stop. Key the skirt at the seamline.
2. Stitch the seam below the placket, backtacking at each end of the seam.
3. Press the seam open. Press the ⅝″ (16 mm) seam allowance of the overlap to the wrong side of the garment. Press ½″ (12.7 mm) of the underlap seam allowance to the wrong side of the garment.
4. Glue the seam allowances of the overlap to the garment.
5. With the garment and zipper right-side-up, position the folded edge of the underlap so that it almost

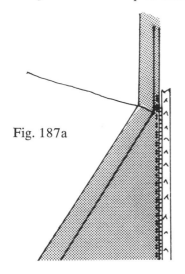

Fig. 187a

touches the zipper teeth, and the keyed lines match at the waistline. Glue or baste the zipper in place if needed. Using a zipper foot, stitch the folded edge of the garment to the zipper tape. If you stitch too close to the teeth, the zipper will be difficult to open. (Fig. 187a)
6. With the garment face-up, tape or baste the placket closed so that the overlap barely covers the stitching line on the underlap. (Fig. 187b)

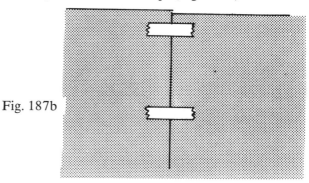

Fig. 187b

7. With the garment wrong-side-up, glue, tape, press, or baste the zipper to the seam allowance of the overlap.
8. Remove the tape or basting from the right side of the garment and open the zipper.
9. With the garment facing right-side-up, stitch the zipper into the garment ½″ (12.7 mm) from the folded edge, using the guideline on the throat plate as a gauge or by using a piece of ½″ (12.7 mm) wide transparent tape along the folded edge of the placket as a guide. (Fig. 187c) Stitch next to the edge of the tape.

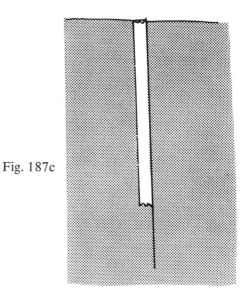

Fig. 187c

Be precise—there is little margin for error when you are stitching ½″ (12.7 mm) from the edge on ⅝″ (16 mm) seam allowance. If you have difficulty catching the seam allowance, cut 1″ (2.5 cm) seam allowances on the garment in the placket area or extend the overlap with a piece of hem tape. (Fig. 187d)

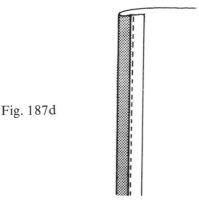

Fig. 187d

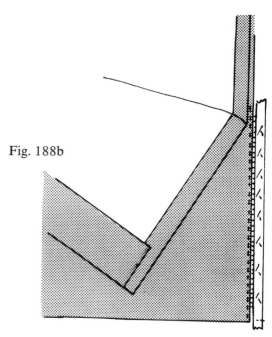

Fig. 188b

Dress with a Facing

Lapped zippers can be inserted in dresses with facings at the center back or underarm. The same technique is used on skirts with faced waistlines.

Easy method

1. Finish the neckline of the dress with a facing for a lapped zipper (see FACINGS). (Fig. 188a)

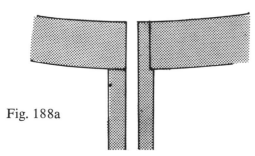

Fig. 188a

2. Key the zipper ⅜″ (9.5 mm) above the zipper stop.
3. Stitch the seam below the placket, backtacking at each end of the seam.
4. Press the seam open. Press the ⅝″ (16 mm) seam allowance of the overlap to the wrong side of the garment. Press ½″ (12.7 mm) of the underlap seam allowance to the wrong side of the garment.
5. Glue the seam allowances to the garment.
6. With the garment sections and the zipper right-side-up, position the folded edge of the underlap so that it almost touches the zipper teeth and the keyed

line on the zipper matches the neckline seam. Fold the facing and excess zipper tape to the wrong side of the garment sections, enclosing the top of the zipper tape. Baste the zipper in place if necessary. Using a zipper foot, stitch the folded edge of the garment to the zipper. (Fig. 188b) The stitching line should catch the folded edge of the facing. (Fig. 188c)

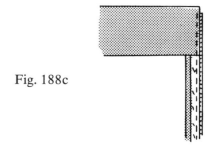

Fig. 188c

7. With the garment sections face-up, tape or baste the placket closed so that the overlap barely covers the stitching line on the underlap.
8. With the garment sections wrong-side-up, glue, baste, or press the zipper to the overlap seam allowance, matching the keyed line on the zipper to the neckline seam.
9. Fold the facing of the overlap and the excess zipper tape to the wrong side of the garment covering the top of the zipper. Glue the facing to the wrong side of the zipper tape.
10. Remove the tape or basting from the right side of the garment sections and open the zipper.

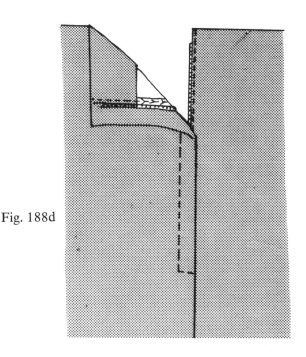

Fig. 188d

11. With the garment right-side-up, stitch the zipper into the garment ½″ (12.7 mm) from the folded edge.

Designer method

1. Key the zipper ⅜″ (9.5 mm) above the zipper teeth. Key the facing at the neckline seamline.
2. Stitch the seam below the placket, backtacking at each end of the seam.
3. Press the seam open. Press the ⅝″ (16 mm) seam allowance of the overlap to the wrong side of the garment. Press only ½″ (12.7 mm) of the underlap seam allowance to the wrong side of the garment.
4. Notch the neck edge of the facing for the underlap ½″ (12.7 mm) from the end and for the overlap ⅞″ (22.2 mm) from the end. Fold the ends of the facing to the wrong side at the notches.

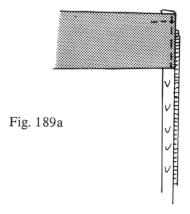

Fig. 189a

5. Stitch the facing sections to the back of the zipper tape, positioning the folded edge next to the zipper teeth with the zipper tape and teeth extending ⅛″ (3.2 mm). Match the keyed lines on the zipper tape to the keyed lines on the facing. (Fig. 189a)

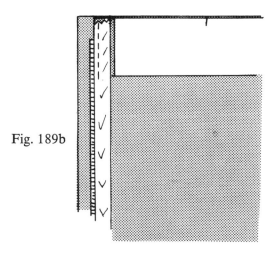

Fig. 189b

6. With the right sides together, place the underlap facing on top of the garment section. The garment will extend ½″ (12.7 mm) at the center back when you match the notches on the neck edge. (Fig. 189b)

Fold ½″ (12.7 mm) of the garment seam allowance to the right side of the garment, enclosing the zipper and facing. Pin and stitch the neckline seam. (Fig. 189c)

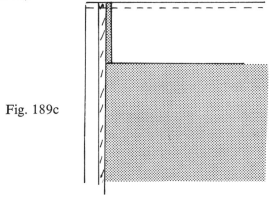

Fig. 189c

7. With the right sides together, place the overlap facing on top of the garment. The garment will extend ⅞″ (22.2 mm) at the center back when you match the notches at the neck edge. (Fig. 189d)
8. Fold the ⅝″ (16 mm) garment seam allowance

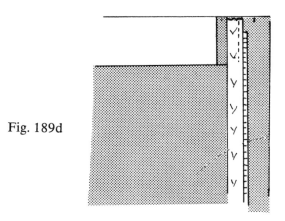

Fig. 189d

so the right side of the garment, enclosing the zipper and facing. Pin and stitch the neckline seam (Fig. 189e)

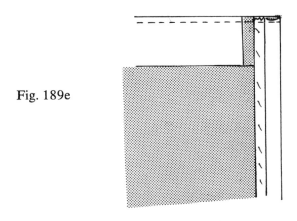

Fig. 189e

9. Turn the garment right-side-out.
10. Understitch, clip, and press.
11. Glue the seam allowances of the placket to the garment sections.
12. With the garment sections face-side-up, stitch the folded edge of the underlap to the zipper, using a zipper foot. (Fig. 189f)
13. With the garment sections face-up, tape or baste the placket closed so that the overlap barely covers the stitching line on the underlap.
14. From the wrong side of the garment, glue, tape press, or baste the zipper to the overlap seam allowance.
15. Remove the tape or basting from the right side of the garment sections. Open the zipper.
16. Stitch the zipper into the garment ½" (12.7 mm) from the folded edge using the guideline on the throat plate as a gauge.
17. Finish the neckline of the garment with a hook and eye.

DRESS PLACKETS

Dress plackets are openings located in the middle of a seam at the side or back. They are usually found in fitted garments.

Make a top stop on the zipper by sewing the zipper tape together just above the teeth by hand or machine. Insert the zipper into the placket with a lapped application.

INVISIBLE ZIPPERS

Invisible zippers are easy to set, and they look terrific on vinyl, suedes, pseudosuedes, lace, velvets, stripes, and plaids. They are great when you can't find a zipper to match the garment color or when another zipper application would detract from the garment or fabric design. Invisible zippers are available with metal teeth and polyester coils.

Use a special invisible zipper foot to set invisible zippers.

Set the zipper into an open seam. Do *not* stitch the seam below the zipper placket until the zipper is set.

1. Open the zipper and press it flat.
2. Key the zipper ⅜" (9.5 mm) above the zipper stop. Key the garment at the seamline.
3. Place the open zipper face-down on the right side of the garment with the zipper teeth on the seamline and the zipper tape in the seam allowance. Match the keyed line on the zipper to the keyed line on the garment.
4. Position the invisible zipper foot at the top of the zipper with the coil under the right-hand groove of the foot. Stitch through the tape and seam allowance down to the zipper tab and backtack. (Fig. 190a)

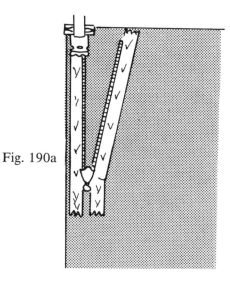

Fig. 190a

If the stitching is too close to the coil, the zipper will be difficult to open and close. If it isn't close enough, the zipper will show.

5. Close the zipper.

6. Place the garment sections right sides together. Position the other side of the zipper face-down on the right side of the garment section; pin it in place. To match stripes, clip the edge of the tape to mark the stripes.

7. If you are matching a large or complicated design, position the garment sections right-sides-up. Fold under the seam allowance of the unstitched side, matching the pattern. Tape the seam together.

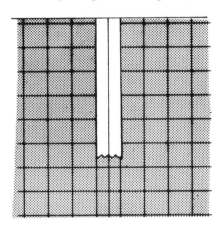

Fig. 190b

(Fig. 190b) Turn the sections over so that the wrong side of the garment is up. Tape the stitched zipper tape to the seam allowance. (Fig. 190c) Remove the tape from the right side of the garment.

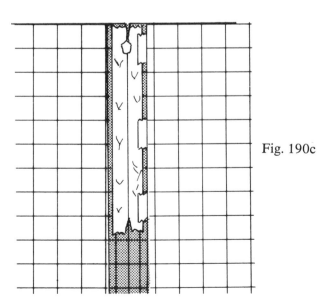

Fig. 190c

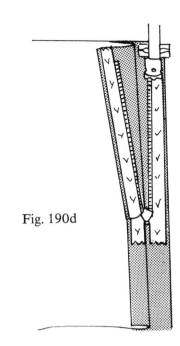

Fig. 190d

8. Open the zipper and position the foot at the top of the zipper with the coil under the left-hand groove. Remove the pin, stitch to the zipper tab, and backtack. (Fig. 190d)

9. Close the zipper. Slide the foot to the left so that the needle is in the outside notch on the right side of the foot. Stitch the seam below the zipper,

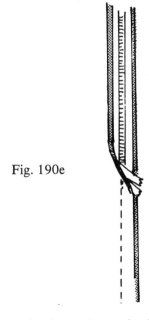

Fig. 190e

beginning ½″ (12.7 mm) above the end of the zipper stitching. Hold the ends of the zipper to the right for a smooth seam. (Fig. 190e)

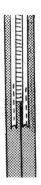

Fig. 190f

10. Stitch the ends of the zipper tape to the seam allowances. (Fig. 190f)

11. Finish the facing. Trim ⅝″ (16 mm) from the ends of the facing. With the right sides together, stitch the facing ends to the garment and zipper with a ⅜″ (9.5 mm) seam. (Fig. 190g)

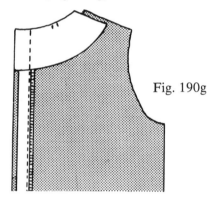

Fig. 190g

12. With the right sides together, match the facing and garment at the shoulder seams and notches to pull the facing into place at the zipper. A fold will form at the back. It sounds confusing but it's guaranteed to work! Pin and stitch the facing to the garment at the neckline. (Fig. 190h)

13. Understitch, trim, and press.

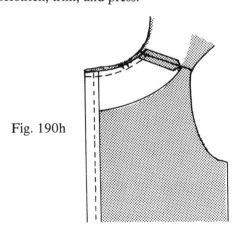

Fig. 190h

FLY ZIPPER

The fly zipper is used on men's and women's pants. The fly laps left-over-right on men's garments. On women's pants, it can lap left-over-right or right-over-left; on other garments it laps right-over-left. A fly placket is longer than a regular placket. Use a 9″ (22.9 cm) zipper.

1. If your pattern has a separate fly extension, pin the fly pattern to the garment pattern on the center-front seamline. (Fig. 191a) Cut the two pattern pieces together in one garment section.

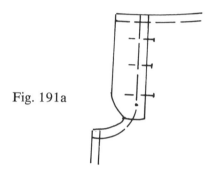

Fig. 191a

2. Mark the garment. Clip the waistline of both sections at the center front. Clip the waistline on the underlap extension ⅝″ (16 mm) from the center notch. Mark both sections at the end of the placket with a pin. (Fig. 191b) Press a line at the center

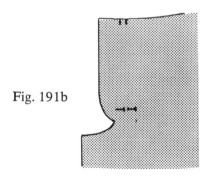

Fig. 191b

front of the overlap. Clip the seam allowance at the bottom of the fly so that it will lie flat. Press a line on the underlap extension connecting the notch at the waistline to the cut edge of the crotch seam. The extension will be interfaced to this line. (Fig. 191c) Mark the center front of the underlap with chalk or soap.

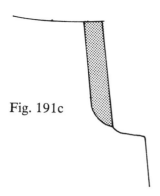

Fig. 191c

3. Use the fly pattern to cut the interfacing. Trim the interfacing for the underlap ⅝″ (16 mm) along the straight edge. Fuse or glue the interfacing to the fly extensions—the interfacing meets the pressed line.

4. Stitch the crotch seam for 2″ (5.1 cm) beginning at the end of the placket which is marked with a pin. Do not stitch to the cut edge, *except* when you're making jeans and children's pants.

5. Position the folded edge of the underlap close to the zipper teeth with the excess zipper at the waist. Using the zipper foot, pin and stitch the underlap to the zipper from the bottom to the top. (Fig. 191d)

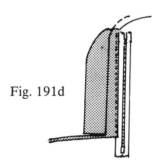

Fig. 191d

6. With the zipper closed, baste the garment sections together at the center front with tape or pins.

7. Turn the garment wrong-side-up. Pin and stitch the zipper tape to the overlap facing. (Fig. 191e)

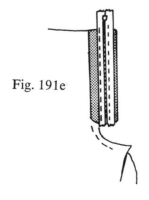

Fig. 191e

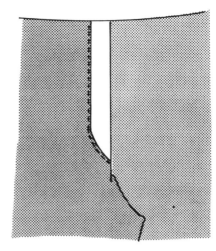

Fig. 191f

8. Pin or glue the fly facing to the wrong side of the garment.

9. On the right side of the garment, indicate the fly stitching line with a cardboard template, soap, or chalk. If you use a template, secure it with double-stick tape. (Fig. 191f) Topstitch the fly.

10. Make a bartack at the end of the fly.

11. Set the waistband to the garment.

12. If the zipper is too long, *open* the zipper, then trim it at the waistline.

HAND-FINISHED ZIPPERS

The hand-finished zipper application is often used on homemade garments that don't deserve this elegant treatment. Hand-finished applications are *only* appropriate on garments made from luxury fabrics. They aren't suitable for inexpensive cottons, polyesters, or washable garments.

The following suggestions will save you time and ensure success when your garment deserves the best —a custom-finished zipper set by hand.

1. Press the seam allowances to the wrong side of the garment. If the seam is shaped, press it over a ham.

2. Working from the wrong side of the garment, baste the zipper into the garment, easing the garment slightly. Open the zipper so that you can baste down one side and up the other, always working so that the edge is in your left hand. (Fig. 192a)

3. Working from the right side of the garment, sew the open zipper into the placket with a prickstitch or tiny backstitch and a single strand of polyester or size-A silk thread—buttonhole twist and topstitching

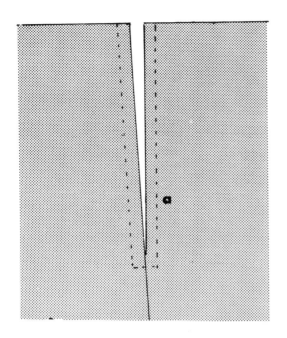

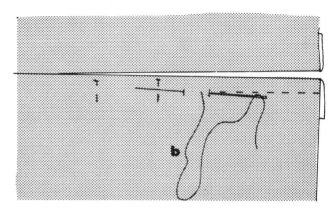

Fig. 192

threads are too heavy for most fabrics. (Fig. 192b) Work from the bottom to the top on the left side of the zipper and from the top to the bottom on the right side.

EXPOSED ZIPPERS

An exposed zipper is not only utilitarian but also decorative. It can be applied where there is no seam. (Fig. 193)

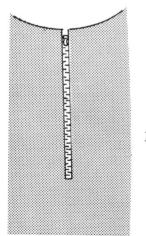

Fig. 193

Slashed Placket
This quick-and-easy application is attractive on knitted fabrics. The zipper can be left exposed on the

wrong side of the garment, or the opening can be faced to conceal the zipper tape.

If the knit will run, cut the garment out so that the fabric will run from the hem up.

1. Allow a ⅜″ (9.5 mm) seam allowance at the garment neckline.
2. With the wrong sides together, press the center of the garment along the fold the length of the zipper plus 2″ (5.1 cm). (Fig. 194a)

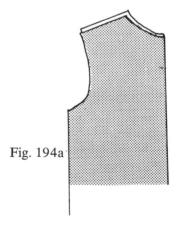

Fig. 194a

3. If the placket will be finished with a hook and eye above the zipper, key the zipper ⅝″ (16 mm) above the top of the zipper stop. If it won't have a hook and eye, key it ¼″ (6.4 mm) above the zipper stop. Key the garment at the seamline.
4. With the garment face-up, place the zipper on

the folded line with the right side up so that the keyed lines on the zipper tape match the keyed lines on the garment. Use a pin to mark the garment at the end of the placket ¼″–½″ (6.4 mm–12.7 mm) below the zipper stop.

This placement will make the opening longer than the finished placket. The excess will be eased to the zipper tape, eliminating a roller-coaster effect on the finished garment.

5. Place the zipper face-down on the right side of the garment so that the bottom of the zipper stop is at the marked point. Tape the zipper in place.

6. Using the zipper foot, stitch across the end of the zipper tape with a very short stitch, beginning $\frac{1}{16}$″ (1.6 mm) before the edge of the coil and ending $\frac{1}{16}$″ (1.6 mm) after it. Stitch back and forth to secure the zipper. (Fig. 194b)

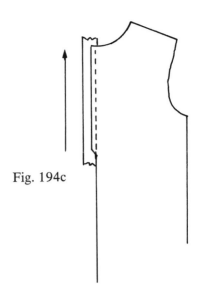

Fig. 194c

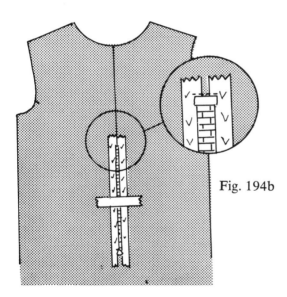

Fig. 194b

7. Hold the zipper in the finished position and check the zipper placement.

8. If the zipper teeth are narrow, slash the placket on the pressed line to the stitched line at the bottom of the zipper. If the zipper is wide, slash toward the stitched line, stopping ½″ (12.7 mm) above it. Clip to the ends of the stitched line.

9. Pull the zipper into place, matching the keyed lines on the zipper tape to the keyed lines on the garment. Pin the zipper to the garment at the neckline. Pin and stitch a ¼″ (6.4 mm) seam from the bottom of the zipper to the neckline with the garment on top. Stitch close to the zipper teeth and ease the garment as you stitch. (Fig. 194c) Repeat on the other side of the zipper.

10. Steam the zipper, using a portable steamer, if you have one.

11. If desired, topstitch around the zipper or face the zipper.

Reinforced Placket

Reinforce the placket opening on woven and knitted fabrics with a line of stitching, then topstitch the zipper in place.

The finished placket width must be wide enough to expose the zipper coil and allow the tab to move smoothly up and down the coil.

If the top of the zipper is to be set even with the finished neck edge, the placket length will be the length of the zipper coil plus ¾″ (19.1 mm). If the placket will be finished with a hook and eye above the zipper, the placket length will be 1″ (2.5 cm) longer than the zipper.

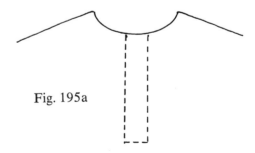

Fig. 195a

1. Mark the stitching lines of the placket on the wrong side of the garment. (Fig. 195a)

2. Staystitch just inside the marked lines. Reinforce the corners with a short stitch.

3. Slash the center of the placket, stopping ½" (12.7 mm) from the end. Clip to the corners. (Fig. 195b)

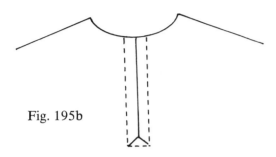

Fig. 195b

4. Press the seam allowances of the placket to the wrong side of the garment.
5. Glue, tape, press, or baste the zipper into the placket so that the zipper is centered with the zipper stop exposed.
6. Using a zipper foot, topstitch close to the folded edge to secure the zipper. (Fig. 195c)

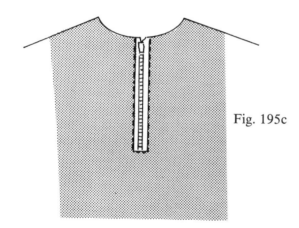

Fig. 195c

Faced Placket
Face the openings on better garments and stretchy fabrics.

1. Mark the opening with a snip at the neckline center and a pin at the end.
2. From a lightweight, firmly woven fabric such as organdy, organza, or sheath lining, cut a placket facing 3" (7.6 cm) wide and 2" (5.1 cm) longer than the finished placket.
3. Mark the stitching lines of the placket on the wrong side of the facing.
4. With right sides together and the facing on top,

match the center marks. Pin or baste the garment and facing together.
5. Stitch the facing to the garment on the marked lines, reinforcing the corners with a short stitch. (Fig. 196a)

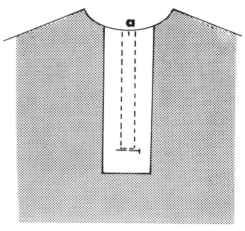

Fig. 196

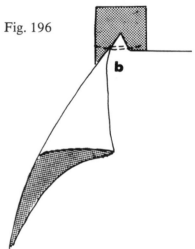

6. Slash the center of the placket, stopping ½" (12.7 mm) from the end. Clip to the corners.
7. Turn the facing to the wrong side of the garment, understitch, and press.
8. Glue, press, or tape the zipper into the placket so that the zipper will be centered with the zipper stop exposed.
9. With the garment face-up, fold the hem up to expose the triangle at the bottom of the placket, the facing section, and the zipper tape. Using a zipper foot, stitch across the bottom of the placket just above the facing-garment seamline. (Fig. 196b) Repeat on each side of the placket, stitching from the bottom to the top of the placket.
10. Press.

Placket Facings

Zippers located on the garment front are often designed to be worn open. The opening will be much more attractive if the zipper tape is hidden by a facing.

1. Make a facing pattern. Trace the center fold and the cut edges of the garment at the neckline and shoulder. Extend the facing 2" (5.1 cm) on the shoulder and the length of the zipper plus 2" (5.1 cm) on the center front.

2. Connect the shoulder and center front. Add a seam allowance to the center front. The width of the seam allowance is equal to the zipper tape width—the distance between the edge of the tape and the teeth. (Fig. 197a)

3. Set the zipper into the garment opening by the method of your choice.

4. Place the right side of the facing on top of the wrong side of the zipper so that the cut edge of the facing seam allowance matches the edge of the zipper tape. With the facing section to the base of the machine, stitch the seam allowance to the zipper tape, using a zipper foot. (Fig. 197b) Repeat on the other side.

5. Butt the folded edges of the facing together below the zipper coil and zigzag them together. (Fig. 197c) Clip the facing, if necessary, to make it lie flat.

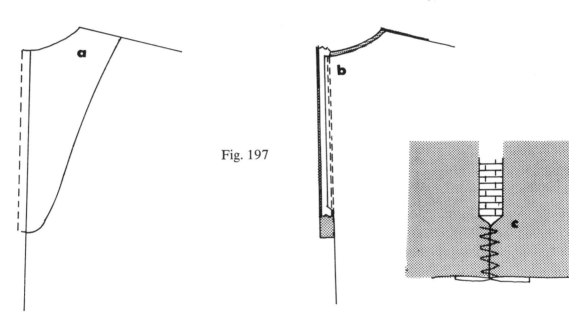

Fig. 197

BUTTONHOLES, BUTTONS, AND OTHER CLOSURES

Buttons and buttonholes are a practical way to open and close garments; they can also be an important design feature. They can beautifully accent a well-made garment or expose a lousy seamstress.

BUTTONHOLES

Bound buttonholes are used on soft-tailored garments. Machine-worked buttonholes are used on casual garments, man-tailored jackets, children's wear, and washable garments. Hand-worked buttonholes are used on delicate and soft fabrics, custom garments, and men's wear.

Buttonholes are located on the right front for women's garments and the left front for men's garments.

Buttonholes should be identical in length and width, spaced evenly and located an equal distance from the edge of the garment.

Buttonhole Size

The buttonhole size is determined by the diameter and thickness of the button. Use a narrow piece of paper to measure around the button, remove the button, and fold the paper in half to determine the minimum length required for the buttonhole. (Fig. 198)

Fig. 198

The button should slip in and out of the buttonhole easily. If it is the least bit tight, the buttonhole is too small and the corners will pull out. Rough buttons require a larger buttonhole than smooth ones, even if they are the same size. Bound buttonholes have a tendency to "shrink" when the facing is finished, so don't be caught short.

Bound Buttonholes

Bound buttonholes are used most often on women's better tailored garments. They are seldom used on children's and men's wear.

Well-made bound buttonholes are flat with even welts and square corners.

They should be made before the facing and lining are attached to the garment. Handling is easier if the buttonholes are made in the garment front before the front is sewn to other sections.

The buttonhole area is always interfaced. *Never* trim away the interfacing in the buttonhole rectangle.

Make bound buttonholes when you are fresh. Always make a sample buttonhole in the same fabric as the garment *and* try the button in it. On the garment, work the buttonholes from the hem up. Your confidence and ability will improve with each buttonhole, positioning the best ones where they are most noticeable.

Your buttonholes will look professional every time if you mark accurately, stitch precisely, clip exactly, and press carefully. There are no other secrets!

Buttonhole size. Select a button that doesn't vary greatly from the size specified on the pattern.

Bound buttonholes should be at least 1″ (2.5 cm) long to look right. If the button is too small for this length, which is rare, the end farthest from the garment center can be slipstitched together to make the buttonhole smaller. There is an exception—bound buttonholes on silk blouses may be very narrow (⅛″ or 3.2 mm total and less than 1″ (2.5 cm) long.

The welts or lips of the buttonhole are usually ⅛″ (3.2 mm) wide, making the finished buttonhole ¼″ (6.4 mm) wide. You may prefer narrower welts in lightweight fabrics and wider ones in bulky fabrics. Always relate the width of the buttonhole to its length. (Fig. 199a) A short, wide buttonhole (Fig. 199b) looks just as ridiculous as a long, skinny one. (Fig. 199c)

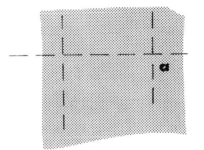

Fig. 200

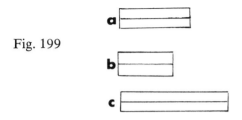

Fig. 199

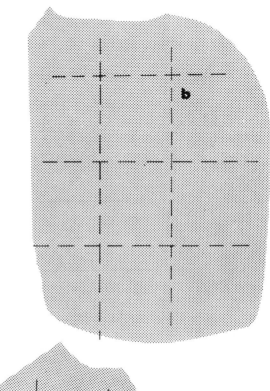

Buttonhole Location

1. If you are using a sew-in or nonfusible interfacing, mark the location for each buttonhole on the right side of the garment with hand basting. Baste using white thread. Use silk thread on fabrics such as silks, piles, and some woollens, which can be marred when pressed.

Hand basting is the quickest, easiest way to get quality results when you are marking the buttonhole locations—machine stitching takes longer to rip out and chalk doesn't hold the fabric and interfacing together.

If you are using a fusible interfacing, mark the buttonhole location with soap or chalk.

2. Place a line of basting through the center of each buttonhole to mark the *location* line. Extend it ½″ (12.7 mm) beyond each end of the buttonhole.

3. Place basting lines at right angles to the location line at the beginning and end of each buttonhole to mark the *termination* lines. They should extend above and below the location line at least 1″ (2.5 cm). Each marked buttonhole looks like an "H." (Fig. 200a) It is easier to baste all termination lines at one time. The finished results will look like a ladder. (Fig. 200b)

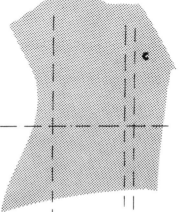

4. Mark the center front of the garment on the right and left sections if you haven't already. The garment center on the right front is located ⅛″ (3.2 mm) from the end of the buttonhole. (Fig. 200c) Match the centers when you fit the garment.

Strip Method

This method is most suitable for use on firmly woven woollens, double knits and nonwovens. As a general rule, do not use the strip method on silks, linens, or other fabrics which will fray badly, unless you're using a fusible interfacing.

Make the buttonholes on the garment from the hem up.

1. Each buttonhole has two welts. Each welt should be the length of the buttonhole plus one inch. The welts are usually cut on the lengthwise grain. Cut them on the bias for stripes, plaids, checks, ribs, piles, and tweed fabrics.

2. To make the welts, trim one side of a fabric scrap on the lengthwise thread (or bias). If you cannot see the grain clearly, pull a lengthwise thread and cut along it. *Make no other cuts at this time.* If your scrap is small, and you have several buttonholes to make, use other scraps; one long strip isn't really necessary, but it is a timesaver.

3. Press a fold along the lengthwise grain (or bias cut) an inch from the cut edge with the wrong sides together. Working with a larger piece like this eliminates that wavy line you often get when you press narrow strips in half. It also prevents burned fingers. Stitch a guideline ⅛″ (3.2 mm) from the folded edge of the welt strip. (Fig. 201a)

4. Trim the strip through both thicknesses so that the stitching line is in the *middle* of the strip. (Fig. 201b) You *must* stitch and trim accurately. If you trim too much, the welts will lap on the finished buttonhole. If you don't trim enough, there will be a gap between the welts on the finished buttonhole. (If the edges of the welt ravel excessively, cut the strip on the bias, use fray-retardant on the edges or use another method to make the buttonholes.)

5. Place the cut edge of the welt strip along the buttonhole location line on the right side of the garment. The welt will extend ½″ (12.7 mm) beyond the termination line at each end. Mark the termination lines on the welt strip with soap or tape to ensure accuracy when you stitch. (Fig. 201c)

6. Set the machine for a short stitch (20 spi or 1.5 mm) so that it won't be noticeable if you are one stitch off. Short stitches will also reinforce the stitching line. Stitch on top of the guideline on the welt, or a hairline toward the fold. If necessary, baste the welt in place by hand to check the placement. Begin and end the stitching with a spot tack or knot the threads by hand. (Fig. 201d)

The stitching must be ended securely at each end. If you can't or don't like spot tacking or knotting, begin stitching in the center of the strip, stitch to the termination line. With the needle anchored in the fabric, pivot. Stitch to the other end on top of the first stitching line, pivot and return to the center. (Fig. 201e)

7. Place the other welt strip so that the cut edge touches the cut edge of the first strip and the location line. Stitch the welt in place. (Fig. 201f)

8. Cord limp fabrics and *all* bias-cut buttonholes so that the buttonhole won't stretch or gap. Thread a tapestry needle with acrylic or wool yarn and pull it through the welt strip. (Fig. 201g)

9. Slash the buttonhole from the wrong side of the garment. Do *not* cut into the welts. Begin in the center of the buttonhole and slash to ¼″ (6.4 mm) short of the end. Carefully clip to each corner, making a triangle at each end. If you don't clip far enough, a pleat will form at the end; if you clip too far, the fabric will fray at the corners. (Fig. 201h)

10. Use fray-retardant at each corner. Be sure to check for spotting on a scrap before using it.

11. To turn the buttonhole, work with the garment face-up. Push the welts through to the underside. (Fig. 201i) Continue with the garment face-up as you straighten the welts; now, admire your work.

12. Baste the welts together with a diagonal basting stitch. (Fig. 201j)

13. With the garment face-up, fold the garment and interfacing back to expose the triangle and welt ends. Use a short stitch to stitch across the end *one* time as closely as possible to the fold of the garment. Swing the stitches in a tiny bit at the corners to catch all cut threads. Too much swing will make a pleat. (Fig. 201k) Stitch the triangle on the other end.

13. Press the buttonhole from the wrong side on a well-padded surface.

14. Trim the welts so that they won't be stitched into the facing seamline. (Fig. 201L)

Fig. 201a

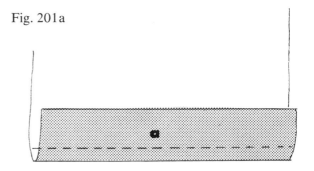

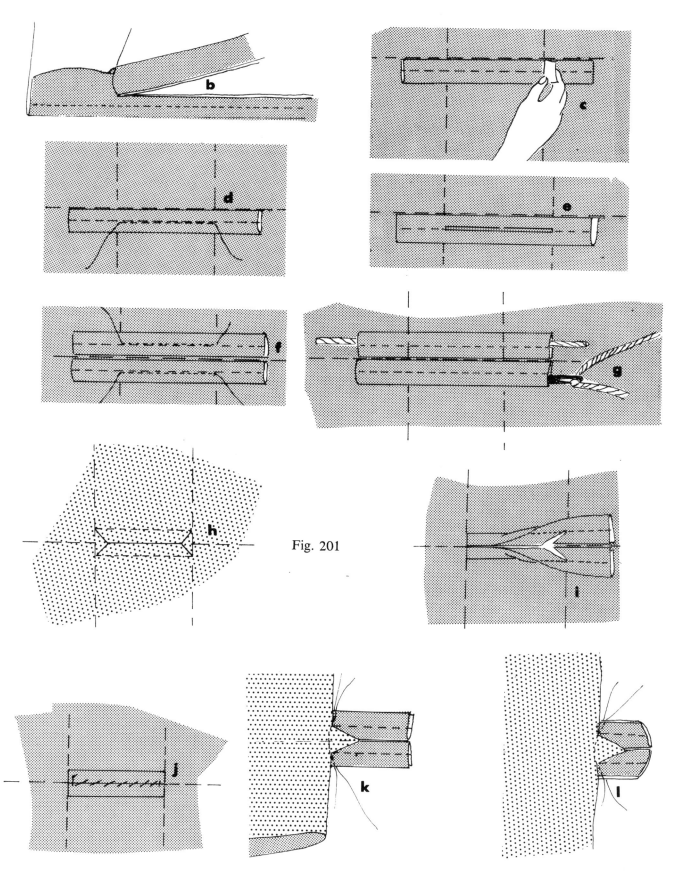

Fig. 201

Patch Method

The patch method for bound buttonholes is suitable for garments made of fabrics that fray easily and are bulky.

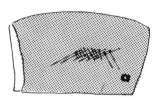

Fig. 202

1. Mark the buttonhole locations.
2. Cut the patch from the fashion fabric on the bias 2″ (5.1 cm) wide and the length of the buttonhole plus 1½″ (3.8 cm).
3. Crease the patch in the center, stretching the patch slightly on the creased line. (Fig. 202a)
4. With the right sides together, place the patch on the garment so that the creased line of the patch is on the location line, stretching it again. Stretching the patch guarantees a perfect, finished buttonhole that won't gap.

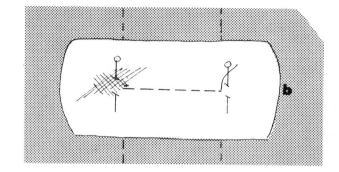

5. Pin the patch in place at each end, with the pins at right angles to the location line. Baste the creased line of the patch to the location line of the garment. (Fig. 202b)
6. Using a short stitch for security and accuracy at the corners and ends, stitch around the buttonhole. Begin stitching in the center ⅛″ (3.2 mm) above the location line; continue in a rectangle around the buttonhole and overlap the stitches at the starting point ½″ (12.7 mm). Pivot at each corner with the needle down. Count the stitches at each end above and below the basted line to ensure that both ends will be stitched the same. (Fig. 202c) Stitch all the buttonholes. Check the rectangles—they should be equal in size and evenly spaced.

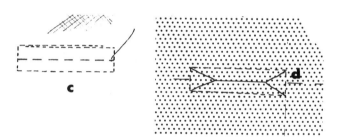

7. Clip the rectangles to the corners. (Fig. 202d) Use fray-retardant on the cut edges. Test before using it on the garment.
8. Push the patch through the slash. The area within the rectangle, the seam allowances, will fill the welts of the finished buttonhole. Working from the right side of the garment, adjust the welts so that they are centered in the opening and equal in width. Pin or glue the welts in place.

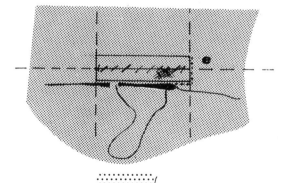

9. Baste the welts together, using a diagonal stitch.
10. Use a fine needle and a tiny backstitch to permanently sew the welts in place. (Fig. 202e)
11. Fold the garment and interfacing back to expose the triangle at one end. Stitch across the end with a short stitch, swinging in slightly to catch the corners. (Fig. 202f) Stitch the triangle on the other end.
12. Press the buttonhole from the wrong side on a well-padded surface.
13. Trim the patch so that it won't be stitched into a seamline.

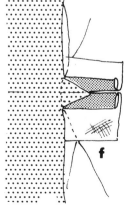

Faced or Window Method

The faced or window method is popular with many home sewers. It is suitable to use on fabrics that fray easily and bulky or stiff fabrics.

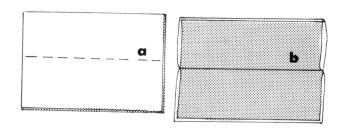

1. Mark the buttonhole locations.
2. Cut a bias patch from a lightweight, tightly woven lining fabric or nylon tricot 2″ (5.1 cm) wide and 1½″ (3.8 cm) longer than the buttonhole.

A lining fabric made of natural fibres can be pressed sharply and makes a better window than a synthetic or permanent-press fabric. Silk organza and cotton organdy make the best patches. Use scraps from another garment or select a lining fabric that is a mixture of synthetic and natural fibres if if you don't have the right color in silk or cotton. The right color can sometimes be obtained by dyeing the patches with permanent-color soft-tip pens.

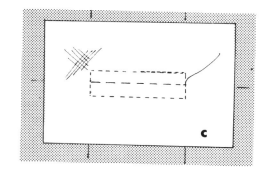

3. Prepare the buttonhole welts. Cut the two welts for each buttonhole on the straight grain or bias 2″ (5.1 cm) wide and the length of the buttonhole plus 1½″ (3.8 cm). With the right sides together, baste the welt centers together on the lengthwise grain or bias. (Fig. 203a) Open the welts so that the right sides are out and press. (Fig. 203b)
4. Baste the facing patch to the right side of the garment on the location line.

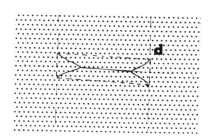

5. Using a short stitch for security and accuracy at the corners and ends, stitch around the buttonhole. Begin stitching in the center ⅛″ (3.2 mm) above the buttonhole, continue in a rectangle around the buttonhole, overlapping the stitches at the starting point ½″ (12.7 mm). Pivot at each corner with the needle down. Count the stitches at each end above and below the basted line to ensure that both ends will be the same. (Fig. 203c)

Fig. 203

6. Clip the rectangle to the corners. (Fig. 203d) Use fray-retardant on the cut edges. Test before using it on the garment.

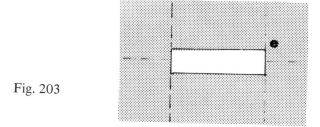

7. Push the facing through the buttonhole. (Fig. 203e)
8. Understitch the long sides of the buttonhole to make pressing easier. Use the inside of the presser foot as a guide to understitch.
9. Press from the wrong side of the garment, rolling the seamline toward the patch.

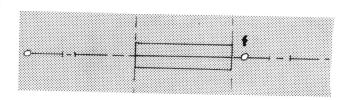

10. Center the welts in the opening or window. This is the most difficult step in the faced method. Glue or fuse the welts to hold them in place when you stitch.

a) Gluing: Working from the right side of the garment, pin the center of the welt section at each

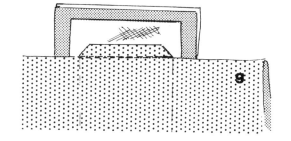

end of the buttonhole. (Fig. 203f) Glue the welt section to the patch.

b) Fusing: Working from the wrong side of the garment, place a short piece of ¼″ (6.4 mm) wide fusible agent on the buttonhole patch. Steam the fusible until it becomes tacky. Don't let the iron touch the fusible. Working from the right side of the garment, pin the center of the welt section at each end of the buttonhole. Press the welt sections into place with your fingers. Steam the garment to fuse the welts.

11. Fold the garment back so that the patch seamline above the buttonhole is exposed. Using a short stitch, stitch on top of this seamline to secure the welt to the patch. (Fig. 203g) Repeat on the line below the buttonhole and at each end. Stitching the welts in place this way instead of stitching a rectangle around the buttonhole ensures square corners instead of rounded ones.

12. Press the buttonhole from the wrong side on a well-padded surface.

13. Trim the welts so that they won't be stitched into a seamline.

Window Method for Nonwoven Fabrics

A variation of the window buttonhole method can be made quickly and easily on nonwoven fabrics.

1. Mark the buttonhole locations. Carefully mark the window around each buttonhole so that it is the exact size of the finished buttonhole. Cut out the window using a mat knife, embroidery scissors, or seam ripper. Be very careful. Do not overcut at the corners and avoid a jagged line. (Fig. 204a)

2. Prepare the buttonhole welts. Cut the welts for each buttonhole 2″ (5.1 cm) wide and the length of the buttonhole plus 1½″ (3.8 cm). With the right sides together, baste the welt centers together on the lengthwise grain.

3. Open the welts so the right sides are out and press.

4. Center the welts in the window. Glue or fuse the welts in place.

5. Edgestitch around the window to secure the welts. (Fig. 204b) If you have used permanent glue or fusible agent, this step can be delayed until the facing is set. Then, when you edgestitch, the facing also will be secured.

Facing Finishes for Bound Buttonholes
Hand finish

1. Set the facing to the garment.

2. Glue or baste the facing to the interfacing around each buttonhole.

3. Place a pin in each end of the buttonhole to indicate the length and location on the facing. (Fig. 205a)

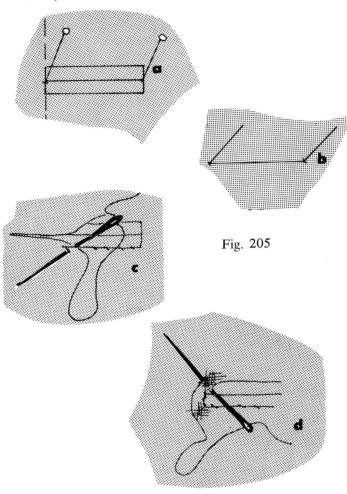

Fig. 205

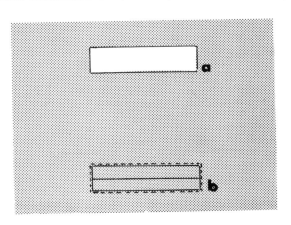

Fig. 204

4. Slash the facing between the pins. (Fig. 205b) Remove the pins and clip 1/16″ (1.6 mm) further at each end of the slash. If you don't slash the facing longer than the buttonhole, the buttonhole will shrink when you slipstitch the facing in place.

If your button is small and does not require a 1″ (2.5 cm) buttonhole, shorten the slash on the end away from the garment center. Use fray-retardant around the slash. Test before using it on the garment.

5. Using a small needle with thread to match the garment, begin in the center of the buttonhole. Turn under a scant 1/8″ (3.2 mm) and slipstitch it to the stitching line of the buttonhole. (Fig. 205c) (It is easier to sew around the buttonhole twice than to make tiny stitches.)

6. Use the point of the needle to shape the facing into a rectangle at each end. Overcast each corner firmly to make it square. (Fig. 205d)

Machine finish. This finish is suitable for garments made of leather, vinyl, suede, or pseudosuede. It can be used on knit fabrics that don't run but it cheapens the garment.

1. Set the facing to the garment.
2. Glue or baste the facing to the interfacing between the buttonholes.
3. Stitch-in-the-ditch around the buttonhole. (Fig. 206a)

If the buttonhole was made by the window method for nonwovens and has been edgestitched, stitch next to the cut edge of the window. If it hasn't been edgestitched, edgestitch around the window.
4. Slash the rectangle in the center (Fig. 206b) or cut out the facing rectangle. (Fig. 206c)
5. On sportswear, you may want to stitch another rectangle around the buttonhole. (Fig. 206d)

Faced finish. Face the facing to finish the buttonhole on difficult-to-handle fabrics.

1. Set the facing to the garment.
2. For each buttonhole cut a bias patch of lining fabric 2″ (5.1 cm) wide and 1″ (2.5 cm) longer than the buttonhole.
3. Pin the patch to the right side of the facing, centering it over the buttonhole.
4. Use pins to mark the corners of each buttonhole exactly on the facing.

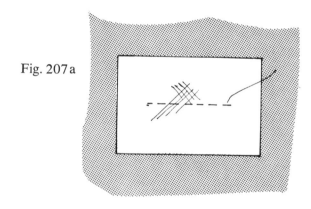

Fig. 207a

5. Baste the patch in place on the location line. (Fig. 207a)
6. Using a short stitch, stitch a rectangle connecting the corners. (Fig. 207b)

Fig. 207b

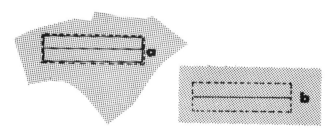

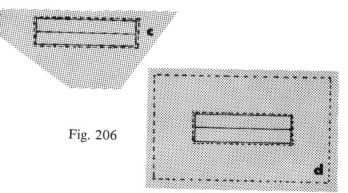

Fig. 206

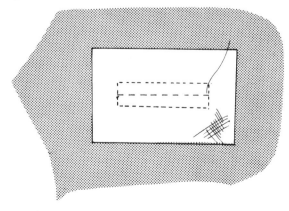

Fig. 207c

7. Slash to the corners and turn the patch to the wrong side of the facing. Press. (Fig. 207c)
8. Use fray-retardant on the cut edges. Test first.
9. Slipstitch the finished edges of the facing to the stitching line of the buttonhole. (Fig. 207d)

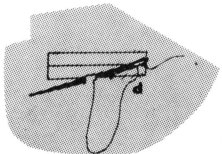

Fig. 207d

Machine-made Buttonholes

⚙ If the buttonhole area is not interfaced, insert a piece of fusible agent that is 1″ (2.5 cm) longer and wider than the buttonhole between the garment and facing.

⚙ Skipped stitches are often a problem when you machine stitch buttonholes. Use a leveller, stitch with paper or use a needle lubricant to eliminate them.

⚙ Loosen the upper tension slightly to make a professional-looking buttonhole.

⚙ Use the seam ripper to slash machine-made buttonholes. Insert the ripper straight down into one end, slash to the center. Repeat at the other end.

⚙ If you prefer using the seam ripper to slash toward the ends of the buttonhole, insert a pin in each end at right angles to the buttonhole to avoid slashing the buttonhole stitches.

⚙ If the interfacing shows when the buttonhole is slashed, use a soft-tip pen the color of the garment to dye the interfacing.

Slashed Buttonholes

This is an easy buttonhole to make on nonwoven fabrics such as suede, pseudosuede, leather, or vinyl.

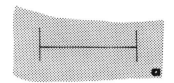

Fig. 208

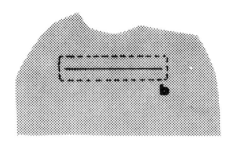

1. Mark the buttonhole length and location exactly with soap or chalk. (Fig. 208a)
2. Using a short stitch, stitch around the buttonhole. Begin stitching at the end near the garment edge ⅛″ (3.2 mm) above the buttonhole; continue in a rectangle around the buttonhole. Overlap the stitches at the starting point ½″ (12.7 mm) and spot tack. Pivot at each corner with the needle anchored. Count the stitches at each end above and below the buttonhole line to ensure that both ends will be equal. (Fig. 208b)
3. Slash the buttonhole through the center with a single-edge razor blade, mat knife, or seam ripper.

BUTTONS

The color and the style of the button are the primary concerns of most home sewers when they select a button. However, the durability and washability are equally important.

Will the finish come off, crack, peel, scratch, or discolor with wear? Will the button become lighter, darker, cloudy, rust, or cause fabric abrasion? Is the dye colorfast to dry cleaning and/or laundering? Will the shank break? Ask these questions every time you select buttons.

Marking the Button Location

1. Fold the garment with the right sides together, matching the neckline, the edges, and the hemline.
2. Place a pin through the end of each buttonhole near the garment edge into the section to be marked.

If the buttonholes are vertical, place a pin in the first buttonhole at the top of the buttonhole. Place a pin in the center of the remaining buttonholes.

3. Carefully lift the buttonholes off the pins without pulling the pins out. The pins mark the button locations.

Sewing the Button by Machine

Sew flat buttons onto children's garments, work clothes, and garments of lightweight fabrics by machine.

1. Tape or glue the button in place on the right side of the garment. If you want a button shank, place a pin or matchstick on top of the button between the holes.
2. Center the button under the zigzag foot or button foot.
3. Lower the foot to hold the button securely.
4. Drop the feed dog.
5. Turn the handwheel manually to adjust the stitch width for the holes in the button.
6. Set the stitch width.
7. Stitch the button in place.

Sewing Buttons on by Hand

Sew the buttons onto all better garments by hand.

1. Cut a length of polyester or silk thread 30″ (76.2 cm) long, that is, an arm's length, to secure the buttons. Wax the thread with beeswax or a white candle to strengthen it.
2. Fold the thread in half and thread the folded end into a crewel needle. (Fig. 209a) Knot the folded and free ends together. (You may prefer to use a length of embroidery floss to sew the buttons in place. Thread all six strands into the needle and knot one end.)
3. Insert the needle into the right side of the garment ½″ (12.7 mm) from the button location. Take a stitch between the garment and facing to the pin that marks the button location. (Fig. 209b) Take several small stitches in place at the button location. Cut off the knot.
4. To avoid an unsightly indentation when the garment is buttoned, sew the button on with a thread shank that is as long as the garment section is thick. The shank may be 1⁄16″ (1.6 mm) long on a silk blouse or ¾″ (19.1 mm) long on a heavy coat.
5. To control the shank length, hold the button in the left hand the desired distance from the garment section while sewing it on. Do not sew the top button through the facing on coats and suits.

You'll need only a few stitches to secure each button since you are using several strands of thread.

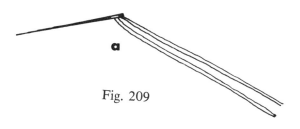

Fig. 209

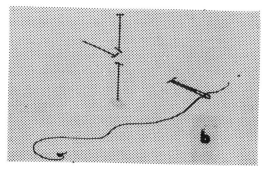

If the button has a shank, the combined thread-button shank equals the garment thickness.
6. Strengthen the shank with several blanket stitches around it.
7. Make several small stitches close to the shank to fasten the thread. Make a knot and take a stitch away from the button with the needle moving between the outer fabric and facing. Hold the thread taut and cut the thread close to the garment. The end will disappear between the fabric layers.

Covered Buttons

Buttons are easier to cover if you wet the fabric before you mould it over the form. Some fabrics are weaker when wet, so don't stretch, pull, or tug too hard.

If the fabric is thin, use an underlining fabric or a double thickness so that the mould won't show through.

Custom-made buttons are very reasonable to have made and are available in many sizes and shapes. This service is offered by many fabric stores and several mail-order companies.

Generally, covered buttons are more appropriate on lightweight blouses and dresses. Try to avoid using them on heavier weight fabrics.

BUTTON LOOPS

Loops are placed along the edge of a garment to fasten edge-to-edge and lapped openings. The loops are usually secured in the garment-facing seam, but they don't have to be.

Fabric Loops Inserted into a Seam

1. Make enough self-filled or corded tubing for all the loops. The tubing doesn't have to be one continuous strip.
2. Cut the tubing for each button loop the finished length plus two seam allowances. Experiment with a length of bias tubing and the button to determine the length of the loop.
3. Make snips on the seam allowance of the right front to indicate the top and bottom of each loop. (Fig. 210a)

4. Pin the loops to the seam allowance on the right side of the garment, matching the cut ends of the loops to the cut edge of the garment. The seamline on the loop should be visible. (Fig. 210b)
5. With the right sides together, stitch the loops to the seam allowance.
6. With the right sides together, stitch the facing to the garment front, enclosing the loops.
7. Understitch if the facing won't be seen.
8. If you are positioning a number of loops, make a gauge in order to position the loops quickly and evenly. (Fig. 210c)

The gauge width is cut equal to the distance between the top and bottom of each loop. The length is equal to the distance between the top of one loop and the top of the next loop. The length of the gauge is also the distance between the buttons.

Fabric Loops Inserted into a Fold

Contrary to popular opinion, loops do *not* have to be secured in a seam—they can be inserted into a folded edge.

1. Make enough self-filled or corded tubing for all the loops.
2. Cut a strip of tubing for each loop that is the finished length plus 1″ (2.5 cm).
3. Using a tapestry or knitting needle, make a hole on the foldline for each end of the loop. Carefully work the threads apart without breaking them. (Fig. 211a)

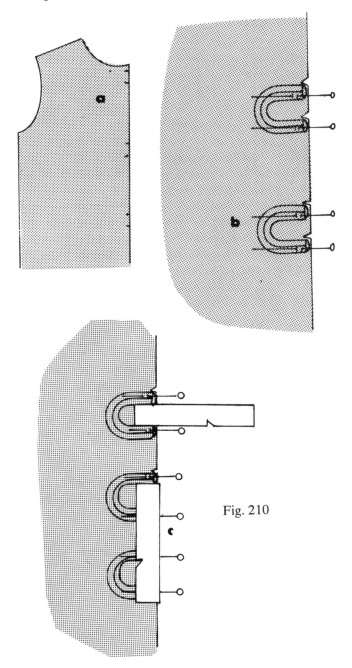

Fig. 210

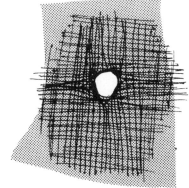

Fig. 211a

4. Insert the loop into the holes from the right side of the garment. (Fig. 211b)
5. Adjust the loop so that it is the desired size.
6. Sew the seam allowances of the loop by hand to the interfacing.

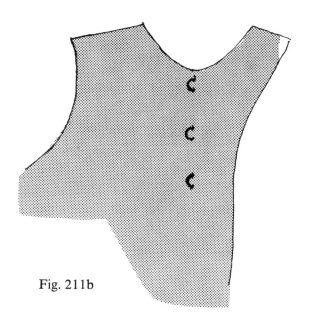

Fig. 211b

Thread Loops

Thread loops are used with buttons on infants' wear and delicate garments. They should be located so that there is little stress on them. The loop can be straight or rounded. It will stretch when it's used so should be made a little shorter to allow for this stretching. The chain or blanket-stitched loops can be made from a single strand of regular thread or silk buttonhole twist.

OTHER CLOSURES

Decorative Closures

Many designs can be finished quickly and attractively with easy-to-apply decorative snaps, frogs, eyelets and grommets.

Hooks and Eyes

Hooks and eyes are strong fasteners which are used to secure the garment inconspicuously. They are usually sewn at the top of a zipper placket or on a waistband, but you can use them to fasten an entire placket instead of using a zipper or buttons and buttonholes.

Regular hooks and eyes are available in several sizes from 0 (small) to 3 (large). Special hooks and eyes and fur hooks and eyes are heavier and designed to withstand the stress of waistband closures.

If the garment is fastened so that the finished edges meet, use a hook and a round eye. If the edges overlap, use a hook and a straight eye.

Application

1. Position the hook so that the end is set back ⅛″ (3.2 mm) from the edge of the fabric. Pin the hook in place; then position the eye in the desired location. (Fig. 212a)

Fig. 212a

2. Sew the eye to the garment using a double thread. (Fig. 212b)

Fig. 212b

On better garments use a single thread to cover the hooks and eyes with a buttonhole stitch or use a thread eye. (Fig. 212c)

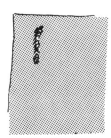

Fig. 212c

3. Check the hook location. Using a double thread, sew the end of the hook under the head, then sew through the two loops. (Fig. 212d)

Fig. 212d

Thread Eyes

The thread eye can be straight or rounded. It stretches when it's used so should be made a little shorter to allow for this stretching.

Using a single strand of thread, make a chain or a blanket-stitched loop.

Lace and Delicate Garments

On lace and delicate garments the hook can be made less conspicuous by bending it so that the two loops are one on top of the other. This isn't difficult to do with pliers. (Fig. 213)

Fig. 213

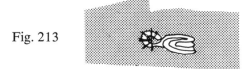

Waistbands

Large regular hooks and eyes or heavy-duty hooks and eyes are used on waistbands.

1. If you are using the regular hooks and eyes, sew two hooks at the top of the placket and another one at the end of the underlap. (Fig. 214a)

2. If you are using the heavy-duty hooks and eyes, sew one set at the top of the placket and another set at the end of the underlap. (Fig. 214b)

Snaps

Snaps are used to secure garments where there is little or no stress. They are available in several sizes from very small (4/0) to very large (4).

Application

1. Position the snap so that the section with the ball is located on the overlap, and the socket section is on the underlap.

2. Using a single strand of thread, secure the knot at the snap location. Do not stitch through to the right side of the garment when you sew the ball section in place.

Make 3–4 stitches in each hole of the snap to secure it. (Fig. 215a) The last stitch in each hole should be straight, not slanted, as you move to the next hole. (Fig. 215b)

3. Arrange the garment in the snapped position. Insert a pin into the center of the sewn-on snap to mark the location of the other snap section. (Fig. 215c)

4. Sew the snap socket to the garment.

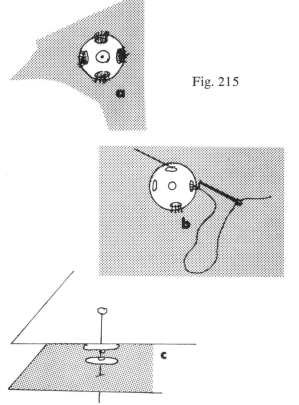

Fig. 215

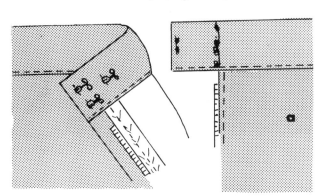

Fig. 214

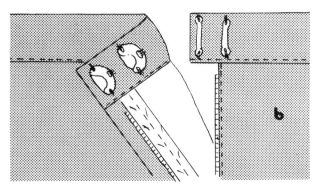

Covered Snaps

Snaps are often used on coats and jackets where they will show when the garment is worn open. Cover these snaps with a lightweight piece of lining fabric to make them inconspicuous.

1. Use large snaps (sizes 1, 2 or 3).
2. Cut a circle of fabric twice the diameter of the snap for each snap section.
3. Baste around the circle with a very small stitch. (Fig. 216a)

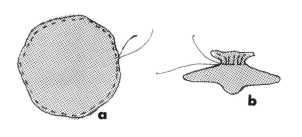

Fig. 216

4. Place the snap face-down in the center of the circle. Pull the basting thread tightly around the snap. (Fig. 216b)
5. Secure and flatten the edges of the circles by sewing over them several times; then secure the thread.
6. Snap the ball and socket together to make a hole in the center.

7. Sew the snap sections to the garment, using the point of the needle to locate the holes around the edges of the snap.
8. If the snaps are too small to cover and the silver or black color is offensive, use clear plastic snaps or "paint" them with permanent-color soft-tip pens.

Snap Tape

Use snap tape on slipcovers, infants' wear, and body suits.

Stitch the tape into a lapped placket, using a zipper foot.

Hook and Loop Tape

Velcro® is the best-known hook and loop fastener. This tape has one side covered with tiny hooks and the other side covered with tiny loops. The two sides stick together when pressed and unlock when pulled apart.

Apply nylon tapes to the garment with Velcro® Adhesive, by machine stitching or by hand sewing.

Use this looped fastener to replace zippers or buttons and buttonholes. It is especially practical on garments for the handicapped or for children who have difficulty dressing.

Nylon tape can ruin other garments when they're washed with it. The hooks on the tape cling to knit fabrics, leaving a fuzzy patch when pulled off. To avoid disaster, press an old nylon stocking to the tape when you put the soiled garment into the laundry basket.

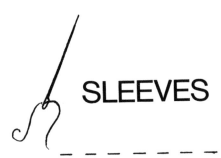

SLEEVES

No special sewing skills are required to set perfect sleeves, just practice, patience, and a little know-how.

RAGLAN SLEEVES
Raglan sleeves are easy to make, they're comfortable to wear, and they are easy to fit. They are often used on coats and jackets. The diagonal seam which joins the sleeve and bodice extends to the neckline or yoke, and it has a seam, gathers, or a dart at the shoulder for shaping. (Fig. 217a)

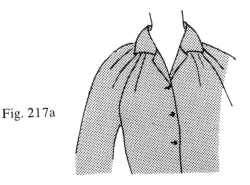

Fig. 217a

There are two methods for constructing raglan sleeves. Most home sewers prefer the flat method; however, the designer method is used on better garments and it is more comfortable to wear.

Flat Method
1. If the sleeve is cut in one piece, complete the dart at the shoulder.
2. With the right sides together, stitch the sleeve to the garment front and the garment back. (Fig. 217b)

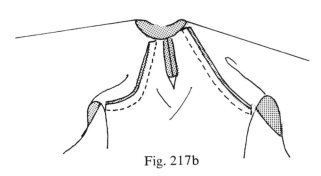

Fig. 217b

3. The seams which join the sleeve to the garment can be pressed open, toward the sleeve or toward the garment. I usually press them toward the sleeve.
4. If the sleeve is cut in two pieces, complete the shoulder seam.
5. Stitch the underarm seam.
6. Reinforce the underarm with a second row of stitches or by taping. If the seam will be topstitched, eliminate the reinforcement.
7. Clip the underarm to the stitching line or tape.
8. Press the seam open.

Designer Method
1. Complete the shoulder dart or shoulder seam on the sleeves.
2. With the right sides together, complete the underarm seams of the sleeves. Complete the underarm seams of the garment.
3. With the right sides together, pin and stitch the sleeves into the garment, matching the notches and seams.
4. Press the seam into the sleeve below the notches and as desired above the notches.

KIMONO SLEEVES

Kimono sleeves don't have an armscye seam. They are cut as part of the bodice. They vary from a full sleeve on a T-shaped garment to a close-fitting sleeve. The T-shaped kimono is very full and has vertical wrinkles at the armscye. When the fullness is reduced to fit the sleeve more closely, a gusset must be added to allow movement and comfort. (Fig. 218)

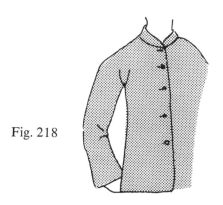

Fig. 218

T-shaped garments. Reinforce the underarm area with a second row of stitches or tape to give extra strength.

Kimono with a gusset. Set the gussets, which are triangular or diamond-shaped, into the slash at the underarm by the shortcut or custom method for stitching an inward corner (see SEAMS).

ANATOMY OF A SET-IN SLEEVE

Basic knowledge of the set-in sleeve is important to its fit and construction. (Fig. 219)

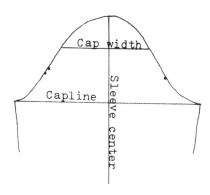

Fig. 219

Sleeve center is usually on the lengthwise grain.
Girth or *capline* is usually on the crossgrain.
Cap is the section of the sleeve above the capline.
Cap height is the distance between the top centerpoint and the capline.
Cap length is the length of the stitching line from the front notch to the back notches.
Cap width is the widest part of the cap on the upper arm.
Armscye or *armhole line* of the sleeve is the stitching line which joins the garment. The front armscye is more deeply curved than the back armscye. The front of the sleeve is always notched with one notch, and the back is notched with two notches. The underarm curve of a classic set-in sleeve should match the armscye curve of the bodice front and back.

Garment armscye (armhole). The lowest point of the armhole is located approximately ½″ (12.7 mm) below the armpit when the arm is down. It is usually at the underarm seam. The armhole is lowered an additional ½″ (12.7 mm) on suits, 1″ (2.5 cm) on coats and ¾″ (19.1 mm) on shirts.

TYPES OF SET-IN SLEEVES

The dimensions of the sleeve cap determine the type of sleeve. Shirt sleeves have a wide, flattened capline (Fig. 220a); tailored coats and suits have deep narrow caps. (Fig. 220b) The sleeves on most garments fall somewhere between these extremes.

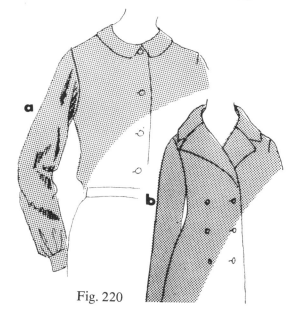

Fig. 220

The type of garment, the desired mobility, the fabric, and the finished appearance are important factors in sleeve construction.

Classic, Set-in Sleeves

The crossgrain of a classic, set-in sleeve is level at the capline and the sleeve hangs in rounded vertical folds.

The armscye seamline appears to be a straight, continuous line from the back notch, across the shoulder, to the front notch. When viewed from the front or back, the vertical foldlines of the sleeve continue the lines of the armscye seamline. (Fig. 220c)

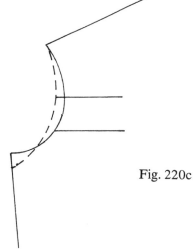

Fig. 220c

Traditionally, classic, set-in sleeves are used in well-tailored garments. If the garment is made of a difficult-to-ease fabric, set-in sleeves with deep caps cannot be set smoothly. In addition, mobility of these sleeves is limited causing the armscye seam to rip or the underarm seam to pull up when the arm is raised. Sometimes a gusset is put in the underarm of set-in sleeves to improve mobility.

Shirt Sleeves

Shirt sleeves are designed for action. They have wide, shallow caps and long underarm seams. The armhole of the shirt is straighter and lower than a regular armhole. Diagonal wrinkles radiate from the armscye seamline to the underarm seam. These wrinkles are more noticeable on long sleeves than on short ones.

SLEEVE PATTERNS
Ease

Most fabrics allow you to ease the sleeve fabric 1⅛″–1″ (2.9 cm–2.5 cm) on the garment without difficulty. Some fabrics, especially woolens and loose weaves, allow you to ease as much as 1½″–1″ (3.8 cm– 2.5 cm). That's quite a difference!

Reducing ease

1. Measure the armscye length on the pattern front and back; place the edge of a see-through ruler or tape measure on the stitching line of the armscye. Measure from the notch(es) to the shoulder seam on each section. Measure the cap length from the front notch to the shoulder point to the back notches.

2. The cap of a regular set-in sleeve should measure at least 1″ (2.5 cm) longer than the armscye. A measurement of 1½″ (3.8 cm) longer than the armscye will produce a smooth sleeve in most fabrics. A measurement of more than 1½″ (3.8 cm) ease will present problems in many fabrics.

3. The cap length of a shirt sleeve should not measure more than ¾″ (19.1 mm) longer than the armscye. Remove some of the ease from the sleeve cap pattern for difficult-to-ease fabrics like leather, vinyl, pseudosuede, suede, and tightly woven fabrics. To remove ease, make a horizontal fold across the sleeve cap. A ⅛″ (3.2 mm) fold will reduce the length of the sleeve cap ½″ (12.7 mm). (Fig. 221a)

4. Redraw the stitching and cutting lines without removing any of the cap width. (Fig. 221b)

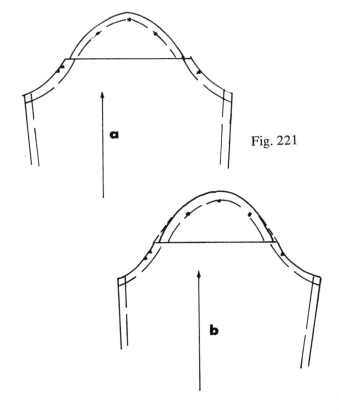

Fig. 221

Marking the Sleeve

Make ⅛″ (3.2 mm) snips at the cut edge of the sleeve to indicate the notches on the front and back, the shoulder point and the matchpoints midway between the shoulder point and the notches. Disregard any matchpoints at the top of the sleeve cap on each side of the shoulder point. Some patterns indicate no ease is to be allowed at the top of the sleeve. Theoretically, no ease is needed; but the sleeve will crush the seam allowances at the top of the sleeve if there isn't any ease and the sleeve cap will be flattened at the shoulder.

CONTROLLING THE SLEEVE EASE

Set-in sleeves have received so much bad publicity that many home sewers avoid them at all costs, without reason. The most important factor in setting any sleeve is controlling the ease. Learn to do this and you will never dread setting sleeves again.

Ease Baste

Ease basting can be used to control the ease on a sleeve made in any fabric or on any garment.

The success of this method is assured by the uneven tension which causes the bobbin thread to float on the underside of the fabric, and the short stitch which prevents pleating. If you accidentally pull the needle thread or stitch from the wrong side of the fabric, you'll have to rip it out and start again.

1. Loosen the upper tension on the sewing machine.
2. Set the stitch length to 10 spi or 2½ mm. Do *not* use a long basting stitch. The fabric will pleat in a long stitch.
3. From the *right* side of the sleeve, place a line of stitching just inside the seamline from one notch, over the cap to the other notch. (Fig. 222) If the sleeve has a deep cap, ease base again ⅜″ (9.5 mm) from the cut edge.
4. Pull the *bobbin* thread to adjust the cap ease in the armscye.

Fig. 222

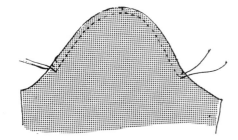

Crimp

Crimping is another method which can be used to control the sleeve ease. It forces more fabric into each stitch than regular stitching would.

1. Set the stitch length at 10 spi or 2½ mm.
2. Position your index finger firmly behind the presser foot. Stitch with the sleeve right-side-up to crimp the cap on the seamline from notch to notch. If the fabric resists crimping, pull the bobbin thread to ease in more fullness. Crimp again ⅜″ (9.5 mm) from the cut edge if needed.

SETTING SLEEVES
Classic Method

The sleeves in all better garments are set by this method. The underarm seams of the garment and sleeve are completed before the sleeves are set.

1. Mark the garment and sleeves with snips at each notch and matchpoint.
2. Ease the sleeve fullness by crimping or ease basting.
3. Complete the sleeve underarm seams, plackets, and cuffs. Complete the underarm seams on the garment.
4. With right-sides-out, insert the sleeve into the armscye. Fold the garment back onto the sleeve so that the right side of the sleeve is facing the right side of the garment.
5. Pin the sleeve into the garment with a pin at each snip and one at the underarm seam. (Fig. 223)

Fig. 223

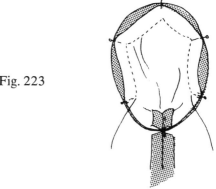

6. Adjust the fullness, distributing it evenly. Secure the bobbin thread at the notches by making a figure eight around the pins.
7. Stitch the sleeve into the armscye with the sleeve uppermost. Use the points of the scissors to adjust

the fullness. As you stitch, hold the scissor points flat on the eased line just in front of the presser foot. The scissor points will flatten the fabric and help to prevent pleating. Use the scissor points to push the sleeve under the presser foot if needed. (This is one of the few times you stitch over pins, but, after you have set both sleeves, throw away the pins *and* the machine needle.)

Some home sewers just can't stitch the sleeve in smoothly with six pins. Do *not* use more pins; baste the cap in by hand with an even basting stitch until you learn to set the sleeve smoothly and confidently with six pins.

8. Set the machine for a narrow, short zigzag (W,1-L,1) and stitch the seam between the notches under the arm. A zigzag stitch will put give into the seam. If you don't have a zigzag machine, use a short stitch under the arm.

9. Do *not* trim the seam allowances of the sleeve. The seam allowance will fill in the cap of the sleeve and improve the sleeve's appearance. If you have been trimming the underarm because the sleeve is too tight, the pattern needs to be altered.

10. Do *not* press the armscye seam open. The seam allowances should stand up under the arm, enabling the sleeve to hang close to the body. If you press the seam open, it will flatten the armscye seam and cause the sleeve to stick out.

Flat Method

Sleeves are easier to set into the armscye before the underarm seams are sewn. The flat method is always used on shirts, and it's sometimes used on sportswear, children's garments, and inexpensive ready-to-wear.

If the sleeve doesn't have a shallow shirt cap, the armscye seam at the underarm will be flattened by the underarm seam and the sleeve won't hang as well as a sleeve set into a circular armhole.

1. Mark the garment and sleeves with snips at each notch and matchpoint.
2. Crimp the cap of the sleeve if needed. A shirt-sleeve cap has so little fullness that it usually won't require crimping.
3. With the right sides together, match and pin the snips of the sleeve to those on the garment. If the sleeve has been crimped, the sleeve is uppermost. If crimping was not needed, position the body of the garment uppermost. Stitch the sleeve into the armscye. (Fig. 224a)

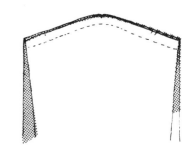

Fig. 224a

4. Finish the seam allowances of the armscye appropriately for the garment and fabric.

Shirt sleeves should be finished with an overlocked, topstitched, quick flat-fell seam or a modified quick flat-fell seam.

To make an *overlocked seam,* trim the armscye seam allowances to ¼″ (6.4 mm) and zigzag the edges together. (Fig. 224b)

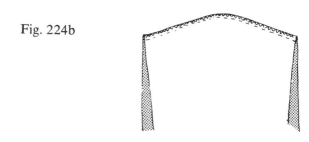

Fig. 224b

To make a *welt seam,* trim the seam allowance of the *garment* to ¼″ (6.4 mm). Clean finish the seam allowance of the sleeve by folding and stitching the raw edge to the *right* side of the fabric. Press the seam toward the garment and topstitch ¼″ (6.4 mm) from the armscye seam. (Fig. 224c)

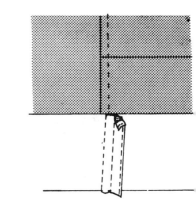

Fig. 224c

To make a *modified quick flat-fell seam,* stitch the seam with the right sides together. Trim the seam allowance of the *garment* to ¼″ (6.4 mm). Fold the seam allowance of the sleeve over the trimmed edge. Turn the garment sections over so that the sleeve is on top and stitch again on the armscye stitching line. (Fig. 224d) Open the garment flat, wrong-

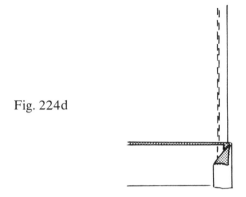

Fig. 224d

side-up, fold the seam toward the garment, and edge-stitch the seam to the garment. (Fig. 224e)

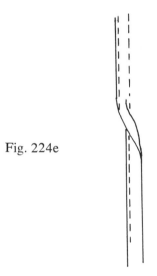

Fig. 224e

To make a *quick flat-fell seam,* position the armscye seam with the right sides together so that the garment is uppermost and the sleeve extends ⅜″ (9.5 mm). Fold the extended sleeve seam allowance over the garment edge. Stitch the seam ¼″ (6.4 mm) from the folded edge. Open the garment flat, with the wrong side up, fold the seam toward the garment, and edgestitch it to the garment.

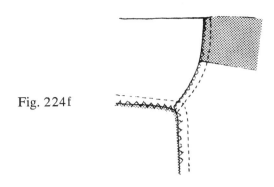

Fig. 224f

5. Complete the underarm seams of the sleeve and garment. Stitching from the lower edge of the sleeve to the hem of the garment, use an overlocked, standing-fell, or quick flat-fell seam (Fig. 224f)
6. Finish the hem or cuff on the sleeve.

Combination Method
The combination method for setting sleeves is almost as quick to use as a flat sleeve and the sleeve fits as well as one set into a circular armhole.

1. Mark the sleeves with snips at each notch and matchpoint.
2. Ease baste or crimp the cap from notch to notch.
3. With the right sides together, pin the sleeve to the garment across the cap, using a pin at each snip. Adjust the fullness, distributing it evenly. Secure the bobbin thread at each end by making a figure eight around the pins. With the sleeve uppermost, stitch the sleeve across the cap from one notch to the other. (Fig. 225a)

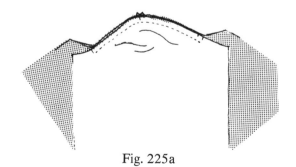

Fig. 225a

4. Complete the underarm seams of the sleeve and garment. Chain stitch to speed from one section to the next. (Fig. 225b)

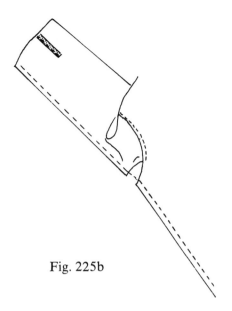

Fig. 225b

5. Complete the underarm of the armscye, using a zigzag (W,1-L,1) or straight stitch. Do *not* trim the seam allowances or press them open.

REDUCING THE EASE
Sometimes the sleeve cannot be set smoothly no matter how hard you try. There may be just too much fullness to be eased into the armhole.

Follow one or more of these tips to get a smooth cap:

✿ Position the front and back notches on the sleeve so that they are ⅛″ (3.2 mm) *below* those on the garment. Ease the shifted ¼″ (6.4 mm) into the *underarm* of the sleeve. (Fig 226a)

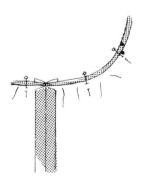

Fig. 226a

✿ Trim the sleeve cap ⅛″ (3.2 mm) at the shoulder point, tapering to nothing at the first matchpoints. Trimming ⅛″ (3.2 mm) will remove ⅜″ (9.5 mm) ease. (Fig. 226b)

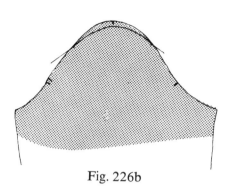

Fig. 226b

✿ Pin the sleeve cap into the armscye so that the sleeve has a ¾″ (19.1 mm) seam allowance at the shoulder point, tapering the seam allowance to ⅝″ (16 mm) at the snips, indicating the matchpoints. The seam allowance on the garment doesn't change.

Increasing the seam allowance of the sleeve at the shoulder point is the same as trimming the sleeve cap; however, if you don't like the way it looks, it's easy to put it back.

SLEEVE HEADS
Sleeve heads are always used in the caps of sleeves of tailored garments, and they can be used to improve the appearance of any set-in sleeve with dimples or gathers.

Sleeve heads can be made with several thicknesses and a variety of materials, depending on the desired effect in the finished garment.

Use lightweight interfacing materials for sleeve heads in blouses. Use domette, cotton flannel, cotton wadding, or polyester fleece in coats and suits. The sleeve heads should have the same washability as the garment.

Single-layer Sleeve Heads
1. Cut a strip 8″ (20.3 cm) long and 1½″ (3.8 cm) wide. Cut it on the bias if it is a woven fabric.
2. Pin the strip into the top of the sleeve cap between the matchpoints so that the cut edge of the strip matches the cut edges of the sleeve and garment. With the garment uppermost, secure the strip by stitching on the original seamline. (Fig. 227)

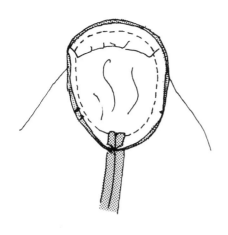

Fig. 227

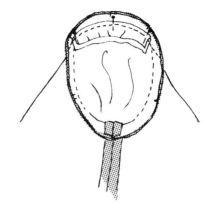

Fig. 228b

Double-layer Sleeve Heads

1. Cut a strip 8″ (20.3 cm) long and 2″ (5.1 cm) wide. Cut it on the bias if it is a woven fabric.

2. Fold the bias strip lengthwise so that one layer is ⅛″ (3.2 mm) wider than the other. (Fig. 228a)

Fig. 228a

3. Pin the strip into the top of the sleeve cap between the matchpoints so that the narrow side of the strip is uppermost and the folded edge of the strip overlaps the seam ⅜″ (9.5 mm). With the garment uppermost, secure the strip by stitching on the original seamline. The finished sleeve head will be four layers thick. (Fig. 228b)

PRESSING

Press the sleeve on a sleeve board or thick, firm roll.

From the wrong side of the sleeve, press the stitched line around the armscye with the point of the iron. Do not allow the point to extend more than ¼″ (6.4 mm) into the sleeve cap. Avoid shrinking out the ease in the cap.

Do not crush the sleeve cap by pressing the armscye seam from the right side of the garment. Use lots of steam and your fingers to press the cap from the right side.

If you start with a flat wrinkle-free sleeve, press as you sew, work carefully, and keep the garment on a hanger or folded neatly when you aren't working on it, very little pressing will be required on the finished sleeve.

SLEEVE PLACKETS
AND CUFFS

Sleeve cuffs are often used to finish the edges of sleeves. The cuff can be cut as part of the sleeve or separately and, with use of tucks and gathers, control the sleeve fullness.

The sleeve placket or vent is an opening at the wrist on a long sleeve which enables you to put the sleeve on comfortably. It is sometimes used on a short-sleeve shirt for design. Sleeve plackets are usually interchangeable. However, the type of placket is related to the cuff and garment style and it is usually completed before the cuff is applied.

Most techniques for sleeve plackets can also be used for neck or skirt plackets. The placket length and width can be modified to suit the garment.

SLEEVE PLACKETS

The sleeve placket or vent is usually located on the back of the sleeve about halfway between the underarm seam and the sleeve center. It is usually completed before the cuff is applied. Since most sleeve plackets are interchangeable, select the one you like and find easy to make.

Hemmed Plackets

Hemmed plackets are often used on inexpensive ready-to-wear. They are sometimes finished by hand and used on designer garments. (Fig. 229a)

1. Notch the sleeve ½″ (12.7 mm) on each side of the placket line before removing the pattern. (Fig. 229b) Clip the seam allowances of the sleeve to the seamline at the notches. Do not slash the placket line.

3. Hem the placket by hand or machine. (Fig. 229c)

4. Stitch the underarm seam of the sleeve.
5. Set the cuff to the sleeve by your favorite method.

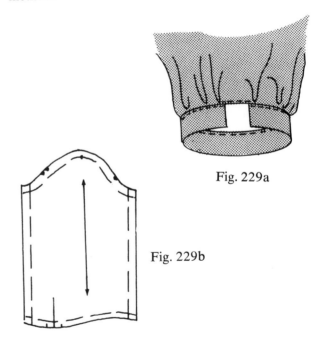

Fig. 229a

Fig. 229b

Fig. 229c

On everyday garments, use a complete cuff for a quick and easy finish. On better garments, use the classic cuff or stitch-in-the-ditch application.

Mandarin Slits

Mandarin slits are sometimes used on better ready-to-wear and designer garments. (Fig. 230a)

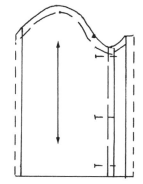

Fig. 230a

If the garment has a two-piece sleeve, the placket is located at the bottom of the seam on the sleeve back. If the placket is used on a regular one-piece sleeve, it is located at the bottom of the underarm seam. Some one-piece sleeves are designed with the seam on the sleeve back instead of at the underarm. Even though it is sometimes used in this location on very expensive garments by Galanos, Christian Dior, and Hanae Mori, it looks and feels awkward.

For a more attractive look and a more comfortable sleeve, reposition the seam so that the placket is located on the sleeve back instead of at the underarm. For best results, the underarm seams of the sleeve pattern should be cut on the lengthwise grain —fitted and flared sleeves are difficult to adapt. Extend the placket line to the sleeve armscye; cut on this line. Match and pin the underarm seamlines together. Add seam allowances to the new underarm seam. (Fig. 230b)

Fig. 230b

1. Finish the seam allowances of the sleeve underarm seam with a clean finish, zigzag, or flat lining (see UNDERLININGS AND LININGS). Be sure that the edge is finished evenly so that it can be used as a guide to stitch the seam.
2. Complete the underarm seam, leaving a 3½″ (8.9 cm) placket.
3. Set the cuff to the sleeve. Use a complete cuff or regular application. If the placket is located at the underarm seam, the cuff can be lapped front-over-back as in Christian Dior garments or back-over-front as in Hanae Mori designs.
4. If desired, edgestitch around the slit to hold the placket in place. It isn't necessary to secure it by hand.

Easy mandarin slit. This variation allows you to set the cuff to the flat sleeve *before* you stitch the underarm seam.

1. Finish the seam allowances of the sleeve underarm seam evenly with a clean finish, zigzag, or flat lining.
2. With the right sides together, pin a completed cuff to the sleeve. Match the notches and allow the sleeve to extend ⅝″ (16 mm) beyond each end of the cuff.
3. Fold the sleeve extension over the ends of the cuff, then stitch the cuff to the sleeve. (Fig. 231a)

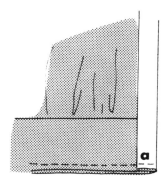

Fig. 231

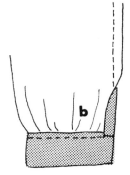

4. Complete the underarm seam, stopping 3″ (7.6 cm) from the cuff. (Fig. 231b)

5. Turn the sleeve right-side-out and edgestitch around the placket and the cuff if desired.

Faced Placket

The faced placket is seldom used on ready-made garments, but it is popular with home sewers, and a few designers use it on the sleeves of dressy garments. (Fig. 232a)

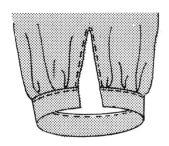

Fig. 232a

This easy-to-make placket doesn't wear or wash as well as other kinds of plackets and should be reserved for garments which will be dry-cleaned. The facing often peeks out or wrinkles around the placket.

1. Measure the placket length. (Example: 3½″ or 8.9 cm.)

2. Cut the facing 1½″ (3.8 cm) wide and 1″ (2.5 cm) longer than the placket slash (4½″ or 11.4 cm). This is smaller than the facing pattern in a commercial pattern. A smaller-sized facing is less likely to peek out and wrinkle around the opening.

3. Finish three sides of the facing with a zigzag or clean finish. Notch the center of the unfinished edge.

4. Slash the sleeve on the placket line 3¼″ (8.3 cm), ¼″ (6.4 mm) less than the placket length. If you are an inexperienced home sewer, stitch around the slash as indicated by the pattern. Otherwise, it isn't necessary.

5. With the right sides together, position the sleeve and placket so that the sleeve is uppermost. Match the slash and notch, then pin the sections together. (Fig. 232b)

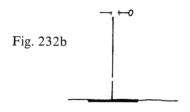

Fig. 232b

Begin stitching at the edge of the sleeve ¼″ (6.4 mm) from the slash. Stitch toward the end of the placket, ¼″ (6.4 mm) beyond the end of the slash. Shorten the stitch length 1″ (2.5 cm) before reaching the end, stitch to the end, make one or two stitches across the end, stitch up the other side for 1″ (2.5 cm), lengthen the stitch, and stitch to the edge of the sleeve. (Fig. 232c)

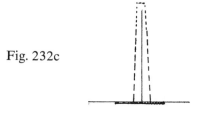

Fig. 232c

6. Slash the facing and garment to the end of the placket. Turn the facing to the wrong side of the sleeve, then understitch around the placket to hold the facing in place and reinforce the placket.

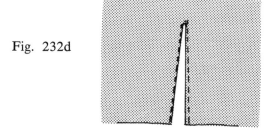

Fig. 232d

7. Edgestitch around the placket (Fig. 232d) or topstitch around the placket ¼″ (6.4 mm) from the slash.

Face the placket facing. This method finishes the edges around the placket quickly and neatly.

1. Face the facing. Measure the placket length. (Example: 3½″ or 8.9 cm.) Cut two facing sections for each placket 3″ (7.6 cm) wide and 1½″ (3.8 cm) longer than the placket slash (5″ or 12.7 cm). Round one end of each section. With the right sides together, stitch the facing sections together with a ⅛″ (3.2 mm) seam. Turn the facing right-side-out and press. Notch the center of the facing on the unstitched side. (Fig. 233)

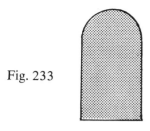

Fig. 233

2. Slash the sleeve on the placket line stopping ¼″ (6.4 mm) from the end of the placket.

3. Position the sleeve and placket with the right sides together and the sleeve uppermost. Pin the sections together, matching the slash and notches. Stitch around the placket.

4. Slash the facing and garment to the end of the placket. Turn the facing to the wrong side of the sleeve, then understitch the facing and seam allowances or edgestitch around the placket.

Lined slash placket. The placket on a lined sleeve is easy to finish quickly and professionally with this clever method featuring a lining to replace the facing.

1. Slash the sleeve and lining on the placket line, stopping ¼″ (6.4 mm) from the end.

2. With the right sides together and the lining uppermost, pin the sleeve sections together. Stitch around the placket. (Fig. 234a)

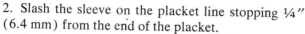

Fig. 234b

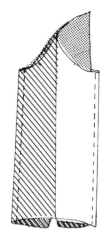

Fig. 234c

Fig. 234a

3. Slash the placket to the end and turn the sleeve right-side-out.

4. Understitch or edgestitch around the placket.

5. Complete the underarm seams of the sleeve and lining separately (Fig. 234b) or together. (Fig. 234c) Press the seams open if you stitched the seams separately.

6. Position the lining in the sleeve with the wrong sides together. Stitch the lining and sleeve together at the wrist and set the cuff to the sleeve.

If the underarm seams of the sleeve and lining are stitched separately, you can sandwich a complete cuff between the sleeve and its lining. With the *right* sides of the lining and sleeve together, position the cuff between them so that the upper cuff is toward the sleeve and the cuff facing is toward the lining. With the sleeve uppermost, stitch the cuff-sleeve seam; then turn the sleeve right-side-out. (Fig. 234d)

Fig. 234d

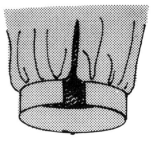

Flat-lined placket. Add a flat lining to the sleeves for comfort and to face the plackets smoothly with minimum effort.

1. Slash the sleeve and lining on the placket line, stopping ¼″ (6.4 mm) from the end.
2. With right sides together and the lining uppermost, pin the sleeve sections together.
3. Stitch around the placket, then stitch the sleeve and lining together at each sideseam with a ¼″ (6.4 mm) seam. (Fig. 235a)

Fig. 235

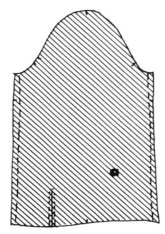

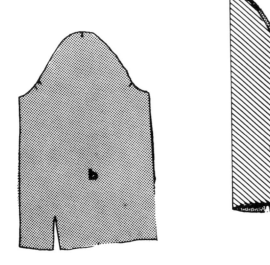

4. Slash the placket to the end and turn the sleeve right-side-out. (Fig. 235b)
5. Understitch or edgestitch the placket.
6. Complete the underarm seam with a ⅜″ (9.5 mm) seam. (Fig. 235c)
7. Stitch the flat lining and sleeve together at the wrist and armscye. Set the cuff to the sleeve.

Hemmed-edge Placket
This placket is quick and easy to make. You'll find it on many ready-made and home-sewn designs. (Fig. 236a)

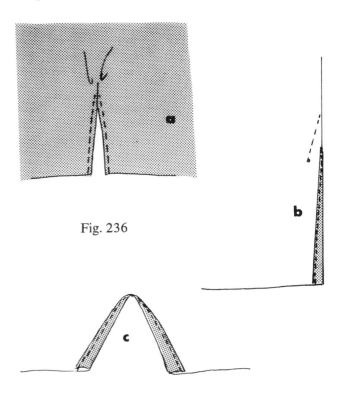

Fig. 236

1. Slash the sleeve on the placket line.
2. Make a very narrow machine hem around the slash. Designers for Christian Aujord and Nina Ricci use a hand-rolled hem.
3. Fold the sleeve with the right sides together, matching the hemmed edges of the placket. Beginning on the folded edge of the sleeve ½″ (12.7 mm) above the end of the placket, stitch a 1″ (2.5 cm) dart so that it ends ¼″ (6.4 mm) from the edge of the placket. Backtack at the beginning and end of the little dart. (Fig. 236b)

Commercial patterns instruct you to stitch the dart before you hem the placket. This procedure is awkward and more difficult.

Eliminate the dart if you want an open look on your design. (Fig. 236c)

Continuous Placket
The continuous placket, sometimes called a continuous-bound or continuous-lap placket, is very strong, launders well, and is used to finish sleeve vents on better ready-made garments. (Fig. 237a)

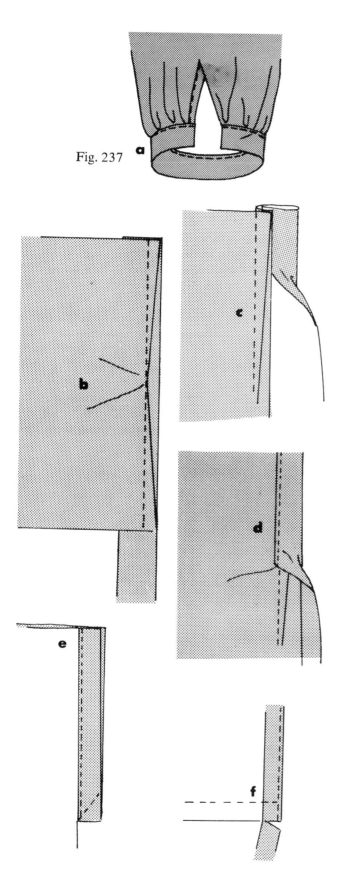

Fig. 237

If you are using this placket on heavy or thick fabrics, use a lighter weight fabric for the placket strip.

1. Slash the sleeve on the placket line.
2. Cut the placket strip the size indicated by the pattern or at least twice the length of the placket and 1¼″–1¾″ (3.2 cm–4.5 cm) wide. It's easier to stitch the placket if you cut it with a tail—allow 1″–2″ (2.5 cm–5.1 cm) extra on the length.

Cut the strip on the lengthwise grain, using the selvage if possible. For stripes and plaids, cut the strip on the bias.
3. Place the sleeve on top of the strip with the right sides of *both* face-up, matching the cut edges of one side of the sleeve slash and the strip.

Shorten the stitch, then stitch the strip to the sleeve so that the seam allowance of ¼″ (6.4 mm) remains even on the strip with the seam allowance on the sleeve tapering to nothing at the end of the placket slash. Stitch carefully to be sure you catch the sleeve and to avoid stitching a pleat at the end of the placket. (Fig. 237b)
4. Fold the selvage or cut edge of the strip to the stitched line so that it is *under* the ¼″ (6.4 mm) seam. (Fig. 237c) Fold the strip again enclosing the cut edges and covering the first line of stitching. Edgestitch the edge of the strip to the right side of the garment. (Fig. 237d)

Watch the grain carefully to avoid a twist in the finished placket. Use the points of the scissors as needed to push the strip up to the needle.
5. Stitch a triangle at the end of the placket strip to hold the placket inside the sleeve when the garment is worn. (Fig. 237e)
6. If the sleeve is to be set to a lapped cuff, fold under the placket on the sleeve front or overlap. If the sleeve is to be set to a French cuff, fold both sides of the placket under. The placket will be held in place with the stitching line which controls the sleeve fullness, gathers, or darts.
7. If the placket strip has a tail and extends beyond the sleeve edge, trim away the excess. (Fig. 237f)

Doubled-strip continuous placket. The doubled-strip continuous placket is even easier to apply than a regular continuous placket. It is especially nice on lightweight fabrics. The folded edge of this placket makes finishing it easy.

1. Slash the sleeve on the placket line.
2. Cut the placket strip on the lengthwise grain or bias 1½″–2″ (3.8 cm–5.1 cm) wide and at least

twice the length of the placket. Fold the strip in half lengthwise with the wrong sides together.

3. Place the sleeve right-side-up on top of the folded strip. Shorten the stitch; then stitch the strip to the wrong side of the sleeve. (Fig. 238)

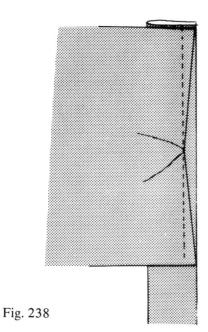

Fig. 238

4. Fold the strip over the cut edges and edgestitch the folded edge to the right side of the sleeve, covering the first line of stitching.

Tailored or Shirtsleeve Placket
The tailored or shirtsleeve placket (Fig. 239a) is used on most expensive blouses and shirts. This placket is surprisingly easy to apply with this hassle-free method.

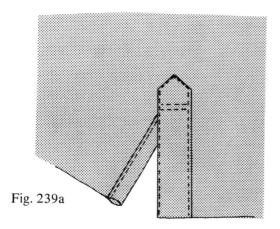

Fig. 239a

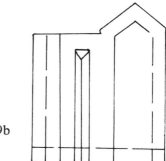

Fig. 239b

The placket pattern included with commercial patterns is shaped so that the home sewer has much needless difficulty setting the tailored placket. The placket pattern is shaped like a house and has a 5/8″ (16 mm) seam allowance on all edges. (Fig. 239b) When the placket is cut, the sides which are cut on the bias are difficult to sew because the bias stretches. A simple reshaping of the placket pattern will make the application easy.

1. Redraw the cutting lines of the placket so that they are square. Notch the longer foldline at the top and bottom. Cut each placket section into two pieces on the long slash line. (Fig. 239c)

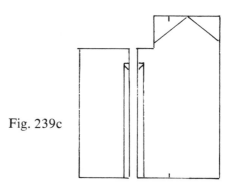

Fig. 239c

2. Slash the sleeve on the placket line, stopping 1/4″ (6.4 mm) from the end.
3. The small placket section will finish the underlap or small side of the sleeve. Wrong-sides-up, place the small section on the sleeve so that the cut edge matches the edge of the sleeve slash.

Stitch the small placket section and the sleeve together 1/4″ (6.4 mm) from the edge. Stop and back-tack 5/8″ (16 mm) from the end of the placket strip. (Fig. 239d)

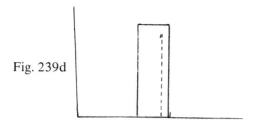

Fig. 239d

4. Wrong-sides-up, place the large section along the sleeve slash so that the cut edge meets the other placket section. Stitch it to the sleeve ¼″ (6.4 mm) from the edges. Stop and backtack even with the end of the stitching on the small placket section. (Fig. 239e)

Fig. 239e

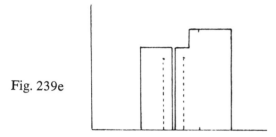

5. Clip the sleeve to the ends of the stitching lines without cutting through the placket sections. (Fig. 239f)

Fig. 239f

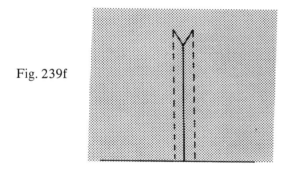

6. Fold the small placket to the right side of the sleeve. Turn under the edge and edgestitch it to the sleeve, covering the stitching line. Stop and backtack ⅝″ (16 mm) from the end of the strip. (Fig. 239g)

Fig. 239g

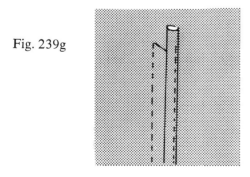

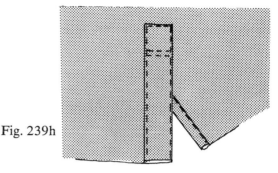

Fig. 239h

7. Fold the large section at the notches with the wrong sides together. Edgestitch along the fold. Stop at a point opposite the end of the stitching line which joins the placket to the sleeve. Spot tack or knot the threads. (Fig. 239h) This edgestitching is eliminated on designer shirts.

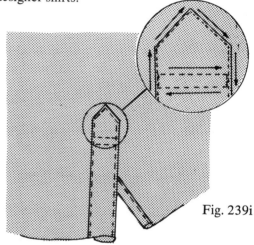

Fig. 239i

8. Tuck the wedge and small section between the garment and placket. Fold the point of the large section into a triangle and glue, tape, or baste it to the sleeve. Beginning at the sleeve edge, edgestitch the placket to the sleeve. (Fig. 239i)

9. If you have difficulty making an even point, use one of these designer details—a square end (Fig. 239j) or a triangle. (Fig. 239k)

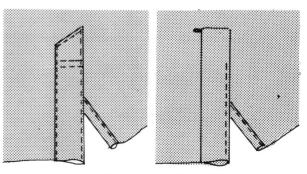

Fig. 239j & Fig. 239k

Easy tailored placket. This easy-to-make placket is a favorite of Saint Laurent, Guy Laroche, and Valentino, and it will be a favorite of yours, too.

1. Cut the placket strip for the overlap so that the width is twice the finished width of the placket plus 1″ (2.5 cm) and the length is equal to the finished length of the placket plus 2″ (5.1 cm). If the placket is 1″ (2.5 cm) wide and the opening is 5″ (12.7 cm) long, cut the strip on the lengthwise grain 3″ (7.6 cm) wide and 7″ (17.8 cm) long. Notch each end of the strip in the center.

2. Slash the sleeve on the placket line.

3. Stitch a narrow hem along the edge of the slash on the back (small side) of the sleeve. (Fig. 240a)

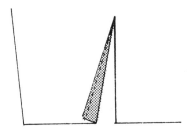

Fig. 240a

4. Wrong-side-up and the placket on top, stitch a ¼″ (6.4 mm) seam to the top of the slash. Back-tack. (Fig. 240b)

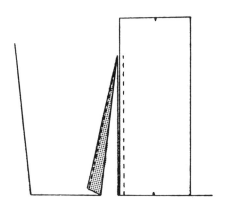

Fig. 240b

5. Clip the sleeve from the end of the slash to the backtack. (Fig. 240c) Do not clip the placket strip.

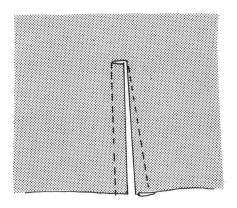

Fig. 240c

6. Turn the placket to the right side of the sleeve. Fold the strip at the notches with the wrong sides together. Edgestitch along the folded edge. Stop and spot tack at the end of the slash. (Fig. 240d)

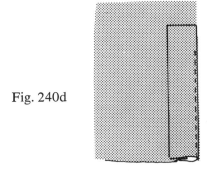

Fig. 240d

7. Fold the point of the placket and glue, tape, or baste it to the sleeve. Turn under the edge ¼″ (6.4 mm) and edgestitch around the placket. (Fig. 240e)

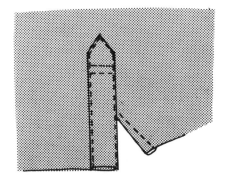

Fig. 240e

CUFFS

Cuffs can be set quickly and professionally when you use the tricks of the trade. Professional methods for setting cuffs rarely employ hand stitches since stitching by machine is more precise and quicker; but many home-sew methods instruct the seamstress to finish the cuff with a hand stitch, leaving a telltale sign of a homemade garment.

If you are reluctant to machine stitch cuffs permanently, master this technique by using basting aids like transparent tape, washable glue, or hand basting to hold the cuff in place while you machine stitch. You'll quickly learn to complete cuffs easily without aids.

Cuff Construction

Cuffs should be cut with the lengthwise grain going around the wrist. The lengthwise grain has little or no stretch, enabling you to set cuffs easily and smoothly. (Fig. 241a)

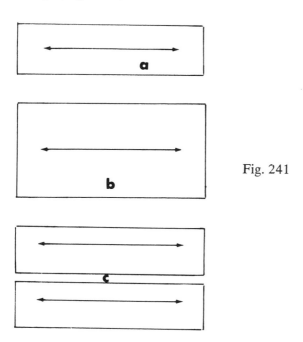

Fig. 241

Straight cuffs and facings are usually cut together in one piece for blouses (Fig. 241b) and separately in two pieces for shirts. (Fig. 241c) Shaped cuffs are always cut with separate facings.

The cuff is usually interfaced. The interfacing is cut on the lengthwise grain unless you want a softer cuff, then it's cut on the bias. Woven, nonwoven, and knitted interfacings with or without fusible backings can be used. The sleeve placket and cuff are usually completed before the sleeve is set into the garment.

One-piece cuffs

1. Notch the cuff on each end at the foldline.
2. Fold the cuff pattern on the foldline to use as a pattern to cut the interfacing.
3. Fuse, glue, or stitch the interfacing to the upper cuff. (Fig. 242a) Or use this easy ready-to-wear

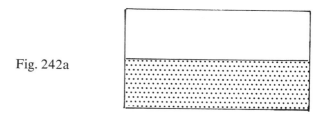

Fig. 242a

technique: Trim away the long seam allowance on the interfacing and stitch the interfacing to the cuff 1″ (2.5 cm) from the edge. (Fig. 242b) On the

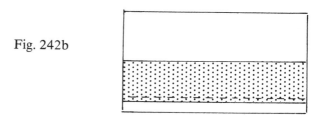

Fig. 242b

finished cuff, this stitching line will be ⅜″ (9.5 mm) from the finished cuff-sleeve seamline. (Fig. 242c)

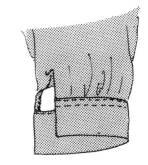

Fig. 242c

Two-piece cuff

1. Cut the interfacing from the cuff pattern.
2. Fuse, glue, or stitch the interfacing to the upper cuff.
3. With the right sides together, stitch the cuff and cuff facing together.
4. Understitch and trim the seam allowances.

From this point, all straight one-piece cuffs and two-piece cuffs are handled the same way.

Cuff Applications

Professional-looking cuffs can be set in a variety of ways. These tips will make setting cuffs easier. Use them whenever possible.

⚙ Cut the garment from a lightweight fabric with a low-fraying quality.
⚙ Cut one-piece cuffs.
⚙ Use a fusible interfacing, omit the interfacing entirely, or cut the interfacing and cuff in one piece.
⚙ Quarter the cuffs and sleeve. Match and pin the quarter marks together.

Complete cuffs. This easy application is often used on less expensive ready-to-wear. It should not be used to finish sleeves which have a lot of fullness at the wrist. The cuff-sleeve seam allowances will be folded *toward the sleeve* in the finished garment.

1. Fold the cuff in half lengthwise with the right sides together and stitch the ends of the cuff. If it is a two-piece cuff, fold the cuff so that the seamline that joins the cuff and facing is toward the facing. (Fig. 243)

Fig. 243

Do not trim away the seam allowances at the corners of the cuff unless the fabric is very bulky. The seam allowances will support the corner to make a sharp point.
2. Turn the cuff right-side-out. To ensure a perfect turn, open the seam allowances at the end of the cuff and place the point turner between them with the point at the corner.
3. Underpress, rolling the seamlines to the underside.
4. Set complete cuffs to the right side of sleeves which have hemmed plackets, Mandarin slits, or complete linings.

Classic cuff and shirtsleeve application. Most cuffs on ready-made shirts and blouses are set by this basic method—the cuff facing is stitched to the *wrong* side of the sleeve, the ends of the cuff are stitched and the upper cuff is topstitched to the right side of the sleeve. The cuff-sleeve seam will be enclosed in the finished cuff. This application and its variation are my favorite methods.

1. Complete the placket and the underarm seam.
2. Trim away the seam allowance on one long edge of the interfacing. Fuse or glue the interfacing to the upper cuff.
3. Fold the 5/8" (16 mm) seam allowance along the long edge of the upper cuff over the interfacing and topstitch 1/4"–1/2" (6.4 mm–12.7 mm) from the folded edge to hold the seam allowance and interfacing in place. (Fig. 244a)

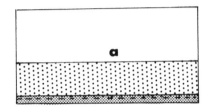

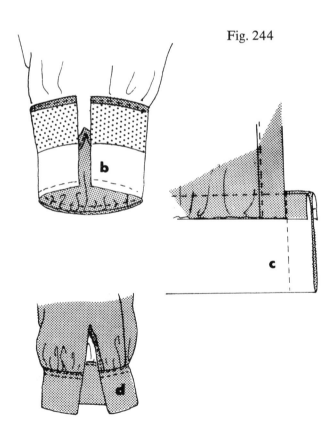

Fig. 244

4. Stitch the right side of the cuff facing to the *wrong* side of the sleeve so that the cuff will extend ⅝″ (16 mm) on each side of the sleeve placket. (Fig. 244b)

5. With the right sides together, fold the cuff in half. Fold the facing-sleeve seam toward the cuff. Adjust the seam allowances at the end of the cuff so that the upper cuff extends ⅛″ (3.2 mm). This trick of the trade ensures success when you topstitch the cuff in place; however, the facing will wrinkle slightly on the finished cuff. Stitch the ends of the cuff very close to the sleeve placket to avoid a step on the cuff. (Fig. 244c)

6. Turn the cuff right-side-out.

7. Use washable glue, transparent tape, or hand basting to hold the cuff to the sleeve. Edgestitch around the cuff using the inside of the presser foot as a guide. Press. (Fig. 244d)

Variation: If the cuff is a lightweight fabric, a one-piece cuff can be cut with an extended self-fabric interfacing. Cut the cuff three times the finished width plus one seam allowance. One width will be the outer cuff; one, the facing; and one, the interfacing. Clip the ends of the cuff to mark the foldlines, then press the folds.

Finish the cuff as above.

Stitch-in-the-ditch application. This easy application is often used on inexpensive blouses. A variation is used on expensive men's shirts by Yves Saint Laurent.

1. Complete the sleeve placket.
2. Fuse or glue the interfacing to the upper cuff.
3. Zigzag or turn under ¼″ (6.4 mm) and clean finish the long edge of the cuff facing.
4. With the right sides together, stitch the upper cuff to the sleeve. The cuff will extend ⅝″ (16 mm) on each side of the sleeve placket. (Fig. 245a)

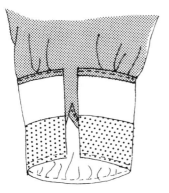

Fig. 245a

5. With the right sides together, fold the cuff in half lengthwise. Compare the ends of the cuff to be sure they will be finished the same width.

6. Fold the cuff-sleeve seam toward the cuff. Stitch the ends of the cuff very close to the sleeve placket to avoid a step on the cuff. (Fig. 245b)

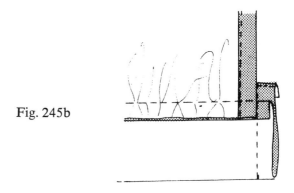

Fig. 245b

7. Turn the cuff right-side-out.

8. Fold under the corners of the facing edge so that they won't show at the placket. (Fig. 245c) Baste

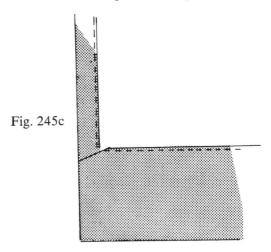

Fig. 245c

the facing in place with washable glue, pins, or hand stitching. Stitch-in-the-ditch to secure the facing. Press. (Fig. 245d)

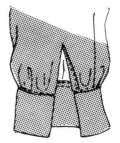

Fig. 245d

Variation: To simulate the expensive finish of YSL, finish the long side of the cuff facing by turning under ½″ (12.7 mm) of the seam allowance. Press or glue it in place.

When the ends of the cuffs are stitched, the folded edge will show ⅛″ (3.2 mm) above the sleeve-cuff seamline. Afterward, when the cuff is turned right-side-out, the cuff facing will cover the cuff-sleeve seamline ⅛″ (3.2 mm).

Wrap cuff application

1. Complete the sleeve placket.
2. Fuse or glue the interfacing to the upper cuff.
3. Fold the cuff in half lengthwise. Divide the cuff into thirds and make two notches on the long sides of the upper cuff and cuff facing. The success of the finished cuff will depend on the two sides being notched *exactly* the same. (Fig. 246a)

Fig. 246a

4. Stitch the upper cuff to the right side of the sleeve so that the cuff will extend ⅝″ (16 mm) on each side of the sleeve placket.
5. Fold the cuff in half lengthwise with the right sides together. Compare the ends of the cuff to be sure they are the same length. Fold the cuff-sleeve seamline toward the *sleeve*.
6. Pin and stitch one end of the cuff from the folded edge to the cuff-sleeve seamline. Stop with the needle in the fabric at the seamline. (Fig. 246b)
7. Pivot so that you can stitch on top of the cuff-sleeve seamline. Arrange the seam allowances of the

Fig. 246b

cuff facing, sleeve and upper cuff so that they are *even* and the sleeve is sandwiched between the cuff and facing. Pin and stitch to the first notch and back-tack. The seam will force the sleeve into the cuff. (Fig. 246c)

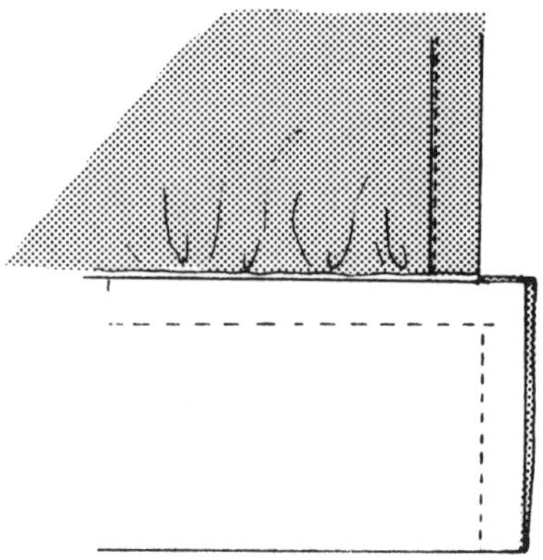

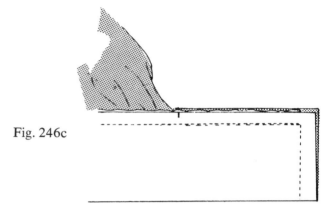

Fig. 246c

8. Trim the corner of the cuff at the pivot point. (Fig. 246d)

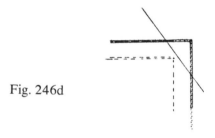

Fig. 246d

9. Turn the end of the cuff right-side-out.
10. Repeat on the other end of the cuff. Press.
11. The opening in the center of the cuff facing can be secured by topstitching the cuff, stitching-in-the-ditch, fusing, gluing, or hand stitching.

Shaped cuff application

1. Complete the sleeve placket.
2. Trim away the seam allowance on the long straight edge of the interfacing. Fuse or glue the interfacing to the upper cuff.
3. Fold the ⅝″ (16 mm) seam allowance along the long straight edge of the cuff over the interfacing. Topstitch ¼″ (6.4 mm) from the folded edge. Press or glue the seam allowance over the interfacing if you want to eliminate the stitched line.
4. With the right sides together, stitch the cuff and facing together. (Fig. 247a) Double stitch the seam and trim it to ⅛″ (3.2 mm).

5. Turn the cuff right-side-out.

6. Underpress, rolling the seamline toward the facing.

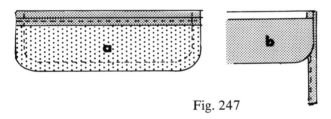

Fig. 247

7. Position the right side of the cuff facing against the wrong side of the sleeve, allowing the placket of the sleeve to extend ⅛″ (3.2 mm) beyond the cuff at each end. (Fig. 247b) Pin and stitch the cuff facing and sleeve together with the sleeve uppermost. Hold or pin the folded edge of the cuff out of the way to avoid catching it in the stitching line.

8. Turn the cuff right-side-out.

9. Push the facing-sleeve seam allowances into the cuff. Adjust the ends to avoid a lump.

10. Position the cuff so that it covers the facing-sleeve seamline, pin and edgestitch it in place.

Chloé cuff application. This super-easy cuff idea was inspired by the expensive designs of Roger Lagerfeld for Chloé.

1. Trim the seam allowances on the ends of the cuff to ¼″ (6.4 mm).

2. Cut the placket strip on the lengthwise grain 1½″ (3.8 cm) wide and twice the placket length plus 1″ (2.5 cm).

3. Slash the garment on the placket line.

4. Use the classic cuff application to set the cuff to the sleeve. The placket has *not* been finished and the ends of the cuff are *raw!* (Fig. 248a)

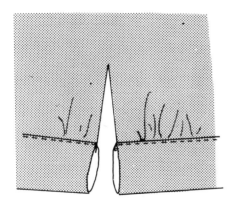

Fig. 248a

5. Finish the placket with a doubled-strip continuous placket. Position the strip so that it extends beyond the cuff ½″ (12.7 mm) on each end. (Fig. 248b)

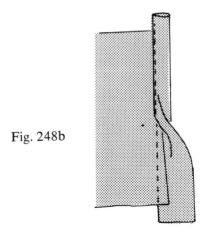

Fig. 248b

6. Fold the ends of the placket strip to the wrong side of the cuff, then fold both sides of the placket to the wrong side of the cuff. Edgestitch around the cuff to hold the placket in place. Press. (Fig. 248c)

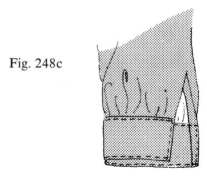

Fig. 248c

7. Add buttons and buttonholes or thread eyes. (Fig. 248d)

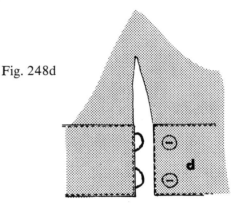

Fig. 248d

CUFFS WITHOUT PLACKETS
Barrel Cuffs
A barrel cuff is one of the easiest cuffs to sew. The cuff is a complete circle and must be large enough to slip over the hand or be made in a fabric that stretches. Look for patterns with this design. (Fig. 249)

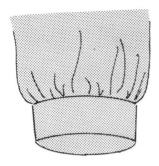

Fig. 249

Shortcut method. This easy method should not be used on better garments or on sleeves which have a lot of fullness at the cuff.

1. Fuse or glue the interfacing to the cuff.
2. With right sides together, stitch the ends of the cuff to form a circle. (Fig. 250a) Press the seam open.

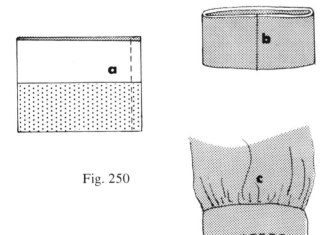

Fig. 250

3. Fold the cuff in half lengthwise with the wrong sides together. (Fig. 250b)
4. With right sides together, pin and stitch the cuff to the sleeve, matching the cut edges. (Fig. 250c)
5. Trim the seam allowances to ⅜″ (9.5 mm) and zigzag the edge.
6. Turn the seam up into the sleeve. Stitch-in-the-ditch at the underarm seam to hold the cuff in place.

Custom method. This method can be used to finish all sleeves attractively; however, it is more time-consuming than the previous method.

1. Fuse or glue the interfacing to the cuff.
2. With right sides together, stitch the ends of the cuff together to form a circle. Press the seam open.
3. Finish the edge of the cuff, which isn't interfaced, with a zigzag or clean finish.
4. With right sides together, stitch the cuff to the sleeve. (Fig. 251a)

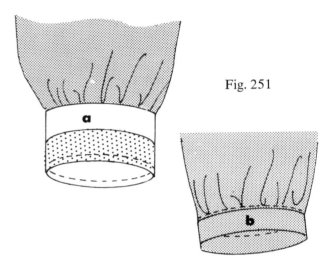

Fig. 251

5. Fold the cuff in half lengthwise with the wrong sides together. Pin or glue the facing in place. Stitch-in-the-ditch to secure the facing. (Fig. 251b)

Fake Cuffs
Sleeves can be hemmed by machine and made to look like real cuffs. (Fig. 252a) Guy Laroche used

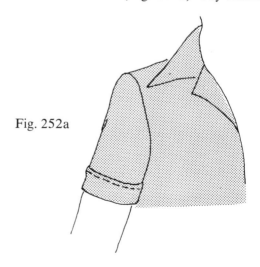

Fig. 252a

this simple finish on a stunning black dress stitched with red.

1. If the sleeve is straight, add ¾″ (19.1 mm) to the lower edge. (Fig. 252b) If the sleeve is shaped,

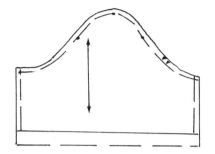

Fig. 252b

slash the pattern above the hemline and insert a strip ¾″ (19.1 mm) wide. (Fig. 252c)

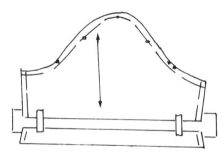

Fig. 252c

2. Fold the hem to the wrong side of the sleeve. (Fig. 252d) Fold the hem again to the wrong side, making a double hem. (Fig.252e)

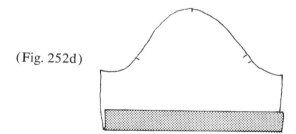

(Fig. 252d)

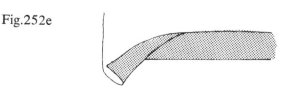

Fig.252e

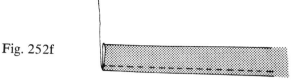

Fig. 252f

3. Stitch ⅜″ (9.5 mm) from the folded edge to make a tuck and to enclose the cut edge of the hem. (Fig. 252f) For variety, edgestitch the folded edge too.

4. Finish the underarm seam with a standing-fell, quick flat-fell, French, or overlocked seam. If you prefer, the underarm seams can be finished before the hem is folded and stitched.

This cuff can also be used to finish slacks.

Fake barrel cuffs. This variation of the fake cuff looks like a barrel cuff. (Fig. 253a)

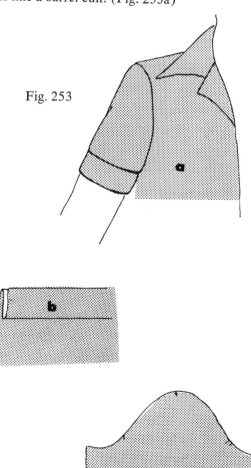

Fig. 253

1. Add ¾″ (19.1 mm) to the sleeve length.
2. Press the hem to the wrong side of the sleeve. Fold the sleeve even with the cut edge so that the *right* sides are together. (Fig. 253b)
3. Stitch ⅜″ (9.5 mm) from the folded edge to make a tuck on the wrong side of the garment. The tuck catches but doesn't enclose the cut edge of the hem. (Fig. 253c)

Turned-Back Cuffs
Add a turned-back cuff in self-fabric or contrasting fabric to finish the edges of sleeves. (Fig. 254a)

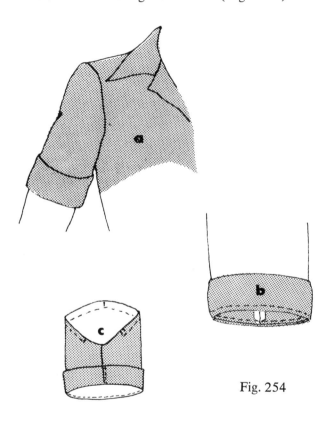

Fig. 254

1. Cut the cuff twice the desired width plus two seam allowances 1¼″ (3.2 cm) and the desired length plus two seam allowances. A finished 2″ (5.1 cm) cuff will be cut 5¼″ (13.1 cm) wide.
2. Reverse the seams on the sleeves which will be under the finished cuff.
3. Make the cuff. With the right sides together, stitch the ends of the cuff to form a circle. Press the seams open. Fold the cuff in half lengthwise with the wrong sides together.
4. Pin and stitch the cuff to the wrong side of the garment with a ⅝″ (16 mm) seam. (Fig. 254b)

5. Understitch the garment and seam allowances.
6. Fold the cuff in place and stitch in the well of the underarm seam to secure it. (Fig. 254c)
   The turned-back cuff can also be used on slacks. It's a great way to lengthen slacks when they're too short.

Cuff a Straight, Hemmed Sleeve
This designer technique is an unusual, but easy, shortcut for a straight sleeve. (Fig. 255a)

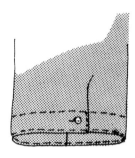

Fig. 255a

The hemmed edge of the sleeve must be cut straight across the crossgrain.

1. Allow a 1½″ (3.8 cm) hem allowance.
2. Clean-finish or zigzag the edge of the hem.
3. Press, pin, or glue the hem to the wrong side of the sleeve.
4. Edgestitch, then topstitch 1¼″ (3.2 cm) from the hemline. (Fig. 255b)

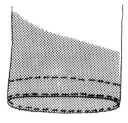

Fig. 255b

5. Mark the center of the sleeve at the hem edge. Fold the sleeve with the wrong sides together at the marked point. Edgstitch along the folded edge from the hemline to the topstitched line. (Fig. 255c)

Fig. 255c

6. Work a buttonhole through the folded sleeve in the center of the hem ½″ (12.7 mm) from the stitched fold. (Fig. 255d)

7. Set the button about 3″ (7.6 cm) from the stitched fold.

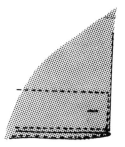

Fig. 255d

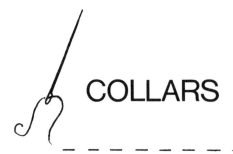

COLLARS

Collars come in a variety of sizes and styles, but there are only three basic shapes—standing, flat, and rolled. The collar shape determines the best method for setting and finishing the collar. Generally, standing collars are self-finished, flat collars are finished with a facing, and rolled collars are finished with a facing or with a facing-self-finish combination. If you have difficulty deciding which finish to use, consider the desired position of the neckline seam allowances in the finished garment—should they be pressed up, pressed down, or pressed open?

COLLAR APPLICATIONS
Standing or Self-Finished Collars
Self-finished collars include tie collars, bias-roll collars, standing collars, and shirt collars. The neckline of the collar is finished by turning the seam allowances up into the collar and securing it by hand or machine. This technique is sometimes called an envelope finish.

Tie collars. Tie collars can be cut on the lengthwise grain, crossgrain, or the bias. They are seldom interfaced and are quick and easy to apply. (Fig. 256a)
1. Cut the collar on the grainline indicated by the pattern. Clip each end on the foldline.

A bias-cut tie collar must be cut exactly—do *not* cheat. If it requires more fabric than you have, use one or more of these ideas to cut the tie: Pretrim the seam allowances at each end of the tie to ⅜″ (9.5 mm); cut the seam at the center back on the bias instead of on the lengthwise grain; shorten the tie length; cut the two ties separately instead of on a double layer of fabric (Fig. 256b); cut the tie on the crossgrain, especially if the fabric is a knit; or cut the tie on the lengthwise grain.
2. Staystitch and clip the neckline of the garment.

3. Stitch the right side of the collar to the wrong side of the garment with the garment on top. Use the staystitching line as a guide.
4. Clip the neckline seam of the collar and garment front at the ends of the stitching line. (Fig. 256c)
5. Trim the neckline seam to ¼″ (6.4 mm) and fold it toward the collar.
6. Fold the ends of the collar with the right sides together, using the clips at each end as a guide. Stitch the end of the collar. (Fig. 256d)
7. With the right sides together, begin stitching one tie end at the *clip,* stitch to the end of the tie and across the end. Stitch the other tie end. (Fig. 256e)
8. Press the seams open. Trim the seam allowances of the tie to ¼″ (6.4 mm). Turn the collar and tie right-side-out.
9. Turn the collar seam allowance under and top-stitch the collar to the garment neckline. Glue, baste, or pin if needed to hold it in place.
10. Finish the neckline between the tie ends with a narrow machine hem—the bow will cover the stitching line. (Fig. 256f)
11. Press *very* lightly to avoid crushing the fold. Pressing can often be eliminated at this stage if you started with a collar section that was wrinkle-free, and if you handled the construction carefully without introducing wrinkles.

Variation: Many garments with tie collars have front openings. For these designs, the neckline at the center front must be finished before the collar is set.

Turtleneck or bias-roll collars. Turtleneck collars are easy to make; however, if they're cut on the bias, they must be cut and sewn precisely to avoid a twist in the finished collar. (Fig. 257a) Turtleneck collars cut in knit fabrics are usually cut on the crossgrain.

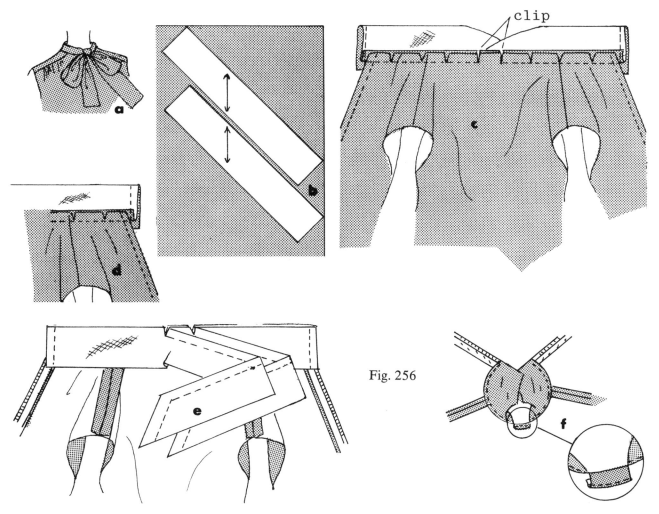

Fig. 256

1. Staystitch and clip the neckline of the garment.
2. Cut out the collar, using the pattern to ensure a correct grainline—do not cheat if it's cut on the bias. Clip the collar at each end of the foldline. (Fig. 257b)

3. If the collar requires interfacing, fold the collar pattern in half and cut the interfacing by the folded pattern. Trim the interfacing ½″ (12.7 mm) at the neckline. Pin, glue, or fuse the interfacing to the upper collar. (Fig. 257c)

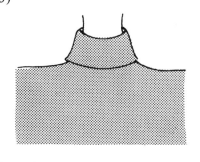

Fig. 257a

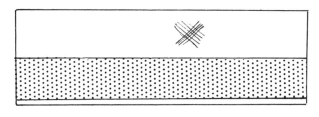

Fig. 257c

Fig. 257b

4. Fold the collar ½″ over the interfacing, stitch ¼″ (6.4 mm) from the folded edge. (Fig. 257d)

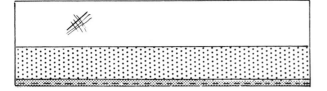

Fig. 257d

5. Stitch the undercollar to the garment so that the right sides are together and the garment section is on top. (Fig. 257e)

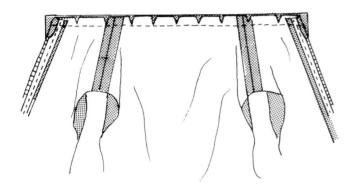

Fig. 257e

6. Trim the neckline seam to ¼″ (6.4 mm) and fold it toward the collar.
7. Fold the collar with the right sides together, using the clips at each end as a guide. Stitch the ends of the collar. If the fabric is bulky, trim the seams to ¼″ (6.4 mm). (Fig. 257f)

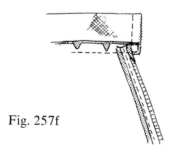

Fig. 257f

8. Turn the collar right-side-out.
9. Glue, baste, or pin the collar so that it covers the stitching line ⅛″ (3.2 mm). Using a zipper foot, stitch-in-the-ditch to secure it. (Fig. 257g)
10. Press the collar *very* lightly.

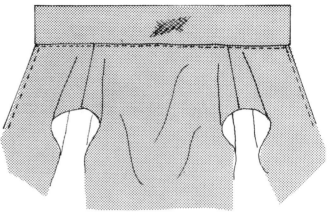

Fig. 257g

Standing collars. Standing collars include Mandarin, Chinese, Nehru, and stove-pipe collars. They are usually self-finished on ready-made garments, but they're often faced on home-sewn apparel. (Fig. 258a)

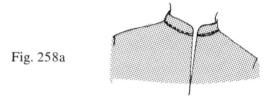

Fig. 258a

1. Cut the collar and collar facing on the *lengthwise* grain—this cut has the least amount of stretch and does not grow when you topstitch in it place.
2. Cut the interfacing on the lengthwise grain or bias. Trim away the neckline seam allowance on the interfacing.
3. Fuse or glue the interfacing to the collar. Fold the seam allowance at the neckline over the interfacing and stitch ¼″ (6.4 mm) from the folded edge. This line of stitching will show on the finished collar. (Fig. 258b) Press or glue the seam allow-

Fig. 258b

ance to the interfacing if you want to eliminate the stitched line.

4. Pretrim the seam allowances around the outer edges of the facing ⅛″ (3.2 mm) to make a ½″ (12.7 mm) seam allowance.

5. Staystitch and clip the garment neckline.

6. Set the machine for a short stitch (20 spi or 1.5 mm). With the right sides together, stitch the collar and facing together with a ½″ (12.7 mm) seam. Double stitch the seam and trim it to ⅛″ (3.2 mm) or make a hairline seam (see SEAMS).

Hairline and double-stitched seams are trimmed very closely, eliminating the need to notch the seam allowances. Shortening the stitch reinforces the curved seam and also allows you to stitch it smoothly.

If you have difficulty stitching curved ends identically, mark the stitching lines with a tracing wheel and tracing carbon or change the design to a square end. (Fig. 258c)

Fig. 258c

7. Turn the collar right-side-out and underpress. (Fig. 258d)

Fig. 258d

8. Pin the right side of the collar facing to the wrong side of the garment. Stitch with the garment uppermost so that the staystitching line can be used as a guide. Align the ends evenly. If necessary, stitch from each end to the center back to avoid a step at the end. (Fig. 258e)

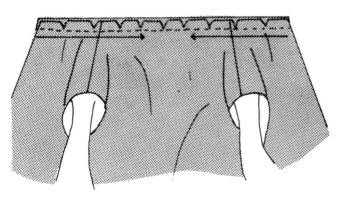

Fig. 258e

9. Trim the seam allowances to ¼″ (6.4 mm) and clip.

10. Glue, baste, or pin the neckline of the collar in place. Stitch the collar to the garment, using the inside of the presser foot as a guide. Again, if necessary, stitch from each end to the center back to avoid a "step." (Fig. 258f)

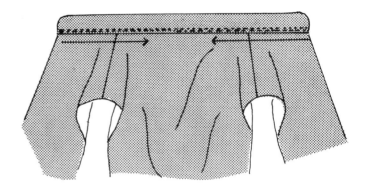

Fig. 258f

Shirt Collars

Dress shirts have collars with separate collar and band sections. (Fig. 259a) They are usually interfaced more crisply than blouse collars.

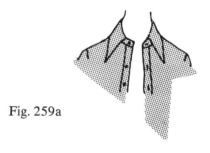

Fig. 259a

Traditional method. This conventional method is used to set most collars on readymade shirts.

1. Cut the collar and band sections on the *lengthwise* grain.

2. If you want the collar to have a soft roll, cut the interfacing on the bias. If you want it to have a crisp roll, cut the interfacing on the lengthwise grain. Trim the interfacing for the band to remove the neckline seam allowance.

If you are making a man's dress shirt which requires a very crisp collar, cut a second piece of interfacing for the collar section from a lightweight or bias fusible. Trim away the seam allowances on this section and fuse it to the collar interfacing or to the undercollar.

3. Fuse or glue the interfacing sections to the collar and neckband. Fold the band over the interfacing at the neckline and stitch ¼″ (6.4 mm) from the folded edge. This stitching line will show when the finished collar is worn open. (Fig. 259b) If you want to eliminate the stitched line, press or glue the seam allowance to the interfacing.

Fig. 259b

4. Pretrim the seam allowances of the undercollar ⅓″ (3.2 mm).

5. Staystitch and clip the garment neckline.

6. With the right sides together, join the long edge of the collar to the undercollar with a ½″ (12.7 mm) seam. You have trimmed the facing ⅛″ (3.2 mm); the turn of the cloth will take up the remaining ⅛″ (3.2 mm). (Fig. 259c) Understitch and trim the seam to ¼″ (6.4 mm).

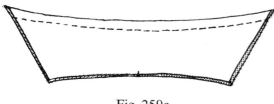

Fig. 259c

7. With the right sides together, fold the collar so the seamline is toward the facing. Stitch each end of the collar with a ½″ (12.7 mm) seam. To allow turning room for each corner, take a stitch or two at right angles to the long edge. Trim the seam to ¼″ (6.4 mm). (Fig. 259d)

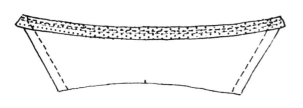

Fig. 259d

8. Turn the collar right-side-out, using a point turner. If the points are very narrow, use an orange-wood stick to turn them.

9. Underpress, rolling the seamline to the underside.

10. Topstitch and/or edgestitch the collar.

11. Key the ends of the collar on the seamline.

12. Sandwich the collar between the band sections, matching the cut edges and notches. The interfaced band will face the *upper collar*. Stitch the collar and band together but do *not* stitch the ends to the band. (Fig. 259e)

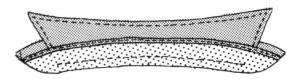

Fig. 259e

13. With the right sides together, pin the neck edge of the garment to the band facing—the band without interfacing. Stitch with the garment uppermost, using the staystitching line as a guide.

14. Clip and trim the neckline seam to ¼″ (6.4 mm); then fold it toward the collar.

15. Using a short stitch, stitch the ends carefully so that the ends are even with the garment and don't make a "step." (Fig. 259f) If you have difficulty

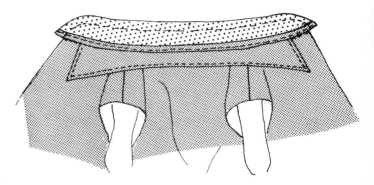

Fig. 259f

stitching the ends identically, mark the stitching lines or square the ends.

16. Stitch the curved section of the stand again 1/16″ (1.6 mm) from the original seamline. Trim close to the second stitching line.

17. Turn the collar right-side-out; underpress.

18. Glue, baste, or pin the neckline of the band to the garment, covering the stitching line. Stitch the band in place. (Fig. 259g)

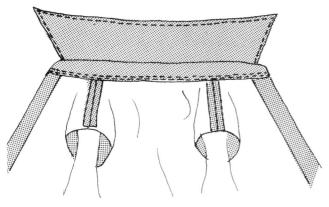

Fig. 259g

Quick-and-easy method. Once you've tried this clever method you'll never use the traditional method again.

1. Cut out and interface the collar.
2. Pretrim the seam allowances of the undercollar ⅛″ (3.2 mm).
3. Staystitch and clip the garment neckline.
4. With the right sides together, join the long edge of the collar to the undercollar with a ½″ (12.7 mm) seam. Understitch and trim the seam to ¼″ (6.4 mm).
5. With the right sides together, fold the collar so that the seamline is toward the undercollar. Stitch each end of the collar with a ½″ (12.7 mm) seam. To allow turning room for each corner, take a stitch or two at right angles to the long edge. Trim the seam to ¼″ (6.4 mm).
6. Turn the collar right-side-out and underpress.
7. Topstitch and/or edgestitch the collar.
8. Key the ends of the collar.
9. With the right sides together, pin and stitch the collar to the interfaced band. Trim the seam to ¼″ (6.4 mm). (Fig. 260a)

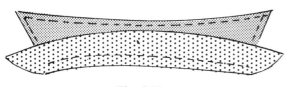

Fig. 260a

10. Position the *garment* between the band sections, so that the interfaced band is next to the wrong side

of the garment. Pin and stitch the garment and band sections together, matching the cut edges and notches. (Fig. 260b)

Many home sewers find this easier to do in two steps. First, pin and stitch the band facing and gar-

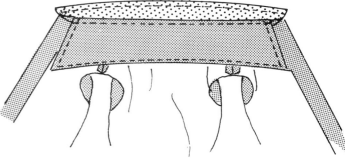

Fig. 260b

ment together with the right sides together. Then, pin the right side of the interfaced band to the wrong side of the garment. Turn the garment over so the band facing is uppermost and stitch the neckline on top of the first stitching line.
11. Clip and trim the neckline seam to ¼″ (6.4 mm).
12. With the right sides together, stitch the ends of the band from the neck edge of the garment to the ends of the collar. Stitch the ends of the band again ¹⁄₁₆″ (1.6 mm) from the seamline, then trim the seam close to the second stitching line.
13. Turn the band right-side-out.
14. Fold under the seam allowance of the outside band and pin, glue, or baste it to the collar. Stitch the band in place. Press. (Fig. 260c)

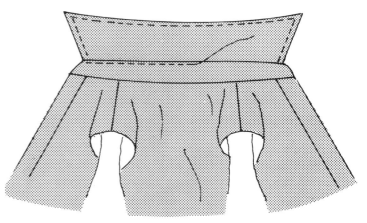

Fig. 260c

Flat or Faced Collars

Convertible collars, notched collars, wing collars, and flat collars (Peter Pan) are usually faced. The facing can be set by sandwiching the completed collar between the garment and facing or by stitching the collar to the facing and stitching the undercollar to the garment. Some collars are finished by combining a facing and an envelope finish.

Complete the collar. When the collar has a facing, the collar is usually completed before it's set to the garment.

1. On the undercollar, pretrim all edges except the neckline edge ⅛″ (3.2 mm).
2. Cut the interfacing by the collar pattern and fuse or glue it to the upper collar.
3. With the right sides together, stitch the long edge of the collar and facing together. (Fig. 261a) Un-

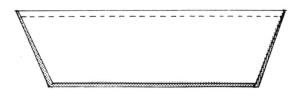

Fig. 261a

derstitch and trim the seam to ¼″ (6.4 mm). Fold the collar with the right sides together and the seamline toward the facing. Stitch the ends, taking a stitch or two at right angles to the long edge to allow turning room. (Fig. 261b) Trim the ends to ¼″ (6.4 mm).

Fig. 261b

If the collar is rounded, use a hairline seam or double-stitched seam to join the collar and facing. These seams are very narrow when they are finished.
4. Turn the collar right-side-out; underpress.
5. Fold the collar in half, lengthwise. Pin the neckline of the upper collar and undercollar together. If you pretrimmed, the edges should match. If they don't match, trim the undercollar as needed. (Fig. 261c)

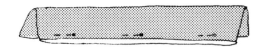

Fig. 261c

Stitch the neckline edges of the collar and facing together if you plan to set the collar with a facing or bias strip.
6. Key the ends of the collar.

Bias strip facing. A double bias strip is a neat finish on a flat collar such as a Peter Pan (Fig. 262a), sailor, or pilgrim collar. Sandwich the completed collar between the garment and bias facing.

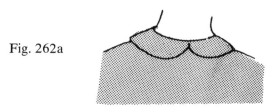

Fig. 262a

1. Complete the collar.
2. Cut a bias strip from a lightweight fabric ¾″–2½″ (19.1 mm–6.4 cm) wide.
3. Staystitch and clip the garment neckline.
4. Place the collar, face-up, on the right side of the garment. Pin and stitch it on the seamline. (Fig. 262b) Trim the seam allowances to ¼″ (6.4 mm).

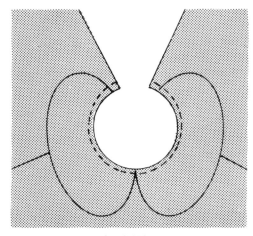

Fig. 262b

5. Fold the bias strip in half lengthwise with the wrong sides together. Place the strip on top of the collar, matching the cut edges. Stitch it in place, understitch, trim, and clip. (Fig. 262c)

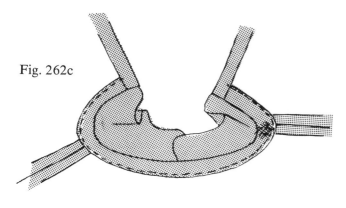

Fig. 262c

6. Fold the bias strip down so that it covers the seam allowances. Use a zipper foot to stitch the bias strip to the garment. Stitch with the foot resting on the bias strip and seam allowances.

This stitching line will be covered by the finished collar except in the center front and/or back where the collar is divided. Leave the bias strip unstitched at the center on dressy garments. The visible stitching line is all right on sportswear and children's wear.

Shaped facing. The collar can be sandwiched between the garment and facing for Peter Pan collars or notched collars on blouses (Fig. 263a) and

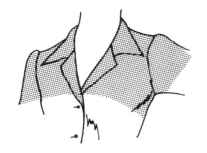

Fig. 263a

blazers. This method is frequently used on blouses and children's wear, but it is used only on inexpensive jackets

1. Complete the collar.
2. Staystitch and clip the neckline.
3. Stitch the front and back facing sections together; press.
4. Pin the finished collar, face-up, to the right side of the garment, matching the edges and notches.

Stitch the collar to the garment with the garment uppermost. (Fig. 263b)
5. Place the right side of the facing next to the right side of the collar. Match the edges and stitch the facing in place. (Fig. 263c) Trim the neckline seam to ¼″ (6.4 mm) and clip as needed.
6. Understitch the back neckline.
7. If desired, topstitch the lapel and garment front. Topstitch with the *lapel face-up*. If the garment fabric has a nap, topstitch in the direction of the nap.
8. If the garment is lined, you can stitch the lining to the facing now, or you could have stitched them together before joining the facing to the garment.

Rolled Collars
Rolled collars are usually finished with a front facing which extends to the shoulder seam and a bias strip, zigzagged seam, envelope finish, or facing at the back neckline. Finish coats, suits, and dresses made from heavy fabrics with a facing or lining. Finish blouses, dresses, and children's wear made from lightweight or knitted fabrics with one of the other methods to eliminate unsightly back-neck facings which often bunch up and stick out.

Overlocked back neckline. The overlocked seam is often used to finish collars on inexpensive garments, children's wear, knits, and lingerie. This quick-and-easy method should not be overlooked when you want to finish everyday garments neatly.

1. Staystitch the garment neckline.
2. Complete the collar and set it to the garment.
3. Stitch the front facing in place. Trim the seam to ¼″ (6.4 mm) and clip as needed. (Fig. 264a)
4. Overlock or zigzag (W,2-L,2) the back-neckline seam allowances. (Fig. 264b)
5. Stitch the back-neckline seam to the garment. (Fig. 264c)
6. Secure the front facing at the shoulder seam. (Fig. 264d)

Bias binding. Bias bindings are frequently used to finish the back neckline on inexpensive garments and children's wear.

1. Staystitch the garment neckline.
2. Cut a bias strip 2¼″–2½″ (5.7 cm–6.4 cm) wide and the length of the back neckline plus 1″ (2.5 cm).

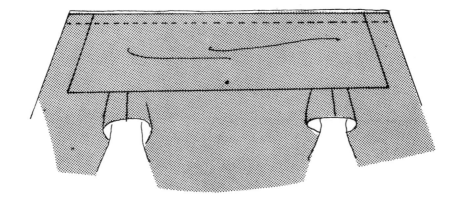

Fig. 263b

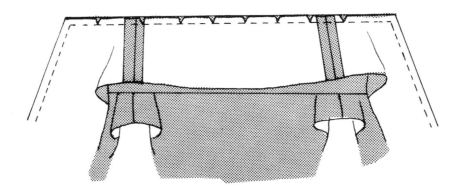

Fig. 263c

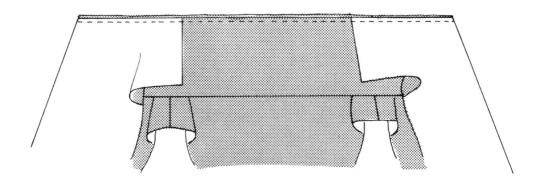

Fig. 264a

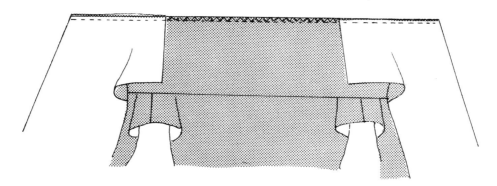

Fig. 264b

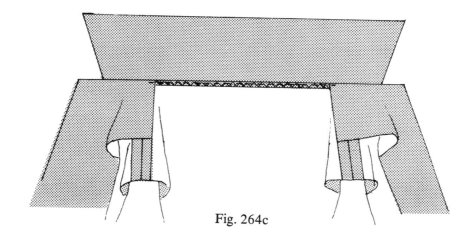

Fig. 264c

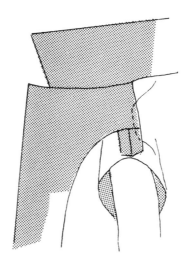

Fig. 264d

3. Complete the collar and set it to the garment.

4. Stitch the front facing in place. Trim the seam to ¼″ (6.4 mm) and clip as needed.

5. Fold the bias strip in half lengthwise with the wrong sides together. Place the strip on top of the collar, matching the cut edges of the back neckline and overlapping the facing ½″ (12.7 mm) at each end. (Fig. 265a) Stitch the bias to the neckline.

6. Understitch and clip the back-neckline seam.

7. Use the zipper foot to stitch the bias strip to the garment back (Fig. 265b) Stitch with the foot on top of the bias. If the collar is a full-roll collar, the finished collar will not cover the stitched line. If it is a partial-roll collar, it will cover the stitched line.

8. Secure the front facing at the shoulder seams.

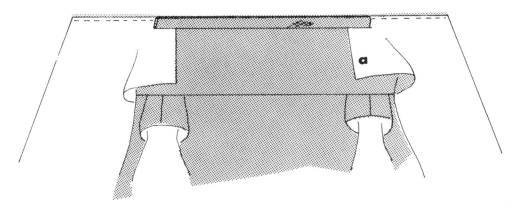

Fig. 265

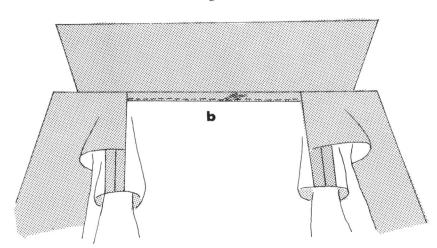

Envelope or self-finish. The envelope or self-finish is an attractive finish for collars on better garments. This quality finish is a favorite of mine—it's easy to master and a snap to sew.

1. Staystitch the garment neckline.

2. Complete the collar.

3. With the right sides together, pin and stitch the edges of the *undercollar* to the garment neckline. (Fig. 266a)

4. Fold the front facing over the collar. Pin and stitch the facing and collar to the garment and undercollar, stopping 1″ (2.5 cm) *before* reaching the shoulder seams. Backtack and clip to the ends of the stitched line. (Fig. 266b)

5. Push the seam allowances of the garment back, undercollar, and front facing into the collar.

6. Turn under the collar seam allowance. Glue, baste, or pin the collar to cover the stitched line. Stitch the collar to the garment. (Fig. 266c)

7. Secure the front facings at the shoulder seams.

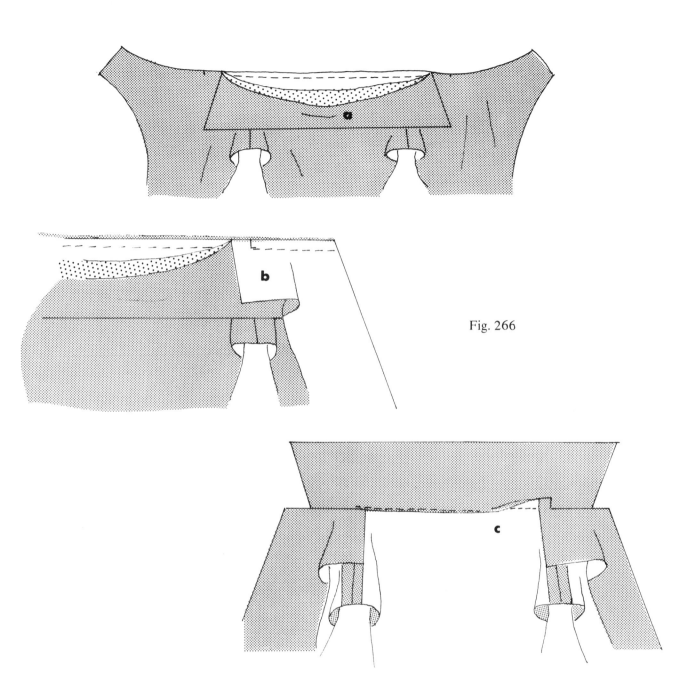

Fig. 266

Facing. Rolled collars on better ready-made garments are finished with facings or linings. The collar facing and garment undercollar seams are stitched separately, then pressed open.

Many of these collars are notched collars. (Fig. 267a) The notch is formed at the point where the collar joins the lapel. This point, where four lines of stitching converge, must be stitched carefully to avoid a homemade-looking garment. These tips will help you stitch this custom-finished collar.

✿ Mark each section—the garment front, front facing, collar, and undercollar—exactly at the matchpoints that indicate the collar notch (usually a small circle).

✿ Stitch away from the notch instead of toward it to prevent bubbles from forming at the notch. Use a zipper foot.

✿ Fasten the threads securely at the notch—a spot tack may not hold. Tie the threads. If you have to rip, a knot is easy to unpick.

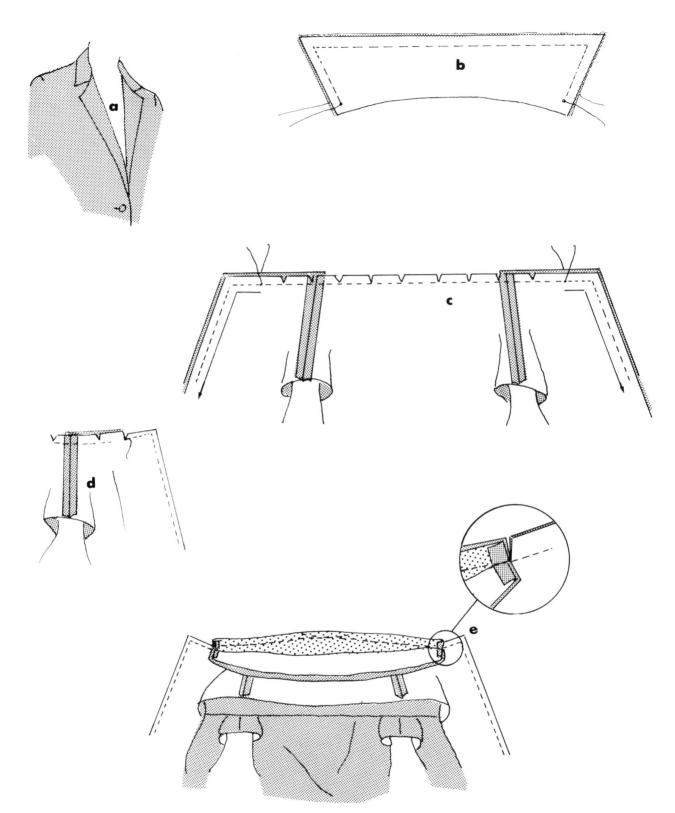

Fig. 267a–e

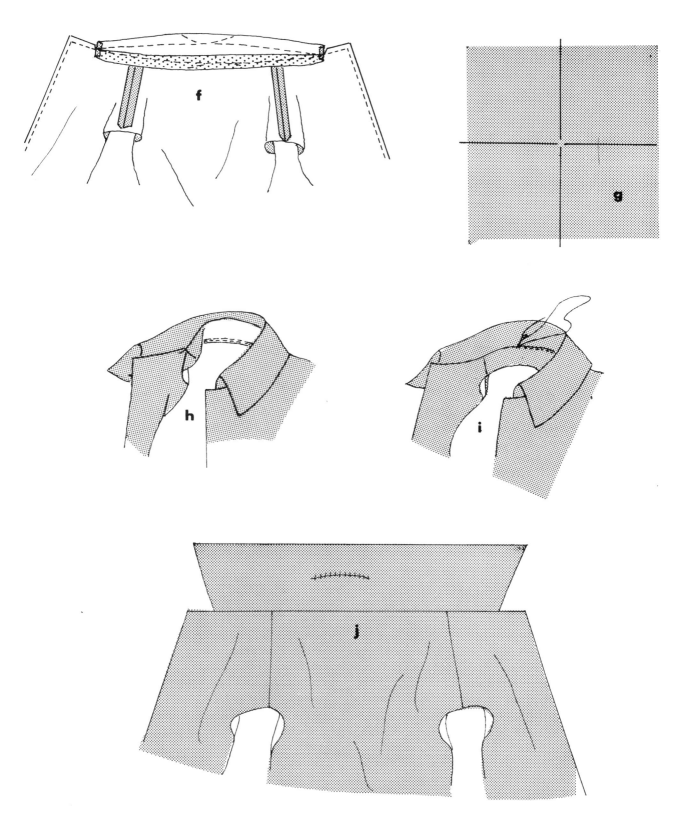

Fig. 267f–j

⚙ Trim the seam allowances as much as needed, but don't overtrim.

⚙ If you are making a jacket or coat, the pattern provided for the undercollar is smaller than the one for the upper collar. For the most part, commercial patterns are designed for mediumweight fabrics.

If your garment fabric is heavy or bulky, or if you are making a garment by a pattern that doesn't have a separate undercollar pattern, you must decrease the length and width of the undercollar to allow for the turn of the cloth. Pretrim the outside edges of the undercollar ⅛" (3.2 mm). The trimmed edges will be matched to the edges of the collar and stitched together with a ½" (12.7 mm) seam.

1. Interface the undercollar and garment on tailored garments. Interface the upper collar on lightweight blouses and dresses.
2. Staystitch and clip the necklines of the garment and facing.
3. With the right sides together and the undercollar uppermost, stitch the undercollar and collar together. Shorten the stitches 1" (2.5 cm) before and after each corner. Begin and end the stitching at the matchpoints indicating the collar notch. (Fig. 267b) Compare the ends of the collar to be sure they are the same.
4. Knot and trim the threads at the matchpoints. Pull the threads firmly to the underside before you knot them to avoid a loose stitch at the notch.
5. Press the collar seams open over a point presser or point turner. Understitch the seam if desired.
6. Trim and grade the collar seam allowances as needed. The finished collar is more attractive if the seam allowances aren't trimmed too closely and support the edges and corners.
7. Turn the collar right-side-out and underpress.
8. With the right sides together, pin or baste the garment and front facings together. Stitch from the matchpoint or collar notch around the lapel to the hem of the garment. Stitch the other lapel, beginning at the notch. (Fig. 267c) Compare the lapels to be sure they are the same. Knot and trim the threads at the notch.
9. Press the seams open over a point presser.
10. Clip the seam allowances to the notch. Trim and grade the lapel seam allowances as needed. (Fig. 267d)
11. Turn the lapels right-side-out and underpress.

12. Using a zipper foot, pin and stitch the neckline of the undercollar to the garment. Begin at each notch and stitch to the center back. (Fig. 267e) Tie the threads securely at the beginning and overlap the stitching at the back.
13. With the right sides together, pin the seamline of the collar and facing together. Place the pins parallel to the seamline. Hold the collar in the finished rolled position to check the collar-facing seamline placement—it should be centered over the undercollar-garment seamline.
14. If the fabric is bulky, the upper collar may be too short and the seamlines won't match. If they are forced to match, the seamline at the outer edge of the collar will show. Adjust the collar by allowing a smaller seam allowance on the collar so that the seamline at the edge will roll to the underside.
15. Using a zipper foot, stitch the neckline of the collar to the facing, beginning at the notch and stitching to the center back. Tie the threads securely at each notch and overlap the stitching lines at the back. (Fig. 267f)
16. Check the stitching lines at each notch—the four lines should look like two lines intersecting at right angles. There will be a small hole at the center. (Fig. 267g) If the lines don't look like an intersection, rip out the line that is out of place and restitch it.
17. Press open the garment-undercollar seam and the facing-collar seam; clip as needed.
18. Trim the seam allowances. If you trim too much at the notch, the lapel will have a dimple. If you don't trim enough, the notch will be lumpy. Trim, then turn the garment right-side-out. Repeat until the notch is trimmed perfectly.
19. The neckline seam of the collar and facing should be centered over the undercollar-garment seam. Reach between the garment and facing; grasp the neckline seam allowances of the facing and garment. Pull them out and stitch the seam allowances together. (Fig. 267h)
20. If the seamline at the edge of the collar shows when the collar-facing seam is centered over the undercollar-garment seam, adjust the collar by sliding the collar-facing seam toward the edge of the collar until the seamline rolls to the underside. Stabstitch the undercollar-garment seam to the garment facing. (Fig. 267i)

If the seamline at the collar edge shows on a finished or ready-made garment, take a small tuck on the undercollar. (Fig. 267j)

WAISTLINE FINISHES

Complete the waistlines of skirts and slacks with a finish that is comfortable to wear and easy to make. Use a band, facing, or elastic to finish the waistline edge.

WAISTLINE SHORTCUTS
WAISTBANDS

If you have mastered cuffs and collars, waistbands will be easy. The sewing techniques for each of these garment sections are almost identical.

The garment placket is usually completed before the band is applied. In addition, you should ease baste the garment on the seamline before you set the band.

Tailored waistbands. The tailored waistband is a neat finish for better garments.

1. Cut the waistband on the lengthwise grain. Make the band 2¾″ (7 cm) longer than the desired finished length and twice the finished width plus two seam allowances. Waistbands will fit more comfortably and more attractively if you measure your waistline honestly and add ½″–1″ (12.7 mm–25.4 mm).
2. Cut the interfacing the length and width of the finished band with seam allowances at each end. Fuse or glue the interfacing to the waistband. (Fig. 268a)

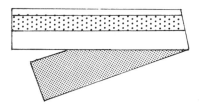

Fig. 268a

The waistband will be applied to the garment so that the interfacing will be toward the outside of the gar-

ment. For clarity, the underside of the band will be called the "facing."

3. Pin or baste the right side of the band facing to the wrong side of the garment, matching the cut edges and the notches. If you have altered the pattern and there are no notches, quarter the band and garment. Stitch them together. (Fig. 268b)

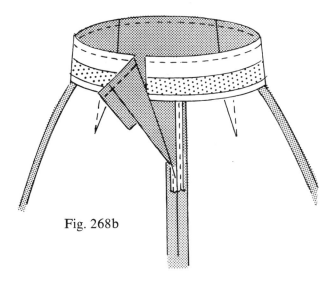

Fig. 268b

4. Fold the waistband seam up and stitch the ends. (Fig. 268c)

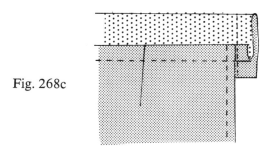

Fig. 268c

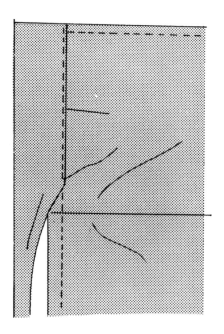

Fig. 268d

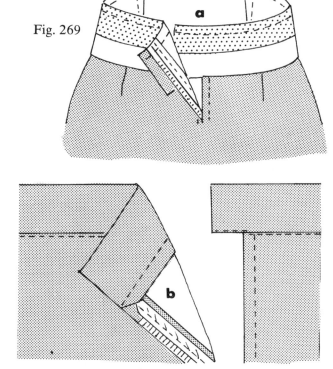

Fig. 269

5. Turn the band right-side-out.

6. Turn the seam allowance under. Pin, glue, or baste the band to the garment, then edgestitch it in place. (Fig. 268d) On the underlap, fold both seam allowances into the waistband and edgestitch them together. (Fig. 268e)

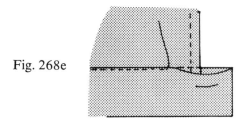

Fig. 268e

Stitch-in-the-ditch or topstitched bands. This easy method is often used on designer skirts and slacks as well as meduim-priced sportswear.

1. Cut the waistband on the lengthwise grain, using the selvage if possible. Make the band 2¾″ (7 cm) longer than the finished length and twice the finished width plus two seam allowances.

2. Fold the waistband pattern in half and cut the interfacing by the folded pattern. Fuse or glue the interfacing to the waistband. If the waistband is cut along the selvage, interface the side *away* from the selvage.

3. If the band isn't cut on the selvage, finish the edge that isn't interfaced with a clean finish or zigzag.

4. With the right sides together, pin or baste the un-

finished edge of the band to the garment, matching the cut edges and the notches. Stitch them together. (Fig. 269a)

5. Fold the waistband seam up and stitch the ends.

6. Turn the band right-side-out.

Fold under the corner of the facing on the overlap and fold the waistband seam allowances of the underlap into the band; pin, glue, or baste the band in place. From the right side of the garment, stitch-in-the-ditch or topstitch ¼″ (6.4 mm) above the waistline seam. If you stitch-in-the-ditch, edgestitch the lower edge of the underlap. (Fig. 269b)

Trouser bands. Waistbands for trousers are assembled with a seam at the center back. They are not only easy to make but easy to alter if you have a fluctuating waistline.

1. Complete the pants, leaving the center-back seam open.

2. Set the waistband to each half of the pants using a tailored, topstitched, or stitch-in-the-ditch application.

3. Stitch the center-back seam. Press.

4. Topstitch the waistband on each side of the seam to secure the seam allowances.

Band with self-fabric to interface. Interfacing with self-fabric is easy and convenient if the band is a lightweight, firmly woven fabric.

1. Cut the waistband on the lengthwise grain. Make the band 2¾" (7 cm) longer than the finished length and three times the finished width plus one seam allowance.
2. Clip the ends of the band to mark the fold lines (Fig. 270a), then press the folds on the band.
3. Pin and stitch the right side of the waistband seam allowance to the wrong side of the garment. (Fig. 270b)
4. Fold the seam allowances toward the waistband and complete the ends. (Fig. 270c)
5. Turn the band right-side-out.
6. Pin, glue, or baste the band in place and edge-stitch.

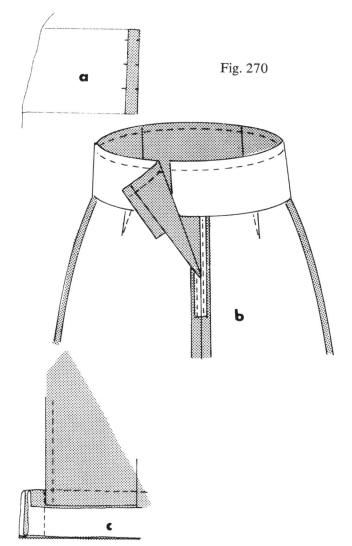

Fig. 270

Band with elastic or waistband stiffening

1. Cut the waistband on the lengthwise grain, using the selvage if possible. Make the band 2¾" (7 cm) longer than the finished length and twice the finished width plus two seam allowances.
2. Cut the waistband stiffening or elastic the finished length of the band.
3. If the band does not have a selvage edge, finish one edge.
4. Pin and stitch the unfinished edge of the band to the right side of the garment, matching the cut edges and notches.
5. If you are using stiffening, pin it on top of the seam allowances so that the edge of the stiffening is next to the seamline and the seam allowances at each end of the band extend beyond the stiffening.
6. If you are using elastic, place the edge next to the seamline and anchor each end in the seam allowances with a pin. Pin as needed to control the stretch. Stitch the stiffening or elastic to the waistline seam allowances.
7. Complete the ends. If you are using elastic, stitch through it on each end; if you are using stiffening, do not stitch through it on the ends—stitch next to it.
8. Turn the band right-side-out.
9. Turn under the corners of the facing at the zipper; glue, baste, or pin the facing in place. Stitch-in-the-ditch from the right side of the garment. Edge-stitch the underlap.

Pull-on garment with a waistband. This band is frequently used on pull-on garments. It is easy to make and comfortable to wear.

1. Cut the waistband on the bias or crossgrain, making the band twice the finished width plus two seam allowances and the finished length plus two seam allowances. If there is no zipper, the fabric must stretch enough to be pulled over the hips.
2. Cut the elastic the length of the waist measurement. Join the elastic, overlapping the ends 1" (2.5 cm). (Fig. 271a)

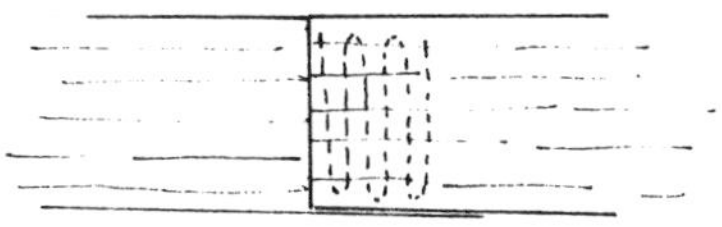

Fig. 271a

3. Stitch the ends of the waistband together and press them open.

4. Place the elastic on the wrong side of the waistband. Fold the band around the elastic, matching the cut edges. Stitch the edges of the band together for easy handling. (Fig. 271b)

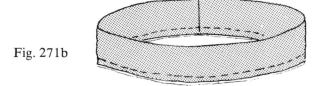

Fig. 271b

5. Divide and mark the garment and band into quarters. Match and pin the cut edges, matching the quarter marks. With the right sides together, stitch the waistband to the garment with a ⅝″ (16 mm) seam. (Fig. 271c)

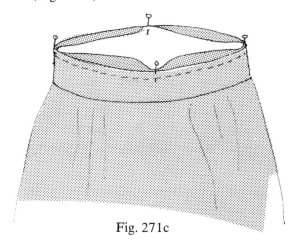

Fig. 271c

6. Trim the seam to ¼″ (6.4 mm) and zigzag the edges.

Variation: Only a few changes are required to adapt this method to a band with a placket. Cut the waistband on any grain. Add 1½″ (3.8 cm) to the length for the underlap and finish the ends of the band before setting it to the garment.

Faced Waistlines

Faced waistlines come and go in the world of fashion. Use a facing, lining, elastic, or grosgrain to face the waistline. The facing is usually set *before* the placket or zipper.

Facing or lining

1. Trim the facing or lining and garment seam allowances at the waistline to ⅜″ (9.5 mm).

2. Stay the garment waistline with tape to prevent stretching and to hold in ease. Stitch the tape to the wrong side of the garment on the seamline. (Fig. 272a)

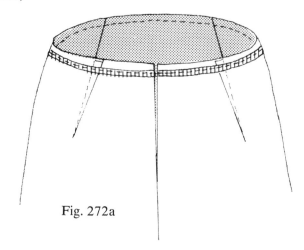

Fig. 272a

3. Finish the unnotched edge of the facing.

4. Stitch the facing or lining to the back of the zipper. (Fig. 272b)

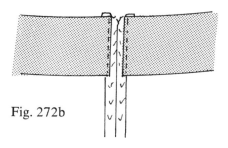

Fig. 272b

5. With the right sides together, pin and stitch the facing or lining to the garment at the waistline with a ⅜″ (9.5 mm) seam. (Fig. 272c)

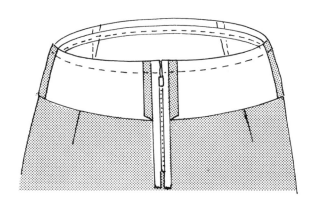

Fig. 272c

6. Understitch, clip, and press.
7. Turn the facing or lining to the wrong side of the garment.
8. If desired, topstitch ¼″ (6.4 mm) from the edge.
9. Set the zipper (see ZIPPERS).

Grosgrain. Select a grosgrain or milliner's ribbon which can be shaped to fit the garment waistline.

1. Allow a ⅝″ (16 mm) seam allowance at the waistline of the garment.
2. Stay the garment waistline with tape, stitching it to the wrong side of the garment on the seamline.
3. Press and shape the grosgrain to fit the waistline curve.
4. Pin or glue the grosgrain to the right side of the garment with the edge of the grosgrain ⅛″ (3.2 mm) above the seamline. Stitch the grosgrain to the garment. (Fig. 273)

Fig. 273

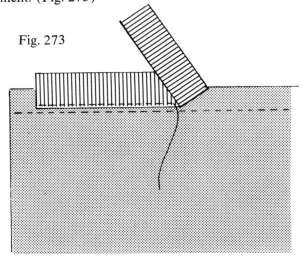

5. Trim and clip the seam allowance.
6. Fold the grosgrain on the inside of the garment.
7. Topstitch ⅛″–¼″ (3.2 mm–6.4 mm) from the edge to hold the grosgrain in place.
8. Set the zipper.

Elastic facings. Use an elastic facing to finish the waistline of slips, skirts, and slacks. Select an elastic appropriate to the garment.

Slips:
1. Allow a ¼″ (6.4 mm) seam allowance at the garment waistline.
2. Cut the elastic the desired length plus two seam allowances. Remember, some elastics don't return to their original length after they are stitched.

3. Stitch the vertical seams of the garment, leaving one seam open.
4. Divide and mark the garment and the elastic into quarters.
5. Pin the elastic to the *wrong* side of the slip, matching the quartered marks. Overlap the edge of the slip ¼″ (6.4 mm) so that the edge of the elastic is even with the garment seamline. Using a straight or zigzag stitch (W,2-L,2) stitch along the edge of the elastic nearer the garment hem. (Fig. 274a) If you

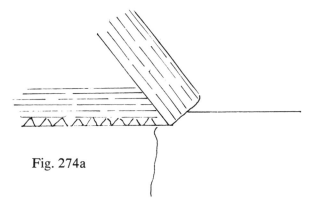

Fig. 274a

use a straight stitch, stretch the fabric and elastic as you stitch.
6. Fold the elastic to the right side of the slip, enclosing the cut edge of the garment.
7. Stitch the free edge of the elastic to the garment, using a straight or zigzag stitch (W,2-L,2). (Fig. 274b)

Fig. 274b

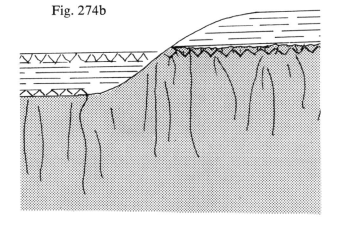

8. Complete the open seam, trim it, if needed, to ¼″ (6.4 mm) and overlock the edge.

Skirts and Slacks:
1. Allow a ⅝″ (16 mm) seam allowance at the garment waistline.

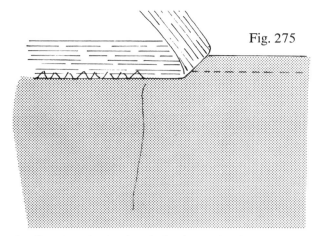

Fig. 275

2. Cut the elastic the desired length plus two seam allowances. Remember, some elastics don't return to their original length after they are stitched.

3. Stitch the vertical seams of the garment, leaving one seam open. If the garment has a placket, leave the seam with the placket open.

4. Place a line of gauge stitching in the seam allowance ⅜″ (9.5 mm) from the cut edge.

5. Divide and mark the garment and the elastic into quarters.

6. Pin the elastic to the right side of the garment with the elastic edge barely covering the gauge stitching, matching the quarter marks. Edgestitch the elastic to the garment. Stretch it as you stitch or use a zigzag stitch (W,2-L,2). (Fig. 275)

7. Complete the open seam. If the garment has a zipper, complete the seam and set the zipper.

8. Fold the seam allowance and elastic to the wrong side of the garment.

9. Topstitch ¼″–½″ (6.4 mm–12.7 mm) from the folded edge to secure the facing. If desired, make several rows of topstitching to create a shirred-band effect.

Bound Waistlines

The bias-binding waistline finish is attractive and comfortable to wear. This unusual finish was a favorite of Coco Chanel. She sometimes finished the skirts of tweed suits with a print fabric to match the suit's blouse.

1. Allow *no* seam allowance at the garment waist-line.

2. Stay the garment waistline with tape to prevent stretching and to hold in ease. Match the edges of the tape and garment. Stitch in the center of the tape.

3. Cut a bias strip 3″ (7.6 cm) wide and the finished length of the garment waistline plus 2¾″ (7 cm). This will finish the garment with a ¾″ (19.1 mm) binding.

4. Fold the bias in half lengthwise with the wrong sides together. Shape the bias with the iron to fit the the waistline.

5. With the right sides together, pin and stitch one edge of the bias to the garment with a ¾″ (19.1 mm) seam. The bias ends will extend ⅝″ (16 mm) on the overlap and 1⅝″ (4.1 cm) on the underlap. (Fig. 276a)

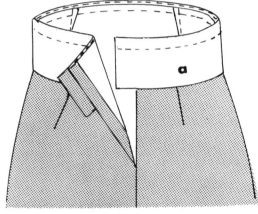

Fig. 276

6. Complete the seams at each end of the binding.

7. Fold the bias up and over the waistline edge to the wrong side of the garment.

8. Set a slot zipper—the tab should be ⅛″–¼″ (3.2 mm–6.4 mm) below the waistline edge.

9. Stitch-in-the-ditch or sew with a small backstitch in the groove of the seam to secure the binding. (Fig. 276b)

10. If the garment is lined, stitch the lining to the free edge of the binding. If it isn't, trim the bias to ⅜″ (9.5 mm).

Variation: If the binding fabric is lightweight, use a doubled-bias strip or French binding. Cut the strip 5″ (12.7 cm) wide for a ¾″ (19.1 mm) finish. Fold the strip in half lengthwise with the wrong sides together, then set it like a single binding.

UNDERLININGS, LININGS, AND INTERLININGS

Linings and underlinings improve the appearance, serviceability, durability, and stability of many garments. Interlinings add warmth.

UNDERLININGS

An underlining, sometimes called a backing or mounting, is cut from the major garment pattern pieces. It is applied to the wrong side of each garment section before the garment is assembled. The fabric and underlining combination is handled as one layer throughout the garment construction. This procedure allows the finished garment to be altered and pressed easily.

Underlinings add body, support, durability, opaqueness, and/or comfort. They reinforce, reduce wrinkling, and conceal construction details from the right side of the garment, but they do *not* finish the inside of the garment.

The choice of underlining fabric is determined by the fashion fabric and the amount of support needed to create the desired effect.

The underlining fabric should be easy to handle, durable, and wrinkleproof. It should have the same care and cleaning requirements as the fashion fabric and be color coordinated to it. The underlining should complement the fashion fabric without overwhelming it.

Generally, the underlining fabric is softer and lighter in weight than the garment fabric so that it won't change the hang or drape of the fashion fabric. The underlining should fit inside the garment without ridges so that you are unaware of its existence from the right side of the garment. Commercial lining fabrics, batiste, organza, cotton flannel, China silk, taffeta, satin, or crepe are used most frequently for underlining.

When the underlining supports the fashion fabric in a silhouette which it could not otherwise maintain, a firm, crisp underlining or an interfacing fabric is needed to back the garment. The shaping fabric shouldn't be so firm and stiff that it buckles and causes ridges that show on the right side of the garment.

Cutting and Applying the Underlining

When backing the entire garment, cut an underlining section for each major garment section. Facings, cuffs, flaps, pockets, belts, and collars will not need underlining unless the underlining influences the color or opaqueness of the fashion fabric.

The underlining fabric is usually cut on the same grain as the fashion fabric. It can be cut on the bias to make it more compatible to knits and loosely woven fabrics.

When an underlining is used to shape the garment, more than one underlining fabric may be required to shape different sections different amounts.

When a garment is underlined for design and also to hide the construction details, two backing fabrics —one for design and one for shape—may be used if needed.

The wrong side of the underlining is usually applied to the wrong side of the fashion fabric. When the underlining is used for design or color as under lace, it is sewn with the right side of the underlining toward the wrong side of the fashion fabric.

✿ When the fashion fabric and underlining fabric

are the same width, you can lay out the two fabrics one on top of the other and cut the garment sections from both fabrics at the same time.

⚙ Mark the construction details on the underlining.

⚙ Use a washable glue stick or permanent glue to glue the underlining to the fashion fabric. Glue the sections together in the seam allowances.

⚙ Hand or machine baste the pick-up line of darts. Extend the basting line 1″ (2.5 cm) beyond the dart point. (Fig. 277)

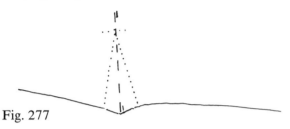

Fig. 277

Underlinings That Shape

Backing fabrics used to shape the garment should be cut slightly smaller than the fashion fabric. The stiff backing fabric must make a smaller circle than the garment so that the backing will fit inside the garment smoothly and won't create ridges on the outside of the garment. The difference between the two layers isn't very large, but it's enough to spell success or failure.

1. Cut the underlining and fashion fabric out separately.
2. Mark the construction and design details on the *right* side of the garment fabric with thread or soap.
3. Trim the backing sections ⅟₁₆″ (1.6 mm) on each lengthwise seam. (Fig. 278)

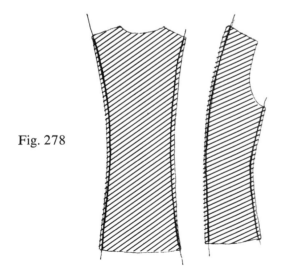

Fig. 278

4. Glue the seam allowances of the underlining and fashion fabric together, matching the *cut edges*. The glued sections will curl toward the underlining.

Partial Underlinings

It isn't always necessary to underline the entire garment. You can underline only a section or part of a section for design or shape. Use a partial underlining on a skirt back to prevent its stretching out of shape, on a bodice front to make it opaque, on sleeves to create a puff, or at the knees of slacks to prevent bagging.

1. Cut a piece of firmly woven lining fabric the width of the garment and the desired length. Shape it as needed to fit the garment outline. If the underlining is used to prevent stretching, cut it so that the lengthwise grain goes *around* the body. Otherwise, the grain is the same as the garment.
2. Finish any edges of the underlining so that they won't be sewn into seams.
3. Glue, pin or machine baste the underlining to the wrong side of the garment. (Fig. 279)
4. Assemble the garment.

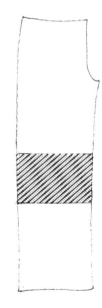

Fig. 279

Flat Linings

Flat lining lightweight fabrics. This easy flat-lining shortcut can be used on lightweight fabrics to back the fashion fabric and finish the edges of the seams simultaneously. Use soft, lightweight underlinings to flat line garments.

1. Cut out the fashion fabric and underlining fabric.
2. Mark any darts on the underlining fabric.
3. Place the underlining on top of the corresponding garment section with the *right* sides together, matching the notches.
4. With the underlining fabric on top, stitch a ¼″ (6.4 mm) seam on all edges except the neckline, armscye, waistline, and hem. The ¼″ (6.4 mm) seam *must* be even; the stitched line will be used as a guide when the garment is assembled. (Fig. 280a)
5. When the garment has a large dart, cut the dart so that each leg of the dart has a seam allowance of 1″ (2.5 cm). Stitch the lining to the fashion fabric at the cut edges of the dart with a ¼″ (6.4 mm) seam. (Fig. 280b) Omit this step when the darts are small.
6. Clip as needed so that the sections will lie flat when turned right-side-out.

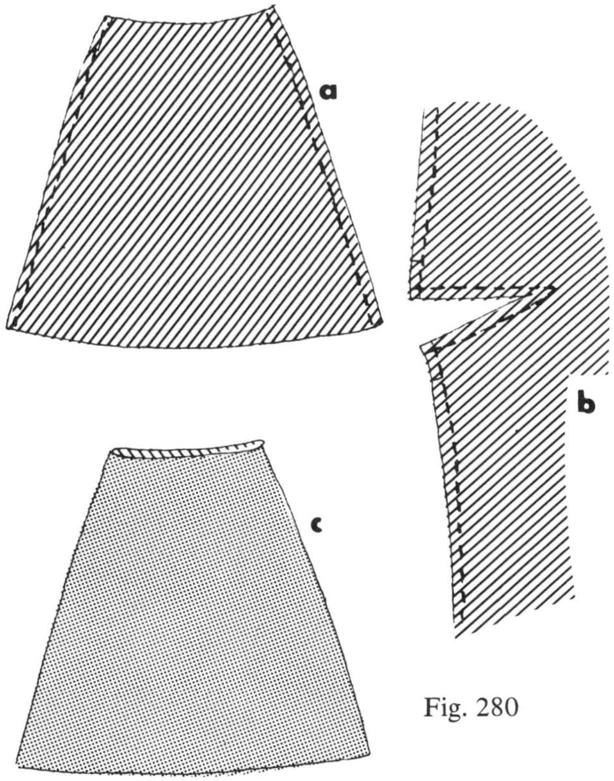

If you don't want narrow seams in the finished garment, cut the fashion fabric and underlining sections with 1″ (2.5 cm) seam allowances, stitch them together with a ¼″ (6.4 mm) seam, and assemble the garment, using a ¾″ (19.1 mm) seam.

Flat lining sleeves is a quick way to make a jacket easy to slip on and off.

Flat lining heavyweight fabrics. To flat line heavyweight fabrics, the underlining can be cut and stitched so bulky seam edges are eliminated. This attractive finish looks like a Hong-Kong finish. Use a soft, lightweight underlining.

1. Cut out the fashion fabric. Mark the construction details on the face-side.
2. Place the garment sections face-down on the underlining, matching the grainlines. (Fig. 281a)

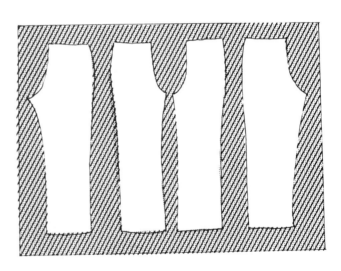

Fig. 281a

Fig. 280

7. Turn the sections right-side-out and underpress them. (Fig. 280c)
8. Assemble the garment, using a ⅜″ (9.5 mm) seam.

3. Mark the cutting lines on the underlining ½″ (12.7 mm) from all edges except the neckline, armscye, waistline, and hem. The cutting line at the neckline, armscye, waistline, and hem is the same as the garment. (Fig. 281b)
4. Cut out the underlining fabric.
5. Match and glue the extended edges of the underlining to the cut edges of the fashion fabric.
6. With the underlining on top, stitch the underlining to the fashion fabric, using a ¼″ (3.2 mm) seam. The seam *must* be stitched evenly.
7. Trim the seam ⅛″ (3.2 mm)
8. Turn the sections right-side-out, wrapping the

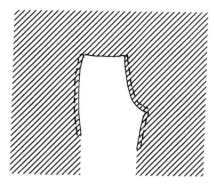

Fig. 281b

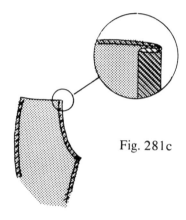

Fig. 281c

underlining around the edge of the fashion fabric. (Fig. 281c)

9. Stitch-in-the-ditch to secure the underlining to the fabric at each seamed edge.

10. Assemble the garment using a ⅝″ (16 mm) seam.

Underlining with Interfacing

When interfacing fabrics, woven and nonwoven, are used to underline, they can shape any fabric into an extreme silhouette. However, seams cannot be pressed flat when many interfacing fabrics such as hair canvas and nonwovens are stitched into them.

Sew-in interfacing shortcut

1. Cut out the fashion fabric and the underlining material.

2. Trim the underlining ¾″ (19.1 mm) on all edges except the armscye and hem.

3. Position the underlining on the wrong side of the garment sections. Secure the underlining permanently to the garment sections, using a ¼″ (6.4 mm) strip of fusible agent, permanent glue, or a hand catchstitch along the edges of the interfacing. Check and double-check to be sure the fusible or glue won't show on the right side of the garment.

Custom method—sew-in interfacing

1. Cut out the fashion fabric and the underlining material.

2. Using the underlining or pattern as a guide, cut a piece of lightweight fabric 1½″ (3.8 cm) wide for all edges except the hem and armscye. It is important to cut around the pattern accurately, but it doesn't matter if the other edge isn't exact. (Fig. 282a)

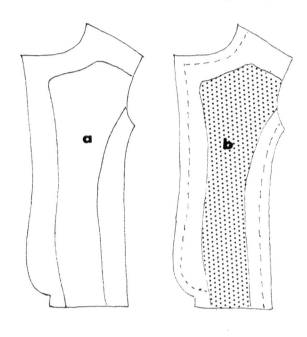

Fig. 282

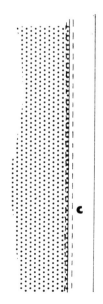

3. Pin these sections to the underlining, matching the cut edges.

4. Stitch the strips in place ⅞″ (22.2 mm) from the edges of the garment. (Fig. 282b)

5. Using embroidery scissors, trim away the outside edges of the underlining close to the stitched line. Assemble the garment with a ⅝″ (16 mm) seam. The stitching line doesn't penetrate the interfacing fabric. (Fig. 282c)

LININGS

A lining is cut from a lining pattern or from the main garment sections. It is assembled separately from the garment, then sewn into the garment by hand or machine so that the wrong sides are together.

This elegant finish preserves the garment shape and increases the life of the garment, but it cannot create the shape or silhouette. It protects the seams from abrasion and the body from abrasive fabrics. It reduces wrinkling and may add design interest or warmth.

The choice of lining fabric is determined by the fashion fabric and the kind of garment. The lining fabric should be easy to handle, colorfast, opaque, static-free, and wrinkle-resistant. It should have the same durability, care, and cleaning requirements as the fashion fabric.

The type of garment determines the qualities desired in a lining. Linings for cold-weather coats should add warmth, and linings for outer garments usually have a smooth, slippery quality, enabling you to easily slide the garment over other apparel.

Avoid white or light-colored lining fabrics in coats and jackets. They soil quickly, requiring more frequent cleaning than the fashion fabric.

Partially Lined Garments

Many garments do not need or require full linings. Line only the desired sections.

Lined yokes. Yokes in blouses are lined to conceal the shoulder and yoke seams. Yokes in jackets are lined to make putting them on easy. Yokes can be lined by several methods, depending on the garment style and finish quality.

Inside-stitched Yoke:
This designer technique can be used to finish any yoke—plain or fancy, inexpensive or luxurious. The stitching is completely concealed on the completed garment.

1. Cut two yoke sections from the yoke pattern with the lengthwise grain *parallel* to the yoke seamline.
2. Sandwich and stitch the front shoulder seams between the two yoke sections. (Fig. 283a)

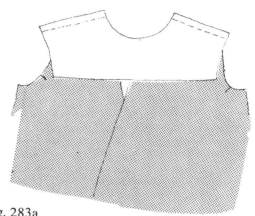

Fig. 283a

3. With the right sides together, pin and stitch the outside yoke and the back together. (Fig. 283b)
4. Place the garment on a table with the yoke sections face-up. Wrap the yoke sections completely

Fig. 283b

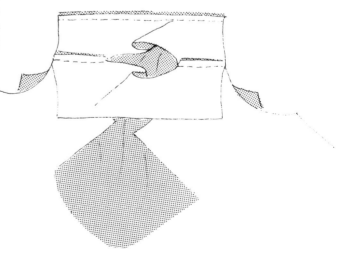

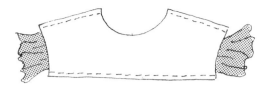

Fig. 283c

around the fronts and the back, matching the right side of the yoke facing to the wrong side of the back. (Fig. 283c)

5. Pin and stitch the yoke seams.

6. Pull the garment fronts and back out gently. The yoke is now lined with no raw seams exposed.

This method can also be used to line the crotch of swimsuits or underpanties.

Topstitched Yoke:
The topstitched yoke is a good method to use on sportswear.

1. Cut two yoke sections from the yoke pattern with the lengthwise grain parallel to the yoke seamline.

2. Fold under the ⅝″ (16 mm) seam allowance on the long edge of the outside yoke and topstitch ⅜″ (9.5 mm) from the folded edge. (Fig. 284a)

Fig. 284

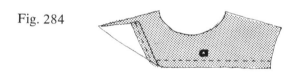

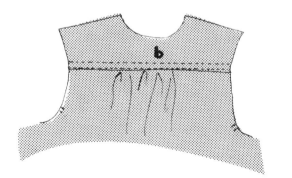

3. Sandwich and stitch the front shoulder seams between the two yoke sections so that the right sides of the fronts and outside yoke face each other.

4. With the right side of the yoke facing next to the wrong side of the back, pin and stitch the yoke seam.

5. Pin or glue the outside yoke in place. Edgestitch the yoke to the back covering the facing-back seamline. (Fig. 284b)

Stitch-in-the-Ditch Method:
This super-simple application was taken from a very expensive dress by Courrèges. It can be used on any garment.

1. Cut two yoke sections from the yoke pattern with the lengthwise grain parallel to the yoke seamline.

2. Finish the seam allowance of the yoke facing with a zigzag or clean finish.

3. Sandwich and stitch the front shoulder seams between the two yoke sections so the right side of the fronts face the right side of the outside yoke.

4. With the right sides together, stitch the yoke and back together.

5. Glue or pin the yoke facing to the yoke-back seam. Stitch-in-the-ditch or topstitch to secure the facing.

Jackets. Unlined jackets may be quicker to make than their lined cousins, but they are harder to put on and not as comfortable to wear. Try this idea from a Vera Maxwell suit—line only the yoke and sleeves.

1. Cut the yoke and sleeves from lining fabric.

2. If your pattern doesn't have a yoke, make a yoke pattern for the lining. Trace the back pattern section on the center foldline and on the cut edges of the neckline, shoulder, and armscye.

3. Mark a point on the center foldline 4″–5″ (10.2 cm–12.7 cm) below the neck edge. Square a line from this point to the armscye. (Fig. 285a)

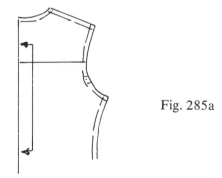

Fig. 285a

4. Cut the sleeve lining by the sleeve pattern, extending the underarm seams 1″ (2.5 cm) into the armscye. This extension allows the lining to go over the underarm seam without mashing the seam.

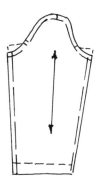

Fig. 285b

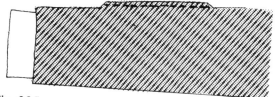

Fig. 285e

5. Trim the lining sleeves at the wrist 1″ (2.5 cm) shorter than the *unhemmed* garment sleeves. (Fig. 285b)

6. If the garment has a yoke, line the yoke by one of the methods in the preceding section.

7. If the garment back is cut in one piece, make a yoke lining. Finish the long edge of the yoke lining; then sandwich the front shoulder seams between the garment back and the lining yoke. Glue or pin the yoke to the wrong side of the back at the armscye.

8. Stitch the underarm seams of the sleeve linings, leaving 8″–10″ (20.3 cm–25.4 cm) open in the elbow area. (Fig. 285c)

Fig. 285c

9. Hem the garment sleeve at the center of the hem allowance.

10. Set the garment sleeve into the garment.

11. Pin and stitch the sleeve lining into the garment, sandwiching the garment between the sleeve and sleeve lining.

12. Position the lining in the sleeve so that the wrong sides are together.

13. Reach into the opening of the sleeve lining, grasp the cut edges of the hem; pull them out; match the cut edges of the hem and sleeve lining, pin and stitch them together. (Fig. 285d) A tuck will form automatically in the lining at the hem.

Fig. 285d

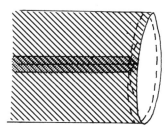

14. Close the lining opening—push the seam allowances to the wrong side of the lining. Fold the lining on the seamline with the seam allowances together. Edgestitch the opening closed. The tiny ridge which will form won't be uncomfortable and it won't show. (Fig. 285e)

Jacket with Cuffed Sleeves

If the sleeves have cuffs, the jacket is even easier to line.

1. Cut the sleeve lining by the sleeve pattern, extending the underarm seams 1″ (2.5 cm) into the armscye. This extension allows the lining to go over the underarm seam without mashing the seam.

2. Complete the underarm seams of the sleeve and lining.

3. Set the garment sleeve into the garment.

4. Pin and stitch the sleeve lining into the garment, sandwiching the garment between the sleeve and sleeve lining.

5. If you're using a faced placket on the sleeve, arrange the sleeve and lining so that the right sides are together and the lining is on top. Complete the placket at the edge of the sleeve. Turn the sleeve right-side-out. If you're using a continuous or tailored placket, position the sleeve and lining with the wrong sides together. Complete the placket.

6. Machine baste the sleeve and lining together at the cuff edge.

7. Set the cuff to the lined sleeve.

Edge-to-Edge Linings

Reversible garments are lined edge-to-edge. The most common mistake made by the home sewer is leaving a large section of the hem open so that the garment can be turned right-side-out. This hem section is difficult to finish by hand so that it looks like the rest of the hem which was finished by machine. Use these shortcuts to eliminate this home-sewn look.

Wrap-around skirt

1. Cut the skirt sections in the fashion fabric and lining fabric. Do not cut facings.

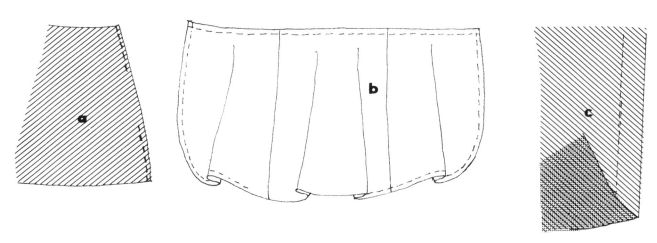

Fig. 286

2. Complete the vertical seams of the skirt and lining, leaving one lining seam open 10″–12″ (25.4
cm–30.5 cm) in the center. Press. (Fig. 286a)
3. Check the garment and lining to be sure they are
exactly the same length.
4. With the right sides together, pin and stitch the
skirt and lining together around the edges. Leave the
hem open about 20″ (50.8 cm). (Fig. 286b)
5. Turn the garment right-side-out.
6. Reach into the open lining seam, pull out the two
hem edges and stitch them together to complete the
hem.
7. Reach into the open side seam, pull out the seam
allowances of that seam and stitch as far as possible.
(Fig. 286c)
8. Slipstitch the remaining 2″–3″ (5.1 cm–7.6 cm)
if the skirt is actually reversible. Omit the slipstitching if it's not going to be worn with the lining out.
9. Press.
10. Topstitch if desired.

Vest
1. Cut the sections of the vest in the fashion fabric
and lining fabric. Cut the lining with a seam at the
center back. Do not cut facings.
2. Complete the center-back seam of the vest and
lining, leaving the seam of the lining open 8″–10″
(20.3 cm–25.4 cm). (Fig. 287a) Complete the
shoulder seams of the vest and lining.
3. With the right sides together, pin and stitch the
neckline and armholes of the vest. If the garment
isn't reversible, understitch.
4. Turn the vest right-side-out and understitch.
5. Stitch the underarm seams. Check the garment
and lining to be sure they are exactly the same size.
(Fig. 287b)

6. Reach into the open lining seam, pull out the
hem of the vest, and complete the hem.
7. If the vest isn't reversible, close the center-back
seam by pushing the seam allowances to the wrong
side. Fold the lining on the seamline with the seam
allowances together. Edgestitch the opening closed.
If the vest is reversible, close the seam with a slipstitch.
8. Press the vest.
9. Topstitch if desired.

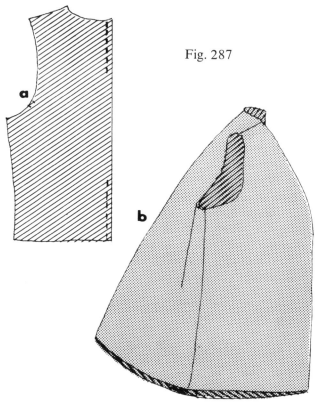

Fig. 287

Slip Linings

Skirts and slacks with a waistband. This lining is attached at the waistline and hangs loosely inside skirts and slacks.

1. Cut the lining from the major garment pattern sections. Do not cut a lining for the waistband.
2. Assemble and press the garment. Set the zipper into the garment.
3. Assemble and press the lining. Press the darts in the opposite direction from those in the garment.
4. With the wrong sides together, match the edges at the waistline, keying the notches and seamlines. Stitch the lining and skirt together at the waistline. (Fig. 288a)

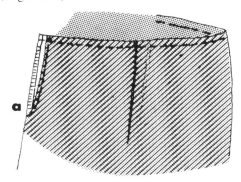

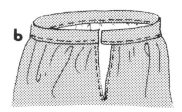

Fig. 288

5. Set the waistband to the skirt. (Fig. 288b)
6. Sew the lining to the back of the zipper.

Skirts and slacks without a waistband

1. Cut the lining and fashion fabric, using the major garment pattern sections, allowing ⅜″ (9.5 mm) seam allowances at the waistline on the lining and garment. Do not cut a facing or waistband from either fabric.
2. Assemble and press the garment. Press the seam allowances of the placket to the wrong side.
3. Stay the garment waistline with tape to prevent stretching and to hold in ease.
4. Assemble and press the lining. Press the darts in the opposite direction from those in the garment. Press the seam allowances of the placket to the wrong side so that ⅞″ (22.2 mm) is folded under

at the waistline, tapering to the seamline at the bottom of the placket.
5. Stitch the lining to the back of the zipper (see ZIPPERS—Centered Application). (Fig. 289a)

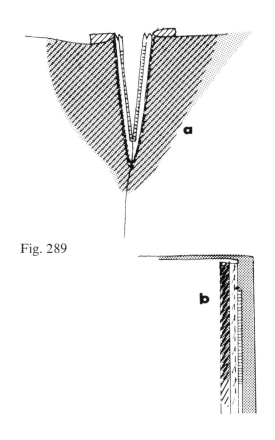

Fig. 289

6. With the right sides together, match the edges at the waistline so that the skirt placket extends ⅝″ (16 mm) beyond the zipper. (Fig. 289b)
7. Fold the seam allowances over the zipper and lining. Pin and stitch the garment and lining together with a ⅜″ (9.5 mm) seam.
8. Understitch and trim.
9. Turn the skirt right-side-out.
10. Stitch the zipper into the garment.

Sleeveless dresses

1. Cut the lining from the major garment pattern pieces. Do not cut facings.
2. Set the slip linings to the sleeveless dress with an all-in-one facing application (see FACINGS). Select the method most appropriate for your garment. Consider the fabric bulk, garment design, and quality when you select the application.
3. Hem the lining so that it is 1″ (2.5 cm) shorter than the dress.

213

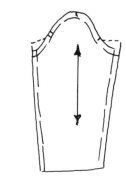

Fig. 290

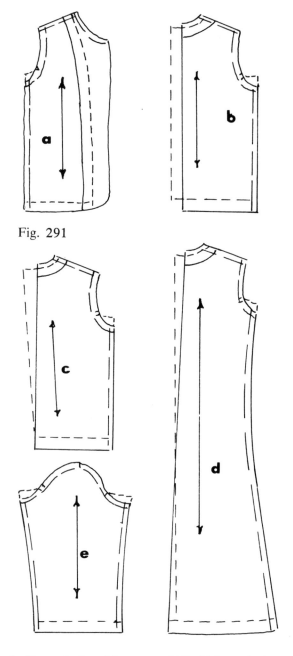

Fig. 291

Jacket Linings

Commercial lining patterns. The lining pattern for a jacket requires a slight adjustment for a professional fit. The sleeve of the jacket will fit and hang better if you make this small change on the lining pattern. Extend the side seams of the front, back, and sleeve ⅝″ (16 mm) into the armscye. (Fig. 290) This extension will allow the lining to go up and over the underarm seam of the garment without mashing the seam.

Drafting lining patterns. Many jacket patterns don't include a lining pattern, but it's often easier to line the garment than to finish the seams attractively, and a lined jacket or coat is usually more comfortable to wear.

Front-lining Pattern:
1. Place the pattern front on top of the front-facing pattern, matching the stitching lines of the front and neckline. (Fig. 291a)
2. Trace the curved edge of the facing.
3. Draw the cutting line for the lining front 1¼″ (3.2 cm) from the edge of the facing toward the center front to allow for a ⅝″ (16 mm) lining-facing seam.
4. Extend the side seam ⅝″ (16 mm) into the armscye. Connect the extended seam to the armscye notch. This will allow the lining to go up and over the seam allowances of the garment, causing the underarm seam and sleeve to hang better.
5. Make the lining pattern 1″ (2.5 cm) shorter than the garment pattern.

Back-lining Pattern:
1. Place the pattern back on top of the back-facing pattern, matching the stitching lines of the shoulder and neckline. (Fig. 291b)
2. Trace the edge of the facing.
3. Draw the cutting line for the lining back 1¼″ (3.2 cm) above the curved edge of the facing.

4. Extend the side seam ⅝″ (16 mm) into th armscye and connect it to the notches.
5. Make the lining pattern 1″ (2.5 cm) shorter tha the garment pattern.
6. Add a 1″ (2.5 cm) pleat to the center bac Lining fabrics are usually more firmly woven wit less stretch than the fashion fabric. The pleat allow the lining to give with the jacket. The pleat usuall extends the length of the garment, but it can tape to nothing at the hemline. (Fig. 291c) The linin of a flared coat can be tapered to less than the widt of the garment. (Fig. 291d)

7. Mark the grainline on the lining back parallel to the center back of the lining.

Sleeve-lining Pattern:
1. Make the lining pattern 1″ (2.5 cm) shorter than the garment pattern unless the sleeve is cuffed. Don't shorten the pattern if the sleeve has a cuff.
2. Extend the underarm seam ⅝″ (16 mm) into the armscye and connect it to the notches. (Fig. 291e)

Hemming Jackets
1. When you are marking and measuring a new garment or altering an old one, hold the lining in place by pinning it to the garment about 10″ (25.4 cm) from the hem. Pin the lining and garment together when the hem is marked or hang the garment on a hanger to pin them together. (Fig. 292a)
2. Trim the lining so that it is 1″ (2.5 cm) shorter than the *unhemmed* garment.
3. Hem the garment at the center of the hem, leaving the unfinished edge of the hem free. (Fig. 292b)

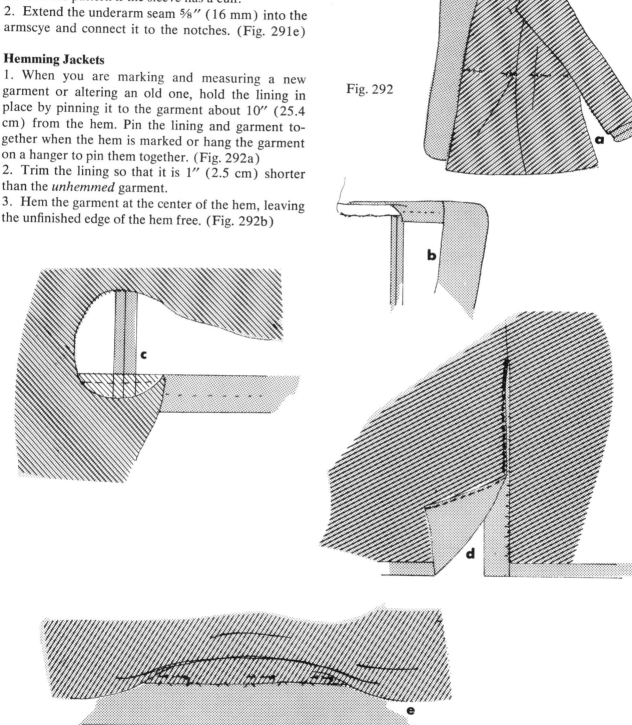

Fig. 292

215

4. If the garment has a vent, leave the vent open until the hem is stitched. Stitch the edges of the lining and garment together with a ½″ (12.7 mm) seam. Begin at the front facing and stitch to the vent. (Fig. 292c)

5. Finish the vent by turning the seam allowances to the wrong side of the jacket. Pin, then edgestitch the lining and fashion fabric together on the underlap and slipstitch them together on the overlap. (Fig. 292d)

6. If the garment doesn't have a vent, stitch from the front facing to the back on each side as far as possible.

7. Complete the lining hem at the center back by hand. (Fig. 292e)

Quick Machine Lining

This easy method requires little time or talent. It can be used on children's jackets and everyday garments. It is not appropriate for better garments.

1. Construct and hem the jacket in the center of the hem. Do not set the facings. Press.

2. Complete the collar. Press.

3. With right-sides-up, pin and stitch the collar to the jacket, matching the notches at the neckline edges. (Fig. 293a)

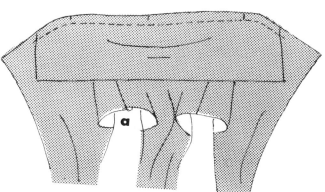

4. Complete the facing and lining. Leave a 12″ (30.5 cm) opening in the center-back lining seam.

5. Pin and stitch the lining to the facing, matching the notches. The lining hem should be folded to the wrong side of the lining. (Fig. 293b)

6. Pin and stitch the facings to the garment so that the collar is sandwiched between the garment and facing. (Fig. 293c)

7. Press the seams open, clip, and trim them as needed.

8. Turn the garment right-side-out.

9. Reach into the center-back opening, pull out the edges of the garment and lining hems, pin, and stitch them together. Stitch the edges of the sleeve hems together.

10. Finish the center-back seam by reaching into the opening, grasping the seam allowances and stitching as far as possible by machine. Close the remainder by hand.

11. Modify this easy method by extending the back lining to the collar, eliminating the back-neck facing to reduce bulk and make a more comfortable garment. Stitch the front facing to the lining front; then complete the shoulder seams by stitching this section to the lining back.

Bagging

Bagging is the method used most often to line jackets and blazers in American ready-to-wear and French *prêt-à-porter* collections. This super-fast finish is used on garments ranging from $50 to $1,000. The method is called "bagging" because the garment forms a bag when you sew the garment and lining together.

1. Cut the garment lining so the body and sleeves are 1″ (2.5 cm) shorter than the corresponding garment sections.

Fig. 293

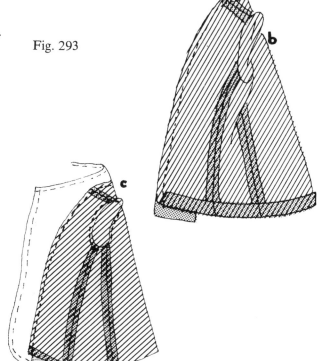

2. Construct the jacket and set the facings. Press.

3. Construct the lining, leaving a 12″ (30.5 cm) opening in the underarm of one sleeve. Begin the opening 1½″ (3.8 cm) from the armhole. Do not press the lining seams open.

4. Hem the jacket and sleeves so that the hemming sttich is in the center of the hem.

5. Match and pin the notches of the facing and lining. Fold the lining hem to the wrong side of the lining, then stitch the lining to the facing. (Fig. 294)

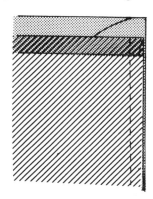

Fig. 294

6. Turn the garment right-side-out and check the lining length at the hem and sleeves.

7. Reach into the open sleeve seam, pull out the sleeve and lining. Pin and stitch the cut edges of the lining and sleeve hem so that the right sides are together. Turn the sleeve right-side-out. Complete the other sleeve.

8. Pull out the hems of the garment and lining. Pin and stitch the edges with the right sides together, beginning and ending 2″ (5.1 cm) from the front facings. Turn the garment right-side-out.

9. Pull out the underarm seams of the lining and garment. Match, pin, and stitch them together.

10. Close the open seam in the sleeve lining. Push the seam allowances to the wrong side of the lining. Fold the lining on the seamline with the seam allowances together. Edgestitch the opening closed.

11. If you have not stitched the underarm seams together, stitch in the well of the underarm seam from the right side of the garment for 1″ (2.54 cm) below the armscye.

Variation:

If you find it difficult to stitch the hem and sleeves by reaching into an open sleeve seam, leave the center-back seam of the lining open 12″ (30.5 cm) instead.

Finish the center-back seam by reaching into the opening, grasping the seam allowances and stitching as far as possible by machine. Stitch from the

bottom to the top so that the small open section will be hidden in the pleat or finish the open seam by hand.

Lining a Vest with an Unfaced Front

Leather, suede or pseudosuede is often used only on the front of a vest for economy and comfort.

1. Cut the vest front from a nonwoven material such as leather, suede, or pseudosuede.

2. Cut the vest back from a woven or knitted fabric that complements the front section. If this is a skirt-vest ensemble, cut the vest back to match the skirt. Allow a 1¼″ (3.2 cm) hem on the back.

3. Cut a lining for the vest back with a seam at the center back and ¾″ (19.1 mm) shorter than the unhemmed vest.

4. Stitch the center-back seam of the lining, leaving 8″–10″ (20.3 cm–25.4 cm) open in the center.

5. Stitch the lining to the back at the lower edge with a ¼″ (6.4 mm) seam.

6. With the right sides together, stitch the lining and back together at the armholes and neckline. (Fig. 295a)

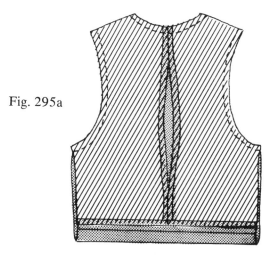

Fig. 295a

7. Insert the front between the back and its lining so that the cut edges of the shoulder seams match. The right side of the front faces the right side of the back. Stitch through the three layers. (Fig. 295b)

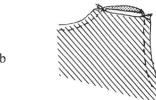

Fig. 295b

217

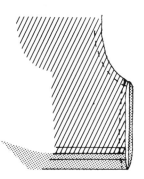

Fig. 295c

8. Repeat at the side seams. (Fig. 295c)
9. Turn the garment right-side-out. Underpress.
10. Close the center-back opening.

Lining by Hand

When you are sewing a jacket or coat lining in by hand, use a running stitch instead of a slipstitch.

1. The lining length is 1″ (2.5 cm) shorter than the unhemmed jacket.
2. Complete the jacket and lining separately.
3. With the right sides together, match and pin the cut edges of the lining and facing. Sew them together with a short, even running stitch. (Fig. 296a)

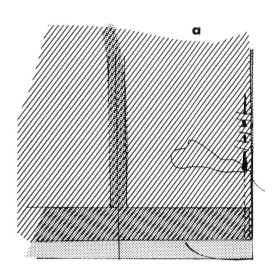

4. Turn the garment right-side-out.
5. Turn the lining hem under ½″ (12.7 mm). Pin the folded edge to the garment ½″ (12.7 mm) below the cut edge of the hem. The cut edges of the garment and lining will match and the lining will bubble. (Fig. 296b)
6. Slipstitch the lining to the garment hem. (Fig. 296c)
7. Remove the pins in the hem; the lining will form a tuck over the stitching line.
8. Hem the lining to the sleeves in the same manner.

INTERLININGS

Interlinings are inserted between the garment and lining to add warmth. They are usually cut by the lining pattern, applied to the wrong side of each lining section and stitched into the lining seams.

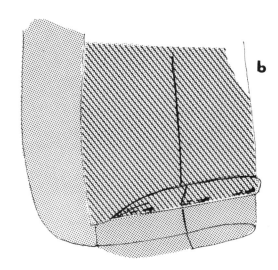

Figs. 296 a-c

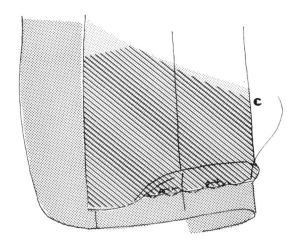

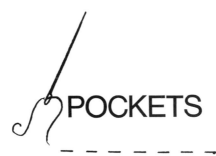

POCKETS

Pockets can be an exciting fashion detail or the mark of a poor seamstress. Careful construction from beginning to end guarantees a quality finish.

PATCH POCKETS

There are at least a dozen ways to make patch pockets. Here are just a few for starters.

Unlined Pockets

1. Cut the pocket by the pattern with notches on each side of the hemline. (Fig. 297a)

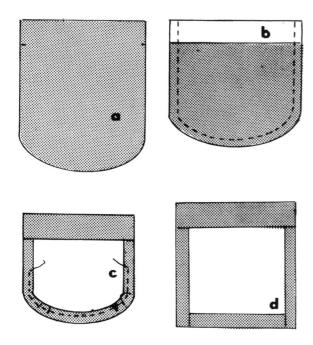

Fig. 297

2. Finish the top edge of the pocket with a zigzag stitch. Use hem tape instead if the pocket will stretch out of shape when it's used or if you don't have a zigzag machine.

3. Fold the pocket at the notched hemline with the right sides together.

4. Stitch around the pocket slightly less than 5⁄8″ (16 mm) from the edge. (Fig. 297b) If the pocket has rounded curves ease baste each curve 3⁄8″ (9.5 mm) from the cut edge.

5. Turn the pocket hem right-side-out.

6. Press the hem and seam allowances to the wrong side of the pocket, rolling the stitched line to the underside.

7. Use a cardboard template the size of the finished pocket to shape pockets quickly and identically. Transfer the stitching lines of the pocket to the cardboard with a stiletto tracing wheel.

8. Place the pocket face-down with the template on top of it. Press the seam allowances over the template. Keep the template in the pattern envelope to use next time you use the pattern.

9. If the pocket has rounded corners, pull the basting thread to draw the seam allowance to the wrong side of the pocket. Put the template in, press, and shrink out the fullness at the curves. (Fig. 297c) Notch the curves with pinking shears if the fabric is bulky.

10. If the pocket is a rectangle, press the seam allowance from the bottom up before pressing those on the sides. (Fig. 297d)

11. Mitre the pocket corners on bulky fabrics and luxury garments.

12. Pin, glue, fuse, or baste the pocket to the garment section.

13. Topstitch the pocket in place or secure it invisibly with a running stitch from the wrong side of the

garment. Many pockets are easier to set with a zipper foot. With the foot positioned on the pocket adjust it to stitch the desired distance from the edge.

Interfaced Pockets

1. Cut a piece of fusible interfacing the size of the finished pocket.
2. Fuse it to the wrong side of the pocket. (Fig. 298)

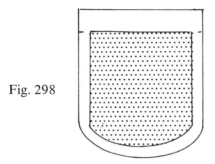

Fig. 298

3. Handle the interfaced pocket like an unlined pocket.

Flat-lined Pockets

1. Cut the pocket by the pattern with notches on each side of the hemline fold.
2. Cut the lining by the pattern for the pocket lining. If the pattern doesn't include a lining pattern, cut the lining ¼″ (6.4 mm) shorter than the finished pocket.
3. With the right sides together, stitch the lining and pocket together with a ⅜″ (9.5 mm) seam. Fig. 299a) Understitch the lining and seam allowances.

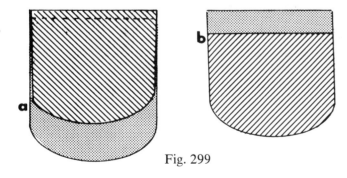

Fig. 299

4. Fold the pocket at the notches so that the *wrong* sides are together. (Fig. 299b)
5. Machine baste the cut edges together just inside the seamline.
6. Press and set the flat-lined pocket like an unlined pocket.

Self-fabric Lined Pockets
Method one
1. Place the foldline of the pocket pattern on the fold of the fabric. (Fig. 300a)

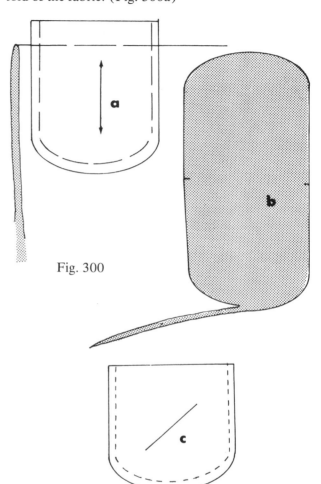

Fig. 300

2. Cut out the pocket and its facing.
3. Notch the pocket on each side at the foldline.
4. Pretrim the seam allowance on the pocket facing ⅛″ (3.2 mm), tapering to nothing at the foldline. (Fig. 300b)
5. With the right sides together, match the cut edges and stitch a ½″ (12.7 mm) seam.
6. Trim the seam to ¼″ (6.4 mm) and notch the curves with pinking shears or double stitch and trim very closely.
7. Make a 1″–2″ (2.5 cm–5.1 cm) slash in the facing on the bias. (Fig. 300c)
8. Turn the pocket right-side-out.
9. Finish the slash by hand or leave it open.
10. Underpress the pocket from the wrong side, rolling the seamline to the underside.
11. Set the pocket to the garment.

Method two

1. Place the foldline of the pocket pattern on the fold of the fabric.
2. Cut out the pocket and its facing.
3. Notch the pocket on each side at the foldline.
4. Pretrim the seam allowance on the pocket facing ⅛″ (3.2 mm), tapering to nothing at the foldline.
5. With the right sides together, match the cut edges and stitch a ½″ (12.7 mm) seam, leaving a 1½″–2″ (3.8 cm–5.1 cm) opening on the bottom edge. (Fig. 301a)

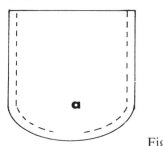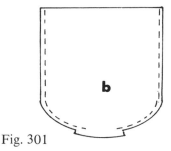

Fig. 301

6. Trim the seam to ¼″ (6.4 mm), leaving a hook at the bottom in the unstitched area. (Fig. 301b)
7. Notch the curves with pinking shears or double stitch and trim very closely.
8. Turn the pocket right-side-out through the hook.
9. Underpress the pocket, rolling the seamline to the underside.
10. Set the pocket to the garment. The opening at the hook will be secured when you topstitch.

Lined Pockets

1. Cut the pocket by the pattern with notches on each side of the hemline fold.
2. Cut the lining by the pattern for the pocket lining. If the pattern doesn't include a lining pattern, cut the lining ½″ (12.7 mm) shorter than the pocket.
3. With the right sides together, stitch the lining and pocket together with a ¼″ (6.4 mm) seam, leaving a 2″ (5.1 cm) opening in the center of the seam. (Fig. 302a)
4. Pretrim the seam allowance on the lining and pocket ⅛″ (3.2 mm), tapering to nothing at the foldline. (Fig. 302b)
5. With the right sides together, match the cut edges and stitch a ½″ (12.7 mm) seam around the pocket. (Fig. 302c)
6. Trim the seams and notch the curves.
7. Turn the pocket right-side-out through the opening in the hem-lining seam. Slipstitch the opening if desired.

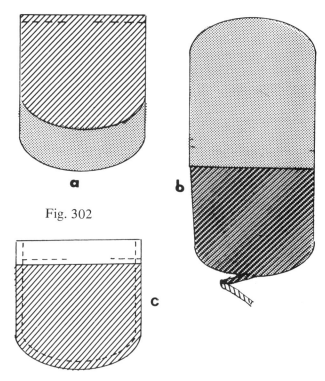

Fig. 302

8. Underpress the pocket, rolling the seamline to the underside.
9. Set the pocket to the garment.

"Invisibly" Stitched Pockets

Invisibly stitched pockets are especially intriguing to the home seamstress. This is an easy, fake method which many manufacturers use.

1. Construct a lined pocket. Do *not* trim the pocket facing seam allowance—it should be the same width as the seam allowance on the pocket. This is one time when you want the facing to be the same size as the pocket or a tiny bit *larger*.
2. Turn the pocket right-side-out.
3. Pin the pocket to the garment. The pins should be located in the center of the pocket, not near the edges. (Fig. 303a)

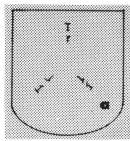

Fig. 303

221

4. Carefully roll back the seamline at the pocket edge, exposing the lining. The pocket will be very bubbly. Set the pocket to the garment by stitching *only* on the lining. (Fig. 303b)
5. Press the pocket to cover the stitching line.

Your friends will really be impressed—you don't have to tell them how easy the pocket is to sew.

Inside-stitched Pockets
This pocket is literally stitched on the *inside* by machine for a smooth finish. It's very popular on men's jackets and ladies' suits.

1. Select a pocket pattern with rounded corners.
2. Make a cardboard template. Trace the finished size of the pocket on cardboard. Mark a line ¼" (6.4 mm) inside the traced line; mark it ⅜" (9.5 mm) inside if the fabric is bulky. Cut out the cardboard template on the inside line and mark it with notches at the sides, curves, and bottom. (Fig. 304a)

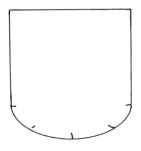

Fig. 304a

3. Mark the right side of the garment by tracing around the template with chalk or soap. Mark the garment to indicate the notches on the template. (Fig. 304b)
4. Flat-line the pocket or finish the edge of the hem.

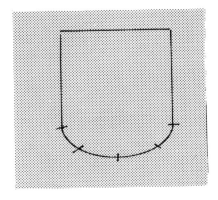

Fig. 304b

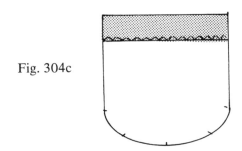

Fig. 304c

5. Make ⅛" (3.2 mm) clips on the pocket to match the notches on the template. (Fig. 304c)
6. Stitch around the pocket ¼" (6.4 mm) from the edge, crimping the curves.
7. Place the pocket face-down on the garment so that the cut edge of the pocket meets the marked line on the garment. Begin stitching at the upper-left corner. (Fig. 304d)

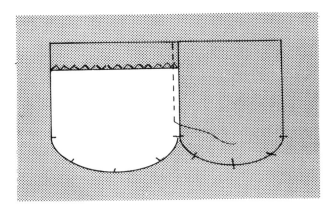

Fig. 304d

8. Stitch ¼" (6.4 mm) from the cut edge of the pocket, matching the notches as you go. If the center notch at the bottom doesn't match, rip back to the last notch that does match.

Allowing a ⅝" (16 mm) seam allowance and stitching ¼" (6.4 mm) puts ease into the pocket so that it will roll over the stitching line without pulling.

Voila! The pocket is set. Stand back and admire your work.

Reinforce the pocket invisibly by hand with a series of cross stitches parallel to the stitching line in the hem area. Sew through the garment, seam allowances, and pocket hem at each corner. (Fig. 304e)

Reinforce by machine with a backtack or bartack at each corner instead, if desired. (Fig. 304f)

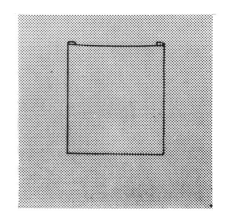

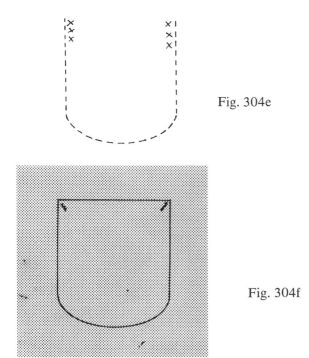

Fig. 304e

Fig. 304f

3. Fold the seam allowance at the bottom under, and pin or baste it in place. (Fig. 305c)

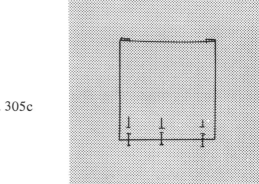

Leave the pocket plain, topstitch, or pickstitch ¼″ (6.4 mm) from the edge.

Fig. 305c

Square Pockets

Inside-stitched square pockets are very difficult to set completely by machine.

1. Make and mark the pocket. Mark the garment.

2. Place the pocket face-down on the garment so that the cut edge of the pocket meets the marked line on the garment. (Fig. 305a) Stitch ¼″ (6.4 mm) from the cut edge, stopping ⅝″ (16 mm) from the bottom of the pocket. Repeat on the other side of the pocket. (Fig. 305b)

4. Turn the garment wrong-side-out and sew the bottom of the pocket in place with a running stitch. (Fig. 305d)

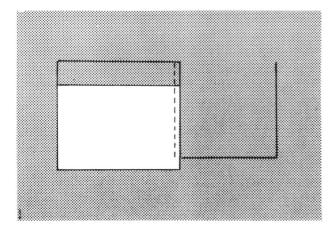

Fig. 305a

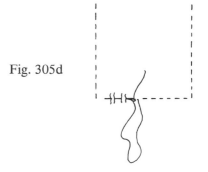

Fig. 305d

Nonwoven Pockets

Patch pockets made in nonwoven materials are easy to set using this cut-edge method. Stitch, then trim the pocket for a professional finish.

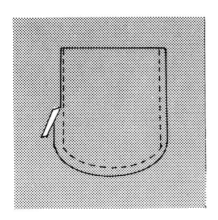

Fig. 306

1. Cut the pocket with ¼″ (6.4 mm) seam allowances. Notch each side of the hemline.
2. Fold the hem to the wrong side of the pocket at the notches.
3. Place the pocket on the right side of the garment section. Fuse or glue it in place. Stitch the pocket to the garment by topstitching ¼″ (6.4 mm) from the cut edges of the pocket.
4. Trim away the seam allowances of the pocket close to the stitched line. (Fig. 306)
5. If desired, topstitch around the pocket again ⅜″ (9.5 mm) from the cut edge.

FLAPS AND TABS
Flaps and Tabs with Topstitching
This method for setting flaps and tabs encloses the seam allowances which are sewn to the garment. It can be used on garments of medium and lightweight fabrics.

1. Interface the flap.
2. Trim the flap facing ¼″ (6.4 mm) at the top.
3. Pin and stitch the edges of the flap, stretching the facing to fit the flap. Trim the seams to ¼″ (6.4 mm) and turn the flap right-side-out. If you want to customize the flaps, taper the seams at the top of the flap. (Fig. 307a)

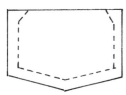

Fig. 307a

4. Underpress the flap, rolling the seamline to the underside.

5. Topstitch if desired.
6. Trim the top of the flap or unstitched edge ¼″ (6.4 mm).
7. Position the flap face-down above the flap location line so that the cut edges overlap the line ¼″ (6.4 mm). Stitch the flap ¼″ (6.4 mm) from the edge. (Fig. 307b)

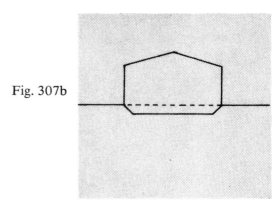

Fig. 307b

8. Fold the flap down, covering the seam. Topstitch across the top of the flap ⅜″ (9.5 mm) from the folded edge. (Fig. 307c)

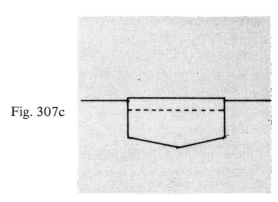

Fig. 307c

Flaps and Tabs without Topstitching
This method is only suitable for lightweight fabrics. The flaps or tabs are not interfaced.

1. Trim the flap facing ¼″ (6.4 mm) at the top.
2. Pin and stitch the edges of the flap, stretching the facing to fit the flap. If you want to customize the flaps, taper the seams at the top of the flap.
3. Trim the seams to ¼″ (6.4 mm) and turn the flap right-side-out.
4. Underpress the flap.
5. Position the flap with the right side up so that the

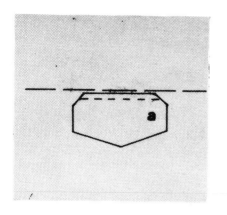
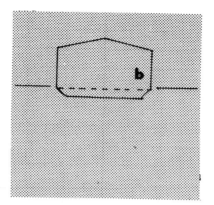
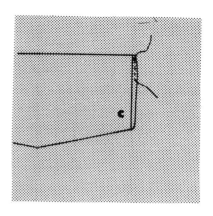

Fig. 308

top edge of the flap is ⅛″ (3.2 mm) below the flap-location line. Stitch across the top of the flap ¼″ (6.4 mm) from the cut edge. (Fig. 308a)

6. Fold the flap up and stitch ⅜″ (9.5 mm) from the folded edge. (Fig. 308b)

7. Secure the ends of the flap to the garment. Hold the flap so that the seamline and facing are exposed on the end. Stitch only on the facing for ½″ (12.7 mm). This is the same technique used on the invisibly-stitched pockets. (Fig. 308c)

WELTS

1. Complete the welt.

2. Position the welt, face-down, so that the seam allowance overlaps the welt-location line ⅝″ (16 mm). Stitch the welt ⅝″ (16 mm) from the cut edge. (Fig. 309)

3. Fold the welt up. Topstitch it to the garment or use the invisible-stitching technique on the facing at each end.

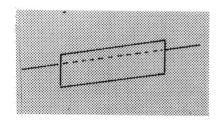

Fig. 309

SLASHED POCKETS—BOUND AND WELT

The key to perfect pockets which are set in a slash is to stitch precisely and clip exactly. These two factors, important in all of your sewing, determine the success or failure of slashed pockets.

Bound pockets—strip method. Bound pockets are sometimes called piped, slashed, or double-welt pockets. If you can make bound buttonholes, you can make bound pockets.

1. Cut two pocket sections the width of the pocket plus 1″ (2.5 cm) and the desired depth. The longer pocket section is cut from the fashion fabric and the other section is cut from lining fabric. If you don't have enough fashion fabric for the pocket section, piece it with lining fabric at the bottom. (Fig. 310a)

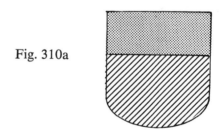

Fig. 310a

2. Glue, pin, or fuse interfacing to the wrong side of the garment in the pocket area.

3. Mark the location line of the pocket on the right side of the fabric with soap or basting thread. The pocket-location line is midway between the stitching lines indicated on the pattern.

4. Make the welts for the pocket. Press a fold along the lengthwise grain or bias 1″ (2.5 cm) from the cut edge of a fabric scrap so that the wrong sides are together. Stitch a guideline ¼″ (6.4 mm) from the folded edge of the welt strip. Trim the strip through both thicknesses so that the stitching line is in the middle of the strip. You *must* stitch and trim accurately. If you trim too much, the welts will over-

lap on the finished pocket. If you don't trim enough, there will be a gap between the welts on the pocket.
5. Cut the welt strips so that they are 1″ (2.5 cm) longer than the finished pocket. (If the edges of the welts ravel excessively, cut the strips on the bias, use fray-retardant or use another method to make the pocket.)
6. To make the pocket, make a large bound buttonhole, using the welt strips. Place the cut edge of one of the welt strips along the location line of the pocket on the right side of the garment. The welt strip extends ½″ (12.7 mm) beyond the termination line at each end. Mark the termination lines on the welt strip with soap or tape to ensure accuracy when you stitch.
7. Set the machine for a short stitch (20 spi or 1.5 mm) so that it will not be noticeable if you are one stitch off. Short stitches also reinforce the stitching line. Stitch on top of the guideline on the welt strip or a hairline toward the fold. Begin and end the stitching with a spot tack or knot the threads by hand. The stitching must be ended securely at each end.
8. Place the other welt strip so that the cut edge touches the cut edge of the first strip and the location line. Stitch the welt in place. (Fig. 310b)

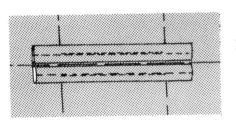

Fig. 310b

9. Cord limp fabrics and *all* bias-cut welts now so that the pocket won't stretch or gap. Thread a tapestry needle with acrylic or wool yarn and pull it through the welt strip.
10. Slash the pocket from the wrong side of the garment. Do *not* cut into the welts. Begin in the center of the pocket and slash to ¼″ (6.4 mm) short of the end. Carefully clip to each corner, making a triangle at each end. If you don't clip far enough, a pleat will form at the end; if you clip too far, the fabric will fray at the corners. Use fray-retardant at each corner. Check for spotting on a scrap.
11. To turn the pocket, work with the garment face-up. Push the welts through to the underside. Continue with the garment face-up as you straighten the welts; now, admire your work.
12. Baste the welts together with a diagonal basting stitch. (Fig. 310c)

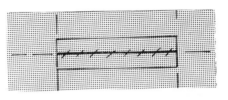

Fig. 310c

13. With the garment face-up, fold the garment edge and interfacing back to expose the triangle and welt ends. Use a short stitch to stitch across the end *one* time as closely as possible to the fold of the garment. Swing the stitches in a tiny bit at the corners to catch all cut threads. Too much swing will make a pleat. Stitch the triangle on the other end.
14. Press the pocket from the wrong side on a well-padded surface.
15. With the wrong side of the garment up, place the pocket lining face-down on the welt strip nearer the garment hem, aligning the cut edges. Stitch the lining and welt strip together. (Fig. 310d)

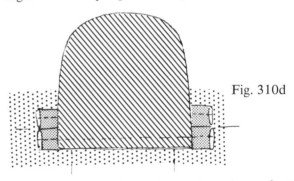

Fig. 310d

16. Stitch the fabric section to the other welt strip.
17. Stitch the pocket sections together. Stitch carefully across the ends of the pocket, catching the triangular end of the garment to the pocket sections. Round the corners of the pocket to avoid collecting lint in them. (Fig. 310e)

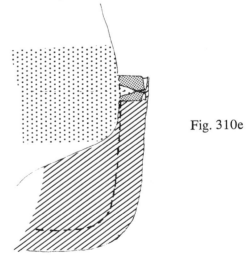

Fig. 310e

Bound pockets—patch method. The patch method for bound pockets is suitable for garments made of fabrics that fray easily or bulky fabrics.

1. Cut two pocket sections the width of the pocket plus 1″ (2.5 cm) and the desired depth. The longer pocket section is cut from the fashion fabric and the other section is cut from a lining fabric. If you don't have enough fashion fabric for the pocket section, piece it with lining fabric at the bottom.
2. Cut the patch for the welt 3″ (7.6 cm) wide and the length of the pocket plus 2″ (5.1 cm) on the bias or lengthwise grain.
3. Pin, glue, or fuse interfacing to the wrong side of the garment in the pocket area.
4. Using a tracing wheel and tracing carbon, trace the stitching lines of the pocket from the pattern onto the interfacing. Machine stitch on the marked lines, connecting the lines at each end, to mark the right side of the garment and reinforce the pocket opening. (Fig. 311a)

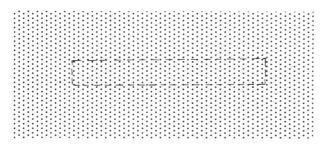

Fig. 311a

5. With the right sides together, center the welt patch over the stitched lines. Pin or baste it in place. With the garment wrong-side-up, stitch on the marked lines, using a short stitch.
6. Clip the garment and patch exactly to each corner. (Fig. 311b) Use fray-retardant at the corners.

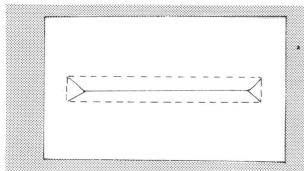

Fig 311b

7. Push the patch through the slash. Adjust it so that the area within the stitched lines fills the pocket welts. Pin the welts in place. (Fig. 311c) Baste the welts together with a diagonal stitch.

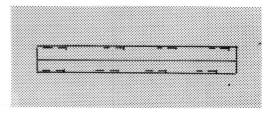

Fig. 311c)

8. With the garment section face-up, fold it back to expose the patch and triangle at one end. Stitch across each end, catching the corners securely.
9. Use a zipper foot to stitch-in-the-ditch around the pocket or use a tiny backstitch to secure the welts. (Fig. 311d)

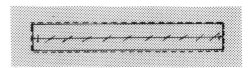

Fig. 311d

10. Press the pocket from the wrong side on a well-padded press board.
11. Stitch the pocket sections to the welts and complete the pockets.

Bound pocket—faced method. The faced or window method is popular with many home sewers. It is suitable for use on fabrics that fray easily and on bulky or stiff fabrics.

1. Follow Step 1, for bound pocket—patch method and mark the pocket locations.
2. Cut a bias patch from a tightly woven lightweight lining fabric or nylon tricot 1½″ (3.8 cm) longer than the pocket and 3″ (7.6 cm) wide.
   A lining fabric made of natural fibres can be pressed sharply and makes a better window than a polyester or permanent-press fabric. Silk organza and cotton organdy make the best patches. Use scraps from another garment or select a lining fabric that is a mixture of synthetic and natural fibres if you don't have the right color in silk or cotton.
3. Cut the two pocket welts on the straight grain or bias the length of the pocket plus 1½″ (3.8 cm) and 3″ (7.6 cm) wide.

4. Prepare the pocket welts. With the right sides together, baste the centers together on the lengthwise grain. Open the welts with the right-sides-out and press.

5. Baste the facing patch to the right side of the garment on the location line.

6. Using a short stitch for security and accuracy at the corners and ends, stitch around the pocket. Begin stitching in the center ⅛″ (3.2 mm) above the pocket, continue in a rectangle around the pocket, overlapping the stitches ½″ (12.7 mm) at the starting point. Pivot at each corner with the needle down. Count the stitches at each end above and below the basted line to ensure both ends are the same.

7. Clip the rectangle to the corners. Use fray-retardant on the cut edges. Test before using it on the garment.

8. Push the facing through the slash. (Fig. 312a)

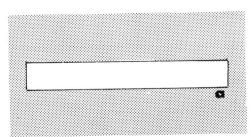

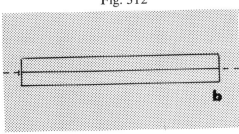

Fig. 312

9. Understitch the long sides of the pocket to make pressing easier. Use the inside of the presser foot as a guide to understitch.

10. Press from the wrong side of the garment, rolling the seamline toward the patch.

11. Centering the welts in the opening or window is the most difficult step in the faced method. Glue or fuse the welts to hold them in place when you stitch. Gluing: Working from the right side of the garment, pin the center of the welt section at each end of the pocket. (Fig. 312b) Turn the garment over and glue the welt section to the patch. Fusing: Working from the wrong side of the garment, place a short piece of ¼″ (6.4 mm) -wide fusible agent on the pocket patch. Steam the fusible, without touching it, until it becomes tacky. Working from the right

side of the garment, pin the center of the welt section at each end of the pocket. Press the welt section into place with your fingers. Steam the garment to fuse the welts in place.

12. Fold the garment back so that the patch seamline above the pocket is exposed. Using a short stitch, stitch on top of this seamline to secure the welt to the patch. Repeat on the line below the pocket and at each end. Stitching the welts in place this way instead of stitching a rectangle around the pocket ensures square corners.

13. Press the pocket from the wrong side on a padded surface.

14. Stitch the pocket sections to the welts and complete the pockets.

Bound pocket with a flap. A flap is often inserted into the bound pocket on men's and ladies' suits. (Fig. 313) This complicated-looking pocket is surprisingly easy to make.

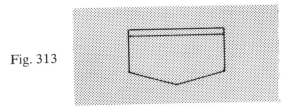

Fig. 313

1. Make the flap. Cut the flap from the fashion fabric and the flap facing from lining fabric. Trim the lining ¼″ (6.4 mm) at the top edge. With the right sides together, pin and stitch the edges of the flap, stretching the facing to fit. Press. Turn the flap right-side-out and underpress.

2. Complete the bound pocket opening by your favorite method. Do not sew the pocket sections in place.

3. From the right side of the garment section, slide the finished flap into the pocket opening.

4. Turn the section over. Align the cut edges of the flap and the cut edges of the top welt. Stitch them together.

5. Stitch the pocket sections to the welts and complete the pocket.

Separate Welt Pocket
If you can make bound pockets, you can make welt pockets.

1. Cut the welt by the pattern. Pretrim the seam allowances to ⅜″ (9.5 mm). Notch the foldline at each end with snips.

2. Cut two pocket sections the width of the pocket plus 1″ (2.5 cm) and the desired depth. One pocket section is cut from the fashion fabric and the other section is cut from lining fabric.

3. Glue, pin, or fuse interfacing to the garment in the pocket area.

4. Mark the stitching lines indicated on the pattern on the right side of the garment with soap or a basting thread. The top stitching line is usually shorter than the lower one; mark and stitch exactly as indicated so that the welt will cover the pocket opening.

5. Fold the welt at the notches with the right sides together. Stitch the ends of the welt with a ⅜″ (9.5 mm) seam. (Fig. 314a)

Fig. 314a

6. Turn the welt right-side-out. If the garment will be topstitched, topstitch the welt ¼″ (6.4 mm) from the edge. Press. If you plan to topstitch the welt to the garment later, edgestitch along the fold ⅟₁₆″ (1.6 mm) from the edge. (Fig. 314b)

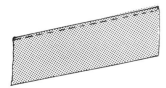

Fig. 314b

7. Place the welt face-down on the right side of the garment. The cut edge overlaps the lower stitching line ¼″ (6.4 mm), allowing ⅛″ (3.2 mm) for the turn of the cloth. Pin or stitch the welt in place. (Fig. 314c)

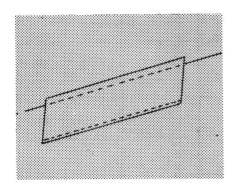

Fig. 314c

8. Place the smaller pocket section on top of the welt, matching the cut edges. The pocket will extend ½″ (12.7 mm) beyond the welt on each side.

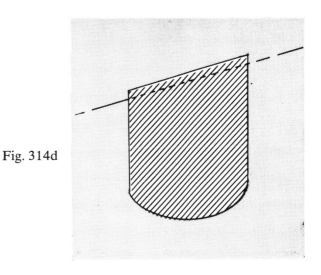

Fig. 314d

9. Stitch the lining and welt to the garment. Begin and end with a backtack at the finished edge of the welt (½″ or 12.7 mm from the cut edge of the lining). (Fig. 314d)

10. Match the cut edge of the other pocket section to the cut edges of the stitched section. Pin it in place. Carefully mark each end of the stitching line on the pocket section. Stitch the upper section to the garment, beginning and ending with a backtack. (Fig. 314e)

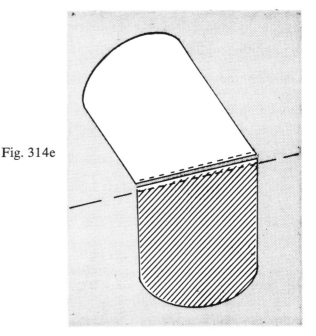

Fig. 314e

11. From the wrong side of the garment, slash the pocket opening and clip precisely to the ends of the stitching lines. (Fig. 314f)

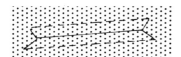

Fig. 314f

12. Turn the pocket to the inside of the garment; press.

13. Edgestitch the welt to the garment or invisibly stitch the welt facing at each end. If desired, top-stitch just below the welt to hold the seam allowances and pocket section in place. Do not stitch through the other pocket section. (Fig. 314g)

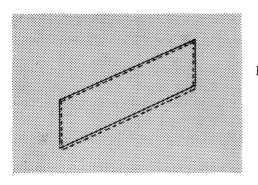

Fig. 314g

14. With the garment face-up, fold one side back to expose the pocket sections. Stitch them together. Stitch carefully across the ends, catching the triangular end of the garment to the pocket sections. Round the corners of the pocket to avoid collecting lint in them.

One-piece welt pocket. The welt won't cover the top stitching line in this easy method. This kind of welt is used on skirts, slacks, coats, and jackets, but it isn't suitable to use as a handkerchief pocket on suits and blazers.

These directions are for a pocket with a welt ½" (12.7 mm) deep and 5" (12.7 cm) wide.

1. Cut the pocket-welt section from the fashion fabric so that it is the desired depth plus 2" (5.1 cm) and the desired width plus 1" (2.5 cm).

2. Cut the other section from the fashion fabric the same width and 1" (2.5 cm) shorter than the pocket-welt section. This section will show when the pocket is used. If you don't have enough fabric, piece the section with lining fabric.

3. Mark the pocket location on the right side of the garment section with soap. This marked line goes through the center of the welt.

4. With the right sides together, place the longer section face-down on the right side of the garment so that the cut edge meets the marked line. Pin the pocket in place. Stitch the pocket to the garment ¼" (6.4 mm) from the edge, beginning and ending with a backtack ½" (12.7 mm) from each side. (Fig. 315a)

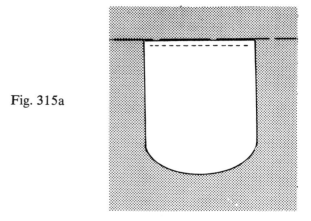

Fig. 315a

5. With the right sides together, match the cut edge of the shorter section to the cut edge of the longer one. Stitch it to the garment ¼" (6.4 mm) from the edge, beginning and ending with a backtack ½" (12.7 mm) from each side. The stitching lines should be equal in length. (Fig. 315b)

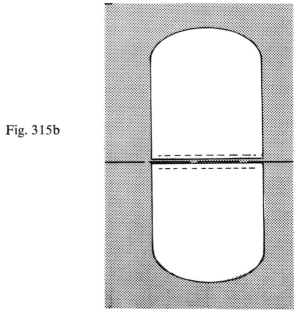

Fig. 315b

6. From the wrong side of the garment, slash the pocket opening and clip to the ends of the stitching lines.

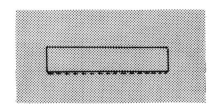

Fig. 315c

7. Turn the pocket to the inside of the garment. Bring the lower pocket up to the top stitching line to form a ½″ (12.7 mm) tuck, making the welt. Secure the welt by topstitching through the garment, seam allowances and pocket section. (Fig. 315c)

If you prefer, the welt can be secured without topstitching. With the garment face-up, fold the garment up, exposing the seam allowances of the lower section. Stitch over the lower stitching line through the pocket section without stitching through the other pocket piece. (Fig. 315d)

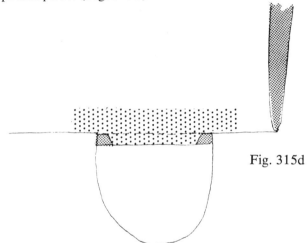

Fig. 315d

8. With the garment sections face-up, fold one side back to expose the pocket sections, stitch them together. Stitch carefully across the ends, catching the triangular ends of the garment and the ends of the welt to the pocket sections.

Inseam Pockets

1. Mark the pocket opening carefully on the wrong side of each garment section.
2. With the right sides together, stitch the pocket to the garment using a ⅜″ (9.5 mm) seam allowance. Understitch the pocket and seam allowances. This step is eliminated when the pocket and garment are cut together in one piece.
3. Stitch the side seam to the pocket opening, stitch around the pocket, and finish the side seam. (Fig. 316a)
4. Press the pocket toward the front of the garment.
5. Press the seam open below the pocket. Clip the seam allowance to the stitching line so that the seam will lie flat. (Fig. 316b)

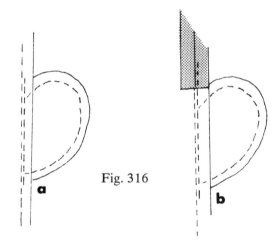

Fig. 316

FASHION DETAILS

BIAS SHORTCUTS
Bias is any diagonal on the fabric. True bias is cut at a 45° angle to the grainline. This 45° cut has the greatest elasticity and flexibility in woven fabrics and in some knit fabrics; it is easy to shape and frays little. These characteristics enable you to make bindings, facings, tubings, and bands quickly and easily. In addition, it enhances the design of garments made of striped, checked, plaid, tweed, pile, and ribbed fabrics.

Bias Strips
1. Fold the fabric diagonally so that the lengthwise grain of the upper layer is parallel to the crossgrain of the lower layer. (Fig. 317a)

2. Cut the fabric along the fold or true bias.
3. Measure strips the desired width parallel to the fold, using a see-through ruler. Mark the width with chalk or soap. (Fig. 317b)
4. Cut the bias strips. Trim both ends so that they are on the same grainline. Ideally, they will be trimmed on the lengthwise grain. (Fig. 317c)
5. Join the strips on the lengthwise grain, using a very short stitch (25 spi or 1 mm). Do *not* match the cut edges; match the stitching lines. (Fig. 317d)

Fig. 317

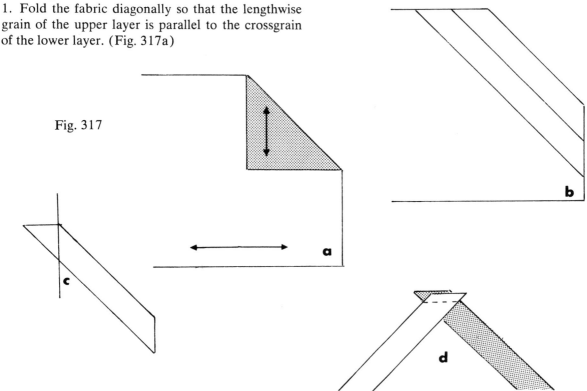

Continuous Bias

If you need a lot of bias, use the continuous bias shortcut to cut the strips. One-third yard of 45" (114.3 cm) fabric will make approximately 10 yards of 1½" (3.8 cm) bias.

1. Cut a rectangular piece of fabric on the straight grain. Find the true bias by folding the rectangle diagonally at one end. Cut along the fold line. (Fig. 318a)
2. Using a very short stitch (25 spi or 1 mm), stitch this triangular section to the other end of the piece along the lengthwise grain. Press the seam open. (Fig. 318b)
3. Mark the bias strips the desired width and parallel to the ends. Accuracy is very important. (Fig. 318c)
4. Pin the straight edges with the right sides together to make a tube. One strip width will extend beyond each end and the tube will have a twist. Stitch a ¼"

(6.4 mm) seam, using a very short stitch (25 spi). Press the seam open. (Fig. 318d)
5. Cut along the marked line to make one long bias strip. (Fig. 318e)

Using a very short stitch when you stitch prevents the strips from ripping apart when they are cut apart.

5° Bias

Most home sewers use a crossgrain cut to make knit bindings. Ready-to-wear manufacturers use a 5° bias which shapes more easily and attractively.

1. To establish the 5° bias, draw a line 5¾" (14.6 cm) long. Mark A at one end and B at the other. Measure up from B ½" (12.7 mm). Mark this point C. Connect AC and BC. (Fig. 319a) Cut out the triangle ABC.

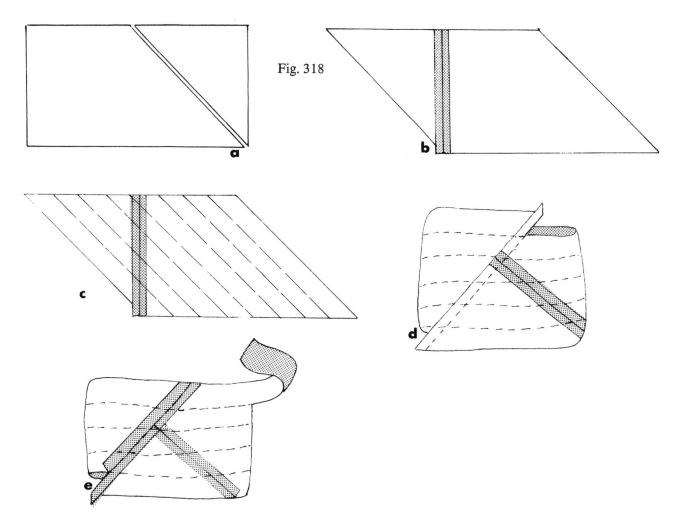

Fig. 318

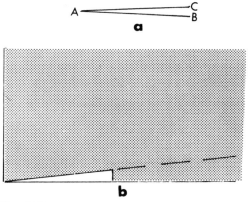

Fig. 319

2. Place the triangle so that AB is on the crossgrain of the knitted fabric.

3. Mark the fabric along the triangle from A to C, extending the line the desired length. This is the 5° bias. (Fig. 319b)

4. Mark and cut the bias the desired width. If needed, piece the binding on the lengthwise grain to make the strip the desired length.

Double-Fold Bias Tape

When you want a beautiful trim in an unusual fabric, make your own bias tape. These directions are for a finished trim ¼″ (6.4 mm) wide. Make the binding any width you want by cutting the bias strip five times the finished width.

1. Cut a bias strip 1¼″ (3.2 cm) wide and the desired length.

2. Fold the strip lengthwise with the wrong sides together so that one side is ⅛″ (3.2 mm) wider than the other. (Fig. 320a)

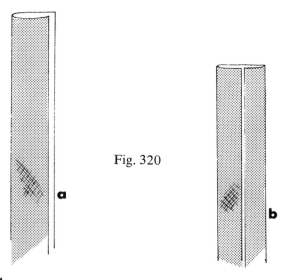

Fig. 320

3. Press the folded edge lightly.

4. Fold the cut edges on each side to the foldline and press lightly. (Fig. 320b)

5. Set the bias to the garment so that the longer fold will be on the underside of the garment.

Self-Filled Tubings:
Spaghetti Straps, Rouleau, and Button Loops

Self-filled tubing as small as a heavy thread can be made for button loops, Chinese ball buttons, and spaghetti straps. The finished size of the self-filled tubing will depend on the weight and texture of the fabric—a lightweight piece of China silk makes a much smaller tubing than a piece of Pendleton wool. The finished tubing is filled by the seam allowances which make it firm and round.

1. Cut a bias strip 1½″ (3.8 cm) wide and the desired length. Short strips are often easier to handle than one long strip.

2. Fold the strip in half lengthwise with the right sides together.

3. Stitch a small funnel at the beginning of the strip; then stitch close to the folded edge, stretching the strip *as much as possible*. Stretching the strip as you stitch will eliminate broken stitches when the strip is turned right-side-out. (Fig. 321a) Make the strip

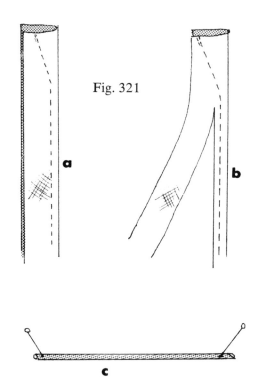

Fig. 321

very narrow when you stitch—it will be wider when you release it from the stretched position.

4. Trim the seam allowances so that the stitching line is in the *center* of the strip. (Fig. 321b)

5. Use a tapestry needle and silk buttonhole twist to turn the strip right-side-out. Buttonhole twist is very strong and won't break when the strip is turned. Secure the thread at the end of the funnel, insert the needle into the tubing and turn the strip right-side-out. Starting the turn is the most difficult step. If the tubing turns too easily, you have stitched the tubing too wide. A wide tubing will be soft and flat instead of firm and round.

6. Wet the strip, squeeze it in a towel, pin it in a stretched position on the press board and leave it to dry. This hint removes any lumps and bumps. Don't worry about water spotting; it won't, even if the fabric is silk. (Fig. 321c)

Unfilled Tubings

Unfilled tubings ¼″–½″ (6.4 mm–12.7 mm) wide can be made quickly and easily to use for straps and ties. They can be made in knitted and woven fabrics.

1. Cut a strip on the true bias for woven fabrics or on the crossgrain for knitted fabrics 1½″–2″ (3.8 cm–5.1 cm) wide. If you are using them for straps, cut them on the lengthwise grain so that they will not stretch.

2. Fold the strip lengthwise with the right sides together. If the end or ends will hang free, finish them by folding ¼″ (6.4 mm) to the wrong side of the strip. Stitch the strip the desired distance from the folded edge. (Fig. 322) Stretch bias strips slightly

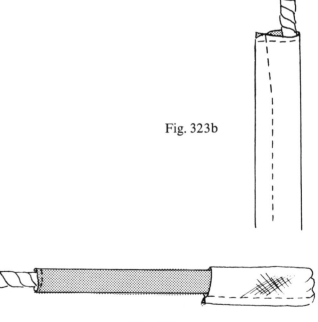

Fig. 322

as you stitch. Use a zigzag stitch (W,2-L,2) to stitch knitted tubings.

3. Trim the seam allowances to ¼″ (6.4 mm).

4. Turn the tubing right-side-out, using a small safety pin or tapestry needle and thread.

Tubings Made with Cord

Use cord in this easy method to help you stitch the tubing evenly and turn it easily.

1. Select cotton cord in the desired size. Cut the cord 1″ (2.5 cm) longer than the finished length of the tubing.

2. Cut a bias strip the desired length and wide enough to go around the cord plus 2″ (5.1 cm).

3. Place the cord on top of the right side of the bias strip with the cord extending 1″ (2.5 cm) at one end. Stitch across the extended end of the cord and the bias strip. (Fig. 323a)

Fig. 323a

4. Fold the bias around the cord. Using the zipper foot, stitch a small funnel at the beginning of the strip, then stitch the bias close to the cord, stretching the strip slightly as you stitch. (Fig. 323b)

Fig. 323b

Fig. 323c

5. Trim the seam allowances to ¼″ (6.4 mm).

6. Holding the end of the cord securely, turn the bias right-side-out. (Fig. 323c)

7. Cut off the end of the tubing that is sewn to the cord and pull the cord out.

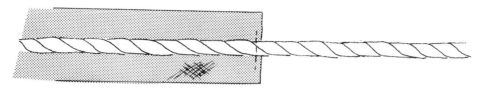

Fig 324

Cord-Filled Tubing

Cord-filled tubing is easy to make for belting, rouleau, spaghetti straps, buttons, and button loops. The cord provides a stay for the tubing and fills it evenly.

1. Select cotton cord or acrylic rug yarn in the desired size. Preshrink the cord. Cut the cord twice the desired length plus 2″ (5.1 cm).
2. Cut a bias strip the desired length and wide enough to go around the cord plus 2″ (5.1 cm).
3. Place the cord on top of the right side of the bias strip so that the cord extends 1″ (2.5 cm) beyond the bias. Stitch the other end of the bias to the center of the cord. (Fig. 324)
4. Fold the bias around the cord. Using the zipper foot, stitch the bias close to the cord; stretch slightly as you stitch. If you stitch too close to the cord, the tubing will be lumpy when you turn it right-side-out.
5. Trim the seam allowance to ⅛″ (3.2 mm) unless the fabric frays badly, then trim to ¼″ (6.4 mm) or use fray-retardant along the edges.
6. Holding the end of the cord covered by the bias securely, turn the tubing right-side-out.
7. Cut off the excess cord.

LACE INSERTIONS

Insert lace à la Dior to transform a plain garment into a fancy one.

1. Mark the location of the insertion on the flat garment section with soap or chalk.
2. Pin or baste the edges of the lace to the right side of the garment.
3. Zigzag (W,2-L,2) the edges on each side of the lace to the fabric. If the fabric ravels excessively, use a shorter stitch.
4. Trim away the fabric under the lace close to the zigzagged stitches. (Fig. 325) Use a fray-retardant along the zigzagged stitches.

APPLIQUE SHORTCUTS

Add an appliqué to make a plain garment fancy. Apply the appliqué to the appropriate garment section before the garment is assembled. Set the appliqué to

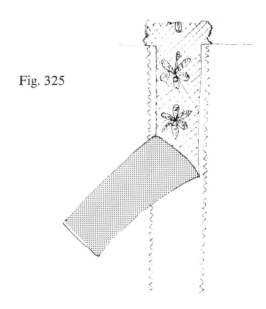

Fig. 325

the section with fusible agent or plastic before zigzagging around it.

Fusible Agent

Set fusible agent to the appliqué before cutting the appliqué sections out.

1. Place the appliqué fabric face-down on the press board. Place a piece of fusible agent over it. Hold a portable steamer 1″–2″ (2.5 cm–5.1 cm) above the fusible agent. Pat the web in place with your hand as you steam it to make it adhere to the fabric.
2. Cut out the appliqués.
3. Place the garment section face-up on the press board. Arrange the appliqués on the garment section with the fusible side next to the garment.
4. Using the steamer, fuse the appliqués to the garment.
5. Zigzag around the edges of each appliqué. A wide, close zigzag stitch (W,4-L,0) makes a pretty satin stitch. Loosen the tension so that the fabric won't pucker. A piece of typing paper placed between the fabric and the feed dog will allow you to guide the work smoothly and easily. A narrow zigzag (W,2-L,2) makes a less conspicuous edge around the appliqué.

Plastic

Use a lightweight plastic such as a dry-cleaning bag to make the applique adhere to the garment section.

1. Cut out the applique in the desired shape.
2. Cut a piece of lightweight plastic slightly larger than the applique.
3. Place the garment section face-up on the press board. Arrange the appliques face-up on the garment with the plastic between the applique and garment section. Cover the applique and plastic with brown paper and press them with a hot dry iron; the excess plastic will adhere to the brown paper.

Do not substitute fusible agent for the plastic in this method—it may leave a residue on the garment around the applique.

DRESS SHIELDS
Pattern

1. Match the stitching lines of the underarm seam on the front and back pattern.
2. Shape the shield by tracing the stitching line of the armscye from the front notch to the back notch and drawing the lower edge. (Fig. 326)

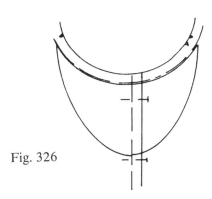

Fig. 326

3. Trace the dress shield pattern and add a ⅜″ (9.5 mm) seam allowance to all edges.

Sleeveless Dresses

Dress shields for sleeveless garments are easy to make from garment scraps.

1. Cut four shield sections from the fashion fabric or two sections from the fashion fabric and two from a more absorbent fabric.
2. With the right sides of two sections together, stitch around the edges, leaving an opening 1½″–2″ (3.8 cm–5.1 cm) wide at the bottom.
3. Turn the shields right-side-out.

4. Edgestitch around the shields or finish the opening at the bottom with glue or by hand.
5. Position the shields so that they show slightly (⅛″ or 3.2 mm) above the armhole. This positioning will enable the shields to catch perspiration and protect your lovely garment.
6. Snap or baste the shields into the garment lining or facing.

Garments with Sleeves

Dress shields are sometimes inserted into dresses, blouses, and jackets to protect them. These garments are usually lined.

1. Cut eight shield sections from the lining fabric.
2. With the right sides together, stitch two sections together at the underarm seam with a ⅜″ (9.5 mm) seam. (Fig. 327) Repeat with two other sections.

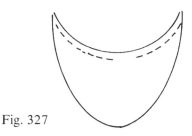

Fig. 327

Stitch the remaining four sections in the same way, leaving the seam open 2″ (5.1 cm) in the center.
3. Make a pair of shields. Each shield has one open seam and one stitched seam. With the right sides together, stitch a ⅜″ (9.5 mm) seam around the edges.
4. Turn the shields right-side-out through the open seam.
5. Snap or baste the shields into the garments so that the open seam is toward the lining.

LINGERIE STRAPS

Lingerie straps are used to hold undergarments in place. They are usually located at the shoulder seam but can be placed at any strategic place. Also, you may need more than one strap on each side.

Seam Binding Straps

1. Cut a strip of seam binding 6″ long.
2. Fold it in half lengthwise.
3. Stitch the length of the seam binding on each side.
4. Fold under ¼″ (6.4 mm) on one end. Place the ball of the snap over the cut edge and sew the snap in

place. Repeat for the other end. Snap the sockets to the balls on each end.

Lingerie straps can be prepared in advance to this point and used when needed.

5. Cut the binding in half.

6. Mark the lingerie strap location on the wrong side of the garment. It is usually on a seam allowance or facing, but it may not be in the center of the shoulder seam. It should be located over the strap which it will hold in place.

7. Sew the socket to the wrong side of the garment on the mark nearer the neckline.

8. Snap the strap in place. (Fig. 328)

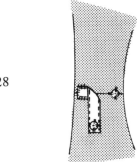

Fig. 328

9. Secure the other end of the strap to the garment, allowing ⅛″–¼″ (3.2 mm–6.4 mm) ease in the strap. If you have a big hollow in your shoulder, allow even more. You don't want the shoulder seam to dip in the center.

10. If necessary, use more than one lingerie strap for each undergarment strap.

Thread Straps

Thread straps should be used on sheer fabrics and garments with very narrow shoulder seams.

1. Mark the lingerie strap location on the garment.

2. Sew the socket on the mark near the neckline.

3. Using buttonhole twist or regular thread, secure the thread on the mark nearer the armscye. Make a chain stitch the desired length.

4. Secure the thread in *one* hole of the snap with several buttonhole or blanket stitches.

Removable Lingerie Straps

If you don't want to have lingerie straps in all of your garments, make a few sets on safety pins to save time.

1. Fold a strip of seam binding in half lengthwise and stitch the length of the binding on each side. Cut a 3″ (7.6 cm) length for each strap.

2. Fold under ¼″ (6.4 mm) on one end and sew the snap socket over the cut edge.

Fold under ½″ (12.7 mm) on the other end and sew the ball over the cut edge. (Fig. 329)

Fig. 329

3. Insert a small safety pin into the loop at the end with the snap ball. Pin the strap to the garment facing or seam allowances.

SHOULDER PADS
Detachable Shoulder Pads

Detachable shoulder pads can be made quickly and easily, and they can be used on more than one garment.

1. Cut two 6″ (15.2 cm) squares from lining or self-fabric. Use a flesh color for pads in transparent fabrics.

2. Cut one 4″ (10.2 cm) square from polyester fleece. Cut the fleece in half on the diagonal. Thicker pads can be made by using several layers of fleece. To avoid a sharp ridge at the edges of thick pads, tear away the fleece at the edges to stagger the edges and to make them thinner. Do not tear the fleece on the long edge.

3. To make each shoulder pad, enclose a fleece pad or pads in a fabric square. Stitch the pad with 8–10 rows parallel to the folded edge. Hold the ends of the pad up in a curved position when you stitch to shape it. (Fig. 330)

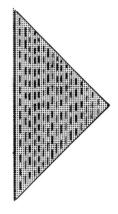

Fig. 330

4. Zigzag and trim or stitch and pink the unfinished edges of the cover.

5. Sew snaps on each pad and on the seam allowances of the garment so that the pad will be centered over the shoulder with the long edge overlapping the armscye seam ½″ (12.7 mm).

Permanent Shoulder Pads
Tailored garments usually require shoulder pads for a professional finish.

1. Make a pattern for the shoulder pads. Pin the shoulder seams of the pattern together. If the garments has darts or fullness of at the shoulder, pin it out. Mark the shoulder seam 1″ (2.5 cm) from the neckline stitching line.
2. Draw the shoulder pad on the pattern front connecting the marked point on the shoulder and the notch on the front armscye; then connect the shoulder point and the notch on the back armscye. (Fig. 331a)
3. Trace the shoulder pad onto pattern paper. Make notches on each side to indicate the shoulder-seam location.
4. Cut four shoulder pad shapes from polyester fleece or cotton wadding. Trim two of the shapes ¼″ (6.4 mm) on all edges except the armscye. Place the smaller shapes on top of the larger ones, matching the notches at the armscye. (Fig. 331b) Be sure to make a pair, not two for the same shoulder, since the pads cannot be interchanged.
5. Stitch several parallel rows on each pad, holding the ends up in a curved position when you stitch.

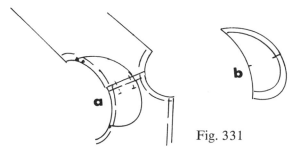

Fig. 331

6. To avoid a sharp ridge at the edges of the pad, tear away the fleece at the edges to make them thinner.
7. Position the pads in the garment, matching the clips on each side of the pad to the shoulder seam. Sew the pad to the shoulder seam or interfacing with a loose basting stitch or stab stitching.
5. If you aren't going to sew the pads into the garment immediately, roll them into a cylindrical shape, pin them together and set them aside until you're ready to use them.

WEIGHTS
Weights ensure that the garment hangs properly. Place them in the hems of jackets and suits at the end of the seamlines.

1. If the weight is too heavy or too large, cut it into a smaller piece with old scissors.
2. Pound the weight flat with a hammer to eliminate ridges and sharp edges.
3. Cut a piece of lining fabric that is three times the width of the weight and three times the length.
4. Place the weight in the center of the lining square. Fold the sides of the lining over the weight, then fold the bottom and top over it.
5. Sew the bag together with a few stitches.
6. Sew the covered weight into the garment on the seam allowances between the garment and hem.

BELTS
Loose-fitting garments without a waistline are quick and easy to sew. Make a belt to complete the outfit.

Braid, Ribbon, or Woven Trim Belts
1. Cut the belt 4″–5″ (10.2 cm–12.7 cm) longer than your waist measurement.
2. To stitch the point, fold the belt in half lengthwise, with the right sides together, and stitch across the end. (Fig. 332a)
3. Turn the point right-side-out. (Fig. 332b)
4. Cut a piece of fusible, nonwoven interfacing slightly narrower than the braid.
5. Fuse the interfacing to the back of the braid.
6. Add a distinctive buckle to finish the belt.

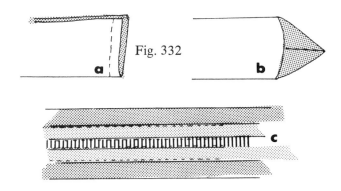

Fig. 332

An attractive belt for a print dress can be made of ribbon in several widths and colors. (Fig. 332c)

Pseudosuede Belt
A pseudosuede belt is a great accessory to add to any garment. A belt gives you an opportunity to sew on

one of these very expensive fabrics with a minimum investment.

1. Purchase the fabric in inches: twice the finished belt width plus ½″ (12.7 mm). A 1″ (2.5 cm) belt will require 2½″ (6.5 cm).
2. Cut the belt 4″–5″ (10.2 cm–12.7 cm) longer than your waist measurement. Notch each end of the belt in the center. (Fig. 333a)

Fig. 333a

3. Fold the belt in half lengthwise with the wrong sides together.
4. Insert a 1″ (2.5 cm) -wide piece of fusible agent between the pseudosuede layers and fuse the three layers together.
5. Shape the point as desired.
6. Topstitch 1″ (2.5 cm) from the folded edge, then edgestitch around the point and folded edge. (Fig. 333b)

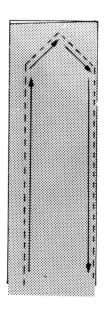

Fig. 333b

7. Trim close (¹⁄₁₆″ or 1.6 mm) to the stitching line with embroidery scissors. (Fig. 333c)
8. Add a beautiful buckle and enjoy this luxurious accessory.

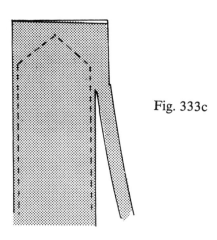

Fig. 333c

This technique for making a pseudosuede belt is the same as the cut-edge facing. Experience has shown that it is difficult to match two cut edges exactly and stitch them together ¹⁄₁₆″ (1.6 mm) from the edge. The above procedure will guarantee success.

Tie Belts: Three Shortcuts
Fold-and-stitch method. This super-easy method can be used to make any topstitched belt.

1. Cut the belt on the lengthwise grain so that it is twice the desired width plus 1″ (2.5 cm) and the desired length plus 1″ (2.5 cm).
2. Fold the seam allowances at the ends of the belt to the wrong side. (Fig. 334a)

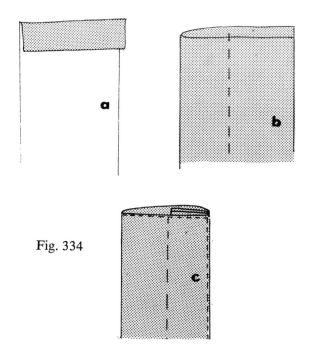

Fig. 334

3. With the *wrong* sides together, fold the belt in half lengthwise. Set the machine for a basting stitch. Stitch the length of the belt 1″ (2.5 cm) from the cut edge. (Fig. 334b) If the needle will leave holes in the fabric, omit this step. After you have made a few belts, you will not need to use this basting aid.

4. Turn in the ½″ (12.7 mm) seam allowances along the length of the belt—the cut edges will touch the basted line. Edgestitch the ends and side of the belt through all layers. Hold the belt firmly so that it won't have a twist. (Fig. 334c)

5. If desired, topstitch the belt ¼″ (6.4 mm) from the edges.

6. Remove the basted line.

Fold-stitch-and-turn method. This clever method is ideal to use when making belts from bulky, difficult-to-turn fabrics.

1. Cut the belt on the lengthwise grain so that it is twice the desired width plus ¾″ (19.1 mm) and the desired length plus 1″ (2.5 cm).

2. Fold the seam allowances at the ends of the belt to the wrong side.

3. With the *right* sides together, fold the belt in half lengthwise.

4. Stitch a ⅜″ (9.5 mm) seam. (Fig. 335)

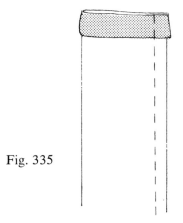

Fig. 335

5. Turn the belt right-side-out.

6. Topstitch if desired.

Stitch-turn-and-stitch-some-more method. Don't let the name of this method or the instructions turn you off—it's really very simple. This time-saving technique can also be applied to seams and hems.

1. Cut the belt on the lengthwise grain so it is twice

the finished width plus ¾″ (19.1 mm) and the desired length plus 1″ (2.5 cm).

2. With the right sides together, fold the belt in half lengthwise. Notch both edges every 10″–12″ (25.4 cm–30.5 cm).

3. Stitch a ⅜″ (9.5 mm) seam across each end and up the side to the first notch. (Fig. 336a)

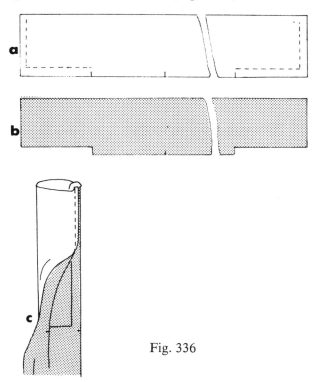

Fig. 336

4. Turn the ends of the belt right-side-out. (Fig. 336b)

5. Fold the belt back over one end enough so that you can grasp the seam allowances. Stitch a ⅜″ (9.5 mm) seam to the center of the belt, matching the notches, and turning the belt right-side-out as you stitch. (Fig. 336c)

6. Repeat from the other end and stitch as far as possible. Although this really looks messy when you are stitching, don't worry, it will come out right if you match the notches as you stitch.

7. Finish the opening by the topstitching around the belt or slipstitching it together.

BELT CARRIERS
Skirt and Slack Waistbands

1. Cut a strip on the lengthwise grain 1½″ (3.8 cm) wide and long enough to make all the carriers. The length of each carrier will be equal to the waistband width plus 1″ (2.5 cm).

2. If the strip is not cut along the selvage, zigzag one edge.

3. Fold the unfinished edge over ½″ (12.7 mm) twice and edgestitch each side of the strip. The inside edge of the strip must be all the way to the fold for the edgestitching to secure it. (Fig. 337a) If you have difficulty catching the inside edge when you edgestitch, topstitch the carrier in the center of the strip instead. (Fig. 337b)

Fig. 337

Setting the belt carriers

1. Place the carriers face-down on the right side of the garment, matching the cut edges of the carriers to the cut edge of the garment waistline. (Fig. 338a)

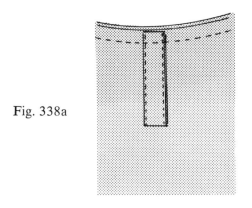

Fig. 338a

2. Pin the carriers in place on the garment. Set the waistband. The lower edge of the carriers will be secured in the waistline seam.

3. Fold the top edge of the carriers under ⅜″ (9.5 mm) and topstitch them in place. (Fig. 338b)

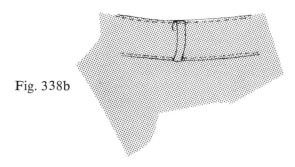

Fig. 338b

Loops and Thread Carriers

Loops made from self-filled or cord-filled tubing make attractive carriers for small belts. Thread chains, made by hand or machine, and blanket-stitched bars make inconspicuous belt carriers. Make machine chains by twisting several strands of thread together and zigzagging over them. Hold the threads taut so that they won't be pulled into the needle hole.

Notch the seam allowances of the garment sections to indicate the locations for the belt carriers. Cut each carrier the desired length plus two seam allowances (1¼″ or 3.2 cm). Sandwich the carriers between the garment sections, matching the cut edges. Pin and stitch the seam.

If a belt is always worn with a garment, the belt carrier can be invisible. It will be located under the belt and snap to the wrong side of the belt.

1. Make a ½″–1″ (12.7 mm–25.4 mm) long thread chain on the garment. Locate it so that it will be hidden under the belt. Finish the chain and sew the ball of a snap on the end.

2. Center the socket on the wrong side of the belt and sew it in place.

3. Snap the belt to the garment.

SPECIAL TECHNIQUES FOR SPECIAL FABRICS

Special fabrics are exciting to wear and most of them are no more difficult to sew than plain fabrics. However, they do require extra thought and planning and they may require additional time and effort. A knowledge of their characteristics and a few suggestions will enable you to sew them successfully and with a minimum of effort.

PLAIDS AND STRIPES
Pattern Design
Designs with curved seamlines are almost impossible to match satisfactorily. Uneven plaids are difficult to match in bias-cut designs. For best results, select a design that is illustrated in plaid on the pattern envelope.

Layout, Cutting, and Marking
The plaid design and its size will determine the amount of additional fabric you will need to lay the garment out attractively and match it correctly. Multiply the length of the repeat by the number of repeats needed for a rough estimate. If the fabric is 45″ (114.3 cm) wide with a repeat of 4″ (10.2 cm), you will probably need 3 lengths for a jacket and 2 lengths for a skirt—a total of 5 lengths. Multiply 5 by the length of the repeat, 4″ (10.2 cm), for a total of 20″ (50.8 cm). You may need less, but you don't want to be caught short.

Avoid fabrics that are off-grain. Fabrics with permanent-press finishes and fabrics manufactured on circular knitting machines cannot be straightened. Don't purchase plaids that are more than ¼″ (6.4 mm) off if you want to match the garment successfully. Sometimes, you can cut off-grain fabrics out and stitch the garments so that the horizontal lines match, but the seams will twist in the finished gar-

ment. Examine a ready-made knit shirt if you haven't had this problem.

Examine the plaid carefully to see if you need to use a "with nap" layout.

Use a complete pattern to cut the garment out accurately. Lay the complete pattern, *face-up,* on the right side of a single layer of fabric. (Fig. 339a)

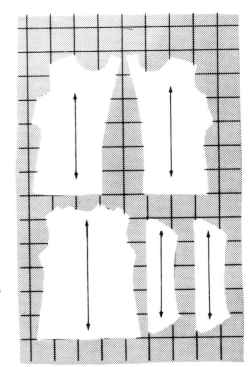

Fig. 339a

Match the *stitching* lines, not the cutting lines of the garment sections. Complicated designs are easier to match if you trim away the seam allowances from the pattern. Lay the pattern on the fabric and mark the cutting lines, using a see-through ruler and soap or chalk, or a dual-wheel tracing wheel. This method takes more time to cut the garment out, but you will save time when you stitch the garment together, and the garment will be easy to match perfectly. (Fig. 339b)

Fig. 339b

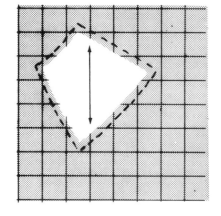

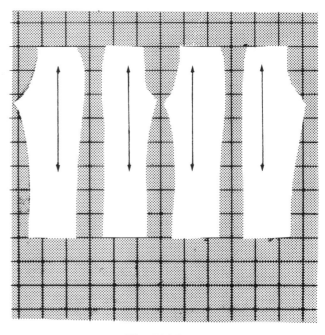

Fig. 339d

☼ If the garment is cut on the bias, match *carefully*. One vertical seam will be matched on the lengthwise grain; the other, on the crossgrain. (Fig. 339c)

Fig. 339c

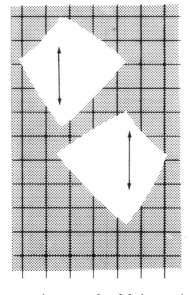

☼ Lay the pattern sections on the fabric so that seam allowances which will be joined together are next to each other. If the fabric is a little off-grain, you will still be able to match the garment successfully. (Fig. 339d)

☼ Cut applied sections—pockets, welts, flaps— after the garment sections to which they'll be sewn have been cut and marked. Lay the pattern for the

applied section on the garment section and mark the fabric pattern on the tissue for easy matching. (Fig. 339e)

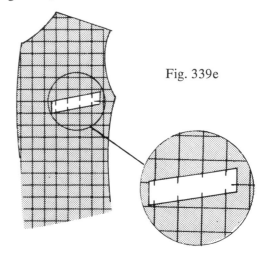

Fig. 339e

☼ Eliminate matching by cutting sections such as pockets, flaps, yokes, plackets, and sleeves on the bias.

You will not be able to match every seamline. Match the most important ones.

Stitching Tips

Stitch with the grain. Use an even-feed foot or roller foot. Stitching with one of these machine accessories will often eliminate the need for basting.

Basting Tips
Baste difficult-to-match seams with one of these methods:

Doublestick tape. Place the tape between the seam allowances out of the line of stitching.

Drafting or transparent tape
1. Mark the stitching lines on the right side of the garment with soap, chalk or gauge stitching.
2. Working from the right side of the garment, turn under the seam allowance of one garment section. Place the foldline so that it matches the seamline and fabric pattern on the corresponding section. Tape the seam together on the right side of the fabric. (Fig. 340)

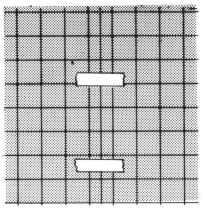

Fig. 340

3. Position the sections with the right sides together, folding the tape. Stitch from the wrong side of the garment on the seamline.
4. Remove the tape and press the seam.

Glue. Paste seams that will not be pressed open with washable glue.

Pins. Insert pins on the seamline. Set them at right angles to the stitching line. (Fig. 341) Remove the pins as you stitch. Do *not* stitch over them.

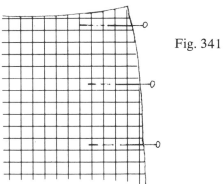

Fig. 341

Machine. If the fabric won't be marred by needle holes, baste by machine from the right side of the garment.

1. Mark the seamline on the right side of the fabric with soap, chalk, or gauge stitching.
2. Working from the right side of the garment, turn under the seam allowance of one garment section. Place the foldline so that it matches the seamline and fabric pattern on the corresponding section. Pin, glue, or tape the seam in place.
3. Loosen the upper tension and lengthen the stitch. Set the machine to make a hemming stitch. Using a zigzag foot or blind-hemming foot, stitch next to the fold—one zigzag stitch will catch the fold every fifth stitch. (Fig. 342)

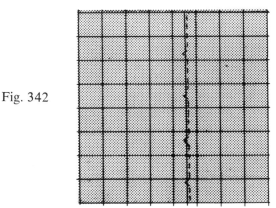

Fig. 342

4. Turn the garment wrong-side-out and stitch the seam permanently.
5. Remove the basting stitch and press the seam.

Hand basting. When all else fails, baste by hand with a slip-basting stitch.

1. Mark the seamline on the right side of the fabric.
2. Working from the right side of the garment, turn under the seam allowance of one garment section. Place the foldline so that it matches the seamline and fabric pattern on the corresponding section. Pin the seam in place. Slip-baste the edges together (see Basic Sewing Skills).
3. Stitch the seam from the wrong side of the garment next to the basted line.
4. Remove the basting threads and press the seam.

Details
Seams are easy to match with lapped seams and invisible zippers, or you can create a new look by inserting piping into the seamlines. If the seam doesn't match exactly, it won't be noticed.

SHEERS AND LIGHTWEIGHT FABRICS
Pattern Design
Avoid patterns that are close-fitting designs. If the fabric is sheer, select a pattern with minimal seaming.

Layout and Cutting
✿ Cover the cutting table with an old blanket or sheet to prevent slippery fabrics from sliding around or use the felt or foam side of your dining room table pads to make a no-slip surface.

✿ Keep your shears very sharp and dry when you cut out the fabric. Perspiration will make a difficult job even harder, and dull shears will make pulls in the fabric.

✿ Slippery fabrics like chiffon, georgette, and crepe are easily pulled out of shape. Use a complete pattern and backing paper to cut them quickly and accurately. Pin a single layer of fabric, right-side-up, to a large sheet of paper. If wide paper is not available, use several strips of wax paper that have been glued or taped together. Lay the complete pattern on the fabric and cut the garment out *with* the backing paper. If necessary, stitch through the backing paper when you stitch the seams; then, carefully tear the paper away.

✿ If the fabric ravels excessively, use fray-retardant on *all* the cut edges.

✿ Use self-fabric, colored organdy, or organza, China silk, flesh-colored nylon tricot, or a fusible knit interfacing to interface the garment.

Stitching Tips
Use universal needles in small sizes and stitch with a light tension. Review the hints for eliminating puckered seams to ensure perfect results (see Basic Sewing Skills).

Seams and Darts
✿ Use the drapery French, French, standing fell, quick flat-fell, or hairline seams on fabrics that unravel, and double-stitched or hairline seams on fabrics that do not unravel or lined garments.

✿ On sheer fabrics, bobbin-stitch darts and tucks or use a hairline seam on them.

Edge Finishes
✿ Use bindings, bias facings, or edge-to-edge linings instead of regular facings to finish the edges of sheers.

✿ Use very narrow hems on flared garments or deep double hems on straight garments. If the fabric is soft and slippery, allow the garment to hang at least twenty-four hours before hemming it.

LACE
Lace can be stitched with narrow seams, it can be underlined and stitched with regular seams, or it can be intricately shaped invisibly by overlapping the seams.

Pattern Design
If the lace is to be underlined or stitched with narrow seams, select a pattern with few seamlines. If the seams are to be overlapped, any design can be sewn attractively; however, you should avoid close-fitting designs.

Alter the pattern before cutting out the garment.

Layout, Cutting, and Marking
Use a complete pattern and an open lay.

Lay the pattern out on the crossgrain or lengthwise grain to utilize the fabric design and position the motifs attractively. If the lace has a scalloped edge, the pattern can be placed with the scallops at the hemline, front edge, sleeve edge, neck edge, or top of the bodice.

Lay out all the pattern pieces before cutting to be sure you have enough lace for your garment. If you are short, piece some sections inconspicuously by overlapping the lace and whipping it together by hand. If you are overlapping the seams, lay the pattern out so there are several inches between the sections.

Underline or flat-line all or part of the garment.

Mark the lace with pins, transparent tape, soap, or bastings. Mark the underlining on sections that are backed.

Stitching Tips
Wrap the toes of the presser foot with transparent tape to prevent their catching in the lace. Stitch with paper between the lace and feed dog to keep the lace from tearing.

Use a short stitch (12–15 spi or 2 mm) and small needles.

Seams
Make narrow seams such as double-stitched, French, drapery French, strap, or hairline seams or overlapped lace seams on sheer garments (see SEAMS).

Flat-line or bind the seams in underlined garments —lace edges can be scratchy.

If the garment is lined, use narrow seams on the lining; the lining seams may be visible under the lace.

Hems and Edge Finishes
Cut the design so that the scallops of the lace finish the edge, or applique motifs or scallops from lace scraps to short or shaped edges, or applique narrow lace trim at the edge by overlapping the lace and whipping it by hand.

Bind the straight edges with bias bindings, ribbon, or braid, or face the edges with a narrow doubled strip of tulle, marquisette, nylon tricot, or silk organza in a matching color or flesh color.

Closures
Use invisible or hand-picked zippers on lined and underlined garments.

On sheer designs, use buttons and loops instead of zippers. Avoid bound buttonholes.

VELVETS AND VELVETEENS
Pattern Design
Select a pattern that doesn't have straight seams on the lengthwise grain—they are difficult to stitch and the nap will divide at the seamline.

Layout, Cutting, and Marking
To avoid creeping when cutting, fold the fabric wrong sides together. Use doublestick tape between the layers to hold them securely or use a complete pattern for cutting. If you make the complete pattern from a commercial nonwoven pattern fabric, it will cling to the fabric, thereby eliminating the need for lots of pins or weights.

Mark the reverse of the fabric with arrows in the direction of the nap. Use a "with nap" layout. Lay the pattern with the tops of all pieces in the same direction. Cut with the nap running up for a deeper, richer color; cut it with the nap running down for a lighter, shinier color.

Never use a crossgrain fold when laying out the pattern.

Place pins only in the seam allowances so that they won't mar the nap. Use snips, soap, or tailor's tacks to mark the garment. A tracing wheel or machine basting may leave holes.

Stitching Tips
Loosen the pressure on the presser foot and use a longer stitch (8–10 spi or 2.5–3 mm); stitch with the nap even though you may be stitching against the grain. Hold the fabric taut when you stitch.

Prevent creeping by stitching with a piece of paper between the feed dog and fabric and/or between the fabric layers, or use a roller foot. Do not use an even-feed foot—it may leave tracks on the fabric.

Do not use doublestick, transparent, drafting, or topstitching tapes on the face side of napped fabrics.

Details
☼ Flat-line or line garments for an elegant finish or finish hems and seams with a bound edge or a Hong-Kong finish to eliminate shedding nap in unlined garments.

☼ Use invisible zippers or hand-stitched zippers. Bound buttonholes and button loops are also attractive on velvet and velveteen garments.

Pressing
Test press a sample of fabric. If you don't have a needleboard for pressing napped fabrics, pad the press board with a thick towel or pressing pad, then cover it with a piece of garment fabric, face-side-up. Don't forget to cover the point presser or ham with a piece of the self-fabric, face-up.

Use a piece of the garment fabric as a pressing cloth. Place the right side of the cloth next to the right side of the garment when you press.

Use lots of steam except on acetate velvets. Lift and lower the iron gently or use a portable steamer. Use very little pressure.

To freshen the nap, hang the completed garment in the bathroom while you shower.

KNITS
Pattern Design
Select a pattern appropriate to the stretch of the chosen knit fabric. Determine the fabric stretch by folding the fabric on the crossgrain. Hold the fabric firmly 2″ (5.1 cm) from the edge with your hands placed 4″ (10.2 cm) apart. Stretch gently.

Stable knits will stretch about ½″ (12.7 mm).

Moderate-stretch knits will stretch about 1¼″ (3.2 cm).

Super-stretch knits will stretch 2″ (5.1 cm) or more.

Patterns for KNITS ONLY *cannot* be used for woven fabrics.

Layout and Cutting
Prewash and dry all washable knits. Many knits are stretched when they are rolled onto the bolt—washing and drying will allow them to return to their original size.

Some knits run. Determine the direction of the run on the fabric and decide whether you want the fabric to run up from the hem or down from the shoulder. The fabric should run *toward* points of stress. If the knit runs up, runs at stress points on the neckline, shoulder seams, and zipper plackets will be eliminated. If it runs down, stress at the hemline won't cause runs. Fray-retardant can be used along the edges to prevent runs.

Use a "with nap" layout—the wales of the knit have a definite top and bottom.

Stitching Tips

For a more elastic stitching line, shorten the stitch so that more thread will be stitched into the seam and loosen the tension on the bobbin and needle threads. A small zigzag stitch will also make a more elastic seamline.

Reinforce seams that undergo stress during normal wear, such as shoulder seams and V-necklines, by stitching twill tape, hem tape, or a piece of lightweight selvage into the seamline.

Stitch the edges of single knits ¼″ (6.4 mm) from the edge to reduce rolling.

Seams and Seam Finishes

Use plain, overlocked or double-stitched seams. Finish the edges of plain seams with a flat finish, such as a cut edge, pinked, zigzagged, or overlocked. Avoid a clean-finished edge—knits are too bulky, and they won't unravel.

Hems

Garments made of knitted fabrics can be hemmed by hand, machine, or fusing or they can be finished with a no-hem finish.

Machine-hemmed garments can be topstitched or blind hemmed or they can be finished decoratively with a satin stitch, lettuce finish, scalloped, or shell hem.

Use a figure-eight stitch, blindstitch, or catchstitch to hem garments by hand. Do not make tight stitches. Do *not* clean finish the edge; use a flat finish like a cut edge, zigzagged, lace, or tape.

Pressing

Use pressing techniques that are appropriate for the fabric content.

VINYL FABRICS AND LEATHER
Pattern Design

Select patterns that require little or no easing. Styles with seams are easier to stitch and shape than those with darts. In the past, home sewers have been advised to use patterns with minimum seaming. This is unnecessary. In fact, leather garments often have many seams because they are cut from small skins.

Kimono and raglan sleeves are easier to assemble than set-in sleeves. If the pattern has a set-in sleeve, measure the ease in the sleeve cap and reduce it to ½″ (12.7 mm).

Make a trial garment; use a pattern you've used before or make a complete pattern in nonwoven pattern fabric so that the pattern can be altered before the material is cut.

Layout, Cutting, and Marking

⚙ Use a complete pattern and a "with nap" layout to cut leather skins.

⚙ Tape the pattern to the material or use weights to hold the pattern in place. If you must use pins, place them only in the seam allowances.

⚙ Mark the fabric or skins with snips, tape, or water-erasable pen.

Stitching Tips

⚙ Use paper clips or transparent tape to baste the seams together.

⚙ Use wedge-point needles to stitch leather and universal needles to stitch vinyls. Lengthen the stitch to avoid splitting the fabric or skins.

⚙ Stitch carefully—needle holes cannot be removed.

⚙ Prevent creeping by using a roller foot or talcum powder on the fabric and machine bed, or stitch with paper.

⚙ To stitch clear vinyl, use nylon filament thread.

Seams and Hems

Use plain seams, lapped seams, or flat-fell seams for nonwovens. Seams cannot be pressed open permanently. Use a permanent glue, rubber cement, or topstitching to hold the seam allowances in place.

Finish hems with a cut edge or Hong-Kong finish. Machine stitch or glue the hem in place.

Use leather needles and a thimble for hand sewing on leather and vinyl.

Details

Invisible zippers are easier to set than regular zippers.

Select the buttonhole of your choice—bound, slashed, or machine stitched.

Pressing

Press with the handle of the scissors. Using short

strokes, press the seam open firmly on the underside, then use them to press the seamline on the right side of the garment.

Pseudosuedes

The most popular pseudosuede is Ultrasuede,® which is distributed by Skinner, a division of Spring Mills. This nonwoven fabric of 60 percent polyester and 40 percent nonfibrous polyurethane took seven years and 14 million dollars to develop. Other pseudosuedes include Amara, Suede 21,™ and Bellesieme.

All of these beautiful fabrics can be used to make casual or dressy garments. For experience and economy, make a garment with a pseudosuede trim— yoke, placket, belt, piping, collar, or cuffs—before you make an entire garment.

Pseudosuedes can be machine washed and dried. They won't shrink, ravel, pill, or crock. They're wrinkle-resistant, lightweight, and won't water spot. They're almost perfect; however, they're very expensive and burn very easily. The tiniest cigarette ash will singe the nap and leave a permanent mark.

These fabrics are very easy to sew but they aren't like wovens and knits.

Planning a Garment

Pseudosuede garments can be constructed by conventional methods or by utilizing the unique no-fray quality of the fabric.

It is important to decide before you begin, even before you purchase the fabric, which method you plan to use to assemble the garment. You may want to use some techniques from each of the methods.

Pattern Design

⚙ Any pattern recommended for corduroy, velveteen, faille, linen, and other crisp fabrics can be used for most pseudosuedes. Select a pattern for soft fabrics if you're using lightweight Suede 21.™

⚙ Avoid patterns designed for pseudosuedes—the seam allowances have already been pretrimmed making the garment difficult to assemble.

⚙ Select patterns that require little or no easing. Styles with seams are easier to stitch and shape than those with darts.

⚙ Kimono and raglan sleeves are easier to assemble than set-in sleeves. If the pattern has a set-in sleeve, measure the ease in the sleeve cap and reduce it to ½″ (12.7 mm).

⚙ Make a trial garment. Use a pattern you have used before or make a complete pattern in pattern fabric so that the pattern can be altered before the material is cut.

Layout, Cutting, and Marking

Prewashing the fabric will make it easier to sew.

Use a complete pattern so that the fabric can be cut out in a single layer or fold the fabric lengthwise with the wrong sides together to cut the pattern out of a double layer.

Use a "with nap" layout. Facings can be tilted off-grain to save fabric. Bias-cut garment sections should be cut on the crossgrain. The crossgrain has more stretch and you will also save fabric.

Use tape, weights, or pins placed in the seam allowances to hold the pattern in place. If you use tape, remove it by pulling down in the direction of the nap.

Mark the fabric with snips, tape, or water-erasable pen.

Interfacing

Many garments won't require interfacing; however, if you want to add body to collars or prevent rippling buttonholes, use a lightweight interfacing. If you are making the garment with conventional seams and edges, use a woven interfacing. If you are using lapped seams and cut edges, use a nonwoven or knitted fusible interfacing. Cut out each interfacing section so that it is ¼″ (6.4 mm) smaller at each edge than the *finished* garment section which it interfaces. If it is cut the same size, the interfacing will show at the edge between the garment and facing. If the interfacing does show at the finished edge, use a permanent-color soft-tip pen to "dye" it.

Stitching Tips

⚙ Use universal needles in sizes 11(75) or 14(90) and needle lubricant. To avoid skipped stitches and a creeping underlayer, review the suggestions for eliminating them.

⚙ Lengthen the stitch to prevent splitting the fabric. If you have to take out stitches, steam the nap and brush it with a toothbrush to hide the needle holes. Obviously, small needle holes are easier to hide than larger ones.

⚙ Use a walking foot, roller foot, glue, or basting tape to prevent the lower layer feeding faster than the upper layer. Do not stitch through basting tape.

⚙ Hold the fabric taut as you stitch.

⚙ Use leather needles and a thimble for hand sewing.

Seams

Conventional seams. Conventional seams can be cut with a seam allowance narrower than the regular ⅝″ (16 mm). The fabric won't fray but alterations will be difficult to make on a finished garment.

Conventional seams cannot be pressed open permanently. To hold them open permanently, press the seams open with a portable steamer and topstitch each side $\frac{1}{16}''$ (1.6 mm) from the seamline (Fig. 343a) or press the seam allowances to one side and topstitch. (Fig. 343b)

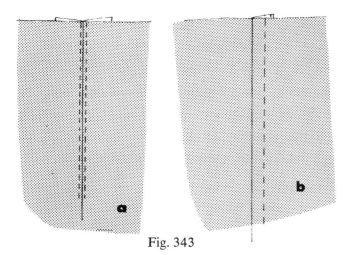

Fig. 343

If you don't want to topstitch the garment, fuse, or use rubber cement to glue the seam allowances to the wrong side of the garment. Rubber cement will not hold when the garment is washed, but the seams will stay "pressed."

Trim enclosed seams to $\frac{1}{16}''$ or $\frac{1}{8}''$ (1.6 mm or 3.2 mm) to reduce bulk.

Lapped seams. Flat lapped seams can be used to assemble garments when you want a sporty look (see SEAMS). These seams require less fabric, enabling you to save money. Prepare the pattern carefully. Lay it out and measure exactly the amount of yardage required *before* making your purchase.

As a general rule, seams are lapped front-over-back and top-over-bottom. Cuffs lap over sleeves, waistbands over skirts, and collars over bodices.

Set-in sleeves, the front and back seams of pants, and pants' inseams should be stitched with conventional seams.

Nonwoven flat-fell seams. If you're unsure about the garment fit or how to lap the seams, use flat-fell seams for nonwovens (see SEAMS).

Hems and Facings
The no-fray quality of pseudosuedes allows you to use no-hem finishes, fused hems, topstitched hems,

and cut-edge facings as well as conventional hems and facings.

Details
Use invisible zippers or set regular zippers with fly, slot, or lapped applications. If you use a slot or lapped zipper, the zipper may look unpressed. Before setting the zipper, apply rubber cement to the wrong side of the garment and seam allowances, let it dry, then press the seam allowances of the placket in place for a crisp finish.

If you're using cut-edge facings to finish a collar with a roll, stitch the collar and undercollar to the garment neckline. Position the collar in the rolled position. The edges of the upper layer may not match the edges of the lower layer. (Fig. 344a) Glue or

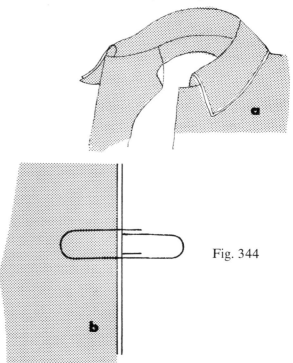

Fig. 344

paper-clip the edges together (Fig. 344b); then stitch and trim the edges. Use the same technique for lapels.

Use the patch pocket application for nonwoven fabrics.

Pressing
Press with a portable steamer if possible. If you are pressing with an iron, do not press the fabric from the face side without a heavy press cloth.

Seams will not remain pressed open after washing. Stitch, fuse or glue them in place so they will remain flat.

Washing and Drying

Pseudosuede garments can be washed and dried by machine if the other fabrics and notions used in them have the same quality.

Wash the garment in cold water, using a cold-water soap. Remove the garment from the washer and shake it briskly. Set the dryer on "Regular."

Place the garment in the dryer. Let it dry for 5–10 minutes, then hang it to finish drying. These fabrics should not be overdried if you want to preserve the beauty of the fabric.

If you get a spot on the garment, be very careful when spot cleaning it. It is easy to rub a hole in the fabric.

INDEX